Margrit Schulte Beerbühl
Jörg Vögele
(eds.)

Spinning the Commercial Web

International Trade, Merchants,
and Commercial Cities, c. 1640–1939

PETER LANG

Frankfurt am Main · Berlin · Bern · Bruxelles · New York · Oxford · Wien

Bibliographic Information published by Die Deutsche Bibliothek
Die Deutsche Bibliothek lists this publication in the Deutsche Nationalbibliografie; detailed bibliographic data is available in the internet at <http://dnb.ddb.de>.

ISBN 3-631-50980-4
US-ISBN 0-8204-6448-1

© Peter Lang GmbH
Europäischer Verlag der Wissenschaften
Frankfurt am Main 2004
All rights reserved.

Printed in Germany 1 2 3 4   6 7

www.peterlang.de

Spinning the Commercial Web

Acknowledgements

From 7 - 9 March 2002 an international conference of economic, social and business historians as well as historical geographers from ten different countries was held at the University of Düsseldorf. The idea for this conference arose from various internal discussions on the public as well as scientific debates on globalization. If an analysis of the emerging world economy is essential for a clearer understanding of the nature of globalization, a systematic approach to the processes which led to the interconnecting of the various social, cultural and economic phenomena into a global network may provide an important instrument for future research. For this purpose, a model was developed to analyse the networking process on three interrelated, macro, micro and actor-oriented levels. Participants from different countries were invited to contribute to one of the three aspects. Each one chose a subject related to his or her own field of research. The international composition of the participants, at the same time, allowed an overview of international research activities.

For financial support we are grateful to the Fritz Thyssen-Stiftung, Cologne. Further support came from the Gesellschaft von Freunden und Förderern der Heinrich Heine Universität Düsseldorf, the Heinrich Heine Universität as well as from the Philosophische and Medizinische Fakultät. We owe thanks to Volkmar Hansen, director of the Goethe-Museum, for putting Schloß Jägerhof at disposal for the opening and reception of the conference.

We thank those who opened the conference and introduced the theme: Alfons Labisch, Michael North and Ulrich Pfister as well as those who chaired conference panels in addition to the participants: Silke Fehlemann, Wolfgang J. Mommsen, Ulrich Nocken and Wolfgang Woelk. During the conference and for the preparation of the conference volume a lot of help was provided by Dominique Behnke, Marita Bruijns-Pötschke, Fritz Dross, Heiner Fangerau, Carmen Götz, Martina Hacke, Thorsten Halling, Nina Jacobs, Ulrich Koppitz, Horst Kroschel, Sandra Lessmann, Eckehart Merholz, Eve Schäfer, Julia Schäfer, Simon Schulte Beerbühl and Michaela Stange. Furthermore, we would like to thank Peter Lang Publishers for the publication of the present volume.

Thanks are due to all who took part in the meeting and helped to organize the conference.

Margrit Schulte Beerbühl and Jörg Vögele

Table of Contents

I. Emergence, Decline and Reconstruction of Networks

a. Maritime networks

b. Inland networks

II. Between Local and Global Networks: the actors

a. Mercantile services and agencies

b. Merchants' networks and empires

III. Merging Local and Global Functions: Port cities

a. At the hub of the nets

b. Migration, politics and people

IV. Appendix

Spinning the Commercial Web. International Trade, Merchants, and Commercial Cities, c. 1640-1939. An Introduction

Margrit Schulte Beerbühl and Jörg Vögele

Introduction

Between the seventeenth and the twentieth centuries the traditional European economies were transformed into a world-encompassing global network. Multinational enterprises and global financial markets have emerged since the beginning of the twentieth century at the latest. The communication revolution within the last quarter of the century, however, has transformed the European economics to an unforeseen dimension and has given rise to a new debate in economic and general history.[1] Apart from questions on the general features of globalisation and its newly arising problems, the central issues in recent research and debates in economic and historical studies are: How and when did the development of an economic world system start? What were the essential economic structural, social or cultural factors which contributed to the emergence of a world economy? The given answers diverge considerably. Braudel and Wallerstein dated the beginning of modern world economy back to the sixteenth or seventeenth centuries.[2] However, as economic growth rates are rather low compared with the latter part of the nineteenth and the twentieth century, the majority of economic historians prefer to see the emergence of a world economy not before the latter part of the nineteenth century.[3] The discovery of the new world, the acceleration of economic growth in the late

---

1 See, for example, M. Waters, *Globalization*, London 1995, or Wolfram Fischer, *Expansion, Integration, Globalisierung. Studien zur Geschichte der Weltwirtschaft*, Göttingen 1998.

2 F. Braudel, *Civilization and Capitalism, 3: The Perspective of the World*, (reprint) London 2002; I. Wallerstein, *The Modern World System I. Capitalist Agriculture and the Origins of the European World-Economy in the Sixteenth Century*, New York 1974.

3 H. Pohl, *Aufbruch der Weltwirtschaft. Geschichte der Weltwirtschaft von der Mitte des 19. Jahrhunderts bis zum Ersten Weltkrieg*, Stuttgart 1989. According to H. Pohl the basic features of the modern world economy did not date before the middle of the nineteenth century. See also R. Robertson, *Globalization*, London 1992, 58-60; J. Foreman-Peck, *A History of the World Economy. International Economic Relations since 1850*, 2nd ed. Oxford 1995; K. O'Rourke and J.G. Williamson, *Globalization and History: the evolution of a nineteenth century atlantic economy*, Cambridge 1999. Concerning growth rates see Ph. Deane and W.A. Cole, *British Economic Growth, 1688-1959*, Cambridge 1962; R. Floud & D.N. McCloskey, *The Economic History of Britain, vol. 1 1700-1860*, 2nd ed. Cambridge 1994.

ninetenth century as well as the communication revolution with the advent of the internet in the twentieth century are crucial watersheds in the history of the world economy. Whatever starting point was chosen in the debates on the beginnings of a world economy, the theories were more or less based on macro-economic quantitative research.

Statistical data on imports and exports, trade or capital flows were collected to assess the development. These quantitative approaches were the outcome of the then prevailing theory of the market, which dominated international historiography and economic research for at least half a century. Statistical approaches based on aggregate data have enabled historians to define and measure historical forces and thereby have given valuable insights into the development of a world economy. However, they could not sufficiently explain how and why changes occurred. Market theory has been an essentially passive approach to historical processes, because it regards markets regulated exclusively by supply and demand and transactions between supplier and buyer as governed by the anonymity of the place and profit orientation. Therefore actors and actions were left out of sight.[4] Jones regarded them as "automatons" of anonymous market forces which had no room to shape or react actively to economic forces.[5] Activities that could not be explained by market theory were at best evaluated as anachronisms or deviations which would be eradicated with the progress of time. The fact that statistics are only able to explain the visible results of economic actions, but not the qualitative forces which shaped economic action, led to a growing discontent.

The failure of economic theory to provide tools with which to analyse the development and growth of business enterprise gave rise to the new institutional economics. This sought above all to fill gaps left by the neo-classical economic theory with respect to firms. The new institutional theory has emanated from the works of J.R. Commons and R.H. Coase and was further developed by D.C. North and O.E. Williamson.[6] At its heart is the concept of transaction costs, which emerge in any economic institution that organises, carries out or controls transactions. It focused its explanation of change on some activities within

---

4   See, for example, D. Hancock, *Citizen of the World*, Cambridge 1995.

5   S.R.H. Jones, 'Transaction Costs and the Theory of the Firm: The Scope and Limitations of the New Institutional Approach', in: *Business History*, 49 (1997), 9; see also W. Reddy, *The Rise of Market Culture*, Cambridge 1998; A. Marshall, 'On Markets', in: G. Thompson et al. (eds.), *Markets, Hierarchies & Networks. The Coordination of Social Life*, London, New Dehli 1991, 24-34; W.M. Reddy, *The Rise of Market Culture. The Textile Trade and French Society, 1750-1900*, Cambridge 1984.

6   J.R. Commons, *Institutional Economics*, Madison 1934; R.H. Coase, 'The Nature of the Firm', in: *Economica* 4 (1934), 386-405; for North and Williamson see the following footnote.

firms.[7] The transaction cost approach is associated notably with North and Williamson and primarily explains the existence of multinational corporations and their internal "governance structures".[8]

Within the last years this approach has been extensively criticized for various reasons.[9] One of the major points of criticism has been that it is hardly able to explain the forces of change and innovation, because its theoretical foundations are still valid within neo-classical economic theory which focuses on conditions of a stable equilibrium.[10] As Jones pointed out, it also fails to identify transactions in an operationally satisfactory way. Like its market predecessors it is a primarily static concept which cannot treat innovatory or evolutionary processes adequately nor does it leave room for the activities of innovating enterepreneurs.[11] Although it is very much concerned with relations it focuses solely on relationships between organisational structures or rule-based internal governance. As relations only exist within hierarchies of institutions, the institutional model fails to take into account inter-organisational relations among different institutions or external relationships with individual customers, suppliers or distributors. Morevoer, relations or transactions are seen by this concept as existing between two parties only. In an economic or industrial society, however, a variety of interdependent relations exists not only dyadic relationships.[12]

---

7 See D.C. North, *Structure and Change in Economic History*, New York 1981; D.C. North, 'Transaction costs in history', in: *Journal of European Economic History*, 14 (1985), 557-76, and R. Thomas, *The Rise of the Western World: A New Economic History*, Cambridge 1973. See also O.E. Williamson, *Markets and Hierarchies: Analysis and Anti-Trust Implications*, New York 1975. For more recent publications, see C. Menard (ed.), *Transaction Cost Economics. Recent developments*, Cheltenham 1997; D.C. North, *Institutions, Institutional Change and Economic Performance*, Cambridge 1994, D.C. North, 'Transaction Costs through Time', in: Menard, *Transaction Costs*, 149-60.

8 M. Casson et. al., *Multinationals and World Trade. Vertical Integration and the division of Labour in World Industries*, London 1986; M. Casson, *The Firm and the Market: Studies on Multinational Enterprise and the Scope of the Firm*, Oxford 1987; A.D. Chandler, *Managerial Hierarchies, Comparative Perspectives on the Rise of the Modern Industrial Enterprise*, Cambridge 1980.

9 A.D. Chandler, *Strategy and Structure*, Cambridge 1962, A.D. Chandler, *Scale and Scope. The Dynamics of Industrial Capitalism*, Cambridge 1990; O.E. Williamson, *Markets and Hierarchies: Analysis and Anti-Trust Implications*, New York 1975, he refined his theory in: *The Economic Institutions of Capitalism*, New York 1985.

10 M. Casson and M.B. Rose, 'Institutions and the Evolution of Modern Business: Introduction', in: *Business History*, 39 (1997), 1.

11 Jones, *Transaction Costs*, 10.

12 J. Johannson and L.-G. Mattsson, 'Interorganisational Relations in Industrial Systems: a network approach compared with the transaction-cost aproach', in: Thompson et al. (eds.), *Market, Hierarchies & Networks*, 261.

The transaction-costs approach highlights the importance of organisation. It attempts to explain the emergence of multinational companies, but even today they comprise only a small part of business behaviour. Inspite of the long predicted death of family firms, they reveal an unforeseen resilience. Family firms do not only characterize the economies of the developing countries, but continue to be an important feature of highly industrialised countries.[13] Trust, cultural and social aspects, ties, values, as well as dynamic interactions ignoring profit-maximizing strategies or transaction-costs efficiency, still account for much of today's business life and change. Jones has therefore characterized the transcactions-cost approach as highly ahistorical and limited.[14] This concept is even less suited to analyse economic developments and changes in the past, when personal and cultural relations dominated economic activities.

In view of the restricted applicability of the new-institutional approach, economists as well as economic historians have turned towards network theory, a concept originally developed in sociology and anthropology.[15] In contrast to the neo-classical theory of the market and new institutional economics, network analysis has many advantages to describe the essential structural elements of an expanding world economy. Network analysis focuses on on-going actions within relations not so much on their outcome. As a result, it offers a useful basis for evaluating the direction, dynamic feature and volume of change.

Social network analysis highlights the importance of relationships between interacting units.[16] It brings to the fore the actor and his actions, but it does not end there. The unit of analysis is not the individual but an entity consisting of an individual merchant, entrepreneur, or groups of them as well as of economic institutions and organisations or even entire networks. Traditional biographical studies are generally written from an atomistic perspective. The choices and decisions individual actors make and their actions are depicted without regard to the social system and therefore do not reflect the extent to which individuals

---

13 Concerning family firms, see G. Cookson, 'Family Firms and Business Networks: textile engineering in Yorkshire 1780-1830', in: *Business History*, 39 (1997), 1-20; A. Colli, *The History of Family Business 1850-2000*, Cambridge 2003.

14 Jones, *Transaction Costs*, 24.

15 The concept was developed, amongst others, by Moreno (J.L. Moreno, *Who Shall survive?: Foundations of Sociometry, Group Psychotherapy and Sociodrama*, Washington D.C.1934; 3rd ed. New York 1978) and Bavelas (A. Bavelas, 'A mathematical model of group structure', in: *Human Organizations*, 7 (1948), 16-30), as well as by anthropologists, such as Barnes (J.A. Barnes, 'Networks and political processes', in: J.C. Mitchell (ed.), *Social Networks in Urban Situations*, Manchester 1969, 51-76) and Mitchell (J.C. Mitchell, 'Social networks', in: *Annual Review of Anthropology*, 3 (1974), 279-299).

16 Stanley Wasserman and Katherine Faust, *Social Network Analysis. Methods and Applications*, Cambridge 1994, 4.

react and interact with the larger economic, social or political processes. The crucial difference between the traditional biographical approach and network analysis is that the latter does not view individuals, firms, social actors or individual units as independent or autonomous. They are embedded in a complex pattern of structured relationships, where the beliefs, actions and perceptions of actors are influenced by other participants in a social unit or system. The nature of this relationships, however, not only shapes individual action, it also provides an opportunity for the actor to shape his or her environment. These relations may be personal, semi-formal or even formal.[17]

As the organisation and structure of relations is the central concept in network analysis, it provides an excellent framework for studying patterns of trade in an expanding world economy. It allows historians to develop a systematic picture of the expanding world economy, as it stresses the linkages between units which tie social, cultural and economic positions into a network. Moreover, as economic relations and transactions can be measured in a long-term perspective, the concept enables researchers to study changes in the core-periphery structure.[18]

The introduction of the network concept in economic history originated from a new interest in the role and function of entrepreneurship and, in turn, of privately owned firms, especially family-based firms. Entrepreneurs and family-based firms were an acknowledged feature of the medieval and early modern period and they lay at the heart of the first Industrial Revolution. Despite their long-predicted death "individual entrepreneurs survived and prospered in an age characterised by anonymous bureaucracies" as Lindsay remarked. Even in corporate and bureaucratic organisations decision-making rests with individuals and their decisions may become an agency of growth and change.[19] Today's economic business interests cannot negate the need for trust and other social values in relation to economic exchange, because, as Edward H. Lorenz has stressed in his research on French firms, human rationality is limited and the environment is uncertain.[20] As entrepreneurship is inseparable from risk-taking, social relationships based on mutual trust and knowledge help to reduce transaction costs.

---

17 S. Sugiyama and L. Grove, *Commercial Networks in Modern Asia*, Richmond 2001, 3; for the concept of embeddedness see M. Granovetter, 'Economic Action and Social Structure: The Problem of Embeddedness', in: *American Journal of Sociology*, 91 (1985), 481-510.

18 See, for example, Wallerstein, *Modern World System*.

19 H.C. Lindsay, 'Entrepreneurial Persistence through the Bureaucratic Age', in: *Business History Review*, 51 (1977), 416.

20 Edward H. Lorenz, 'Neither friends nor strangers: informal networks of subcontracting in French industry', in: Thompson, et al., *Markets Hierarchies & Networks*, 183-192.

Entrepreneurship is seen by representatives of the concept of new entrepreneurship, like Mark Casson or Mary B. Rose, as the main source of business dynamism and innovation. Family firms fostered trading, financial and marketing skills.[21] Their informal, semi-formal or formal networks of business associates lowered transaction as well as information costs, because they often relied on extended family ties and trusted partners also united by a common value system and cultural expectations.[22] They also co-ordinated resources through cooperative strategies.[23]

The usefulness of network analysis has been widely accepted by a variety of social, economic and historical disciplines, and it has been widely used in migration historiography. Although the literature on networks has increased considerably in certain fields of economic and business history, there are still many lacunae to be filled. Networks have been discussed intensively in economic and business theory, but apart from studies on the economic development of Modern Asia or in historical geography, historical research on networks has hardly started, although it is generally acknowledged that they played a vital role in the expanding commerce of the early modern period. There are some local or regional studies, such as Gilliam Cookson's analysis of Yorkshire textile engineering firms during the Industrial Revolution or the comparative research by Mary Rose on the British and American cotton industry, to name only two, but there are still too few case studies to provide sufficient detail for an in-depth analysis of how such network practices actually contributed to the development of trade.[24] Even in research at a local level few attempts have been undertaken to examine the business population of a locality systematically in its entirety, i.e. in terms not only of its economic, but also its religious, social, political, familial, or cultural linkages.[25] Nor has any systematic

---

21 See, for example, the study of N. McKendrick on Josiah Wedgwood, in: N. McKendrick, J. Brewer and J.H. Plumb (eds.), *The Birth of a Consumer society. The Commercialization of Eighteenth-century England*, London 1982, 100-145.

22 For the role of trust in economic relations, see F. Fukuyama, *Trust. The Social Virtues and the Creation of Prosperity*, New York 1996, also N. Luhmann, *Trust and Power*, New York 1979; for trust as foundation of the early modern culture of credit see C. Muldrew, *The Economy of Obligation. The Culture of Credit and Social Relations in Early Modern England*, Basingstoke 1998.

23 A. Godley and D.M. Ross, *Banks, Networks and Small Firm Finance*, London 1996, 4.

24 M.B. Rose, Firms, *Networks and Business Values. The British and American Cotton Industries since 1750*, Cambridge 2000; G. Cookson, 'Family Firms and Business Networks: Textile Engineering in Yorkshire 1780-1830', in: *Business History*, 39 (1997), 1-20.

25 R. Pearson and D. Richardson, Business Networking in the Industrial Revolution, in: *Economic History Review* (2001), 659.

approach been undertaken to view networks on different levels in the period of the expanding world economy.

Networks happen not only in socially, economically and historically defined spheres, but also in geographically determined areas.[26] They have a spatial as well as hierarchical structure. They not only provide tools to analyse economic patterns on a micro, local or regional level, but also on macro or national or transnational levels. The expansion of the world economy, however, was not only a macro-level affair transgressing political as well as geographical boundaries. It was a multi-layered process occurring on different local, regional or national levels, as well as between them, and connecting remote and previously autonomous trading places or regions into a common network. The interconnectedness between the different levels has been hardly researched in economic historiography although this aspect is a central element in network analysis for it provides tools for analysing economic activities systematically. It is the aim of this volume, therefore, to examine the development of international trading networks on three interconnected levels in a long-term perspective, in order to elaborate the complexity and interrelations of historical developments. In view of recent debates on globalisation the present volume not only aims to analyse the causes of long-term developments, but also seeks to offer insights into the emergence and functioning of the multilayered links within this process. The focus is on the way in which individuals and groups created ties to facilitate the movement of commodities, money, information and people across shorter or longer distances.

The book is divided into sections which provide a tripartite approach for analysing the networking process of an expanding world economy at three different levels, on a macro or regional or international level, an individual or group level, as well as on a local level. The book, however, does not provide a comprehensive analysis of these processes, but by bringing together an international group of scholars it offers international and interdisciplinary insights into the complex and multi-layered process of economic expansion. By exploring aspects of growth and change in a coordinated way the contributions offer valuable insights and hopefully open up an agenda for future research.

Trading networks are flexible and represent fluid patterns of relations with no fixed boundaries. At the periphery their ends are highly loose and unstable. The net itself does not have a smooth or homogenous texture. It may consist of one or more cores or nodes, which may be either of equal or hierarchical nature. Not only the periphery of the net but also the cores are in a constant process of

---

26 Concerning the spatial structure of networks, see P. Haggett and R.J. Chorley, *Network Analysis in Geography*, London 1969.

change. Cores may fade and disappear, while others gain in strength or new ones emerge. Equally important are the disconnecting forces at the boundaries of the networks. Old established commercial links may be dropped at any time for better and more profitable ones. Others may be strengthened or extended to incorporate even previously independent or distant commercial spheres.

Emergence, Decline and Reconstruction of Networks

In the first section (Emergence, Decline and Reconstruction of Networks) some of the general features of networks in the early modern period will be discussed, in terms of their extension and geographical concentration, the diversification of their linkages and clusters, as well as their connecting and disconnecting forces. This section is devided into two parts: while the first one concentrates on the maritime networks, the second one focuses on the inland networks. Contrary to the long established view in historical research that the decline of the old Mediterranean trading world was caused by the retreat of the leading families of Venice to their manorial estates Alexander Nützenadel demonstrates that their involvement in new industrial ventures on the mainland was responsible for their increasing abandonment of traditional trading interests. The penetration of the new enterprising mercantile groups from the northwestern European countries into the Mediterranean economy led to a reorganisation and modernization of the old Ionian trade. By establishing new demand structures and financial provisions English merchants successfully integrated this part of the Mediterreanean into their own emerging commercial web (Sakis Gekas). Cátia Antunes uses the example of two rising trading centres on the Atlantic coast as a case study to develop a complex multi-layered network model to analyse the repercussions of the emergence of new trading connections on the local and regional hinterlands of Amsterdam and Lisbon, two of the main port cities in the early modern periods. Each city had been at the core of independent Atlantic and colonial networks.

The rapid expansion of international trade since the seventeenth century had diverse repercussions on old established inland as well as overseas trading groups and originated the development of new ones. The articles in the second part of this section reveal that no single or uniform answer can be given as to the fate of networks in the face of these changes. In the case of the Silesian merchants Marcel Boldorf shows that the concept of "feudalization" can be applied. For the changes in the international textile market as well as a lack of innovative spirit caused the Silesian merchants to give up their international commercial connections and invest in country estates. Christiane Reves highlights the role of migration for the establishment of new international networks. Century-old established commercial networks did not always fade out silently, as Laurence Fontaine demonstrates in her article on the European pedlars. They showed an astonishing resilience and adaptability to the challenge of commercial and industrial changes.

Between Local and Global Networks: the actors

The second section (Between Local and Global Networks: the actors) explores the commercial activities of individuals and groups who were responsible for the creation of networks and the commercial infrastructure. Recent literature on entrepreuneurs re-affirmed the importance of these actors as 'the engines of economic growth and innovation'.[27] This section of the book deals with the information and service agencies created by merchants as well as with the networks of merchant groups or individuals. The first part explores the maritime services provided by commercial and entrepreneurial networks to optimize the flow of information, capital and goods. The provision of adequate and reliable information has been a key function in reducing transactions costs not only in hierarchical organisations, but even more so in entrepreneurial networks. Within the framework of principal-agent-theory the problem of gaining reliable information has generally been researched from the principal's perspective. Jari Ojala argues that the monitoring process in order to ensure the reliability of information was as much the agent's as the principal's problem. Agency theory should therefore be reconsidered from the agent's point of view by stressing the interdependencies between the two parties. The flexibility and creative strength of maritime shipping agents and their principals for developing new strategies in the face of external events, such as the Napoleonic Wars, is emphasized by Silvia Marzagalli. As established maritime service networks were based on personal relationships, changes in the membership and composition of such

---

27 For the recent evaluation of the entrepreneur see, for example, S.A. Zahra, G. George and D.M. Garvis, *Networks and Entrepreneurship in Southeast Asia: The Role of Social Capital and Membership Commitment*, in Godley and Ross, *Banks, Networks*, 39; M. Casson also regards entrepreneurship as inseparable from innovation (Casson, 'An economic appproach to regional business networks', in: J.F. Wilson and A. Popp (eds.), *Industrial clusters and regional networks in England 1750-1970*, Aldershot 2003, 60; see also T.A.B. Corley, 'The Entrepreneur: the central issue in business history?', in: J. Brown and M.B. Rose, *Entrepreneurship, Networks and Modern Business Entrepreneurship*, Manchester 1993, 11-29; see also among older literature A.H. Cole, who remarked that "to study the entrepreneur is to study the central figure of in modern economic development" (*Business enterprise in its social setting*, Cambridge 1959, 28)).

agencies, which also influenced social relationships, could vitally affect their work. In a case study on the Mersey Dock & Harbour Board Adrian Jarvis showed how the change in the age-structure of the members, involvement in their businesses and their increasing volunteer activities in social and religious institutions were the causes for partial inefficiency of the Board.

The second part of this section explores the role of individual merchants as well as merchant groups and their changing commercial networking activities over the three centuries. It starts with Peter Edwards case study on the English arms dealers in the period of the Puritan Revolution. The dependency of the belligerent parties on arms supplies from foreign markets forced seventeenth-century arms dealers to include new groups of general merchants into their networks and expand their trading connections to new overseas territories. In face of the rapid expansion of the British Empire since the late seventeenth century the leading port cities of London or Bristol became the entrepots of international commerce. Asa Eklund, Chris Evans, Göran Ryden demonstrate in their study on Graffin Prankard from Bristol that the enterprising spirit not only of groups but also of individuals played a key role in the growth of the British Empire. He started his mercantile career as an Atlantic merchant and later on extended his trading relations into the Baltic, thereby integrating both regions into a single trading net. The networking activities of the overseas merchants connecting distant parts of the world gave rise to the big merchant empires of the nineteenth century. Their appearance with the progress of commercialisation and industrialisation represented the peak in the development of international family enterprises. Their networks were essentially based on family and kinship ties, where trust and reliability remained the key elements of business activity. In contrast to their eighteenth century predecessors, they had diversified into a wide range of economic and non-economic activities such as manufacturing or banking and had established a variety of social, cultural, religious and political linkages.[28] A systematic analysis of such a diversified network is provided by Dittmar Dahlmann's analysis of Ludwig Knoop's empire. Like other well-known British merchant-bankers of German descent, Ludwig Knoop and his sons established a mercantile empire which stretched from Russia via Britain and Germany across the Atlantic.

---

28 For the concept of diversification in networks see R. Pearson, Collective diversification: 'Manchester Cotton Merchants and the Insurance Business in the Early Nineteenth Century', in: *Business History Review*, 65 (1991), 379-414.

Merging Local and Global Functions: Port cities

The last section (Merging Local and Global Functions: Port cities) concentrates on ports and commercial cities. They were nodes of commercial networks where local, regional and overseas networks merged. Essential features of commercial expansion can only be explained from a local perspective, for urban activities vitally influenced the dynamic of expansion. Jürgen Nagel shows how the penetration of the Verenigde Oostindische Company (VOC) to the Malay Archipelago caused a major change of the traditional trading pattern in southeast Asia. Integrating the concept of 'centrality' into network analysis he demonstrates how under the impact of the VOC a shift in traditional trading routes took place and to what extent new and old trading centres declined and rose outside as well as under the influence of the Company.

Research on urban history has concentrated its analysis mainly on processes which operated within the urban boundaries and thereby largely neglected the relationship towards the hinterland. However, port and commercial cities in particular were not self-contained units but extended their influence into the immediate hinterland and even further. Three case studies take up this largely neglected aspect of research on port city-hinterland relations. Jon Stobart shows in a case study on Chester how merchants and the local commercial institutions shaped the links and channels towards the hinterland and other local centres or regions. He highlights the importance of assured local networks for securing a reliable commercial information flow beyond local borders into wider business linkages across the country and beyond. Although the north-eastern region of England had several large ports, their importance has been for a long time overshadowed by the country's West ports of Liverpool and Bristol. Graeme Milne shows that the coal trade and shipbuilding industries were central to the development of the region and inter-connected the port cities with the hinterland and other parts of Europe and the world. The commercial elite had a defining influence on the economy, the society and culture of the North East. Therefore the activities of the port cities should be seen not only in a commercial context but also as administrative and governmental interfaces between ports, regions, and nations. In his case study on the port city of Bremen Robert Lee stresses the role of political factors in shaping the relation between port city and region. The persistence of the federal structure in Germany with its diverse tariffs and taxation policies even after the unification in 1871 prevented a full integration of the port city with its hinterland. Nevertheless with the considerable expansion of overseas commerce the port city of Bremen created a complex system of interaction between city and hinterland in terms of migration, information dissemination or flows of goods that determined the patterns of commercial and cultural change in the urban hinterland. As gateways to international commerce on the one hand and interfaces to the hinterland port cities played a pivotal role in the expanding world economy. With the changes in transport technology in the twentieth century, however, as Henk van Dijk stressed, port cities underwent a de-industrialisation. It ensued a radical transformation of their internal as well as external network structure in the twentieth century.

The expansion of trade from Europe to the remotest parts in the world cannot be understood solely in economic terms. The last part of this section deals with the non-commercial social and cultural values which accompanied the flow of goods. As long as the transport of commodities is organised by human beings, cultural and social values are inextricably integrated in the exchange of goods and capital. The commercial and the geographical range of activities is most apparent, but by introducing new goods, merchants and businessmen introduced new styles, new habits and cultural values. They established economic as well as social or charitable institutions in distant parts of the world and with them they transformed old-established infrastructures and established new ones. In other words, the expansion of the European commercial networks generated 'social capital'.[29] The flow of goods also created a web of social relationships, cultural norms of behaviour, obligations and trust which gave rise to a cosmopolitan pattern of behaviour. It gave birth to what Friedrich Meinecke called the "Weltbürger"[30] long ago or more recently Hancock called "Citizens of the World". The relationship between commerce and culture is explored in Eva Stolbergs paper on the integration of Russia into the Western Hemisphere. For the intensification of commercial relations between Europe and Russia, as well as the migration and settlement of members of the West-European commercial and industrial elites into the Russian empire, was accompanied by an eager adoption of west-European cultural values and patterns of behaviour by the Russian élite. In cases like Boston integration into a wider network did not happen without conflict and clashes at a local level (Sharon Rodgers). The spread of a cosmopolitan commercial culture was necessary precondition for commercial ventures beyond national and cultural lines and it manifested itself in structural similarities on the political, administrative and social level in port

---

29 Concerning "social capital" see F. Fukuyama, *Trust: the social virtues and the creation of prosperity*, Hammondsworth 1995; Luhmann, *Trust and Power*; M. Fiedler, 'Netzwerke des Vertrauens: Zwei Fallbeispiele aus der deutschen Wirtschaftselite', in: D. Ziegler (ed.), *Großbürger und Unternehmer. Die deutsche Wirtschaftselite im 20. Jahrhundert*, Göttingen 2000, 93-115.

30 F. Meinecke, *Weltbürgertum und Nationalstaat: Studien zur Genesis des deutschen Nationalstaates*, 4th ed., Munich 1917.

cities as far apart as Bremen and Boston or New York and other American port cities, as Sam Mustafa shows in his paper.

Taken together the contributions in this volume provide different explanations as to how networks expanded or degenerated in the period under review. Although they differ in emphasis and approach the chapters address a number of common aspects which are complementary to the recent theoretical developments in commercial and entrepreneurial network concepts. By addressing various facets of commercial networking and its linkages at different operational levels and in different countries, the studies address many of the issues which have become focal points for the recent debate on the emerging world economy.

I.

Emergence, Decline
and Reconstruction of Networks

Coping with Decline. Commercial Networks, Merchants and the Regionalization of Trade in Eighteenth Century Venice

Alexander Nützenadel

Introduction

If we refer to the sixteenth and seventeenth centuries as the initial stage of globalization,[1] then Venice figured among the first losers of this process. As well known, the leading European sea and trading power entered into a severe crisis after the discovery of new trading routes in the Atlantic, the emergence of new maritime powers in Europe and the disintegration of its colonial empire in the Eastern Mediterranean.[2] The crisis of long-distant trade was closely linked to the decline of urban manufacturing since the early seventeenth century. Production of silk and wool fabrics, glass, printing and ship building decreased dramatically, as the domestic industry was less and less able to keep up with the prices and quality of the English, French and Dutch competitors. Scholarship has referred to the declining productivity and unwillingness of the urban artisanship to adopt new manufacturing techniques.[3] The strict rules and market regulations of the guilds, which once had guaranteed the high quality of Venetian products, proved to be a suffocating corset. Moreover, the merchant elites withdrew from commercial activities and invested their money in splendid palaces and an extravagant life-style.

There have, however, been doubts whether decline was an irreversible process lasting until the end of the Republic in 1797. While this picture prevailed in historiography for a long time,[4] more recent studies have questioned this interpretation. They point to the fact that during the eighteenth century, Venice still figured among the wealthiest cities in Europe and represented an important centre of regional trade. They thus prefer to speak of a relative decline at most and point to the reorganization of regional economy during the eighteenth century.[5]

1   See I. Wallerstein, *The Modern World System*, vol. I: *Capitalist Agriculture and the Origins of the European World-Economy in the Sixteenth Century*, San Diego 1974.

2   *Aspetti e cause della decadenza economica veneziana nel secolo 17*, Venice / Rome 1961.

3   R.T. Rapp, *Industry and Economic Decline in Seventeenth-Century Venice*, Cambridge (Mass.), London 1976; D. Sella, *Commercio e industrie a Venezia nel secolo XVII*, Venice 1961.

4   See e.g. G. Quazza, *La decadenza italiana nella storia europea. Saggi sul Sei-Settecento*, Turin 1971, 35-51; Amintore Fanfani, 'Il mancato rinnovamento economico', in: *Storia della civiltà veneziana*, vol. 9: *La civiltà veneziana del Settecento*, Florence 1960, 27-67.

5   M. Costantini, 'Commercio e marina', in: P. del Negro and P. Preto (eds.), *Storia di Venezia*

This article confirms this more optimistic view and explores the economic transformation between the late seventeenth century and the end of the Republic in 1797. The first part analyses the quantitative development of Venice's trade in the context of regional integration. The second part explains how and why economic activities shifted from Venice to the mainland and in which way this was linked to trade regionalization. The third part inquires about the role that the old merchant elites played in the economic transformations during the last hundred years of the Republic.

Regional integration has come to the fore in the last years in both the literature of economics and geography, since spatially defined productive systems have been discerned as important elements of economic growth and development. In this context, Alfred Marshall's concept of "industrial districts" has been rediscovered and discussed with particular regard to Italy, where regionally based economic development seems to have played an important role.[6] Industrial districts are defined as networks of mostly small and specialized firms which are located in close proximity and are embedded in local institutional structures that support a dynamic mix of cooperation and competition.[7] A significant feature of industrial districts is that they are conceived as a social and economic entity. This implies that various aspects of regional governance and institutions have to be considered, including informal cooperation, networking and partnerships as well as the social and cultural context.[8] There are obvious reasons to apply this theoretical framework to the regional development of eighteenth century Venice, as has been recently suggested by Walter Panciera.[9] Even though formal model testing can hardly be

---

dalle origini alla caduta della Serenissima, vol. VIII: L'ultima fase della Serenissima, Rome 1998, 555-612, 577-581; W. Panciera, 'The geography of trade from the Battle of Lepanto to the Fall of the Serenissima', in: G. Barbieri (ed.), L'Europa e le Venezie. Viaggio nel giardino del mondo, Cittadella 1997, 250-251; see also D. Sella, 'Crisis and Transformation in Venetian Trade', in: B. Pullan (ed.), Crisis and Change in the Venetian Economy in the 16th and 17th Centuries, London 1968, 89-105.

6   G. Becattini, Distretti industriali e made in Italy: le basi socioculturali del nostro sviluppo economico, Turin 1998; F. Pyke, G. Becattini and W. Sengenberger (eds.), Industrial Districts and Inter-Firm Cooperation in Italy, Geneve 1992; M. Bellandi, 'The Industrial District in Marshall', in: E. Goodman and J. Bamford (eds.), Small Firms and Industrial Districts in Italy, New York 1989, 136-152.

7   S. Brusco, 'The Emilian Model: Productive Decentralization and Social Integration', in: Cambridge Journal of Economics, 6 (1982), 167-184; Ch. Sabel, 'Flexible Specialization and the Re-Emergence of Regional Economies', in: P. Hirst and J. Zeitlin (eds.), Reversing Industrial Decline, Oxford 1982, 17-70.

8   See, for example, M. Danson, G. Lloyd and S. Hill (eds.), Regional Governance and Economic Development, London 1997.

9   W. Panciera, L'Arte matrice. I lanifici della Repubblica di Venezia nei secoli XVII e XVIII,

carried out, since information on industrial development, social structures, communication and trade networks are still sketchy for this period, this model may help to understand the profound transformations of Venetian economy during the eighteenth century. Moreover, it provides useful insights into the complex interaction between global linkages and regionalization processes.

Venice and the Regionalization of Trade

By the mid-seventeenth century, Venice had lost her role as the hub of the Mediterranean.[10] However, commercial activities of the emporium were still considerable, and after the end of the Cretan War in 1669, long-distant trade was slowly recovering. Reliable trade statistics are not available for this period. But the receipts from the anchorage tax show an increase of about 70 per cent between 1670 and 1702, and a similar rise is revealed by some import statistics: 68,000 bales of merchandise entered the port of Venice in 1675, 83,000 five years later, 110,000 in 1725.[11] After the end of the war against the Turks, Venice was partly able to revive her trade with the Levant. While the European markets in France, England and the Netherlands were irretrievably lost, Venetian merchants were able to regain a foothold on the German markets after the end of the Thirty Years War. The increase in trade may also be attributed to the fact that Venice abandoned protectionism and drastically lowered her import tariffs in 1662.[12] The experiment of a free port (terminated in 1684) was the first of a whole series of political initiatives devised to restore Venice's former maritime power. Even if this goal was never achieved, mercantile and commercial politics contributed at least to a temporary recovery of trade and helped to prevent further decline.

J. Georgelin has calculated an overall trade index for Venice in the eighteenth century (*Figure 1*).[13] Although his figures are based on diverse data sources and

---

Treviso 1996, 310; C. Poni, 'Per la storia del distretto industriale serico di Bologna (secoli XVI-XIX)', in: *Quaderni storici*, 73 (1990), 93-168; see also S. Ciriacono, 'Protoindustria, lavoro a domicilio e sviluppo economico nelle campagne venete in età moderna', in: *Quaderni Storici*, 52 (1983), 57-80; M. Mirri, 'Formazione di una regione economica. Ipotesi sulla Toscana, sul Veneto, sulla Lombardia', in: *Studi Veneziani*, 11 (1986), 47-59.

10 S. Ciriacono, 'The Venetian economy and its place in the world economy of the 17th and 18th centuries. A comparison with the Low countries', in: H. J. Nitz (ed.), *The early modern world system in geographical perspective*, Stuttgart 1990, 120-135.

11 See Sella, Crisis, 100; J. Georgelin, *Venise au siècle des lumières*, Paris, La Haye 1978, 68-69.

12 M. Costatini, 'La regolazione dei dazi marittimi e l'esperienza del "portofranco" a Venezia tra il 1662 e il 1684', in: A. di Vittorio (ed.), *La finanza pubblica in età di crisi*, Bari 1993, 77-88.

13 Georgelin, *Venise*, 1008-1011; see also the figures in Costatini, *Commercio*, 577-581.

therefore have to be treated cautiously, they provide a rough picture of the long term trends.

Figure 1: Commerce of the port of Venice 1700-1800
(Index, constant prices)

Source: Georgelin, *Venise*, 1008, Annexe 17

According to the estimates, trade volume rose considerably up to about 1710, followed by a marked decline, especially after the foundation of the free ports in Triest and Fiume in 1719. In the mid-1730s Venetian trade recovered again, probably due to the tariff reform of 1736 and the introduction of government subsidies for the domestic merchant fleet.[15] During the second half of the 1740s, the markets of Rialto took advantage of the Austrian war of succession, as the neutrality of the Republic made the port attractive for foreign merchants and shipping companies. After a period of stagnation, trade recovered again during the early 1760s as a consequence of the commercial treaties that Venice stipulated with the Kings of North Africa. In general, trade activities of the city remained considerable during the whole eighteenth century. According to the older estimates of Giordano Campos, the emporium's trade in the second half of the eighteenth century was, in constant prices, more or less equivalent to the trade turnover at the peak of the late fifteenth century.[16] This evidence supports

---

14 Georgelin, *Venise*, 1008-1011; see also the figures in Costatini, *Commercio*, 577-581.
15 D. Beltrami, 'La crisi della marina mercantile veneziana e i provvedimenti del 1736 per fronteggiarla', in: *Rivista Internazionale di Scienze Sociali*, 50 (1942), 304-318.
16 G. Campos, 'Il commercio esterno veneziano della seconda metà del 1700 secondo le statistiche ufficiali', in: *Archivio Veneto*, ser. V, vol. 29 (1936), 145-183, 153-155; see also G. Luzzatto, 'Le vicende del porto di Venezia dal primo Medievio Evo allo scoppio della guerra

the interpretation that commerce declined in relative rather than in absolute terms.

Table 1: Regional distribution of Venetian commerce 1789/90 (in thousand ducats)

Regions	Imports	%	Exports	%
Levante estero (Constantinople, Egypt, Cyprus, Morea ecc.)	1,505.1	*11.4*	578.3	*7.0*
Golfo estero (Turkish Albania, Apulia, Pontifical harbours)	973.3	*7.4*	325.8	*4.0*
Terraferma estera (Lombardy, Piedmont, Bologna ecc.)	463.0	*3.5*	652.1	*7.8*
Germania alta e bassa (German territories including Trieste)	1,292.2	*9.8*	546.1	*6.6*
Ponente alto (Netherlands, England, France, Portugal, Spain)	1,702.0	*12.9*	223.9	*2.7*
Ponente basso (Genua, Livorno, Malta, Naples, Sicily)	451.3	*3.4*	249.7	*3.0*
Levante suddito (Zante, Cefalonia, Corfu, Cerigo, Santa Marta)	1,174.1	*8.9*	221.0	*2.7*
Golfo suddito (Dalmatia, Istria)	1,409.5	*10.7*	681.6	*8.2*
Terraferma veneziana (including the Venetian Lombardy)	4,214.5	*32.0*	4,806.6	*58.0*
Total	13,185.0	*100.0*	8,285.1	*100.0*

Source: Caizzi, *Industria*, 265

However, structure and regional distribution of trade had changed considerably. Based on custom registers, Bruno Caizzi drew up a statistic which illustrates the regional distribution of Venice's trade fairly accurate (see Table 1). The data shows that commercial activities of Venetian merchants focused on the

---

1914-1918', in: G. Luzatto, *Studi di storia economica veneziana*, Padua 1954, 1-35, 18.

Republic's colonies and the *Terraferma* as well as on the adjoining territories in Northern Italy. In 1789/90, 35.5 per cent of the imported goods arrived from the Italian mainland, 18.1 per cent from the Adriatic, and 8.9 per cent from the colonies in the eastern Mediterranean. 34.1 per cent were imported from Germany, Western Europe and the Levant, while the rest came from other Italian port cities such as Naples or Genova. Export numbers reflect an even stronger trend towards regionalization. Venice exported 68.5 per cent of her goods to the *Terraferma* and the colonies, while only 16.3 per cent were directed to Northern and Western Europe and the Levant. During the second half of the century, Venice had to face an increasing trade deficit, which amounted to little less than 5 Million silver ducats in 1789/90. While the city's demand for consumer products remained high, the domestic industries were less and less able to sell their products abroad. Transit trade - once the most important business for Venetian merchants - continually declined. Venice imported mainly raw materials and agrarian products as well as textiles from the mainland. Exports to the Levant and the Adriatic consisted principally of textiles and paper from the mainland, while the traffic towards Holland, England and the Iberian Peninsula was dominated by locally produced commodities such as books, silk and Murano glass. To the German-speaking territories, the city sold olive oil, raisins and small amounts of silk cloth and glass products. Long-distant traffic did not disappear entirely, although the port served more and more as a market for raw materials, foodstuff and manufactured products from the *Terraferma*.

The trend towards regional integration is also reflected by the fact that the trading centres of the *Terraferma* gained importance during the seventeenth century.[17] Especially Padua, Vicenza, Bassano and Verona hosted important regional markets. The fairs of Bolzano played a crucial role in the commerce between Northern Italy, the Alpine Region and the German territories. An increasing share of the regional trade - especially between the eastern provinces and the adjoining territories - was transported by land and inland navigation. Verona was by far the largest inland port of the region with the Adige linking the Po valley, the ports of the Adriatic and the German-speaking territories.[18]

---

17 Panciera, Geography, 250-251.
18 T. Fanfani, 'L'Adige come Arteria principale del traffico tra nord Europa ed emporio realtino', in: G. Borelli (ed.), *Una città e il suo fiume. Verona e l'Adige*, Verona 1977, 569-629.

Population, Rural Economy and Industrial Development in the Venetian Mainland

There is reason to believe that the regionalization of trade was closely linked to the economic development of the *Terraferma*. While industry in Venice never fully recovered from the severe crisis of the seventeenth century, there was a remarkable development of agriculture and (proto-)industrial production in the hinterland. Agriculture had undergone a far-reaching transformation since the middle of the seventeenth century. Supported by investments from Venice and co-ordinated by new government magistracies, land reclamation projects had extended the area of arable land.[19] Beltrami estimated that in the sixteenth century about a third of the agricultural area of the republic was lying fallow. About 60 per cent of that area were turned into productive land during the seventeenth and eighteenth centuries.[20] In addition, the liquidation of communal property, which the Venetian government had started to sell for fiscal reasons in the mid-seventeenth century, led to more intensive forms of land cultivation.[21] The expansion of arable land facilitated the spreading of new crops. Corn, which had been introduced from Germany in 1536, was especially important because of the high yield per acre. In the province of Verona and in the Polesine farmers began cultivating rice on such a large scale that considerable amounts could be exported.[22] Viticulture expanded as well, and the same goes for mulberry plantations and silkworm farms, which became important branches of agriculture, especially around Padua, Verona and Treviso. The intensification of agriculture was a slow process depending on technical know-how as well as on external capital.[23] It was accompanied by a substantial demographic growth, while the population of the old urban centres stagnated or even declined.[24]

Closely linked with the agrarian development was the emergence of new industrial agglomerations in the small towns and rural areas of the *Terraferma*,

---

19 R. Cessi, *I lavori pubblici nella Repubblica veneta*, Roma 1925.

20 D. Beltrami, *Saggio di storia dell'agricoltura nella Repubblica di Venezia durante l'età moderna*, Venice / Rome 1955, 30-36.

21 G. Ferrari, La legislazione veneziana sui beni comunali, in: *Archivio veneto*, 36 (1918), 38-58.

22 M. Fassina, 'L'introduzione della coltura del mais nelle campagne venete', in: *Società e storia*, 15 (1982), 31-59; M. Lecce, *La coltura del riso in territorio veronese*, Verona 1958.

23 G. Borelli, *Città e campagna in età preindustriale XVI-XVIII secolo*, Verona 1986; C. Salvatore, 'Investimenti capitalistici e culture irrigue. La congiuntura agricola nella Terraferma veneta (secoli XVI e XVII)', in: A. Terraferri (ed.), *Venezia e la Terraferma attraverso le relazioni dei rettori*, Milan 1981, 123-158.

24 See D. Beltrami, *Storia della popolazione di Venezia dalla fine del secolo XVI alla caduta della Repubblica*, Padua 1954.

depending mainly on the growth of the silk industry. Silk weaving had constituted an important branch of the Venetian economy since the Middle Ages.[25] Manufacturers in the city had specialized in the production of high quality products. They relied on the importation of large amounts of raw silk from Spain, Southern Italy and the Balkans. Since the sixteenth century the production of raw silk expanded in the Venetian Republic, especially in the hilly region of the Alpine foothills. By the beginning of the seventeenth century, the Venetian Republic had become one of the largest producers of raw silk in Europe with an output peaking at about 500,000 pounds yearly.[26]

The development of the mainland's sericulture was fostered by mercantilist politics. In 1634 the Venetian Senate passed a bill which aimed to promote the construction of water-driven silk mills in the country, a technology that had been introduced from Bologna in the sixteenth century already.[27] The decree granted tax exemption for machinery, allowed the free use of water ways, abrogated some of the strict guild regulations and abolished the internal tariff on silk yarn. Even though rural domestic work continued to play an important role, power spinning took a growing share of silk manufacturing. By the middle of the eighteenth century about 160 modern silk mills existed in the Veneto, most of them in the rural areas of the Alpine foothills.[28]

Only part of the raw silk and silk thread was sold on the regional market. Large amounts were exported to other Italian cities and to the rapidly growing industries in Western and Central Europe, while manufacturers in Venice continued to import raw silk from Greece and Syria. Silk-weaving forcefully expanded on the mainland during the eighteenth century, especially in the *Vicentino*. Of the 2,390 looms counted throughout the Republic in 1790, almost half were located in this area, compared to only 674 in Venice.[29] Economic rather than political factors were responsible for the rise of the mainland silk industry. The pre-alpine region offered both water power and cheap labour in abundance. Guild regulations which hampered new initiatives in Venice and other towns of the *Terraferma*, were absent or less restrictive. Close proximity of sericulture and raw silk production kept transportation costs low. Finally, the

25 L. Mola, *The Silk Industry of Renaissance Venice*, Baltimore 2000.

26 L. Mola, 'The spice and silk routes: export trade in the Veneto from the 14th to the 16th century', in: Barbieri (ed.), *Viaggi*, 248-50.

27 C. Poni, 'Archéologie de la fabrique: la diffusion des moulins à soie "alla bolognese" dans les États vénetiens du XVIe au XVIIe siècle', in: *Annales,* 27 (1972), 1475-1496, 1486.

28 D. Sella, 'Contributo alla storia delle fonti di energia: i filatoi idraulici nella Valle Padana durante il secolo XVII', in: *Studi in onore di Amintore Fanfani*, vol. V, Milan 1962, 621-623.

29 Numbers in B. Caizzi, *Industria e commercio della Repubblica veneta nel XVIII secolo*, Milan 1965, 116, 124.

long tradition of rural domestic work and small industries guaranteed the availability of technical know-how and skilled labour. The combination of a rapidly growing new industry and the proto-industrial transformation of substantial rural areas proved to be a decisive local advantage.

The rural areas of the *Terraferma* ousted Venice from her former leading position in yet another sector: the production of woollen cloth. Cloth-making in Venice had collapsed in the seventeenth century and remained insignificant thereafter.[30] A more complex picture is provided by the cities of the mainland. While the production of woollen cloth suffered from a severe crisis in Verona and Vicenza, Padua and Treviso could hold their position as important centres of production.[31] At the same time, however, cloth making boomed in the countryside, especially in the northern regions of Treviso, Vicenza and Bergamo. Again, low wages, absence of strict guild regulations and the horizontal integration of different stages of production provided favourable conditions for new industries. A similar situation characterized the production of cotton fabrics as well as hemp and canvas making, which also flourished in rural areas and small towns. An outstanding example is the linen factory of Giacomo Linussio, founded in 1720 in Tolmezzo, a small town in northern Friuli. Flax production abounded in the surroundings of Tolmezzo, based primarily on rural domestic work. In 1725 the Linussio company produced 15,000 metre of linen already and employed 200 weavers and 2,500 spinners. 35 years later the company had raised its production more than ten-fold and was able to export a large share of its output aside from serving the local market.[32] Other entrepreneurs in the region followed Linussio's lead, e.g. Tommaso Del Fabbro and Lorenzo Foramiti, who also set up large linen mills in Tolmezzo. Another important sector which combined both regional basis and integration into the international market was paper production and printing. Paper production concentrated in the pre-alpine areas, particularly around the Lago di Garda and the provinces of Treviso and Vicenza.[33] In the mid-eighteenth century, 85 paper mills were in operation throughout the Venetian territory, some of them producing a considerable output. High quality paper was partly delivered to the still outstanding printing industry of Venice, partly to new enterprises emerging in the *Terraferma*. One of the centres of printing evolved in Bassano di Grappa, where the Remondini brothers ran one of the foremost printing industries in

---

30 Caizzi, *Industria.*, 34 and 50.

31 Panciera, *L'Arte*, 13-22.

32 Caizzi, *Industria*, 167-170; see also G. Ganzer, *Arte e impresa nel Settecento in Carnia: Iacopo Linussio*, Udine 1991.

33 I. Mattozzi, *Produzione e commercio della carta nello stato veneziano settecentesco. Lineamenti e problemi*, Bologna 1975.

Europe, employing 2,400 workers in 1767. The company was able to export a large share of its output to the Levant, Spain and to other European countries.[34]

Venetian Merchants and the Economic Development of the Hinterland: Capital Investments, Entrepreneurship and the Reconstruction of Commercial Networks

It has been disputed whether the development of the *Terraferma* was influenced by the policies and economic activities of the capital. For a long time, scholarship has pointed solely to the negative aspects of Venetian policies. According to that view, the capital had exploited the natural resources of the mainland (for example by cutting the forests for the Venetian construction and shipbuilding industry) and hampered the *Terraferma*'s economic growth through high taxes and discriminating policies for trade and industry.[35] At the same time the Venetian aristocracy had bought land on a large scale but showed little interest in running their own estates. This opinion has been challenged by recent studies.[36] They stressed the fact that in the eighteenth century, Venice increased her efforts to integrate the territory and promote the establishment of new industries in the region.[37] Because of her still important port, wealth and high demand for food stuffs, raw materials and semi-finished products the metropolis did remain a relevant economic centre for the hinterland. Finally, Venetian merchants invested capital in agriculture and the new industries thus contributing to the economic upswing of the *Terraferma*.

Already in the fifteenth century, Venetian nobles had begun to build magnificent estates in the *Terraferma* where they and their families spent the summer months. Since the middle of the seventeenth century, the demand for real estate on the mainland grew strongly, a fact that was linked to the crisis in long-distance trade and the imminent loss of the colonies in the Eastern Mediterranean.[38] Both the cultivation of new land and the privatization of communal property enabled Venetian patricians to buy large estates and gain an

---

34 M. Infelise, *I Remondini di Bassano. Stampa e industria nel Veneto del Settecento*, Bassano 1980.

35 M. Berengo, *La società veneta alla fine del Settecento. Ricerche storiche*, Firenze 1965, 1-42; Caizzi, *Industria*, 5-40.

36 See e.g. Georgelin, *Venise*.

37 See W. Panciera, 'L'economia: imprenditora, corporazioni, lavoro', in: Del Negro and Preto (eds.), *Storia*, 479-533, 482.

38 S. J. Woolf, 'Venice and the Terraferma: Problems of the Change from Commercial to Landed Activities', in: Pullan (ed.), *Crisis*, 175-203.

economic foothold in the hinterland. About 40 per cent of the communal land alienated between 1646 and 1726 was bought by families from the capital. Between the tax surveys of 1636 and 1740 the percentage of agricultural land owned by Venetians grew from 11.7 to 22.2 per cent.[39] In provinces close to the metropolis such as Padua, Venetians owned as much as half of the land. The 1722 tax census counted 1,000 Venetians as tax-paying landowners. At the top figured big landowners like the Pisani family with a property of 4,600 hectares, the Contarini family with 3,000 hectares or Ludovico Manin, father of the last Doge, with estates amounting to roughly 6,000 hectares.[40] By the mid-eighteenth century almost every patrician family owned landed property in the *Terraferma*. Some historians have referred to the concept of a "feudalization" of the Venetian aristocracy, who shifted investments from trade to landed property and built luxurious country estates. Indeed, 739 stately mansions were erected in the Veneto during the seventeenth and eighteenth centuries, many of whom outshined Central European palaces in terms of size and splendor.[41]

However, it would be wrong to consider the purchase of land as a misinvestment of capital and as a sign of an increasing economic immobility of the aristocracy. Studies analyzing the economic activities of Venetian families show that the low but secure ground rent served to counterbalance the risks related to fluctuating trade returns.[42] For example, Guiseppe Gullino's study of the Pisani dal Banco and Moretta has demonstrated that the acquisition of real estate played an important role in the financial strategies of Venetian nobles.[43] Diversification and spreading of risks were based on rational investment behaviour of the patricians who wanted to secure and enlarge their wealth.[44]

---

39 D. Beltrami, *La penetrazione economica dei veneziani in Terraferma. Forze di lavoro e proprietà fondiaria nelle campagne venete dei secoli XVII e XVIII*, Venice, Rome 1961, 75, 141.

40 Beltrami, *penetrazione*, 127f.

41 M. Brusatin, *Venezia nel Settecento: stato, architettura, territorio*, Turin 1980, 52-53.

42 R. T. Rapp, 'Real Estate and Rational Investment in Early Modern Venice', in: *The Journal of European Economic History*, 8 (1979), 269-290.

43 G. Gullino, *I Pisani Dal Banco e Moretta. Storie di due famiglie veneziane in età moderna e delle loro vicende patrimoniali tra 1705 e 1836*, Rome 1984; J. Cushman Davis, *A Venetian Family and its Fortune (1500-1900). The Donà and the Conservation of their Wealth*, Philadelphia 1975; R. Derosas, 'I Querini Stampalia. Vicende patrimoniali dal Cinque all'Ottocento', in: G. Busetto (ed.), *I Querini Stampalia. Un ritratto di famiglia nel Settecento veneziano*, Venice 1987, 43-87.

44 P. Burke's examination of the tax records shows that the income of the aristocracy was considerably higher in the mid-eigthteenth century than in the sixteenth century; P. Burke, *Venice and Amsterdam: A Study of Seventeenth-Century Elites*, London 1974, 102.

Those strategies were especially important during the eighteenth century with its almost continuously rising prices for land and agricultural products.[45] Furthermore, the real estate boom in the hinterland led to a significant influx of capital, which very likely had an effect on the economic development of the region as well. The aristocratic country estate had not only a representative function, but very often also served as "the heart of a manorial farm".[46] Many nobles were heavily involved in the economic development of their country estates. Some of them fostered the intensification of agriculture by cultivating fallow land, constructing drainage canals and fencing open fields.[47] Often these farms focused on labour- and capital-intensive products such as viticulture, flax, hemp and mulberry trees.[48]

Investments and entrepreneurial activities of the patricians evidently played a major role in the development of new industries in the small towns and rural areas of the *Terraferma*.[49] Paradigmatic is the case of Niccolò Tron (1685-1772), member of one of the most influential and wealthy Venetian families. The Tron family owned a large estate in Anguillara in the Polesine, a fertile region in the eastern Po valley. Niccolò Tron carried out the extensive draining of the land employing a steam-driven engine, which he had imported from England.[50] Through high investments, the family estate became one of the largest and most advanced farms in the region, cultivating 415 hectares with 360 workers.[51]

---

45 For prices of agricultural products in the Veneto see Georgelin, *Venise*, 1048-1074. Another economic motive for investment in real estate might have been price inflation; Woolf, Venice, 195f.; see also R. Derosas, 'Aspetti economici della crisi del patriziato veneziano tra fine Settecento e primo Ottocento', in: G.L. Fontana and A. Lazzarini (eds.), *Veneto e Lombardia tra rivoluzione giacobina ed età napoleonica. Economia, territorio, istituzioni*, Bari 1992, 80-132.

46 E. Sereni, *Storia del paesaggio agrario italiano*, Bari 1961, 197; see also A. Ventura, 'Aspetti storico economici della villa veneta', in: *Bollettino del Centro Internazionale di studi di architettura Andrea Palladino*, 11 (1969), 65-77.

47 G. Gullino, 'Venezia e le campagne', in: Del Negro and Preto (eds.), *Storia*, 651-702; a survey of the land reclamation in the Venetian Republic is provided by S. Ciriacono, 'Fiumi e agricoltura nella Repubblica di Venezia nel Settecento', in: *L'uomo e il fiume dal mito alla storia*, Milan 1989, 51-64.

48 J. Georgelin, 'Une grande exploitation en face à la révolution agricole: Bottenigo (Venise): 1755-1791', in: P. Bairoch (ed.), *Les passages des économies traditionelles européennes aux sociétés industrielles*, Geneve/ Paris 1985, 257-283.

49 See Caizzi, *Industria*, 43-127 and 165-194.

50 G. Gullino, 'L'anomala ambasceria inglese di Niccolò Tron (1714-1717) e l'introduzione della macchina a vapore in Italia', in: *Non un itinere. Studi storici offerti dagli allievi a F. Seneca*, Venice 1993, 185-207.

51 G. Georgelin, 'Une grande propriété en Vénétie au XVIIIe siècle: Anguillara', in: *Annales*, 23 (1968), 483-519.

But the entrepreneurial ambitions of Tron were not confined to agriculture. Even more important were his activities in the woollen industry. As Venetian ambassador in London between 1714 and 1717 he had learned English manufacturing techniques. After his return to Venice his proposal to reform the Venetian woollen industry met with heavy resistance by the craft guilds and was finally rejected by the *Consiglio dei Dieci*.[52] Those obstacles induced Tron to shift his activities from Venice to the *Terraferma*. He finally decided to invest in the woollen industry in Schio, a small town north of Vicenza. Schio offered both cheap labour and abundant raw material in the vicinity. On the plateau nearby (*Altopiano dei Sette Comuni*) about 200,000 sheep provided wool of a medium quality.

There already existed several small manufactories employing a large number of workers who had been producing fabrics of low quality almost exclusively for the local market. The development of Schio's industry had been restricted by the guild regulations of Vicenza permitting Schio to produce only a certain type of cloth of minor quality. By the beginning of the eighteenth century the woollen industry of Vicenza had almost collapsed and Schio was granted the privilege to produce high quality mechandise for the domestic and foreign markets.[53] Niccolò Tron founded a wool mill in Schio in 1719, which was managed by local merchants. During the first years, the enterprise had only limited success. However, by constantly enlarging production and introducing new weaving techniques, he became one of the most successful entrepreneurs in the region. Tron employed skilled workers from France and England. He introduced the English flying shuttle to Italy, a technique which was rapidly taken over by other companies of the region.[54] His factory, which for some time employed more than 2,500 workers, laid the foundation for the lasting success of the textile industry in the provinces of Vicenza and Treviso.[55]

During the first three decades of the eighteenth century, manufacturers in Schio produced mainly for the regional market. Their fabrics were traded at the fairs in Lombardy and in the Marche, but they played no role in the overseas

---

52 Caizzi, *Industria*, 62; see also G. Gullino, Jacobo Linussio, 'Nicolò Tron ed una possibile manovra di politica economica agli inizi della protoindustria veneta', in: B. Bertoli (ed.), *Chiesa, società e Stato a Venezia. Miscellanea di studi in onore di Silvio Tramontin nel suo LXXV anno di età*, Venezia 1994, 197-206.

53 Panciere, *L'Arte*, 83

54 W. Panciera, 'Articolazione della produzione e livelli technologici delle manifatture laniere di Schio nella seconda metà del XVIII secolo', in: *Quaderni Storici*, 59 (1985), 403-426, 417.

55 Caizzi, *Industria*, 62-65; see also W. Panciera, *I lanifici dell'Alto Vicentino nel XVIII secolo*, Vicenza 1988; for the geographical distribution of the manufactories see Georgelin, *Venise*, 1118, Annexe 76.

commerce, because they could not compete with the quality and prices of the Flemish, French and English fabrics. However, as early as 1739 Tron had set up a new factory with 44 weaving looms (*Associati della fabrica di panni ad uso estero in Schio*), where local wool was mixed with imported Spanish wool and woven into high quality cloth. By the 1740s, the merchants of Schio already exported part of their production and gained a foothold on the markets in Constantinople and Alexandria.

In 1767 about 6,000 people worked in the manufactories of Schio, and in the surrounding villages and towns (Thiene, Valdagno, Arzignano, Leguzzano, Torrebelvicino) new manufactories were set up as well. By that time, Schio had become the centre of Venetian cloth-making accounting for about half of the overall cloth production in the Republic.[56] In 1794, 350 weaving looms were counted in Schio and roughly a hundred more in the villages in the vicinity. Moreover, in almost every house of the city manual spinning was carried out.[57]

Since about 1750, new centres of woollen cloth-making emerged in the small towns and villages north of Treviso (e.g. Valdobbiadene, Castelfranco, Follina, Crespano).[58] Locational factors (low labour costs, no compulsory guild member-ship, raw material in the immediate vicinity) were similar to those in Schio, but again entrepreneurial initiatives and capital investments from the outside were necessary to establish modern production methods in the quaint villages.

It is difficult to assess how many Venetian merchants were involved in the industrial boom in the *Terraferma*, but there are indications that Niccolò Tron was not the only one. For example, a group of Venetian nobles founded a woollen manufactory near Treviso in the early 1720s, managed by Lambert de Micheraux, an expert in cloth-making from Belgium. The *Compagnia di nuova istituzione* was quite successful in adopting Flemish techniques of cloth-making, although the factory was closed after a few years and de Micheraux established his own business in Pieve di Soligo near Treviso in 1730.[59] In Soligo, Alberto Pezzi, a Venetian merchant and former partner of Niccolò Tron, founded a new wool mill around 1750. At the same time, Giorgio Stahl, a German-born merchant from the *Fondacco dei Tedeschi* in Venice, set up a wool factory in Follina, where only eight years later 4,000 people worked on 100 weaving stools.[60] Stahl, who had been manager of one of Niccolò Tron's factories in

---

56 See the figures in Panciera, *L'Arte*, 350.
57 Caizzi, *Industria*, 69.
58 Caizzi, *Industria*, 75-78; Panciera, *L'Arte*, 186-188.
59 Caizzi, *Industria*, 80-82; see also M. Pitteri, 'Lana e seta a Pieve di Soligo nel secolo XVIII', in: D. Gasparini (ed.), *La pieve di Soligo e la Gastaldia di Solighetto dal Medioevo all'età contemporanea*, Pieve di Soligo 1997, 105-120.
60 Caizzi, *Industria*, 76-77; see also W. Panciera, A. Follina, 'Da Schio e dall'Europa: la

Schio, brought the technological know-how as well as a considerable amount of capital to Follina, which Tron had made available. Stahl's factory mainly produced for the regional market, but was also able to export about 12 bales of cloth to Cairo and Constantinople via Venice every month. But success was short-lived. After Stahl's death the factory was sold and Tron removed his financial support. Stahl's successor, Giorgio F. Faber, another merchant of the *Fondacco dei Tedeschi*, was not able to continue the outstanding success of his predecessor.[61] However, a number of new smaller manufactories emerged in Follina during the 1760s and the 1770s, which adopted the techniques that Tron and Stahl had introduced. Capital investments and knowledge transfer depended largely on networks and partnerships between local merchants and businessmen from Venice and other commercial centres of the region.

Conclusions

There is strong evidence that the Serenissima regained some of her former glory and wealth once she had overcome the severe crisis of the seventeenth century. This was achieved partly by reconstructing former trade networks, especially with the Levant and the German territories. More important, however, were the expansion of regional trade, the intensification of agriculture and the blooming of the wool and silk industry in the *Terraferma*. The new industries mainly developed in the Alpine foothills, which once had figured among the most backward regions of the Republic. Abundance of natural resources, cheap labour supply and the absence of guild restrictions created favourable conditions and attracted external capital. In addition, there had been a long tradition of rural domestic industry which was integrated into the production cycles of cloth manufacturing and guaranteed the supply of skilled labour.

There was thus a complex interaction between rural proto-industry, urban artisanship and factory production, partly based on advanced techniques. Production was, as Walter Panciera has rightly pointed out, characterized by an "eclectic structure".[62] There are good reasons to assume that the economic reorganization of the Venetian Republic was achieved by intensifying horizontal and vertical linkages between different groups of actors throughout the region. The neo-marshallian concept of "industrial districts" thus provides a useful

---

compagnia Tron - Stahl', in: W. Panciera, A. Follina and D. Gasparini (eds.), *I lanifici di Follina. Economia, società e lavoro tra medioevo ed età contemporanea*, Verona 2000, 161-177.

61 Caizzi, *Industria*, 75-78.
62 Panciera, *L'Arte*, 310.

theoretical framework to understand the patterns of economic transformation in the eighteenth century. This refers to "productive co-operation" through networks and partnerships, the importance of diversified industries and markets as well as the cultural and social embeddedness of a primarily regional economy.

There are many indications that the old commercial elites played a crucial role for the development of the region.[63] Wealthy merchants such as Niccolò Tron provided not only the financial capital, but also the technological know-how without which the rapid rise of the new industries would have been impossible. Moreover, the involvement of Venetian merchants was decisive for integrating the new products into the domestic and international trade networks. Finally, members of the Venetian aristocracy could rely on their political connections with the government in order to receive privileges and subsidies. Although more research into family and business history is required, it seems to be evident that the picture of the Venetian patricians as a backward and luxury-loving class living idly on inherited money must be revised. Surely, many aristocrats strongly reduced their commercial activities during the crisis-ridden decades of the seventeenth century, but this was the result rather than the cause of the economic problems of the Republic.[64] When conditions changed at the end of the century, many were obviously willing to invest into new, lucrative businesses and to take on entrepreneurial risks. But even those who bought land without being involved in the management of their estates, contributed to the economic development by transferring capital into the rural areas. The enormous wealth, which had been accumulated in Venice over centuries, served not only as a source of capital, but also created the demand for products from the *Terraferma*.

The example of Niccolò Tron clearly shows that entrepreneurship and a baroque aristocratic life-style were not a contradiction. Tron neither managed the family estate in Anguillara nor his factories in Schio and Follina, but rather left those posts to administrators or business partners. He spent most of the year in his magnificent palace in the city or in the family villa in Cittadella near Padua. However, this does not prevent us from seeing him as a prototype of the "dynamic entrepreneur", whom Joseph Schumpeter described 150 years later as the driving force of economic progress.

---

63 For a general account of this problem, see 'How do city networks contribute to regional development', in: Danson, Lloyd and Hill (eds.), *Regional Governance*, 85-108.

64 See Costantini, *Commercio*, 563.

The Merchants of the Ionian Islands between East and West: Forming international and local networks

Sakis Gekas

Introduction

This paper focusses on the geographical area of the central Mediterranean, the Ionian Islands. The commercial networks established between the port towns of the islands and markets on the east and west of the islands are discussed in the first part, while the second part is mainly concerned with the increasing competition and tensions evoked by the anticipated union of the islands with Greece.

Any discussion of port cities and commercial networks between the islands and other markets cannot ignore and will have to be placed in the context of the literature on the Greek diaspora merchants, a field which is directly linked with the issue of commercial networks in the Mediterranean and the Black Sea, the Ionian Islands and the Greek peninsula. The main focus of this paper will be on these areas. Greek diaspora merchant communities in the Mediterranean and the Black Sea ports have been substantially researched.[1] The Greek Orthodox merchant groups have been studied in the context of foreign communities or *nations*, the members of which were closely associated with each other due to economic interests, religion, language, culture, and in the cases of some merchant houses, intermarriage as well. The above traits enabled these communities to maintain an internal coherence and unity, as the studies mentioned above have amply demonstrated.

The Greek merchant communities declined mainly due to external European and global economic developments, which permanently altered the development

---

1   The literature is extensive. Only the studies used for this research are mentioned here. O. Katsiardi-Hering, *H Elliniki paroikia tis Teryestis (1750-1830)* [The Greek paroikia of Trieste], Athens 1986, on Alexandria X. Xadziiosif, 'Emporikes paroikies ke anexartiti Ellada: erminies ke provlimata' (Merchant paroikiae and independent Greece: interpretations and problems), in: *O Politis*, 62 (1983), 28-34, on Odessa and the grain trade: V. Kardasis, *Ellines Omogeneis sti Notia Rosia 1775-1861* [Ethnic Greeks in south Russia], Athens 1997. D. Vlami, *To fiorini, to sitari ke i odos tou kipou. Ellines emporoi sto Livorno 1750-1868* [The florin, the grain and the garden street. Greek merchants in Livorno], Athens 2000; A. Mandilara, *The Greek Business Community in Marseille, 1816-1900. Individual and Network Strategies*, Ph.D.-thesis, Florence 1998.

of the ports where the communities had been established.[2] These studies emphasise the extensive commercial networks on which the success of the communities' members was based.

However, the port cities examined never became part of the Greek Kingdom which emerged during the third decade of the nineteenth century and matured while expanding, in the following decades. A notable exception is the work of V. Kardasis on Syros and its development into one of the most important ports of the eastern Mediterranean around the middle of the nineteenth century.[3] In this paper, a similar attempt is made to locate the commercial networks established between the Ionian Islands and markets eastwards and westwards, while focusing on the port of Corfu, the commercial and administrative capital of the Ionian State.[4]

The research conducted so far does not yet allow comparisons between the economy and society of the two ports of Syros and Corfu, which both declined after the 1870s due to the rapid rise of the ports of Piraeus and Patras, but this would definitely be a project worth undertaking.[5] This paper draws on the above-mentioned historiography, and is based on research in both the Historical Archive of Corfu and the Public Record Office in London. The commercial networks established during the period of Venetian rule are examined first.

From Venetian to British Rule

The changes introduced in the latter period under Venetian rule (sixteenth until late eighteenth centuries) and the economic developments of the islands determined the pattern of agricultural production for centuries to come. The economy of the Ionian Islands became dependent on monoculture and the

---

2   These developments included above all the peripheral role of the Mediterranean in the world economy and the redundancy of free ports as stations for the storage of grain from the east and of British manufactured goods on their way to the Levant, that followed the technological innovations of the steamer and the telegraph.

3   V. Kardasis, *Syros. Stavrodromi tis anatolikis Mesogiou* [Syros, crossroads of the eastern Mediterranean], Athens 1987.

4   The Ionian State was a quasi independent State since according to the constitutional charter granted to the islands by the Treaty of Paris (1815), they were placed under the exclusive protection of Great Britain.

5   For these two ports and their 'take off' during the nineteenth century, see N. Bakounakis, *Patra 1828-1860. Mia elliniki protevousa ston 19o aiona.* [Patra. A Greek capital in the 19th century], Athens 1988, and V. Tsokopoulos, *Pireas, 1835-1870. Eisagogi stin istoria tou ellinikou Manchester* [Pireus. Introduction to the history of the Greek Manchester], Athens 1984.

production of export commodities e.g.: olive oil, currants and wine. This monoculture, according to Fernand Braudel, was "destructive of local balance", since "in the Venetian islands in the Levant [there was] external demand for raisins and strong wines to be consumed as far away as England". According to Braudel, the Ionian Islands belonged to what he calls "marginal economies"[6]. Adjusted to the needs of the Venetian economy and its mercantilist considerations, Corfu was turned into an island producing large quantities of olive oil, which were sent to Venice for home consumption or production of soap and exported to areas as far as Germany.[7] The production of olive oil increased as the eighteenth century advanced, and the Ionian Islands became more important for Venice in an attempt to balance its income losses on the international markets.[8] Merchants from Corfu (some of the wealthiest being Jewish with extended networks of credit relations with the agricultural producers of Corfu) settled in Venice and Trieste and operated from there.[9] Corfu became even more important among the Venetian possessions after the loss of Crete to the Ottoman Empire in 1669. This is evident in the increased port activity of Corfu from the middle decades of the seventeenth century onwards. The port of Corfu became the destination of ships from Venice bringing luxury goods in exchange for olive oil, as well as the centre of an extensive trade with south Italian ports.[10]

---

6   F. Braudel, *Civilisation and Capitalism 15th-18th Century*, Vol. III, London 1984, 36 (English translation).

7   S. Ciriacono, 'Venetian economy and commerce in modern times: the case of olive oil production in Corfu', and M. Constantini, 'The trade policy of Venice towards its possessions in the eastern Mediterranean', in: A. Nikiforou (ed.), *Kerkira, mia Mesogiaki synthesi: nisiotismos, diktia anthropina perivallonta 16os - 19os aionas* [Corfu, a Mediterranean synthesis: insular, networks, human milieu, 16-19th centuries], International Conference Proceedings, Corfu 22-25 May 1996, Corfu 1998, 76. The year 1599 is of particular importance; the Venetian Senate allowed olive growers to own the land on which they would plant olive trees. As a result of the 'planned' economy and agricultural production of olive oil, the islands experienced a permanent deficit in grain production; the consequences were felt in the nineteenth century as will be discussed later. During Venetian rule the Ionian Islands grain supplies generally came from the Morea and the opposite mainland.

8   Between 1760 and 1766 Corfu produced more than 50% of the total oil production, S. Ciriacono, 'Venetian economy and commerce in modern times: the case of olive oil production in Corfu', 110.

9   Ciriacono,'Venetian economy', 115.

10   In the middle decades of the seventeenh century, 28% of the ships that entered Corfu port came from the Italian peninsula and Sicily, from Otranto, Messina, Ancona, Brindisi and Taranta. See A. Nikiforou, 'H diakinisi tou emporiou sto limani tis Kerkiras ton 17o aiona' [The movement of mercantile navy in the port of Corfu during the 17th century], in: Nikiforou (ed.), *Kerkira*, 86.

Zante and Kefalonia, which were strategically and economically less important for Venice and therefore under lesser control,[11] were the currant producing islands. Until the 1580s Anglo-Venetian trade was largely carried out by Venetian vessels that brought currants and olive oil to England in exchange for wool, cloth and tin.[12] From the late sixteenth century onwards, English merchants increasingly circumvented the high tariff trade imposed by the Venetian Republic, by clandestinely making for the islands *directly* to buy the luxury products.[13] A favourable political climate, created by the commercial treaties with the Ottoman Sultan allowed merchants to trade in Smyrna. As there was peace with Spain, and, above all, the fact that Venice was no longer indispensable as a market for goods from the Levant, merchants in English and Dutch vessels were enabled to operate in the south-east Mediterranean and the Levant, and e.g. in the case of Zante currants to steer to the place of production directly . The currant trade compensated the Venetian economy to some extent for the losses from duties, with the increased circulation of specie in the local economy.[14]

Nevertheless, the pattern of trade in currant remained almost unchanged for two centuries. In 1793, Spiridon Foresti, the British consul in Zante and currant factor, did extensive business with merchants in Amsterdam, Bristol, Trieste, Venice and Hamburg. Many merchants still bought their currants from Venice (and paid the required duty), but Foresti offered his services in Zante, so that they paid commission only to him and not to the Venetian authorities.[15] His resourcefulness in trying to persuade the foreign merchants is impressive. Foresti's arguments must have been quite persuasive, because he was in the position to provide essential information which merchants abroad could not have obtained otherwise. This included progress of the harvest each year, news concerning outbreaks of plague in the mainland opposite the islands that could destroy a good crop, and, last but not least, news about movements of gunboats in the area during troubled times.[16]

---

11 M. Constantiti,'The trade policy of Venice towards its possessions in the eastern Mediterranean', 77.

12 A. Tenenti, *Piracy and the Decline of Venice 1580-1615*, Berkeley 1967, 59.

13 F. C. Lane, *Venice, A Maritime Republic*, Baltimore 1973, 386 and 401.

14 Constantini,'trade policy of Venice', 78.

15 Commercial Letters, Public Record Office (PRO), FO 348/1.

16 In 1793 for instance the Anglo-French war hindered the currant trade causing the island of Zante to suffer, as it damaged its already shrinking trade, overtaken by the more profitable Morea currant trade. Morea is the old nam+e of the area called Peloponnese today. Both the war and excessive duties had driven currant merchants to the Morea where they could buy at a much lower price, leaving the Ionian islands for the end of their buying trips, as long as their

The commercial relations, based on trading routes and the islands' agricultural production established in the previous centuries survived well into the nineteenth century and provided the basis for economic exchange until the period of British rule. Most of the olive oil production was still exported to Venice and Trieste while currants, the staples of the Ionian State and the principal source of revenue, were exported to Great Britain, mainly by 'foreign merchants', as we are informed by contemporary sources, e.g. John Davy and the statistical information of the Ionian State.[17] Substantial economic relations existed between Corfu, the mainland opposite, and Trieste. Several Ionians had migrated to Trieste, settled and become members of the Greek merchant community there from the middle decades of the eighteenth century onwards.[18] Greeks, of course, had long been present in the Italian ports of Venice, Ancona or Livorno, but it was not until the eighteenth century that the Greek merchants expanded their trade.[19] Around the turn of the nineteenth century two types of trading networks could be distinguished: the first stretchingfrom the northern ports of the Adriatic sea (Trieste, Venice) and south-east Italy to the ports on the mainland opposite the Ionian Islands[20] and to areas of the Ottoman empire. The second type of network covered the long-distance trade, conducted between north-west European ports and the port towns of Argostoli (in Kefalonia) and especially Zante. However, the writings of Foresti show that old trade patterns survived until the period of British rule.

The geopolitical reasons for the gradual occupation of the Ionian Islands (1809-1814) by the British navy and the final cession of the islands to British

---

ships could still load more cargo before they sailed to the north-west. See A.C. Wood, *A History of the Levant Company*, London 1964, 161.

17   J. Davy, *Notes and observations on the Ionian Islands and Malta*, Vol. 2, London 1842, 64, and Ionian Islands Blue Books, PRO, CO 136 / 1392-1423.

18   Katsiardi-Hering, *H Elliniki paroikia tis*, 402.

19   This has been attributed largely to the declaration that the Adriatic was open to the navigation of all ships, by Charles VI of Austria. T. Stoianovich, 'Conquering Balkan Orthodox Merchant', in: *Journal of Economic History*, 20 (1960), 234-313. In this classic work, Stoianovich discusses the identity of "Greek" merchants of the seventeenth and eighteenth centuries, concluding that the sources concerning merchants who came from the area of Epirus do not distinguish between Greek Orthodox and Albanian Orthodox merchants, since Greek was the language of business in many areas of the Habsburg and Ottoman empires, and therefore was widely used. The term "Greek merchants" for those merchants who moved to the Ionian Islands from Epirus is used in the same sense in this paper as well.

20   These were the Venetian outposts for centuries until the late 1790s and early 1800s. The last of these 'dependencies', as they were called, was the port of Parga, which remained independent after the cession of the Ionian Islands to Britain, only to be 'sold' to Ali Pasha, warlord of Epirus in 1819 for 150.000 Pounds Sterling.

protection need not be explored here as they have been examined in the context of the antagonism of the Great Powers in the Mediterranean.[21] It is worth noting though, that from the date the Ionian State was established, its citizens and the vessels carrying the Ionian flag could enjoy British status, one of the privileges of protection.[22] From the early years of British rule, as J. Chircop argues, the area of the Ionian Islands was part of the British project that should lead to their integration into a strategic and economic imperial network, together with Gibraltar and Malta.[23] British-manufactured goods first appeared on the islands *en masse* during the period of the Napoleonic wars, when the British navy seized three of the islands and replaced the French as 'protectors' of the islands.[24] However, it was not until the establishment of the Ionian State (1815) that this process of integration into the 'imperial network' began to take shape.

According to Chircop the Ionian 'narrow-sea economy' (Ionian Islands and the adjacent area) was transformed when British-made goods, mainly large quantities of cheap cotton products flooded the area as they were distributed from Corfu to neighbouring ports.[25] While this is true, extensive research in the archive of Corfu has shown that despite the 'invasion' of British manufactured products and the rapid changes in business organisation and in the institutional framework in general (to be discussed shortly), there were nevertheless continuities. The *negozianti*, the wholesale merchants who had settled in the ports of the islands, imported products made in Britain, which were then distributed in the neighbouring ports.[26] At the same time, other merchants

---

21 Bayly for instance believes that the occupation of Sicily (1806-1815) and the Ionian Isles "...were acts of pre-emption designed to keep the Bonapartists out of the Mediterranean, and prolonged in Ionia by suspicion that Imperial Russia saw itself as a successor to the Ottoman empire as ruler of the Orthodox Greek populations of the Balkans and the Levant.", C. A. Bayly, *Imperial Meridian. The British Empire and the World 1780-1830*, London 1989, 102-3.

22 The Times, 1 December 1815.

23 J. Chircop, *The British Imperial Network in the Mediterranean 1800-1870. A study of regional fragmentation and imperial integration*, Ph.D.-thesis., Essex 1997, passim.

24 J.B. Williams, *British Commercial Policy and Trade Expansion 1750-1850*, 1972, 413-4. The policy first applied in 1809 was to bring British goods from Malta instead of Venice.

25 Chircop, *British Imperial Network in the Mediterranean*, 71.

26 The resident C. Napier (representative of British authority in Kefalonia) remarked about the prospects offered by the Ionian economy for British goods: "when I say that the influence of a British government in the midst of these barbarous and unsettled countries ought to have an imposing effect by affording a ready protection to our trade, I do not mean such protection as the two letters I give copies of in the appendix bespeak. If our protection was well administered, we should find the islands afford a good market for our manufactures; my reason for saying so is that the islanders (particularly the Cefalonians) drive a considerable retail trade: for example a vessel is freighted thus - the owner, the master, the sailors, and all their friends, contribute in money or goods and when the vessel is loaded with a variety of articles, away she

continued to trade with the Dalmatian and Albanian coasts, Epirus, and the south-western coasts of Greece as in the past, and they did so *because of* the rise in imports of British made goods.[27] The transformation of the regional economy was a rather silent one, it changed from one of relative autarky to one of strong dependence, from a 'narrow-sea' to a broader imperial one. The imperial dimension of the Ionian economy manifested itself in the increasing dependence of the Ionian State revenue on the currant trade, for Ionian currants were almost exclusively exported to Britain. At the same time, the dependence indicates the enduring orientation of commercial interests towards the west. In the early nineteenth century Ionian economy oscillated between British imperial requirements on the one hand and the habitual patterns of trade that had persisted for centuries, on the other.

It has been argued that the economic and social structures of the islands dud bit duffer significantly in the first third of the nineteenth century.[28] Forms of business organisation, simple partnerships with limited capital remained unchanged, as evidence from the 1820s and the correspondence of family firms of Corfu show.[29] From the 1830s onwards though, the project of accelerating the progress of the islands was promulgated by the Lord High Commissioners, the supreme authority of the Ionian State and the representative of British power and

---

sails, a floating shop, directing her course to all places where the master and crew think a demand may be found for any portion of their cargo. If this vessel is large, she goes to Constantinople, to the Black sea, to Smyrna, to Alexandria, to the coast of Italy &c. ; and if small, she runs up a thousand little creeks, and traffics with the villages on the Greek and Dalmatian coasts: in this way an extensive traffic is carried on". A very good description of the range and variations of the maritime trade conducted by Ionians. C. Napier, *The Colonies, Treating of their value generally, of the Ionian Islands in particular: The importance of the latter in War and Commerce*, London 1833, 15.

27 In 1857 the Greek consul in Corfu was writing in his report to Athens that "...*the majority of textiles are re-exported in Epirus, Patras and Messolongi*", Ionian Senate file, Royal Greek Consulate, Corfu Historical Archive (hereafter CHA), Document 2842, fol. 1.

28 See for instance the interesting periodisation and conclusion of Yannoulopoulos that "the changes were almost exclusively political. The social infrastructure, the social relations of production remained virtually unchanged. The tenant farmers went on working the land and paying their dues to the landlords, and the members of the middle class went on about their business as merchants, shopkeepers, lawyers, doctors etc.". G. Yannoulopoulos, 'State and Society in the Ionian Islands 1800-1830', in: R. Clogg (ed.), *Balkan Society in the age of Greek Revolution*, 1981, 56.

29 A very rich source is the archive material of the Vassila family in the CHA. The Vassila family originated from Epirus, settled in Corfu in 1820 and rose to one of the major commercial houses there. The family's activities were based on long-established commercial ties with Trieste.

interests in the region, in accordance with the increasingly predominant liberal ideology in Great Britain itself.[30] The intentions of the British 'protective' power become obvious with the declarations of 1825 and 1830[31] which gave Corfu the status of a free port, a common pattern of imperial expansion.[32] In the following years under the administration of several High Commissioners, the 'developmental' project of British imperial principles, summarised in the idea of 'progress', took on different forms with varying degrees of intensity. Part of this development and 'civilizing' process was also the establishment of a number of institutions to advance commerce and lead Ionians to economic and social prosperity. On the other hand, the involvement of Ionians in the Black Sea grain trade demonstrates the development of new commercial routes and a web of economic relationships expanding eastwards. However, in currant trade certain continuities dating from the Venetian period can be discerned in the existing commercial network. For this reason the importance of the networks for the islands and the merchants situated in the port towns is discussed first.

The Currant Trade

During the Greek war of independence Morea became one of the main scenes of war and the currant-producing areas were ravaged. Consequently, the currant trade of the Ionian Islands rocketed.[33] The profits decreased during the 1830s and

---

30 By region of course we do not mean only the immediate and restricted geographical area of the Ionian Islands but we are dealing (just as British administration did) with a larger geographical area that extends from the entrance of the Adriatic sea to the southern Peloponnese, and of course the south-west Greek mainland opposite that during the 1820s was in turmoil due to the Greek war of independence from the Ottoman empire. The Ionian State officially remained neutral to the belligerent parties, although this volatile balance shifted according to the sympathies of the High Commissioner in office.

31 CO 136/56 5 March 1830, P.R.O.

32 J.B. Williams, *British Commercial Policy and Trade Expansion 1750-1850*, 78.

33 "The failure of the Greek corps, in consequence of the revolution, led to a great scarcity of currants in 1822 and subsequent years, so that, notwithstanding the enormous import-duty of 44s. 44d. per cwt., into this country, which had remained unaltered since the war (between England and France), the price in the islands rose to Spanish dollars 96 per 1000 lbs.", J. Davy, Notes and observations on the Ionian Islands and Malta, Vol. 2, 91. Napier, the Resident (local administrator) of Kefalonia did not fail to note the boom in the currant trade in his memoirs: "the currants of Cephalonia became from the year 1821 the staple commodity of the island, because at this period a monopoly begun, in consequence of the Greek revolution, which prevented the cultivation of currants at Patras and Corinth, and thereby threw the whole trade into the hands of the islanders, and the price mounted up from 13 dollars, to 100 dollars, the 1000pounds weight, the produce likewise increased in quantity from 4 millions, to 11 millions

1840s when currants from Morea were back on the market, but for the Ionian State currants continued to form between 50-60% of the total exports, thus constituting one of the principal sources of the State's revenue.[34] The majority of the crop was exported to England, but also to Holland, the German states and Italy. In 1862 for instance, two years before the union of the Ionian Islands with Greece, 75-80% of the currant shipments from the islands of Kefalonia and Zante were sent to England, in particular London; Liverpool and Falmouth were other common destinations.[35] Foreign merchants exported the larger bulk of the produce, one of their several business activities. A few examples will suffice. Ernest Toole, the manager of the Ionian Bank branch in Kefalonia, exported 40% of all currant shipments from that island in 1863.[36] Barff & Co had a share of 22% of the exports from Kefalonia and 38% of the exports from Zante and were also extensively involved in the currant trade in Patras, opposite Zante. Although the Fels company exported only 7% of the total exports of Kefalonia in 1863, it was more significantly involved in business activities in Corfu than in the currant trade. Another merchant called Van Lennep had a share of 28% of the currants sent from Zante to Antwerp, while Gerasimo Lucato who exported 25% from Kefalonia that year, also imported wheat from the Black Sea.[37] Despite the limitations posed by one year's data, these figures show that a few merchants dominated the currant market, their influence on the local economy and society of the islands still have to be investigated.

The notoriously volatile and insecure cultivation and production of these agricultural commodities[38] and the awareness that the State revenue was totally dependent on the currant trade, induced several High Commissioners to ask for the reduction of the import duty of currants in Britain.[39] The reduction of high

---

of pounds weight." Napier, *The Colonies*, 338. This 'boom' in the currant trade is of course very different from the first expansion of the cultivation and export of currants to England and the rest of western Europe in the late sixteenth century. For an excellent account of the currant trade in the early modern period, see M. Fusaro, *Uva Passa. Una guerra commerciale tra Venezia e l' Inghilterra, 1540-1640*, Venezia 1996.

34 Ionian Islands Blue Books of Statistics, PRO, CO 136 / 1392-1423.

35 *Ionian Islands Government Gazette* (hereafter *IIGG*), 1863, Statistics compiled from the issues for the months September to March.

36 *IIGG* (1863), Statistics compiled from the issues for the months September to March.

37 *IIGG* (1863), Statistics compiled from the issues for the months September to March.

38 A sudden shower during late August or early September, when the grapes dried, could damage the whole crop, while substantial quantities of olive oil could be produced only every two years.

39 It was considered impossible to reduce the extremely high export tariff of 19.5% on the islands without seriously jeopardising even further the revenue of the Ionian State, constantly in

import duties was in the interest of both sides, of the currant merchants on the islands and of those in London. In 1833, the "merchants of London trading with the Mediterranean, exporters of British Manufactures and importers of the produce of the Ionian Isles and the Morea" asked for the immediate reduction of the import duty.[40] The next attempt in 1844 was supported more strongly as it originated from 'principal Landholders and Merchants of Zante' [41] and 'currant growers of Kefalonia'.[42] Results were disappointing: The reduction did not fulfill expectations as a favourable duty policy towards Greek currants, the main competitor, followed shortly after 1846. Nevertheless, the currant trade continued to play an important part on the islands' economy and established conctacts between the islands and west European markets, while at the same time a different solution was found to the centuries old problem of deficit in cereal production: the establishment of a rapidly growing commercial network between the islands and the Black Sea.

The Black Sea Grain Trade

During the second and third decades of the nineteenth century a major change in the Mediterranean and indeed European economy took place, far away from the Ionian Islands, but with a substantial impact on the economic life of Ionians: the Black Sea grain trade.[43] Several Ionian merchants contributed to the establishment of the Greek economic power and domination of the Anglo-

---

deficit. The main reason for the permanent deficit was the extremely high percentage of the expenditure paid for the 'military establishment' meaning the expenses for maintaining the 3,000-4,000 strong British garrison in Corfu, and also for conducting several fortification works during the existence of the protectorate.

40 Merchants to the Treasury, 29 April 1833, PRO, CO 136/68.

41 Petition enclosed in Seaton to Stanley, No 16, 2 June 1843, PRO, CO 136/120.

42 Petition enclosed in Seaton to Stanley, No 11, 11 May 1843, PRO, CO 136/120.

43 So far the issue has been examined in the historiography of Greek merchant communities settled in the wheat-exporting ports. These are extremely useful studies, which are mostly concerned with the Greek *paroikia* of Odessa, Tangarok, and Black Sea ports in general, as well as of other Mediterranean ports. For the commercial operations and the constitution of the Greek merchant community in Odessa and the Black Sea in general, see V. Kardasis, *Syros. Stavrodromi tis anatolikis Mesogiou*, Athens 1987, For a more detailed exploration of *diaspora* merchants see G. Harlaftis, 'The Role of the Greeks in the Black Sea Trade, 1830-1900', in: L.R. Fischer and H.W. Nordvik (eds.), *Shipping and Trade, 1750-1950: Essays in International maritime Economic History*, Yorkshire 1990, and for the Greek shipping in general see G. Harlaftis, *A History of Greek-Owned shipping*, London 1996.

Russian[44] and Mediterranean grain trade. In the early nineteenth century merchants from Kefalonia and Ithaca,[45] usually with little experience or capital, decided to look for better business prospects in the Black Sea.[46]

Contemporary observers were impressed by the magnitude of the Kefalonian merchant navy; reports mention up to 300 vessels of large and smaller tonnage.[47] These accounts inform us of the ways in which a maritime commerce developed from rudimentary business practices, and how Ionian entrepreneurs made use of all commercial opportunities to form new commercial networks in a very profitable trade. The following example of the Vallianos family from Kefalonia is representative of what G. Harlaftis has called the 'Ionian phase' of Greek shipping.[48] Born in 1808 Marinos Vallianos, the eldest of three brothers, settled in Tangarok, where he and his partner Avgerinos managed to rapidly and effectively establish themselves as principal merchants. V. Kardasis considers him to perhaps be the first Greek of the *diaspora* who combined trade and shipping in a single commercial activity.[49] Favoured by the boom caused due to the Crimean War, Vallianos bought large quantities of grain at a very low price and sold them after the end of the war at a huge profit. Having opened a house in Istanbul in 1849, his range of activities expanded to London in 1858 and Marseilles in 1869.[50]

---

44 The Anglo-Russian grain trade was largely carried out by Greek firms with offices in London, such as the Rallis, Rodocanachis and Scaramagas merchant houses, S. Chapman, *Merchant Enterprise in Britain*, 1992, 246.

45 Ionian shipping began to emerge from the late eighteenth century on the island of Kefalonia in particular. Freed from Venetian interventionism and monopolistic restrictions, people from Kefalonia developed a substantial maritime trade and other shipping activities, such as maritime insurance.

46 Once business opportunities were created by the rapid increase of the grain trade, the parameters of success for the Ionians were the privileged status of their vessels' flag provided by British protection, their status as Orthodox Christians, as well as their familiarity with the loose business organisation of these areas (the lack of organised credit establishments for instance). These 'golden years' of commerce in fact started when Russia occupied the southern territories around the Black sea and welcomed foreign merchants, among them many Greeks; see Kardasis, *Syros. Stavrodromi tis anatolikis Mesogiou*, Athens 1987. These developments of course were directly related with the corn laws in Britain which did not allow free import of grain in order to support British agricultural production; they were abolished in 1846. S. Fairlie, 'The Corn Laws and British Wheat Production, 1829-76', in: *Economic History Review*, 22 (1969), 88-116.

47 J. Davy, *Notes and observations on the Ionian Islands and Malta*, Vol. 2, London 1842, 63-4.

48 G. Harlaftis, 'The Role of the Greeks', chapter 3.

49 V. Kardasis, *Syros*, 229.

50 V. Kardasis, *Syros*, 229.

Less wealthy and less connected Ionians also involved in the grain trade employed more elementary business methods such as joint venture.[51] These methods aimed at securing profit with the least possible risk. The grain trade was apparently a very lucrative one and the image of the rags-to-riches captain - merchant of grain was depicted quite often and is perhaps not far from truth, as the several examples of Greeks in the Black Sea who started in the manner described by Davy demonstrate. 'Wandering' in the Mediterranean until the necessary capital was raised, buying wheat from the Black Sea ports and then travelling up to Livorno until the cargo was sold, was the answer to the lack of credit that the anonymity of these merchants entailed. Lacking the surname of a Ralli or a Rodocanachi, or even a connection with one of these houses, meant that other business practices had to be employed in order to overcome the problems of network limitations and lack of information. In 1838, a merchant-ship owner from Ithaca travelled to Odessa, where he bought grain from another Ihaca merchant stationed there, and he tried to evaluate the price at which he would be able to sell by the number of Ionian vessels in the port of Odessa. Returning to the islands, he travelled from port to port trying to sell the cargo at the best possible price, because that was where he had his connections.[52]

The grain trade had important effects on the merchants who settled on the islands as well. By the early 1840s when the volume of the grain trade increased, agents of the principal grain trade merchant houses of the Black Sea were appointed in the Ionian Islands, particularly in Corfu. This was due to the function of Corfu's port as an entrepôt and warehouse for grain from the Black Sea during British rule.[53] Agents of the houses of Ralli, Rodocanachi, Scaramanga and Avgerinos were positioned in Corfu linking this port to the rest of the grain trade chain. Moreover, as already mentioned, due to the production

---

51 John Davy, a contemporary observer, provides a very detailed description of the business organisation of the grain trade conducted by Ionian mariners, and his description is worth quoting at some length: "The manner in which it is conducted is in every way rude and primitive. Each ship employed commonly belongs to its captain and 2 or 3 other proprietors; and as the purchases of grain are chiefly made with real money, seldom by barter, and never on account or credit, they have to advance the sums requisite, with the understanding that the profits are to be divided between the owners and sailors in certain proportions; so many shares to each owner; so many to the captain; so many to the mate; and to the sailors individually so many, according to their respective merit. The sailors receive no pay nor wages; but they are allowed to take small investments on their own, to the amount of from 15 to 20 dollars' worth, with which they trade on their own account. Many of the ship owners and merchants are said to be quite illiterate, unable either to read or write." Davy, *Notes and observations on the Ionian Islands*, 64.

52 V. Kardasis, *Syros*, 122-3.

53 Chircop, *British Imperial Network*, 71.

of export commodities (currants, wine, olive oil) and the deficit in cereal production,[54] the supply of grain was not sufficient in the Ionian Islands for more than 3-4 months and had to be imported. It constituted the bulk of imports in the Ionian State.[55] Unlike the convergence of interests between the High Commissioners and merchants on the issue of reducing the import duty on currants in Great Britain, the interests of the merchants and the State were usually in conflict over grain trade and led to a heated debate.[56] Grain importers time and again protested against the attempts of the central government to regulate the grain trade by establishing a grain administration. While the government aimed at avoiding scarcity of wheat and famine during extremely tense periods such as the years of the Crimean war, merchants on their part claimed that they were in the position to provide the State with the indispensable grain. The merchants used their strong connections and established commercial networks with the Black Sea ports as proof of their ability to cater for the populations' needs for bread.[57]

In this first part of the paper the impact of the rapidly increasing currant trade on the Ionian economy, and the formation of a new commercial network based on the grain trade, have been explored. The Ionian State attempted to regulate the grain trade and maximise profits from the currant exports for its own administrative and fiscal needs. To achieve these ends the State inevitably converged and diverged with the merchants of the islands, who of course were at the heart of the development of these 'old' and 'new' networks.

---

54 S. Asdrahas, 'Feoudaliki prosodos ke geoprosodos stin Kerkira tin periodo tis Venetokratias' (Feudal revenue and land revenue in Corfu during the period of Venetian rule), in: S. Asdrahas, *Oikonomia kai Nootropies* [Economy and Mentalities], Athens 1988, 69.

55 Interesting comparisons can be made with Leghorn, the other porto franco of the time and with very similar characteristics, where the grain trade was of significant importance for the port's prosperity; D. Loromer, *Merchants and Reform in Livorno*, 1987, 31-2.

56 A public debate on the issue took place in the official State newspaper and in petitions of merchants to the High Commissioner. These documents and the language used demonstrate the degree of agency of the merchants specialising in the import and re-export of grain as they articulate and pursue their interests collectively and against the will of the central administration.

57 In their argumentation against what they called 'the monopoly of the Government' the merchants used theories of political economists, as well as the example of Great Britain as the first country to teach free trade to the rest of the world. Petition 31, PRO, CO 136/661.

The Merchants of the Ionian Islands: Diversity and Cohesion

The merchants of the Ionian Islands were one of the most diverse groups in the Ionian society.[58] Despite the scarcity of information on the merchant group of the town ports in general and Corfu in particular during this first period of British rule (1810-1830), the picture presented by contemporary sources is a rather 'multicultural' one.[59] Merchants from places as far as Bordeaux and England resided in Corfu town, while the presence of Theodoro Ralli e compagnia from the island of Scio (Chios), member of the famous commercial house of Ralli, should be noted. In later years the merchant group was joined by merchants from Epirus and other areas of the Ottoman Empire, merchants from the Italian states, Malta, Britain, Holland and even Switzerland.[60]

---

58 This is probably one of the reasons why their role during the nineteenth century has never been thoroughly researched. In the historiography of Corfu and the Ionian Islands merchants have been viewed as part of a 'rising bourgeoisie'. While some of them fervently supported the prolongation of the status of Corfu as a British protectorate, cf. Chircop, *The British Imperial Network in the Mediterranean*, 111, others became increasingly dissatisfied with British rule and supported union with Greece; see for instance *History of the Greek Nation*, Athens 1975 Vol. 11, passim. Another common pattern in literature follows contemporary accounts in an almost orthodox manner (Newspaper *Patris* No. 5, 12 February 1850), regarding "merchants-capitalists" as the evil moneylenders who exploited the peasant population by lending at usurious rates of interest; see for instance, D. Hannel, 'The Ionian Islands under the British Protectorate: Social and Economic Problems', in: *Journal of Modern Greek Studies*, 7 (1989), 115. On occasions merchants appear to fit in both categories as members of the rising bourgeoisie with commercial and usurious activities, G. Yannoulopoulos, 'State and Society in the Ionian Islands, 1800-1830', in: R. Clogg (ed.), *Balkan Society in the Age of Greek Revolution*, London 1981, 49. For the only explicit association of merchants with the 'bourgeoisie' of the islands, see L. Zamit, *H oikonomia tis Eptanisou tin periodo tis Vretanikis prostasias* (1815-64), [The economy of Eptanisos under British protection], Corfu 1994, 49. Notable exception in the relevant literature is the work of E. Prontzas that draws attention to the issue of institutions and social conflict by arguing that new social groups 'seek their role in the new economic institutions as political administration is directed by the imperial power', E. Prontzas, *Trapeza h Ioniki, «xarin tis Ellados»*, [Bank The Ionian 'in favour of Greece'], Thessaloniki (forthcoming).

59 The two registers of Corfu town (1812 and 1818) found so far give an idea of the registered *negozianti* of the town, the wholesale principal merchants who are clearly distinguished from the *mercanti*, and the *bottegai*, the retailers and shopkeepers. Town Population Register 1812-1814, CHA, Executive Police 1319; and Register of Corfu Merchants, Corfu 1818, CHA, Ionian State 232a.

60 A. Mousson, *Kerkira ke Kefalonia. Mia periigisi to 1858*. [Corfu and Kefalonia. A tour in 1858], Athens 1995 (Greek translation), 41. English merchants though had long been present in the southern Ionian Islands, especially Zante, from the sixteenth century onwards. Their wealth,

These merchants settled on the islands of Corfu, Kefalonia and Zante after the expansion of British rule, either establishing their own firms or acting as commercial agents. Omnipresent were Jewish traders (mainly in Corfu and Zante), local merchants and merchant families from Parga in the mainland opposite Corfu.[61] This merchant group comprised merchants not only of different origin and ethnicity but also of different religions. Roman Catholics had a strong presence in the town, due to the centuries-old Venetian rule. It was only after the occupation of the islands by the Republican French (1797) that the large Jewish population, and the Jewish traders in particular, were granted any rights and a certain representation in the municipality.[62] A number of other differences cut across this merchant group: different fields of business activity, specialisation in long distance trade (wholesale merchants), retailing (shopkeepers), and commercial specialisation (coal, grain, currants, olive oil, foodstuffs, British manufacture, etc.). The same merchants took over other functions as well, serving as commercial agents for Italian, Austrian and British companies and as consuls.[63] The urban society of port cities has quite often been analysed by using the concept of 'merchant community'.[64]

The above features of the Corfu merchants indicate that such a term is inadequate and that the 'merchant community' of Corfu might have been more

---

evident in the houses they built and in the tombs they left behind has been proverbial. See M. Pratt, *Britain's Greek Empire*, London 1978, 57.

61 Approximately 1,500 people from Parga found refuge in Corfu when it was ceded to Ali Pasha of Epirus in 1819. Among them were several merchant families involved in trade with Trieste and Venice, as for instance the Vassilas family; Vassilas Family Archive, CHA.

62 However, Jewish Ionians were not granted civil rights until union with Greece in 1864, when all Ionians became 'Greek citizens' regardless of their religion. Approximately one fifth of the Corfu town population during the nineteenth century were Jewish. The Jewish merchants were heavily involved in trade and port activities in general; for instance, approximately 80% of the porters of Corfu were Jewish. Eklogikos Katalogos 1864, Egxoria Diaxirisi 1544, [Electoral List 1864, Domestic Administration 1544], CHA.

63 Friedrich and Martin Fels, for example, were exporters of currants from Zante, importers of coal in Corfu, commercial agents of the Liverpool and Mediterranean Steam Ship company, IIGG, No 509, 11 February 1861, and also Consular Agents of the Papal States (IIGG No. 104, 12 December 1852), of the Netherlands (IIGG No. 558 23 December 1862), and of the free Hanseatic Towns of Bremen, Lubeck and Hamburg (IIGG No.579, 28 April 1862). They were also involved in maritime insurance granting sea loans.

64 Other historians have tackled similar problems. O. Katsiardi-Hering, investigating the function and role of the Greek paroikia in Trieste, focuses more on the activities of members of this group, rather than on the group of merchants as a whole. L. Romer explores the reform efforts of the merchant community in Livorno, and attributes the cohesion of the community to diffusion of a 'merchant ideology' (as well as to economic reasons).

fragmented than originally believed. The existence of a merchant identity, if any, during the period of British rule, should be traced in the process which brought these people under a common framework of action. This process was the establishment of a number of economic institutions.[65]

The introduction of commercial legislation in 1840[66], the founding of the Exchange in 1841, the establishment of the Chamber of Commerce in 1851, the function of a Commercial Tribunal under the new legal framework, and new forms of business organisation, such as joint-stock and limited liability companies, are extremely important institutions for structuring and facilitating networks. These essential commercial mechanisms facilitate exchange, aim at minimising commercial risk and 'modernising' the economy and patterns of trade, and, ultimately, regulating commercial behaviour. More significantly, the involvement of merchants in the arbitration of commercial disputes is an example of what Braudel has called "a privileged form of justice for merchants, which safeguarded class interests."[67] Towards the end of the period examined here the merchants-agents of the commercial houses involved in the grain trade, for instance, all held posts as president or council members of the Chamber of Commerce in both Corfu and Argostoli.[68]

In order to demonstrate the importance of these new institutions for the merchants of the islands and their role in forging established and new

---

65 The literature on institutions is already vast. Instead of exploring into the discussion of historical institutional analysis it will just be noted that the institutional context is perceived here as being "not only the economic institutions, i.e. mechanisms to co-ordinate economic activities, but also formal and informal rules, conventions, codes and systems." See research project on "Entrepreneurship and Institutional Context in a Comparative Perspective", N.H. Posthumus Institute, http://www.kun.nl/posthumus/index.html.

66 The introduction of the Commercial Code in 1840 provided the *modus operandi* for limited liability and joint-stock companies, defining who could be considered a merchant, and specified the mechanism for recovering commercial debts. The Commercial Code, of Napoleonic origin, had already been introduced in the Greek kingdom by the Bavarian authorities, and the British authorities were keen to follow in the context of 'progress' that aimed at advancing the islands' economy and society. The merchant world embraced and supported the introduction of legislation in the form of a code, which would replace the sparse laws of the State and would thus provide a framework for commercial activities, such as joint-stock companies of maritime insurance, for the production of wine, etc.

67 F. Braudel, *Civilisation and Capitalism 15th-18th Century. The wheels of Commerce*, Vol. 2, London 1982, 81.

68 Ionian Islands Government Gazette [on Chamber of Commerce elections]. This is a recurrent phenomenon in towns-cities dominated by merchant elites. The networks formed become even more evident if we consider that members of the same commercial houses (Rodocannachi) were members of the Chamber of Commerce council in Livorno and Marseilles. For the Greek merchant community of Livorno see D. Vlami, *To fiorini, to sitari ke i odos tou kipou. Ellines emporoi sto Livorno 1750-1868*, 207 and passim.

commercial networks two examples of commercial mechanisms will be used: the Ionian Bank and the maritime insurance companies. These forms of business activities were related to the currant and grain trades discussed above, but were also linked with the political issue that dominated the life of the islands from the 1850s onwards: the issue of a union with Greece.

In 1839, before the establishment of the legal framework, the Ionian Bank was established which advanced the monetarisation of the economy and facilitated trade. The supposed virtues of the Ionian Bank and its advantages for the Ionian economy were promulgated excessively in the speeches of H. Douglas, Commissioner of the islands from 1835-1841, and principal supporter of the whole project. The bank's functions were: "current accounts, discounts, exchanges, letters of credit".[69] Founded in London in 1837, the Ionian Bank Company was the first joint-stock company on the islands, established by British interests and with British capital. It commenced business with three branches on the islands of Corfu, Kefalonia and Zante two years later. The bank is an example of the expanding British financial capitalism reaching this corner of the empire. It is very doubtful whether a British bank would have been established in the area, had the islands not been under British rule ('protection', to use the exact diplomatic term). After several failed attempts to raise local capital due to the refusal of local merchants to get involved in the enterprise, Douglas turned to City merchants of London to finance a project first envisaged by his predecessors as a bank which would grant loans to farmers and free them from their dependence on local capital holders and their usurious practices.[70]

Banking proved to be very attractive to Ionians. The insurance companies which sprang up like mushrooms due to the Black Sea grain trade and the rapid increase of shipping activity, also offered banking services such as current accounts and discounting bills of exchange. Although they provided the same services as the Ionian Bank there were significant differences. The Ionian Bank held the privilege of issuing bank notes (strictly forbidden to any other company and renewed in 1859, twenty years after it was originally granted). These companies also lacked the capital and the backing of the British power, which always loomed in the background or was even stated explicitly when decisions

---

69　*IIGG*, No. 478, 10 February 1840. Notification of Ionian Bank commencing operations.

70　Adam, High Commissioner first conceived the idea in 1830, and Nugent, his successor, in fact established a state fund for loans to 'agriculturalists'. Ionian Bank Archive, 2/1, British Library of Political and Economic Science, London School of Economics. In fact, the bank served as a financier of the Ionian State, whose budget was almost permanently in deficit, and wages (extremely high for the upper echelons of the administration) had to be paid urgently.

such as the renewal of the privilege were to be made or for any other reason.[71] Thus, competition between the supporters of the local joint-stock companies and the Ionian Bank was not averted as the issue was one of national identity as well, both when the "foreign" British bank was first established in 1837,[72] and especially when the National Bank of Greece stepped into the field in the early 1860s.

The merchant networks structured around the Ionian Bank and other joint-stock companies were shaped by British interests, the currant trade involved both local and British merchants as well as capital. The issue towards the end of the period is directly linked to the agitation for the union with Greece. Evidence concerning the shareholders of the Ionian Bank, the founders and shareholders of the maritime insurance companies, the National Bank of Greece, correspondence and the reports of the Greek consul in Corfu, reveals that quite clear lines were drawn among merchants as to their preferences. While the Ionian Bank established itself firmly as an essential financial mechanism of the Ionian economy, it never received the support of Ionian merchants, either in the form of buying shares or having frequent transactions with them. The bank largely facilitated the currant trade of Kefalonia and Zante and the foreign merchants involved in it, and served as a place of deposit for current accounts and exchanging currency.[73] Members of the old aristocracy and the new bourgeoisie of the islands, landed proprietors, politicians[74] and members of the professions were the principal shareholders of the Ionian Bank and attended the annual general meetings of the shareholders in London frequently.[75] 888 out of 5,000 shares of the British-owned and administered company were available for sale on the islands but local merchants were very reluctant to buy shares. They were

---

71 See for instance the complaints of the bank managers in London to the Colonial Office, for lack of support from the Ionian State at a moment of crisis for the bank, when a sudden panic caused by the tumultuous events of 1848 resulted in a run on the bank. "Appeal of the Ionian Bank to the Right Honourable the Secretary of State for the Colonies, dated London 29 April 1848", CO 136/128.

72 J. Davy, *Notes and observations on the Ionian Islands and Malta*, 71, and Ionian Bank Archive 6 / 29, BLPES, LSE.

73 Only occasionally were merchant houses involved in the grain trade such as Rodocanachis and Rallis doing business at the Ionian Bank branches, but these of course were not the 'average' trading company or merchants, but rather the 'multinationals' of their time.

74 The interesting point is that both *reformists*, aiming at reform but not at an end of British protection and *protectionists*, supporting the continuation of the regime, were among the shareholders of the Ionian Bank. Ionian bank Shareholders, 1860. Emporodikeio, 699 [Commercial Tribunal], CHA.

75 Lists of Proprietors, Company Reports and Accounts 2/1, Ionian Bank Archive, BLPES, LSE.

more eager to do business with the bank, as it facilitated trade as mentioned above.

A further network was formed around the maritime insurance business and eight joint-stock companies established on the islands between 1841 and 1863. Old elementary forms of business organisation were replaced by joint-stock companies aiming at reducing commercial risk and securing profit. Although the building costs of a ship were covered after only four journeys, there was no guarantee that a ship would run as long as that due to the vagaries of the sea. For the sailors it has always been the *Black Sea, Efksinos Pontos* in Greek, meaning the "Hospitable Sea", an euphemism no doubt given the shipwrecks time and time again. It is not surprising that merchants and other capital holders in the Ionian Islands developed their own maritime insurance companies. Spread of entrepreneurial spirit and business ideas could at least be traced back to 1816, when merchants from the Ionian Islands were involved in founding an insurance company in the Black Sea.[76] The first one was founded in 1841, but insurance business did not spread before the 1850s, when eight companies were founded on the Ionian Islands, two on the island of Corfu, three on Kefalonia, one on Zante and two also on the tiny island of Ithaca.[77] The geographical dispersion of these companies reflected the commercial specialisation and orientation of each island, and the sea loans contracted between these companies and merchants confirm the case.[78] The organisation as joint-stock companies involved a large section of the Ionian urban society. Members of the 'old aristocracy' and the new capital-holders of the islands, i.e. the principal merchants, invested in them. However, other social groups found the prospect of investment attractive and lucrative, and this change has been described as the "maritime insurance mania".[79]

The expansion of insurance companies on the Ionian Islands coincided with the rapid rise of the grain trade, and with the role of Corfu as a port of distribution. An analysis of the company documents, and in particular on the shareholders, has so far shown that local capital holders preferred to 'support' the Ionian companies, and not the 'foreign' (as contemporaries called it) Ionian

---

76 V. Kardasis, *Syros*, 133.

77 The history and role of these companies in the transformation of the Ionian economy and society remains to be explored. For a very good account of the organisation, operations and other information on these companies see N. Vlassopoulos, *H naftilia ton Ionion Nison (1700-1864)* [The Ionian Islands Shipping], Vol II, Athens 1995, 115-147.

78 This is part of an ongoing research that looks at the constitution of these companies in different islands, their deeds of settlement, the lists shareholders and the actual sea loans granted to shipmasters.

79 E. Prontzas, *Trapeza h Ioniki, «xarin tis Ellados».*, Thessaloniki (forthcoming)

Bank. On the other hand, merchants who had migrated to Corfu from the mainland opposite and who supported the idea of an expanding Greek kingdom that would include the Ionian islands, were the first to respond to attempts by the National Bank of Greece to establish a branch in Corfu. This development was another type of credit network under formation.[80] The most important attempt was a plan in 1860, envisaged by Scaltsouni, a Kefalonian lawyer and entrepreneur involved in maritime insurance, to establish a rival bank with the support of the Greek bank, which would attract the number of merchants required by Ionian State law to subscribe the necessary capital.[81] While this first attempt failed, another more organised move to establish a bank in 1864, achieved the support of more than 80 merchants and landed proprietors in Corfu, only a few days before union with Greece officially took place. This time the agent of the National Bank of Greece in Corfu, M. Paramithiotis proved more efficient than Scaltsounis a few years before.[82]

In 1858 on the other hand, 71 shareholders from Corfu and 60 from Kefalonia bought Greek Steam Navigation Company shares, one of the first important Greek enterprises of the new kingdom.[83] The presence of Ionians as investors in the Greek Steam Navigation Company is interesting because it indicates the overlapping of business interests with national sentiments. This is further substantiated by evidence from the Greek consul's reports sent regularly to Athens. The same merchants who were shareholders of the Greek Steam Navigation Company were also supporters of the establishment of a Greek bank under the aegis of the National Bank of Greece. At the same time, the wives of some of those merchants were regular subscribers to the fund for an orphanage established in Athens by Queen Amalia of the Greeks.[84] The Greek consul reported that merchants from the Ionian Islands involved in insurance had informed him that they were seriously considering the merging of several Ionian

---

80 The National Bank of Greece was established in Athens in 1841.

81 Prontzas, *Trapeza h Ioniki*, 77-87.

82 Paramithiotis came from Ioannina, in the mainland opposite Corfu and had migrated in the port in the early years of the protectorate. He was involved in several business activities, insurance and banking being but one of them. These activities were very profitable indeed, as his will shows; M. Paramithiotis' will, Aspreas notary documents, Notaries 605 b, CHA.

83 V. Kardasis, *Apo tou istiou eis ton atmon. Elliniki Emporiki Naftilia, 1858-1914*, [From sail to steam. Greek Merchant Shipping], Athens 1993, 32.

84 The letter of the president of the society for the administration of the orphanage asks the consul to thank on his part the 'patriotic members of the society residing in Corfu', Arhio Ioniou Gerousias, Elliniko Vassiliko Proxenio, CHA , Ionian Senate Documents / Greek Royal Consulate File 26, document 2867.

with Greek companies, something that according to them would be welcomed by both sides.[85]

Overall, the economically most powerful businessmen, politicians and members of the professions seem to have been shareholders of the Ionian Bank without rejecting investment in Ionian insurance companies, and some of them even in the Greek Steam Navigation company. On the other hand, the merchants and capital holders who were not involved in the Ionian Bank, found the prospect of developing networks with companies and business of Greek interests in the 1850s and the 1860s attractive, on the other hand they continued to invest in maritime insurance companies in their own local financial milieu.[86]

The decline and final disintegration of the Venetian Republic's power enabled merchants in the Ionian Islands to expand their activities, although the centuries old relationship had created networks strong enough to survive up to the nineteenth century. As the economy of the islands was transformed and adjusted to British imperial requirements, merchants from and in the islands maintained traditional patterns of trade while establishing new commercial networks with both the east and the west. This was largely due to the boom in currant trade and the rapid increase of the Black Sea grain trade. The development of new economic institutions and mechanisms of exchange contributed substantially to the construction and adoption of the networks described. These institutions were established with the agency of merchants and the co-operation between the merchant elite and the British authorities, both aiming at promoting the liberal idea of progress through commerce. However, competition between capital holders intensified towards the end of the period of British rule, as Greek economic interests appeared on the stage and as networks of merchants looking ahead of their time were formed with both the National Bank of Greece and maritime insurance interests in Greece. Throughout the centuries old networks gradually gave way to new ones, as changes in the economy and in the power politics of the time directed the regional, but increasingly internationalised, economy of the Ionian Islands.

---

85 According to the Greek consul, the merchants involved had already found the name of the new company: "Greek Insurance". CHA, Ionian Senate Documents / Greek Royal Consulate File 26, document 2867.

86 Prontzas, *Trapeza h Ioniki*, 100.

Urban Links, Trade Networks and Globalisation in the Early Modern Period: Amsterdam and Lisbon, 1640-1705 – a Case Study

Cátia A. Pereira Antunes

Theoretical Approach

The goal of this paper is to determine if the concept of globalisation can be applied to the Early Modern period. To achieve this goal, I use a case study centred in the economic relationship established between two European cities in the second half of the seventeenth century. The choice fell on Amsterdam and Lisbon because of their position as maritime powers and their importance in the European urban web at the time. The period 1640-1705 was chosen because of historical circumstances. In 1640 Portugal restored its sovereignty after 60 years of Spanish rule and 1705 marked the period right after the signature of the Treaty of Methuen.

The problem with the definition of globalisation is threefold. First, social scientists cannot agree on a common definition of globalisation for the modern times, or even acknowledge its existence.[1] Those who believe that a concept such as globalisation is viable have decided to establish a set of criteria that may help to sharpen their concept. The problem so far has been that each scholar comes up with a different set of criteria.[2] Second, globalisation has mostly been accepted as a static concept applied in a particular time and space. Third, although scholars of the main disciplines have accepted or criticised the concept of

---

1   D. Held, A. McGrew, D. Goldblatt and J. Perraton, *Global transformations. Politics, economics and culture,* Stanford (Calif.) 1999, 1.

2   For arguments about globalisation and counter-arguments see: P. J. Katzenstein, 'International interdependence in some long-term trends and recent changes', in: *International Organization,* 29-4 (1975), 1021-1034. M. Panic, *National management of the international economy,* London 1988, 161-194. B. J. Cohen, 'The political economy of international trade', in: *International Organization,* 44-2 (1990), 261-281. R. J. B. Jones, *Globalization and interdependence in the international economy. Rhetoric and reality,* London 1995. P. Treanor, 'No globalization', in: http://web.inter.nl.net/ users/Paul.Treanor/globalization.htm (originally published at Telepolis as *Globalisierung – ein Mythos? World nationalism: normative globalism as pan-nationalism. Global open society and the Long Boom*). A. Kleinknecht and J. ter Wengel, 'The myth of economic globalisation', in: *Cambridge Journal of Economics,* 22 (1988), 637-647. J. G. Williamson, 'Globalization, convergence and history', in: http://cs/muohio.edu/Announcements /global.shtn. P. Hirst and G. Thompson, *Globalization in question. The international economy and the possibilities of governance,* Cambridge 1996.

globalisation, historians are still lagging behind. This almost permanent refusal to discuss globalisation in history derives from the fact that the Early Modern historian's world is still dominated by the 'world system' theory created by Wallerstein.[3]

I would argue that the creation of a new concept of globalisation would surely be bound to bring more disruption than consensus, and it seems to me that that has already been achieved with the very extensive literature on the subject. But a definition is still needed. I would say that my idea of globalisation fits the essence of the definition by Held, McGrew, Goldblatt, and Perraton. They argue that globalisation is the increasing world interconnectedness of all aspects of social life.[4] To clarify this notion of world interconnectedness I would add that globalisation also has to be defined as total, dynamic, interdependent and planetary.[5] But this definition is given in a broad sense, without a proper analytical framework it stays very vague. On the basis of the studies already available, Held e.a. found an analytical framework common to all the specialists. They systematically present a set of five issues that must be addressed by those wishing to characterise globalisation properly. Those issues are: conceptualisation of the word, causal dynamics of the process, the socio-economic consequences of globalisation, the implications for state power and governance, and the historical background of the concept.[6]

Different schools have addressed the above-mentioned issues differently. We can conclude that there are mainly three groups involved in the globalisation debate. The hyperglobalisers, amongst whom Ohmae[7] and Guehenno,[8] the sceptics, gathered around people like Hirst, Thompson,[9] Ruigrok, Van Tulder,[10] Boyer, and Drache[11]; and a third group built around the works by Castells,[12] Hoogvelt[13] and Sassen,[14] often referred to as transformationalist.

---

3 I. Wallerstein, *The Modern World System*, 3 vols., New York 1980.

4 Held et al.,*Global transformations*, 2.

5 M. Castells, *European cities, the informational society, and the global economy*, Amsterdam 1992.

6 Held et al.,*Global transformations*, 3.

7 K. Ohmae, *The end of the nation state: the rise of regional economies*, New York 1995.

8 J.-M. Guehenno, *The end of the nation state*, Minneapolis 1995.

9 P. Hirst and G. Thompson, *Globalisation in question*.

10 W. Ruigrok and R. van Tulder, *The logic of international restructuring*, London 1995.

11 R. Boyer and D. Drache, *States against markets: the limits of globalization*, London 1996.

12 M. Castells, *The rise of the network society*, Cambridge (Mass.) 1996.

13 A. Hoogvelt, *Globalisation and the postcolonial world: the new political economy of development*, 1997.

14 S. Sassen, *Losing control? Sovereignty in an age of globalization*, New York 1996.

The hyperglobalisers base their arguments mainly on general economic logic. They argue that economic globalisation is synonymous with losing national identity and power. The national influence over politics and economics is transferred to transnational networks, which dominate the decision making process in fields like production, trade and finance. As an immediate consequence of this transnational power, the hyperglobalisers identify an economy without frontiers, in which national governments become the intermediate elements of economic policy controlled by a supranational structure. National economic and political institutions end up victims of a growing conflict between local, regional and global means of governance and therefore tend to lose power and influence. This group has a neo-liberal wing that identifies and explains the rise of a single global market by explaining how the national level is being slowly but steadily replaced by the global.[15]

The sceptics are more moderate in their arguments. They make use of heavy statistical evidence on world trade and flows, some of them dating back to the nineteenth century, to emphasize the fact that twentieth century globalisation is not a historical novelty and that interdependence processes were all active much before the discussion over globalisation had ever arisen. Their historical data confirms the high levels of internationalisation, i.e., the growing interaction between local and regional economies. But in the end of their arguments there is always the deep conviction that globalisation is a myth as is put forward by the hyperglobalisers. In fact, the only element that they accept as integrated and global is the market. They base this claim on the growing regional divisions in the global mechanisms of today, i.e., the clear division in geo-economic trade blocs, such as Europe, Asia-Pacific, and North America on a move that they have called regionalisation of the world economy.[16]

The third group is the transformationalist. The transformationalist thesis states that globalisation is a very important force of quick change of all aspects of society. Globalisation is believed to deeply change societies and individuals at all levels of their existence. One of the most important claims presented by the transformationalists is that the traditional core-periphery theory forwarded by Wallerstein[17] is no longer a geographical concept, but a social one.[18] Subsequently they argue that the strength of globalisation is to be found on the

---

15 Held et al.,*Global transformations*, 2-4.

16 Held et al.,*Global transformations*, 5-7.

17 I. Wallerstein, *The modern world system*, 3 vols., New York 1980.

18 A. Hoogvelt, *Globalisation and the postcolonial world*, XII.

interconnectedness of all social transformations, based in a growing interdependent world.[19]

So far, we were able to understand that hyperglobalists speak of a global age characterised by clear signs of global capitalism and governance, in which national states hold no power and therefore promote the replacement of some national structures by global mechanisms of control and decision making. The sceptics, on the other hand, refuse to acknowledge the hyperglobalist world. They argue that earlier historical periods, namely the end of the nineteenth century, were more interdependent and less regional than the world today. They base their statement on the trading blocs they have identified has strongholds of the national governments' economic interests, and the uneven economic development throughout the world. Finally, the transformationalists state clearly that globalisation has been a historical process but the world has never experienced the levels of interconnectedness and integration that it enjoys today. This level of interdependence has brought along a new restructuring of societies, where integration and fragmentation can co-exist.

Following the transformationalist trail, and considering their framework to analyse globalisation as a historical process we have built the following table, based on the structure by Held et al.[20]

Table 1: Historical forms of globalisation – an analytical framework

Key Dimensions	Key Characteristics
Spatio-temporal dimensions	- Extensity of global networks - Intensity of global interconnectedness - Velocity of global flows - Impact propensity of global interconnectedness
Organisational dimensions	- Infrastructure of globalisation - Institutionalisation of global networks and the exercise of power - Pattern of global stratification - Dominant modes of global interaction

This analytical framework works in two different dimensions: the spatio-temporal and the organisational. The spatio-temporal dimension is used to

19 Held et al., *Global transformations*, 7-9.
20 Held et al., *Global transformations*, 20.

measure globalisation at three levels: extensity, intensity and velocity. Extensity is used to measure the coverage of globalisation of different aspects of social life using different networks to determine the outcome. Intensity shows how deep globalisation has been felt and therefore reflects the levels of interconnectedness and interdependency established between the networks. And velocity expresses the speed to which the global flows produced by the networks and brought closer by phenomena of interconnectedness spread throughout the world. These three levels of measurement together determine the impact of globalisation in a specific period of time. This means that the three dimensional relation between extensity, intensity, and velocity determine the success of globalisation as a historical process.

Based on this spatio-temporal dimension, and considering the three levels of extensity, intensity and velocity and their impact, Held e.a. have identified four types of historical forms of globalisation.[21]

Table 2: The spatio-temporal dimension: types of historical globalisation

Type	Features	Historical Period
1. Thick globalisation	High extensity High intensity High velocity High impact	19th century
2. Diffused globalisation	High extensity High intensity High velocity Low impact	20th century
3. Expansive globalisation	High extensity Low intensity Low velocity High impact	Early Modern period
4. Thin globalisation	High extensity Low intensity Low velocity Low impact	Medieval period

Type 1 has been identified as the nineteenth century. Thick globalisation means that the reach of the global networks extended throughout the world at

---

21 Held et al., *Global transformations*, 21-25.

high speed and covering all components of a society. The net result: a strong impact of globalisation. The twentieth century is associated with diffused globalisation. This second type is characterised by a good internal functioning of the networks, associated with a large interdependence movement between them at a high speed. However, the impact of these features is quite low. This has something to do with the permanent disputes between local, regional and supranational power structures that have been retarding a higher impact of the phenomenon of globalisation.

Type 3 and 4 are deeply connected with pre-industrial forms of globalisation. Type 3 is linked with the Early Modern period in general. At that time, the movement of general expansion of the socio-economic networks throughout the world was not enough to cover for the difficult permanence of long-term interdependencies and a speedy spread of those networks, mainly due to the deficient infrastructural system. Nonetheless, the Early Modern expansive globalisation had a high impact, mainly for two reasons: first, the creation, development and dynamics of different networks brought together different production outlets and consumption markets; second, the proximity of different cultures and habits greatly shaped tastes, fashions, and general civilization developments.

Type 4 is the beginning of historical globalisation. This thin globalisation is presented almost as incidental. It refers mainly to the long distance commercial circuits of luxury products that travelled from the Far East into Western Europe, without having much of an impact, except on the individuals directly involved in these networks. The big question is: can we accept that this thin globalisation is the beginning of globalisation as a historical process? If one answers 'yes', then we ignore all history before the Middle Ages, and that seems to me too much of an easy way out. If one argues 'no', then it is worthwhile thinking about the historical periods that preceded the Middle Ages and see if this framework can or cannot be applied. In case the framework can actually be used before the Middle Ages, I would argue that it would be very interesting to see if what preceded a period of thin globalisation was a period of diffused globalisation, which was preceded by an epoch of thick globalisation and so on, and so forth. If that was the path of the process, then one might start talking about the behaviour of globalisation in the *long-durée*.[22]

This typology of historical globalisation concludes that all forms of globalisation put forward by the various groups involved in the debate have their

---

22 The concept of *long-durée* was brought into history by the hand of F. Braudel, *La Mediterranee et le monde mediterraneen à l'époch de Philippe II*, 2 vols., Paris 1966. F. Braudel, *Civilisation matérielle, économie et capitalisme*, Paris 1979.

place and are justified by a historical approach to the concept. Thick globalisation expresses best the feelings of the sceptics, who deeply believe that the nineteenth century was far more integrated than any other historical period. Diffused globalisation justifies the arguments of the hyperglobalisers on what concerns the extensity, intensity and velocity of the globalisation process, but the sceptics have a point when they argue that the contemporary world is developing into a more regional unit, divided by blocs of interest, where socio-economic and political-military success differs between developed and underdeveloped areas. Expansive and thin globalisation reflect clearly the transformationalist thesis according to which globalisation has been a forgotten historical concept systematically ignored and that scholars should not fear the idea that signs of globalisation were already present in the pre-industrial world.

The second level of this theoretical framework is the organisational dimension. This level is divided into four issues: infrastructure, institutionalisation, stratification, and modes of interaction. The infrastructures of globalisation are the means through which flows move in the networks. Held e.a. have identified three types of infrastructure: physical, legal and symbolic. The physical infrastructures include the infrastructures available for transportation, which can increase or decrease the velocity of globalisation and its impact. The laws governing certain networks compose the legal infrastructures. They promote better or worse conditions for the creation, development and success of a network. The symbolic infrastructure is connected with the means of communication throughout the networks, for example languages and cultural differences, which may deeply influence the impact of globalisation in any period of time. The performance of the infrastructures is therefore connected with the higher or lower extensity and intensity of certain domains of a particular network during a period of time.[23]

The level of institutionalisation observes the frameworks used by the governing powers to control and regulate the networks. This institutionalisation of the networks is in every sense positive. In fact, the higher the institutionalisation the better chance the network has to unify and promote financial flows, labour force migration, and so on. One may still argue that the growing efficiency of the network, achieved by increasing levels of institutionalisation, ends up making a large difference not only for the impact of globalisation in time, but also in space.

While the good conditions of the infrastructures and the high performance of the institutional framework can change the impact of globalisation, once globalisation is in motion there is still the question to which extent that

---

23 Held et al.,*Global transformations*, 19.

phenomenon is a true achievement. That is exactly why the level of stratification is important. Stratification became the means through which one may identify the organizational changes operated throughout the networks after being included in a globalisation process. These changes often assume the side of contradiction in globalisation. They express the asymmetries and discontinuities present among the networks and can be seen in a spatial and a temporal dimension.[24]

Finally, one ought to mention the modes of interaction. They characterize the relationship established between two or more networks. Held e.a argue that there are for types of interaction: imperial or coercive, cooperative, competitive, and conflictual. Some of these concepts can be immediately related to certain periods of world history. But what seems important at this level is the correct description and characterisation of the relationships established between networks involved in the globalisation process.[25]

So far one may conclude that the analysis of historical globalisation should be done through a spatio-temporal and an organisational dimension. The outcome of each one of these dimensions is the net product of the dynamic elements of each one of their levels. The performance achieved by each one of those levels determine the characteristics of each dimension, that is afterwards used to describe and classify types of globalisation, which differ according to historical events and developments.

The Case Study: Analytical framework

The type of globalisation that will be reflected by our case study is the model of expansive globalisation. As it has been pointed above, expansive globalisation is characterised by high extensity, low intensity, low velocity and high impact. This means that the Early Modern world brought together Europe, Africa, America, Asia, and Oceania, a political / legal infrastructure based on diplomatic relations, and a low level of dynamics through the networks and between them, due to the slow means of transport available. The global flows and networks that reflect this are mainly political, military and economic. This is a period generally characterised by a political and military expansion and the creation, development and growth of economic contacts throughout the world. Finally, the high impact of the time had more to do with economic and cultural/civilizational contacts then with strong institutionalisation or stratification of the networks.

---

24 Held et al.,*Global transformations*, 20.
25 Held et al.,*Global transformations*, 20.

The centre of my Early Modern case study involves the analysis of the role of two cities as economic bridges between several networks. Amsterdam and Lisbon assumed four major roles:

1. they were the points of contact between the hinterland and the rest of the world;
2. they were key players in the regional networks connecting the whole of Europe;
3. they became strong international performers immediately after the general European expansion overseas;
4. both cities recognised their inability to control each other's networks. For that reason, they became very eager to promote a long-term bilateral relationship that could improve their socio-economic development.

Amsterdam and Lisbon achieved a good performance during the second half of the seventeenth century. This was made possible because both cities were able to sustain and expand the interpenetration of their networks. The result of this process was the growth of both cities' participation in the globalisation process. Their success brought hinterlands, regions, and continents closer.[26]

I have faced a difficult problem in defining network from an urban history point of view. Several debates have ensued over this particular concept. The first one concerns the existence, or not, of urban networks. Historians and geographers such as Christaller and Lösch argue that the way cities relate to their hinterlands and to each other is mainly hierarchical. The argument runs that a city is part of a system and the level of economic and political development it can achieve depends mainly on the place it occupies in the hierarchy. This implies, that the city on the top of the pyramid is not only the most influential, but is also the one that dominates the others, withdrawing from this relationship the bigger profit.[27]

This sort of parasite theory has been questioned by a wave of historians and social scientists, such as Hohenberg and Lees, who put emphasis on the importance of equal relations, where not only the top of the pyramid gets profits from its contacts with the outside, but also the smaller urban units can promote

---

26 I. Geiss, 'The intercontinental long-distance trade. A preliminary survey', in: *Itinerario*, 10-2 (1986), 33-51. D. A. Irwin (ed.), *Trade in the Pre-Modern Era, 1400-1700*, 2 vols., Cheltenham 1996.
27 A. Lösch, *The economics of location*, New Haven 1954. W. Christaller, *Central places in Southern Germany*, transl. C. W. Baskin, reprint. Englewood Cliffs (N.J.) 1966.

themselves by relating to the centre, or to other urban units of their own size. This idea of promotion creates an impression that all the cities would be eager to have contacts with their hinterlands and their fellow cities. The optimal situation would be when all the cities could withdraw the same amount of profit from their networks and transfer it to the relationship with other cities.[28]

Recently these views have been taken into reflection by De Vries. He argues that the acceptance of one of the schools does not necessarily imply the rejection of the other. An attempt to bring these theories together has resulted in formulating a new analysis. It is perfectly acceptable for a city to be the top of a regional pyramid by building a hierarchy not only of direct rural hinterland, but also of other cities. Of course, the boundaries of this pyramid would eventually surpass regional and national borders. Nonetheless, the existence of a regional hierarchy does not necessarily compromises the existence of an international urban network, where the tops of several hierarchies would relate to each other, taking into account their personal profit and the profit of their enlarged hinterlands. One would then have a hierarchical network.[29]

My research has shown that the relationship Amsterdam-Lisbon was built on a set of contacts, based on the interdependencies secured by the economic needs of each city and of its networks. However, I cannot ignore the fact that Amsterdam had not only a larger hinterland, but a larger and stronger entrepreneurial basis as well, if compared to Lisbon. Nonetheless, the Early Modern city was not self-sufficient in what concerns its 'centrality' in the world economy. So, even the stronger urban economy would heavily rely on its relationship with the outside world, i.e., other urban economies. This interdependence created, in the long run, socio-economic and political ties typical of an interdependent and integrated global economy.[30]

So far we have seen that Amsterdam and Lisbon made part of an urban network, therefore it is now important to limit our focus to five criteria, which will give us the basic arguments to show that the networks developed by, and around, these two cities give strong signs of globalisation in the Early Modern period. The five criteria that I have found important for such an analysis are:

---

28 P. M. Hohenberg and L. H. Lees, *The making of Urban Europe, 1000-1994,* Cambridge 1996.

29 Statements presented during the Crayborgh Colleges, Department of History, University of Leiden, during the Spring of 2000. These ideas were already somehow put forward in J. de Vries, *European urbanization, 1500-1800,* Cambridge 1984. A similar model of explaining the connection between urban networks and urban hierarchies has been published by C. Lesger, *Hoorn als stedelijk knooppunt. Stedensystemen tijdens de late middeleeuwen en vroegmoderne tijd,* Hilversum 1990.

30 New attempts have been made to bring together this concept of socio-economic networks linked to a global and integrated society. See: Castells, *rise of the network society.*

1. Geography,
2. Trade,
3. Integration of production outlets and consumption markets,
4. Capital,
5. People.

The first criteria will concern the geographical space that gives the physical framework to the creation and spread of the networks. Geography acquires an extremely important role as a factor of analysis due to the limitations of movement, speed and communication technology available in the Early Modern period.[31] Although very limited in these technical domains, the Early Modern man, especially the businessman and the merchant, made all the possible efforts to overcome these difficulties by improving not only the transportation system, but also the speed with which information spread. Therefore, space and time became key factors for pre-industrial entrepreneurs.

A second important factor of analysis is trade. Trade was the largest activity connecting local, regional and international markets. At a first level, it will be important to analyse the quantitative nature of the trade flows, but the qualitative issues cannot be set aside. In fact, the capacity to deliver products in a certain geographical space, during a period of time, required skills to keep trade running both in quantity and quality.[32]

The integration of production outlets and consumption markets seems to be a major factor worth examining. The importance of the market integration is enormous. The measurement of contacts and interdependencies established between the two ends of the commercial net are essential for the understanding of the dynamics of production, trade and consumption. These become increasingly important for the breakdown of the structure surrounding the Early Modern process of globalisation.[33]

---

31 About the importance of geographical notions to define globalisation see: A. J. Scott, *Regions and the world economy. The coming shape of global production, competition, and political order*, Oxford 1998.

32 E. Mata and N. Valério, 'Alguns dados e notas sobre o comércio europeu e mundial nos finais do século XVII', in: *Revista de História Económica e Social*, 2 (1978), 105-122. I. Geiss, 'The intercontinental long-distance trade', in: D. A. Irwin (ed.), *Trade in the Pre-Modern Era*. R. C. Feenstra, 'Integration of trade and disintegration of production in the global economy', in: *Journal of Economic Perspectives*, 12-4 (1998), 31-50.

33 R. Gilpin, *The challenge of global capitalism. The world economy in the 21st century*, Princeton 2000.

If one speaks of trade and markets, one can hardly avoid the word capital. In fourth place, capital appears an unavoidable issue to come to terms with this idea of global economy. Capital will be mainly taken into account as means of delivering payments, establishing credit lines, and promoting foreign investment. These three dimensions, associated with a specific space, a growing trade volume, and the interpenetration of markets will bring the concept of Early Modern globalisation a step further.[34]

Last, but not least, one has to mention people. People were, in fact, the engines of globalisation. They were both producers and consumers. They fulfilled their role as middlemen, merchants, entrepreneurs, and businessmen. But the function of the human element does not stop here. The movement of people around implied other demands then the ones connected to business. Migratory movements in Early Modern Europe were heavily connected with religions persecutions and the search for specific labour markets. In this case, we can also spot growing development of an international labour market, deeply linked with the formation of specialists and the lack of particular skills, in different networks.[35]

The Case Study: Empirical findings

In the second half of the seventeenth century Amsterdam and Lisbon were two of the main port cities in Europe. Amsterdam witnessed a boom in the first half of the seventeenth century due to economic expansion and the increase of the urban population. This boom was, on the one hand, the immediate consequence of the fall of Antwerp as the largest international market, and of Amsterdam's stronghold in the Baltic trade and her part in the overseas expansion of the Republic, on the other. Lisbon had been growing very slowly since the end of the sixteenth century. In fact, the city had suffered a severe blow on her hold of international trade, due to growing competition fuelled by the Dutch Republic, England, France and Spain. However, the capital of the Portuguese empire was far from declining, although, by the second half of the seventeenth century, her growth was put under pressure due to the wars of restoration against the Spanish

---

34 M. Obstfeld, 'The global capital market: benefactor or menace?', in: *Journal of Economic Perspectives*, 12-4 (1998), 9-30.

35 J. G. Williamson, 'Globalization, labor markets and policy backlash in the past', in: *Journal of Economic Perspectives*, 12-4 (1998), 51-72.

and the overseas wars against the European powers that were trying to conquer the Portuguese controlled areas in Africa, South America, and Asia.[36]

On a local level, Amsterdam had, in the second half of the seventeenth century, a very large hinterland. This hinterland provided the city with basic foodstuffs to feed the growing population, but also with a labour force able to fit the demands of Amsterdam's growing role as the centre of the world's commercial and financial transactions. Amsterdam provided the hinterland with the ideal market place for the export of its production, not only into the urban market, but also into the regional and international markets. Farmland and the industrial cities around Amsterdam, such as Haarlem, Leiden, and Delft composed the first ring of the hinterland.[37] The second ring was fulfilled by the other port cities of North and South Netherlands. Although those cities were Amsterdam's traditional competitors, economic pressure, political developments and military interventions ended up dictating the conjunctural relationship developed between them and Amsterdam. The third and final ring included the East borders of the Republic, well into Germany, following the route of the main waterways. If the first ring supplied the city with foodstuffs and industrial goods, either for urban consumption or for the regional and international export markets, the second ring was the easiest access to the hinterland of other smaller port cities, whose capacity of market redistribution was smaller then Amsterdam's. Finally, Germany provided the perfect spot to form new consumer markets for the products coming from the regional and the international routes and the best labour provider in the whole hinterland. The general high salaries of the Republic combined with a serious economic crisis in Germany made Amsterdam the perfect migratory destination for German youngsters. In fact, the Amsterdam's marriage registers show that 18.5% of the seamen married in the city were Germans in the period 1661-1665.[38]

On the other side of Europe, Lisbon was keeping a slow pace of growth mainly due to the political and military instability both inside and outside the European domains of the new King of Portugal. The region directly served by the Tagus river dominated the hinterland. Although the river was not navigable for a long distance inland, this was one of the most fertile areas of the Portuguese Kingdom. The city could easily withdraw from the immediate agricultural hinterland enough foodstuffs to feed the urban population, as well as

---

36 J. de Vries, *European Urbanization, 1500-1800,* Cambridge 1984, 271 and 278.

37 C. Lesger, 'Clusters of achievement: the economy of Amsterdam in its golden age', in: P. O'Brien, D. Keene, M. 't Hart and H. van der Wee, *Urban achievement in Early Modern Europe. Golden ages in Antwerp, Amsterdam and London,* Cambridge 2001, 78.

38 P. C. van Royen, *Zeevarenden op de koopvaardijvloot omstreeks 1700,* Amsterdam 1987, 129.

create some stocks, which could later on be introduced in the regional and international networks. On the other hand, this area was also a big producer of wine and salt, not only sent into the urban markets, but also aimed at the export markets. The natural position of the city and the specific dynamics of the Portuguese economy at that time made all the possible developments of a second and third rings of hinterland impossible to sustain. The other Portuguese harbours preferred to use the local foreign communities to connect with the regional and international networks.[39] Furthermore, Lisbon did not have enough harbour infrastructures to support any stock pilling of products for a long time. After all, the city was still working with the infrastructures built and developed during the second half of the sixteenth century.[40]

At a regional level, Amsterdam was exploiting the strong hold conquered in the Baltic and Scandinavia during the end of the sixteenth and the beginning of the seventeenth century. This trade network was essential for the development of Amsterdam as the largest and most prosperous European city of the seventeenth century. The Baltic depended on the Amsterdam carriers to supply luxury articles from the international trade, but also other rather more essential items from the regional network. The Baltic and Scandinavian fishing industry depended heavily on the salt brought from the South of Europe by the Dutch, as well as consumption goods such as wine and fruit. On the other hand, Amsterdam's role as a local, regional, and international redistribution post made it the perfect warehouse for the grain produced in the Baltic area, as well as the wood and fish output from Scandinavia. Although the overall imports of Scandinavian fish and wood were directly consumed in the Republic, first in Amsterdam, than through the several rings of her hinterland, some of these imports were sent to the second regional network controlled by Amsterdam: the Western European and Mediterranean trade.[41]

The first item of exchange in the Amsterdam-Baltic/Scandinavian trade was salt. I already addressed the vital importance of salt to these two regions, but it is still important to mention the necessity for the Baltic grain production in the West European and Mediterranean areas. The seventeenth century general grain shortages gave the Amsterdam middlemen the vital function of feeding entire cities. In the 1640s, Amsterdam's grain exports to Lisbon amounted to 11% of

---

39 J. R. Magalhães, *O Algarve económico: 1600-1773*, Lisbon 1988.
40 L. F. Costa, 'Carpinteiros e calafates na Ribeira das Naus: um olhar sobre a Lisboa de Quinhentos', in: *Penélope: fazer e desfazer a História*, 13 (1994), 37-55. I. Moita, 'A imagem e a vida da cidade', in: *Lisboa Quinhentista. A imagem e a vida da Cidade. Exposição temporária, Museu da Cidade*, Lisbon 1983, 22.
41 C. Lesger, 'Clusters of achievement', 68.

the total grain purchased by the Dutch in the Baltic. By 1677-1685 that percentage had increased to 18%, although the number of ships involved in this trade had decreased from 76% to 61% of the total fleet trading in the route Amsterdam-Lisbon-Amsterdam.[42] On the way back, they would transport the salt to balance the regional transactions. Scandinavian wood was also of great importance due to the fact that ships became the fastest and best means of communication and transport between medium and long distance trading partners. Once again, the balance of trade claimed for the supply of salt to complement fishing activities.[43]

The regional network provided Amsterdam with far more products. Wine, fruit, olive oil, raw materials (wool, cork), sugar, tobacco, spices, precious stones, exotic raw materials and silver were available to Amsterdam's merchants. The products of European origin were mainly used in the urban consumption, the provision of raw materials for the industries of the hinterland, and the fulfilling of the demand of the first regional ring, i.e., the Baltic and Scandinavia. On the way back, Amsterdam was willing and able to provide these areas with warfare materials, books and fish, assembled in the city itself, manufactures and agricultural products from her hinterland, as well as grain, fish and wood collected from the Baltic/Scandinavian trade. Finally, the products of international origin were brought into this regional network due to the fact that these areas of Western Europe and the Mediterranean were losing their hold on the consumption markets, which were now being supplied through the North Atlantic axis, dominated by Amsterdam.

At a regional level, Lisbon assumed the role of the major Atlantic harbour of Iberia connecting the North Atlantic and the Mediterranean. The city was able to gather in her urban market two groups of products attractive to the Mediterranean world: first, the goods in transit from the North of Europe, and carried to Lisbon, until the first quarter of the eighteenth century, by Dutch middlemen, mainly from Amsterdam; second, the city's withdrawal from her own international network. The products brought into Lisbon from the North Atlantic axis were mainly manufactures, grain and raw materials (wood, copper), which Amsterdam would gather from her hinterland and regional networks. Lisbon was, then, a destination market and a bridge to the Mediterranean world,

---

42 Calculations based on: Arquivo Nacional Torre do Tombo (ANTT), *Inquisição de Lisboa*, Livros 804, 805 and 806. J. T. Lindblad, 'Foreign trade of the Dutch Republic in the seventeenth century', in: K. Davids and L. Noordegraaf (eds.), *The Dutch economy in the Golden Age. Nine studies*, Amsterdam 1993, 243.

43 J. T. Lindblad, 'Foreign trade of the Dutch Republic', 242. V. Rau, *A exploração e o comércio do sal de Setúbal: estudo de história económica*, Lisbon 1951. V. Rau, *Os holandeses e a exportação do sal de Setúbal nos fins do séc. XVII*, Coimbra 1950.

which would send as return cargo wine, luxury products and silver.[44] In 1680 the
level of employment in the Dutch shipping activities was 50.000 people. Of
those, 18.500 were directly involved in the European trade networks. The
Spanish-Portuguese-Mediterranean route represented 32.4% of the European
trade. In fact, this route gathered the majority of the workforce available in this
activities, directly followed by the England and Norway route, which
represented 21.6% each of the total jobs linked to the European trade networks.[45]

Amsterdam had still a third line of trade: the international trade network.
This was the means through which the city imported several luxury products,
spices, textiles, tea, and porcelain from Asia, tobacco, sugar, and wood from
America, and some exotic products from Africa. These products were brought to
Amsterdam through the commercial companies put together in the beginning of
the seventeenth century, the Verenigde Oostindische Compagnie (VOC) and the
West-Indische Compagnie (WIC), and some single entrepreneurs, based on
personal deals. Once arrived in Amsterdam, all these products were kept in
warehouses and later on redistributed through the hinterland and the regional
network, especially the branch connecting the city to the Baltic and to
Scandinavia.[46]

Lisbon's international dimension consisted of her overseas controlled areas.
The city would send to Africa all sorts of cheap products and foodstuffs (mainly
used to feed the Portuguese administration there) and bring back gold, which
declined to quite negligible proportions during the late seventeenth century. The
city was also the departure point of all the foodstuffs sent into Brazil (wine, cod
fish, grain) and the receptacle of exotic raw materials (Brazil, wood, pastel),
sugar, tobacco, precious stones, and towards the end of the seventeenth century,
gold. Asia was the last destination of the Portuguese foodstuffs and precious
metals, used to buy luxury products, spices, precious stones, porcelain, jewels,
and tea. Very often, all the products mentioned above, destined to the overseas
territories were accompanied by some shipments of war materials, imported
from the North Atlantic axis.[47] For example, during the seventeenth century, the

---

44 M.-C. Engels, *Merchants, interlopers, seamen and corsairs: the 'Flemish' community in
    Livorno and Genua (1615-1635)*, Hilversum 1997.
45 J. I. Israel, *The Dutch Republic. Its rise, greatness, and fall, 1477-1806*, Oxford 1995, 623. J. de
    Vries and A. van der Woude, *Nederland 1500-1815. De eerste ronde van moderne
    economische groei*, Amsterdam 1995, 472.
46 F. S. Gaastra, *De Geschiedenis van de VOC*, Leiden 1991. H. den Heijer, *De geschiedenis van
    de WIC*, Zutphen 1994.
47 F. Mauro, *Portugal, o Brasil e o Atlântico, 1570-1670*, 2 vols., Lisbon 1988. J. Serrão and A.
    H. de O. Marques (dir.), *Nova História da Expansão Portuguesa*, vol.VII: F. Mauro (coord.), *O
    império Luso-Brasileiro, 1620-1750*, Lisbon 1991. F. Bethencourt and K. Chaudhuri (dirs.),

Dutch and the Portuguese were able to send 1,923 ships to Asia. They dominated together 65% of the European shipping in this part of the world, while the English and the French together held only 32% of that same shipping.[48]

At this point, it seems important to conclude that these cities had a three dimensional function. At the first level, they were the gatherers of the hinterland production and the market place for the hinterland consumption. On the second level, they were the regional recipients of products around Europe, which were not only spread through the city and the hinterland, but also through the regional network as a whole. Thirdly, Amsterdam and Lisbon were the receptacles of overseas products, collected from the international network, and brought into the hinterland and the region.

The need for a bilateral relationship between Amsterdam and Lisbon developed because neither the former nor the latter were able to fully control production outlets and consumption markets throughout their networks. Therefore, both cities became bridges between three different rings of commercial contacts (hinterland, regional and international), using each other to gain access to the output of the other's networks. So, we can very simply say that the salt, wine, fruit, olive oil, raw materials (wool, cork), sugar, tobacco, spices, precious stones, and exotic raw materials received by Lisbon from all her networks, were sent to a smaller or larger extent to Amsterdam and from there spread into Amsterdam's hinterland, regional and international networks. The same happened with Amsterdam. Products such as manufactures, grain, raw materials (wood, copper), war materials, fish, books, and agricultural products, would be gathered in the city coming from the city's hinterland, regional and international networks, and sent to Lisbon, where they would spread into her own networks.[49]

História da Expansão Portuguesa, vol. 2: *Do Índico ao Atlântico, 1570-1697* and vol. 3: *O Brasil no balanço do império, 1697-1808*, Lisbon 1998.

48 F. S. Gaastra and J. R. Bruijn, 'The Dutch East India Company's shipping, 1602-1795 in a comparative perspective', in: J. R. Bruijn and F. Gaastra (eds.), *Ships, sailors and spices. East India companies and their shipping in the sixteenth, seventeenth and eighteenth centuries*, Amsterdam 1993, 183.

49 In this context is difficult to place the example of this case study in P. O'Brien's statement that between 1450 and 1750 commerce was made at a small scale. See: P. O'Brien, 'European Economic Development: the contribution of the periphery', in: *Economic History Review* (2nd ser.) 35-1 (1982), 3. However, he recognises that the volume of trade increased dramatically after 1650. See: O'Brien, 'European Economic Development', 4.

Figure 1: Visualising Early Modern globalisation: urban networks and trade flows

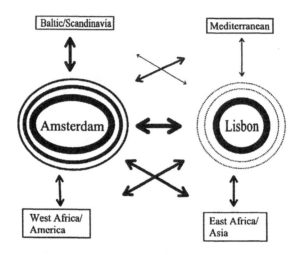

So far we were able to see how geographical networks were constituted to form a natural vehicle for trade. This ability to trade at different levels in different geographical spheres promoted a shortcut between production outlets and consumption markets. The growing dynamism of the geo-trading networks and the fast developing interconnection between production and consumption contributed heavily to an increasing interdependence and cooperation between both ends of the market.

But the geographical networks were not only composed by flows of products, but by flows of capital and people as well. My research has shown that there were two kinds of capital flows. First, the capital moved alongside with the products in direct connection with them due to the need for payments. These payments could be made instantly during the act of buying or through means of short or medium credit[50]. Second, capital was also used for investment. This investment acquired three forms. First, direct investment in the international companies of the time. For example, on the 13 December 1650, Luis Mendes, merchant in Lisbon, used 2 bills of exchange to invest 10,000 Flemish pounds in

---

50 Good examples are the bills of exchange. See: Gemeentearchief Amsterdam (GAA), *Notarial Archives* (NA), 1105, fol. 57 (23 July 1653). GAA, *NA*, 2892B, fol. 965 (5 July 1663). GAA, *NA*, 2892B, fol. 1145 (7 August 1663). GAA, *NA*, 3681, fol. 362 (12 December 1673).

the WIC, delegation of Amsterdam.[51] On the other hand, according to a contract dated 6 June 1643, Corens van Teylingen had invested 3,000 guilders in the Companhia Geral do Comércio do Brasil.[52] Second, the investment in species or goods to promote a particular enterprise.[53] And finally, the capital investment throughout the networks by promoting better means of transportation, broader systems of insurance, or improvement of the social networking, for example.[54]

Concerning the flows of people they moved along with trade and capital flows. Early Modern people were as eager to move around as people nowadays. Early Modern migration was also the consequence of religious persecutions or economic hardships. The various religious movements in Europe at the time drove thousands out of their cities. Two of the best examples of such a migratory flow were the South European Jews and the Huguenots.[55] When these people moved they took with them their capital, and therefore capacity of investment, and their skills. If the regions from where they left got poorer, the ones they arrived at prospered. In fact, some Portuguese historians have often claimed that the departure of the Jewish Sephardic community from Lisbon first to Antwerp, then to Amsterdam, Hamburg and London, weighted heavily on the low capacity of the Portuguese cities to produce net investment.[56]

Religious problems were not the only driving force behind migration. The second largest reason was economic disruption often provoked by military actions or political instability. That is how Amsterdam got so attractive to the German youth who barely survived the difficult first half of the seventeenth century.[57] The city was also attractive to the specialised Scandinavian workers, mainly skilled sailors and captains, who moved into Amsterdam due to the traditional high salaries practiced throughout the Republic. This was the case of the Scandinavian seamen who represented 31.25% of the married seamen in the

51 GAA, *NA*, 2189B, fol. 1133-1134.
52 GAA, *NA*, 1067, fol. 86.
53 It was the case of weapons, ammunitions and horses sent to Lisbon by several merchants, after permission of the States General and the Admiralty of Amsterdam. See: ARA (Algemeen Rijksarchief), *Archief van de Admiraliteiten*, Resolutien van de Admiraliteit Amsterdam, No. 1387, 1388, 1399, 1400, 1401, 1402, 1403, 1404 (1641-1649).
54 For insurance see: GAA, *NA*, 3713, fol. 457 (27 February 1693). GAA, *NA*, 5896, fol. 803 (4 May 1705).
55 For the Jews see: J. I. Israel, 'The economic contribution of Dutch Sephardi Jewry to Holland's Golden Age, 1593-1713', in: *Tijdschrift voor Geschiedenis*, 96 (1983), 505-535. J. I. Israel, *European Jewry in the age of Mercantilism, 1550-1750*, Oxford 1985. About the Huguenots see: de Vries and van der Woude, *Nederland 1500-1815*, 99.
56 A. J. Saraiva, *Inquisição e Cristãos-Novos*, Lisbon 1994.
57 P. C. van Royen, *Zeevarenden*, 129.

city between 1661 and 1665.[58] On the other hand, Lisbon was eager to receive a whole range of specialists, who would earn well above average in comparison to their Portuguese counterparts. In fact, the lack of engineers and other warfare specialists, as well as a whole range of administrative workers, such as bookkeepers, kept the migration flow between Amsterdam and Lisbon in good health. This was the case of Johannes Korbagh, who was hired by Nicolas Simons & Co., bankers in Lisbon, to be their bookkeeper for a period of 5 years, earning 300 rijksdaalers per year.[59]

There is a third group of 'migrants' that I doubt that they could or should be called migrants: the diplomatic personnel. Diplomats were themselves movers due to their professional activity. But they were also the source of flows of credit and investment. These credits and investments, far from the normal capital movements already mentioned above, often meant loans and compensations at the highest political level. This was the case of the Portuguese ambassadors in The Hague, the Portuguese agents in Amsterdam, and the Dutch consuls and agents in Lisbon.

Conclusion

At this point I would argue that the relationship Amsterdam-Lisbon between 1640 and 1705 is a good example of Early Modern globalisation. We have been able to confirm the diversity of flows (trade, credit/investment, and labour/migration) that justify the high extensity pointed out earlier as a prime characteristic of an expansive globalisation process. The second characteristic of this process is the low intensity. That means that the level of interconnectedness of the networks was quite small. I can agree with this only to a certain extent. The levels of credit and investment, and the amount of population migrating as a social or a labour movement are difficult to account for, and it seems clear that only a very small percentage of the population at the time had the chance to move. However, I must say that the interdependencies developed by Amsterdam and Lisbon on what concerns their bilateral trade relationship and their relationship with the different networks give a clear sign of strong interconnectedness, and therefore of a higher intensity than expressed by the model presented earlier. Furthermore, if we consider the issue of integration of markets, and although statistic approaches on this subject are almost impossible

---

58 P. C. van Royen, *Zeevarenden*, 129
59 GAA, *NA*, 3361, fol. 993 (14-15 November 1703). About the warfare specialists see: ARA, *Archief van de Staten Generaal*, Lias Portugal, 7011, 7037 and 7038.

to gather, one may argue that the qualitative integration of markets also gives a push to the intensity of globalisation. This means that the spread of new habits and tastes created, developed and shaped new dynamic elements throughout the networks.[60]

The model also states that expansive globalisation develops at a low speed. I guess that the speed to which global flows move is deeply linked with the infrastructures available and the level of institutionalisation around and in the networks. Ships were slow and so was the transmission of information. Credit and investment were not a general practice and did not move enormous amounts of capital. But one may still argue that Early Modern men achieved all the possible infrastructural and institutional developments possible at the time, taking in account the technology available. And therefore, one may have to use the model in a more flexible way to address the issues connected to the scale and scope of the globalisation process in different historical periods. However, it is undeniable the high impact of the whole process: continents came closer, trade developed rapidly, fashion and habits moved along with economic networks and the world became 'smaller'.

A historical model can only provide some improvement to define a certain reality if one can find enough case studies to support it. In this particular case, it would be of great use to replace the two cities mentioned above by other two cities, and see to which extent the proposed model can be applied or not. It would be ideal to take in account the relationship established between 'City A' and 'City B' in the Early Modern period and study the development and relationship with their networks, each other, and to see how far the influence/control and participation/integration of these two cities in the expansive model of globalisation are of some consequence or not.

---

60 The production of sugar for the export markets grew from +/- 800.000 *arobas* in 1650, to +/- 1.600.000 *arobas* in 1670. This growth reflects the increase in the number of sugar engines, which grew from +/- 350 in 1650 to +/- 520 in 1670. This overall growth of means of production and output for the export markets provoked immediate consequences at the other end of the markets. First, the price, in silver, of each *arroba* of sugar in Brazil decreased from 1650 to 1670, which reflects the increase in the production sector. Second, the prices of sugar throughout the distribution networks developed accordingly, i.e., the price of sugar was, in 1670, +/- 50 gr. of fine silver each *arroba* in the production outlet (Brazil), +/- 95 gr. at the middleman's hands (Lisbon), and +/- 110 gr. in the consumption market (Amsterdam). These prices had been equally decreasing throughout the networks, since the 1650s. See: J. Serrão and A. H. de O. Marques (dirs.), *Nova História da Expansão Portugesa*, vol. 7, 221. F. Mauro, *Portugal, o Brasil*, vol. 2, 285.

The Rise and Fall of Silesian Merchant Guilds in the International Trade Net (1700-1850)

Marcel Boldorf

The beginnings of the Silesian linen exports date back to the early sixteenth century. Merchants from *Oberdeutschland* (Nuremberg, Augsburg, Ravensburg etc.) signed collective contracts with the craft guilds of Silesian towns, thus fixing a certain output of linen at an arranged price (*Zunftkäufe*).[1] Furthermore, many traders from Western Europe came to Silesia. They acted as factors for Dutch and English companies and bought the linen on the public markets before exporting it. Already in 1601, Silesian merchants asked the Viennese court to discriminate against the foreign linen buyers because such activities meant a serious threat for their own business.[2] Although Vienna imposed a rise in duties for foreigners' exports, the businesses of Silesian merchants were too small at that time to begin long-distance trade. However, from 1602 onwards, foreign factors were obliged to buy the linen only from local merchants and retailers or to acquire the freedom of a Silesian town.

After the Thirty Years' War, the situation became much more favourable for the local merchants. The number of foreign exporters had diminished during the war. Meanwhile the linen production in the countryside spread out fast and new trade centres arose. In the town of Hirschberg (*Jelenia Góra*), the merchant class grew so strong that in 1658 it split from the all-craftsmen-guild (*Vielhandwerkerzunft*) which had included all kinds of crafts before. At the same time, the foreign factories (*Faktoreien*) were forbidden within Silesian towns.[3] The only chance for these merchants to maintain their business was to settle down in one of the trade towns. The Silesian exporters in towns like Hirschberg, Landeshut (Kamienna Góra) and Greifenberg (Gryfów Śląski) expanded their export business to distant trade places.

---

1   H. Aubin and A. Kunze, *Leinenerzeugung und Leinenabsatz im östlichen Mitteldeutschland zur Zeit der Zunftkäufe. Ein Beitrag zur industriellen Kolonisation des deutschen Ostens*, Stuttgart 1940; H. Aubin: 'Die Anfänge der großen schlesischen Leineweberei und -handlung', in: *Vierteljahrschrift für Sozial- und Wirtschaftsgeschichte*, 35 (1942), 148-149.

2   A. Zimmermann, *Bluethe und Verfall des Leinengewerbes in Schlesien. Gewerbe- und Handelspolitik dreier Jahrhunderte*, 2nd edition, Breslau 1885, 6.

3   S. Kühn, *Der Hirschberger Leinwand- und Schleierhandel von 1648 bis 1806* (Breslauer Historische Forschungen 7), Breslau 1938, reprint Aalen 1982, 46. The decree was re-enforced in 1678 and 1685.

The demand for Silesian linen grew in the western and southern European countries and their colonies, as these territories could not satisfy the demand by home production. The coarse Silesian cloth was good enough to clothe plantation workers. It was also used for packaging, canvas and canvas bagging. In the eighteenth century, the European linen industry developed into an annex of the expanding Atlantic trade.[4] Hamburg became the main export harbour for Silesian textile goods. As a consequence of the Navigation Act of 1651, the trade with the colonies in the Americas was mainly organized as re-export trade. The transport by ship to the overseas territories was only allowed on English vessels. Following the English example, other maritime powers tried to transport more linen on their own fleets. Sometimes, the differences in taxation were maintained for political reasons. For instance, the Spanish discriminated Silesian goods by demanding higher tolls for them than for French linen.[5] Thus, most of the Silesian linen exports were traded via Hamburg to London until the 1770s. The English Capital was the most important place of transhipment for the transatlantic trade to America and the West Indies. Four fifth of the English exports ran via London.[6]

During the eighteenth century, the Silesian merchants intensified their trade relationships with foreign wholesale traders. Most of the wealthy merchants charged carters to bring the linen to the Leipzig fair or to seaports like Hamburg itself. There is no evidence from the sources that the Silesian merchants used ships of their own for the transport overseas.[7] Only a small number of them settled abroad. Nearly all of the linen cloth – which was Hamburg's first export good – was transported on English, Spanish or Portuguese ships. In 1745, Christian Mentzel, who was one of the most important merchants from Hirschberg, had stocks in the warehouses of six Hamburg wholesalers.[8] Sometimes, the linen was kept on stock in Lüneburg, some kilometres down the Elbe. In this town, the Silesian exporters were allowed to store the goods as long as they wanted, whereas in Hamburg they had to pay a toll of 37.5 percent after six months of storage. From there, they offered samples of cloth to the Hamburg merchants and waited for orders. When the overseas merchants were interested

---

4   P. Kriedte, H. Medick and J. Schlumbohm, *Industrialisierung vor der Industrialisierung. Gewerbliche Warenproduktion auf dem Land in der Formationsperiode des Kapitalismus*, Göttingen 1978, 86.
5   A. Zimmermann, *Bluethe und Verfall*, 142.
6   R. Davis, *The industrial revolution and British overseas trade*, Leicester 1979, 31; F. Braudel, *Sozialgeschichte des 15. bis 18. Jahrhunderts*, vol. 3: *Aufbruch zur Weltwirtschaft*, German transl., Munich 1986, 504.
7   Kühn, *Hirschberger Leinwand- und Schleierhandel*, 88.
8   Kühn, *Hirschberger Leinwand- und Schleierhandel*, 90.

in purchasing the linen, it could be delivered immediately from the Lüneburg stocks. The Silesian merchants mostly sold the cloth to the Hamburg exporters. A direct sale to the merchants of the re-exporting nations was very rare. In these cases, the sellers often had to wait for a long time before receiving the payment.

During decades of trade relationships, the ties between the Hamburg and Silesian merchants strengthened. Although the distance between the seaport and the production region was quite far, most of the larger Silesian merchants kept close contacts to their Hamburg business partners, which enabled Silesian suppliers to get credit for outstanding deliveries. When the overseas trade stagnated because of the American War of Independence, a Silesian *Kriegsrat* suggested in 1782 sending the whole output to one Hamburg trader named Ohmann & Cie.[9] The government official hoped to guarantee the incomes of the poor weaver population. But the Hirschberg merchants rejected his plans because they had no interest in storing the cloth for a longer time. They feared that keeping stocks in the seaports might lead to a decline of prices if the Hamburg warehouses were overstocked. They preferred to stop buying linen on the markets. As a consequence, the weavers had no opportunity to sell their cloth.

Such behaviour was typical of the Silesian linen merchants. The supervision of the production process was guaranteed by institutional arrangements which were only favourable for their purchase in bulk. Despite their participation in the worldwide free trade, the linen merchants organised the trade and the production sphere by a scheme of harsh restrictions. When the Hirschberg merchants established a trade guild in 1658, they immediately gave themselves a charter.[10] Applicants were admitted under the condition that they possessed the freedom of the town, were of honourable birth and of good reputation. The guild members elected leaders, who were called aldermen (*Kaufmannsälteste*). General meetings took place four times a year under the supervision of Hirschberg's lord mayor. In the domain of trade, solidity and reliability were indispensable as well as the prohibition of unfair competition and the duty to buy well-fabricated cloth from the weavers who came to the linen markets. Two years later, a similar guild was

---

9   Kühn, *Hirschberger Leinwand- und Schleierhandel*, 90.
10 M. Göbel, *Die Hirschbergische Kaufmanns-Sozietät 1658-1933. Ein Ausschnitt aus der Wirtschaftsgeschichte des Hirschberger Tals. Dargestellt zur Feier des 275-jährigen Bestehens der Sozietät*, Hirschberg [1933], 10-13; G. Cassel, *Die Hirschberger Kaufmanns-Sozietät (von 1658-1740). Ein Beitrag zur Geschichte der Weberei im Riesengebirge im Rahmen der österreichischen Merkantilpolitik in Schlesien*, Hirschberg 1918, 18-20.

founded in the neighbouring town of Landeshut.[11] The regulations of the two institutions transferred the traditional ideas of the craft guilds to the trade sphere. The town-based merchants tried to maintain a system of institutionalised trade relations that was centred around the market towns. On the privileged markets, the wholesale trade was monopolised. With the help of a lobby-association, the *Gebirgshandelsstand,* the guilds managed to convince the state to install a survey system for rural trade. Three *Leinwand- und Schleier-ordnungen* of 1724, 1742 and 1788[12] contained various regulations for linen production and trade. According to these restrictive instructions, the small rural traders were neither allowed to cross the Silesian borders with linen goods nor to keep linen or yarn on stock. As a result of these measures, no putting-out-system (*Verlagssystem*) developed in the largest parts of the proto-industrial region. Thus, the innovative organisation of eighteenth-century rural trade was practically unknown in Lower Silesia.[13]

The production of coarse linen, which was on demand overseas, required little skill. Before being brought to market, the cloth was quickly inspected in the villages for its length, breadth and quality. An inspection system called *Leinwandschau* guaranteed a minimum quality standard of the manufactured goods.[14] Despite the state's efforts, the production of higher qualities, for which there was a domestic demand, could not be promoted. The introduction of fine linen like dowlas (creas) or damask failed because the export-merchants did not want to include them into their range of products. They stated that these goods changed fashion too often and that trading them would mean a threat to the stability of their income.[15] The production of damask, for instance, would have led to the investment of a higher rate of fixed capital and to the introduction of a putting-out system. The Silesian merchants feared the risk of these changes. They insisted on their refusal even when the Silesian government tried to force

---

11 O. Schumann, *Die Landeshuter Leinenindustrie in Vergangenheit und Gegenwart. Ein Beitrag zur Geschichte der schlesischen Textilindustrie,* Jena 1928, 17-18.

12 A. Zimmermann, *Bluethe und Verfall des Leinengewerbes in Schlesien,* 37-43, 79-82, 176-182.

13 Yet, Silesia was an exporting gregion and had a growing weving population like other proto-industrialised regions. For the peculiarities of the Silesian development see: Kriedte / Medick / Schlumbohm, *Industrialisierung,* 51, 54. More details in: M. Boldorf, 'Märkte und Verlage im institutionellen Gefüge der Leinenregion Niederschlesien des 18. Jahrhunderts', in: C. Wischermann (ed.), *Die Wirtschaftsgeschichte vor der Herausforderung durch die New Institutional Economics* (in print).

14 M. Boldorf, *Institutional barriers to economic development: The Silesian linen proto-industry, 17th to 19th century* (Institut für Volkswirtschaftslehre und Statistik der Universität Mannheim, Beiträge zur angewandten Wirtschaftsforschung, Discussion Paper 566), Mannheim 1999.

15 For the correspondence about it see: Archiwum Pañstwowe w Jeleniej Górze (APJG), Konfraternia Kupiecka w Kamiennej Górze (Landeshuter Sozietät) No. 15 [1766-1780].

them. In 1764, the Silesian minister von Schlabrendorff gave the order for a police intervention in the houses of the Hirschberg and Schmiedeberg (Kovary) merchants to break their obstructive behaviour.[16] As such coercive measures were not practicable in the long term, product innovation did not expand nor did the introduction of fine linen or cotton.

The economic development of Silesia during the eighteenth century may be characterised by two points:

1.) lack of process innovations – i.e. innovations leading to a more efficient arrangement of the social and economic institutions,

2.) lack of product innovations – i.e. innovations leading to a change in demand, resulting in the development of new branches.

With the expansion of trade, a number of linen merchants made a political career on the local level. They became mayors or gained other official honours and powers in their home towns.[17] Like many other members of the bourgeois classes, they were keen on achieving the same way of life as the nobility.[18] During the last decades of the eighteenth century, some of the established merchants of Hirschberg and other trade towns abandoned their business and retired to the countryside. They bought agrarian estates in order to live from their rents as landowners. At his death in 1748, the above mentioned Hirschberg linen merchant Christian Mentzel, one of the wealthiest men in town, left a large amount of capital, warehouses and a luxurious residential building in town. Besides that, he owned two manors in the nearby countryside.[19] Mentzel can be seen as an example of many Silesian merchants who bought rural estates. By 1795, the bourgeois classes owned 7.4 per cent of the 4,000 Silesian manors.[20] Becoming landowner was more beneficial for the self-image of the merchants than investing the money in the arising industrial sector.

---

16 Zimmermann, *Bluethe und Verfall*, 130.

17 Kühn, *Hirschberger Leinwand- und Schleierhandel*, 116-131. H. Teichgraeber, E. Zimmermann and A. Kunze, *Greiffenberger Leinenkaufleute in vier Jahrhunderten*, Görlitz 1938, 30-42.

18 K. Gestwa, 'Protoindustrialisierung und „Judenfrage" in Schlesien', in: *Zeitschrift für Ostforschung*, 38 (1989), 77. For a more general perspective see: R. Koselleck, *Preußen zwischen Reform und Revolution. Allgemeines Landrecht, Verwaltung und soziale Bewegung von 1791 bis 1848*, 2nd edition, Stuttgart 1975.

19 Kühn, *Hirschberger Leinwand- und Schleierhandel*, 121; H. Weczerka (ed.), *Handbuch der historischen Stätten: Schlesien*, Stuttgart 1977, 300.

20 J. Ziekursch, *Hundert Jahre schlesischer Agrargeschichte. Vom Hubertusburger Frieden bis zum Abschluß der Bauernbefreiung* (Darstellungen und Quellen zur schlesischen Geschichte 20), 2nd edition, Breslau 1927, reprint Aalen 1978, 47.

The continental blockade during the Napoleonic wars led to a sharp economic crisis, which was due to the continental blockade.[21] Napoleon wanted to exclude British trade from the continent and at the same time, England prevented all the ships belonging to France's allies from sailing to the British Isles. Thus, the overseas trade to America broke down. The consequences of the embargo were particularly hard for Silesia's exports, as one can see in the slump of Landeshut's exports during the Napoleonic wars.

Figure 1

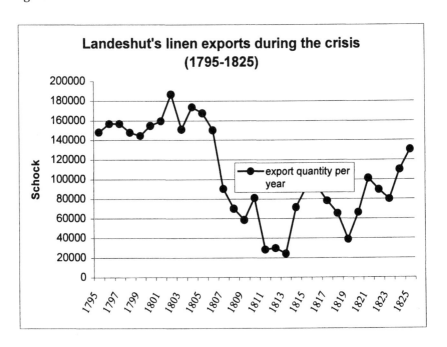

Source: Otto Schumann, *Die Landeshuter Leinenindustrie in Vergangenheit und Gegenwart. Ein Beitrag zur Geschichte der schlesischen Textilindustrie*, Jena 1928, 128.

During the decade from 1795 to 1805, the exports remained at the high level of the period before. But in the following years – in particular from 1811 to 1813

21 E. Fehrenbach, *Vom Ancien Régime zum Wiener Kongress* (Oldenbourg Grundriss der Geschichte 12), 4th edition, Munich 2001, 95-108.

and in 1819 – they dropped dramatically before they started to recover in the 1820s. As sales opportunities were lacking, the export merchants stopped buying the cloth on the linen markets – they often reacted in this way in times of an economic crisis.[22] The absence of foreign demand led to a loss of income among the spinners and weavers who then scraped a bare living.

As a result of the turmoil of the Napoleonic wars the efficiency of the state's control of rural trade and industry diminished. In times like these, small rural retailers tended to expand their trade activities. As a consequence, countryside-based merchants from remote areas became severe rivals of the city-based merchants in the field of export. The effects of this development can be seen in the following table.

Table 1: Turnovers of Silesian linen exporters in the Breslau Department (1808)

Turnover [in Prussian Taler]	Turnover more than 20,000 Tlr.	more than 5,000 Tlr.	more than 1,000 Tlr.	more than 500 Tlr.	less than 500 Tlr.	Local number of exporters
Landeshut [443,857 Tlr.]	10	6	6	.	1	23
Waldenburg [322,828 Tlr.]	6	9	9	3	13	40
Wüstewaltersdorf [238,739 Tlr.]	5	4	10	3	35	57
Obergiersdorf [201,012 Tlr.]	3	6	10	3	6	28
Charlottenbrunn [82,364 Tlr.]	.	.	5	1	3	9
Gottesberg [47,838 Tlr.]	.	.	3	.	2	5
Liebau [38,800 Tlr.]	.	1	.	.	1	2
Friedland [28,270 Tlr.]	1	1	1	.	.	3
Freiburg [10,698 Tlr.]	.	2	.	.	1	3

Source: APJG, Konfraternia Kupiecka w Jeleniej Górze, No. 275. [1808] Turnovers of linen exporters (Breslau Dept.). Annotation: In some of the localities (especially Obergiersdorf), exporters who lived in other trade towns (Waldenburg, Landeshut) were also listed.

---

22 APJG, Konfraternia Kupiecka w Kamiennej Górze No. 82, Breslau, 17 May 1764. Letter from the Breslau government (*Kriegs- und Domänenkammer*) to the town council of Landeshut. Geheimes Staatsarchiv - Preußischer Kulturbesitz Berlin (GStA-PK), I. Hauptabteilung (HA), Repositur (Rep.) 120, D V 2c, No. 3, vol. 1, 128-132. Breslau, 4 February 1815. Letter from *Regierungsrat* Bothe to the Prussian minister of finance von Bülow.

In 1808, one of the first crisis years, Landeshut (around 3,300 inhabitants) could export only 70,095 *Schock* of linen[23] with a value of 443,857 Prussian *Taler* (Tlr.). In comparison to previous years, this result was rather unsatisfactory (see figure 1).

The Landeshut export sector was dominated by a group of about ten wealthy merchant houses whose turnovers exceeded 20,000 Tlr. per year. One of the most important of them, Cramer & Co. alone had a turnover of 95,581 Tlr. in 1808. The second ranking town of Waldenburg (Wałbrzych, around 2,000 inhabitants), member of the *Gebirgshandelsstand* like Landeshut, had an influential merchant guild, too. The biggest linen exporters in that town were Töpfer & Co. with a turnover of 51,375 Tlr. The former leading trade centre Hirschberg (more than 6,000 inhabitants), which does not figure in table 1 because it was in the Liegnitz Department, had higher losses. The town's export value decreased to 205,451 Tlr. in 1808.[24]

While the established markets suffered from the drop in demand, the countryside villages made a good performance. Wüstewaltersdorf (Walim) had a little more than 1,100 inhabitants,[25] but counted 57 linen exporters in 1808. The majority of those (35 traders) ran very small business. They had an annual turnover of less than 500 Tlr. and exported only some pieces of cloth which were presumably partly self-produced. At the same time, five prosperous export merchants with an annual turnover of more than 20,000 Tlr. lived in the small village. Their businesses continued to grow even during the time of crisis. In two other villages of the Waldenburg district (*Kreis*), the situation was similar. A considerable number of linen exporters also lived in Charlottenbrunn (Jedlina Zdrój) and Obergiersdorf, both as small as Wüstewaltersdorf. In the latter village, a large number of the merchants were not residents but came from distant places like Breslau (Wrocław) or sometimes from Landeshut and Wüstewaltersdorf.

As a further step, freedom of occupation (*Gewerbefreiheit*) was introduced in Prussia.[26] After this reform of 1810, everyone holding a licence was free to start

---

23 One *Schock* was equal to 40 yards, cf. Kühn, *Hirschberger Leinwand- und Schleierhandel*, 100.

24 E. Michael, *Die Hausweberei im Hirschberger Tal* (Heimarbeit und Verlag in der Neuzeit 7), Jena 1925, 36.

25 H. Weczerka, *Handbuch der historischen Stätten: Schlesien*, 576. The number of village residents was 1,102 in 1785 and 1,349 in 1825.

26 'Edikt über die Einführung einer allgemeinen Gewerbe-Steuer (2 November 1810)', in: *Gesetzessammlung für die Königlich Preußischen Staaten*, 1810, 79. Generally see: B. Vogel, *Allgemeine Gewerbefreiheit. Die Reformpolitik des preußischen Staatskanzlers Hardenberg 1810–1820* (Kritische Studien zur Geschichtswissenschaft 57), Göttingen 1983.

a business in the sectors of trade or handicraft. This led to the abolition of the former privileges of the city-based merchants. For instance, they were no longer obliged to give proof of a certain asset to start export trade. The restrictions on rural trade were no longer applicable. As a consequence of the new regulations, a flood of new buyers and sellers crowded the countryside and town markets.[27] Originally, these people were pub owners or brewers who tried now to succeed in a new branch of trade. The old export merchants saw in their activities "*das Verderbniß von Manufactur und Handel*" (the ruin of manufacture and trade).[28] They argued that the newcomers lacked of knowledge of the production process, which lead to a poorer quality of the cloth. The weavers would be driven away from the linen markets on which the merchants as the regular buyers would lose their purchase opportunities. As a result, the connections to the international markets would be cut.

This argument can be pursued after the end of the Napoleonic wars. In 1816, the old trade town of Hirschberg exported linen for 258,922 Tlr., whereas the small village of Wüstewaltersdorf achieved a turnover of 475,962 Tlr. This was more than twice the amount of 1808 and exceeded the Hirschberg sum by more than 200,000 Tlr.[29] Hirschberg's exports only ran up to a quarter of the amount before the crisis.[30] As the wholesale prices for linen declined, the profits went down. This represented an excellent opportunity for small traders to build up their own export business. These merchants sometimes exported little more than the goods that they produced themselves. Furthermore, a number of countryside-based exporters succeeded in extending their business during the crisis.

As the depression persisted, a lot of the established merchants in the old export towns went bankrupt. In 1816, four of the most important Hirschberg exporters stopped business (Kießling, Jentsch, Schneider and Contessa).[31] Similar cases were reported from other traditional trade towns which were associated in the *Gebirgshandelsstand*. The Schmiedeberg *Handelsherren*

---

27 APJG. Konfraternia Kupiecka w Jeleniej Górze (Hirschberger Sozietät), No. 279. Waldenburg, 10 December 1816. Report on the actual development of the linen manufacture and its future. See also: GStA-PK, I. HA, Rep. 120, B II 1, No. 3, vol. 2, 8. Breslau, 18 October 1814. Letter of the Breslau merchant Moriz Eichhorn to the Berlin ministry of commerce.

28 GStA-PK, I. HA, Rep. 120, D V 2c, No. 3, vol. 1, 128-132. Breslau, 4 February 1815. Letter from *Regierungsrat* Bothe to the Prussian minister of finance von Bülow.

29 GStA-PK, I. HA, Rep. 120, D V 2 c, No. 3, vol. 1. Reichenbach, 25 April 1817. General report from the Reichenbach *Regierungspräsident* von Lüttwitz on the Silesian linen manufacture.

30 In 1796, Hirschberg's linen exports had a value of 1,430,000 Prussian Taler.

31 GStA-PK, I. HA, Rep. 120, A V 2, No. 3. Berlin, 24 November 1818. Kunth's rapport on Silesia (Reichenbach district), sent to von Bülow, state minister for trade and commerce. See also: A. Zimmermann, *Bluethe und Verfall des Leinengewerbes in Schlesien*, 274.

(prosperous merchants) left the town and withdrew to the countryside.[32] In Landeshut, the number of large linen export-"firms" decreased from 22 in 1807 to 17 (1812) and 13 (1820).[33] Many of the wealthy merchants gave up trade and retired to agrarian estates as their ancestors had done in the eighteenth century.

The drop of Silesia's linen exports changed the patterns of trade in two ways. Firstly, the retired merchants left a vacuum in the export trade of the traditional centres. Secondly, newcomers who usually lived in the countryside were taking the remaining opportunities. Starting at a low level, they built up a business which sometimes led to a remarkable success within one or two decades. This exchange had lasting consequences for Silesia's involvement in international trade. The majority of the direct trade relations to the Hamburg wholesalers were given up. The new traders tried to make a profit in nearby places like the fairs of Breslau or Leipzig. Thus, the trade relations with the seaports were hardly ever renewed. As a result, the Silesian linen region lost its connection to the net of international trade.

In the period of early industrialisation, the introduction of fine linen and mechanisation of the spinning process failed in Lower Silesia. This was a consequence of the above-mentioned lack of innovations. Other regions like the northern Irish province of Ulster made a good performance during the 1820s, but Silesia could not successfully follow the path of industrialisation. Silesia's exports overseas never regained the pre-war importance as the Americas, for instance, build up their own textile factories.[34] During the crisis, the number of handlooms in the rural industry had decreased from 22,000 in 1805 to 13,000 in 1819. In the two following decades, it remained on that low level and in 1840, 12,000 looms were registered in the former proto-industrialised region.[35]

The Silesian merchant class generally remained uninterested in starting initiatives to found industrial enterprises. The town-based merchants had been a dynamic factor at the beginning of the proto-industrial regional development. Now, on the threshold of the age of industrialisation, they were responsible for a belated development or even for a de-industrialisation of the textile sector. After having lost connection to the net of international trade, they were no longer interested in continuing their business in the linen handicraft sector. On the one hand, the terms of international trade turned against worldwide linen exports. On the other hand, there was the alternative of investing capital in the newly

---

32 Michael, *Hausweberei im Hirschberger Tal*, 36.

33 Schumann, *Landeshuter Leinenindustrie*, 38.

34 N. Lamoreaux: 'Entrepreneurship, business organization, and economic concentration', in: S. Engerman, L. Stanley and R.E. Gallmann (eds.): *The Cambridge Economic History of the United States*, vol. 2: The long nineteenth century, Cambridge (Mass.) 2000, 404-407.

35 Zimmermann, *Bluethe und Verfall*, 448-455.

developed technical processes. However, the roots of the traditional Silesian merchants in the production sphere were too weak to be a real alternative for them. The possibility of a further financial engagement in the textile industry offered no viable perspective. Except for a few examples like the merchant Alberti from Waldenburg,[36] who received large sums of money from the Prussian state, or the clothier merchant Kramsta,[37] no pioneer entrepreneur could be found in Lower Silesia.

The following de-industrialisation of Lower Silesia had severe consequences for the population that lived by spinning yarn or weaving. The import of machine-spun yarn led to widespread unemployment among the hand-spinners.[38] The handloom-weaving sector recovered in the 1820s, but in the 1830s and 1840s the competition of the mechanized industry grew in importance. The rural industries suffered a deep crisis during that time. The weavers' incomes fell below subsistence level, leading to distress and hunger among the population living at the foot of the Silesian Giant Mountains. By the end of the 1840s, handloom weaving had become more and more a part-time occupation.[39] From the 1850s on, the number of looms decreased and the rate of industrial employment sunk.[40]

---

36 H. Blumberg, 'Ein Beitrag zur Geschichte der deutschen Leinenindustrie von 1834 bis 1870', in: H. Mottek et al. (eds.): *Studien zur Geschichte der industriellen Revolution in Deutschland*, Berlin (GDR) 1960, 105-106.

37 GStA-PK, I. HA, Rep. 120, A V 2 No. 3. Berlin, 24 November 1818. Kunth's rapport on Silesia (Reichenbach district), sent to von Bülow, state minister for trade and commerce.

38 A. Schneer, *Über die Not der Leinen-Arbeiter in Schlesien und die Mittel ihr abzuhelfen*, Berlin 1844, re-printed in: L. Kroneberg and R. Schloesser (eds.): *Weber-Revolte 1844. Der schlesische Weberaufstand im Spiegel der zeitgenössischen Publizistik und Literatur*, 2nd edition, Cologne 1980, 114-143.

39 Zimmermann, *Bluethe und Verfall*, 452-456.

40 K.H. Kaufhold and U. Albrecht (eds.): *Gewerbestatistik Preußens vor 1850. Vol. 2: Das Textilgewerbe* (Quellen und Forschungen zur historischen Statistik von Deutschland 6), St. Katharinen 1994, 53-56.

Italian Merchants of the Eighteenth Century in Frankfurt and Mainz: Circumstances contributing to their socio-economic ascent

Christiane Reves

Introduction

„[...] at the beginning they came as lemon and seville [orange] pedlars, carrying around in every city their lemons and sevilles under their arms, [...] whereas now they allow themselves to be bought out with large sums of money, [... and] transport their fortune back to Italy [...]".[1]

This was the impression that the native merchants in Frankfurt had regarding the ascent of the Italian merchants from Lake Como, who resided in the city at the end of the seventeenth century, selling sevilles, spices and other rare commodities with great success.

Regarding the beginnings of Italian commerce north of the Alps, the image of the impoverished fruit pedlar carrying a backpack full of lemons to Germany in order to improve his financial situation by trying to sell his wares is one that was not only predominant in the seventeenth and eighteenth centuries, but that exists even in present day historiography.[2]

These pedlars became successful wholesalers by the middle of the eighteenth century, in supposition, exclusively through the sale of their goods. But such a change in their financial situation based on only this sole factor would constitute quite a leap. The fact that these "poor" Italian merchants became wealthy wholesalers in the middle of the eighteenth century raises the question: what are the true origins of the success of the merchants from the region surrounding

---

[1] Institut für Stadtgeschichte / Stadtarchiv Frankfurt a.M. (ISG Ffm), Handel Ugb Nr. 191, 103v: „[...] anfangs Citronen und Pomerantzen Gängler gewesen, so ihre citronen und Pomerantzen unter dem Arm in jeder Stadt herumb getragen, [...] lassen sich aber an ietzo mit großen Summa Geldes auskauffen, [... und] transportiren ihren Reichthumb nach Italien [...]".

[2] A. Schindling, 'Bei Hofe und als Pomeranzenkrämer: Italiener im Deutschland der Frühen Neuzeit', in: *Deutsche im Ausland – Fremde in Deutschland. Migration in Geschichte und Gegenwart*. Hrsg. v. K.J. Bade, 3rd edition, Munich 1993, 287-294; J. Augel, *Italienische Einwanderung und Wirtschaftätigkeit in rheinischen Städten des 17. und 18. Jahrhunderts* (Rheinisches Archiv 78), Bonn 1971, esp. 72-105; A. Dietz, *Frankfurter Handelsgeschichte*, vol. 4.1, Frankfurt 1925, 238-365.

Lake Como, a success they enjoyed not only in Frankfurt and Mainz, but also in many other places north of the Alps?

Since the middle of the seventeenth century, citrus fruit merchants, or "Pomeranzenkrämer", were commonplace in the Holy Roman Empire.[3] These merchants, who for the most part came from small villages southwest of Lake Como, were referred to in certain source material simply as "Italian merchants".[4] They could be found in large commercial centres such as Frankfurt, in medium-sized residencies such as Mainz and also in rural areas, where these salesmen chiefly peddled their wares. Apart from seville oranges and lemons, they also mainly dealt in wholesale and retail rare commodities, such as spices and tobacco, but also in other products such as fish, paints and dies, perishable goods for the practicing of lent, and, to a certain extent, various kinds of fabrics.[5]

The social and economic categorization of these merchants is a relatively difficult undertaking, since these include not only pedlars, but also retailers and large-scale cross-border wholesalers, who imported and exported goods in large quantities.[6] In addition to the merchants from the Lake Como region, there were also notable groups of merchants active in cross-border commerce from the Lago Maggiore region, the Dukedom of Savoy, as well as certain merchants from traditional commercial centres such as Lucca or Venice, who were also commercially active beyond the Alps.[7]

The following focuses solely on those merchants whose region of origin is Lake Como.[8] The great success of these merchants was based on several factors, for instance

1. Place of origin situated on a traditional trade route;
2. Tradition of trade and migration;

---

3   A. Schindling, *Bei Hofe und als Pomeranzenkrämer*, 290; J. Augel, *Italienische Einwanderung*, 187-203.

4   ISG Ffm, Handel Ugb 191, Specerey und Würtzkrähmer Acta contra die Italianische Beysaßen und deren Handel da 1671 a 1736.

5   Lists of the commodities sold by "italian merchants" can be found in contemporary dictionaries as well as in inventories: C.G. Ludovici, *Eröffnete Akademie der Kaufleute oder vollständiges Kaufmanns-Lexicon* [...], 3. Teil (H-M), Leipzig 1754; J.H. Zedler (ed.), *Großes vollständiges Universallexikon aller Wissenschaften und Künste*, [...].Leipzig vol. 1 (1733) - vol. 63 (1750); an example for an inventory is the one of Stephano Brentano (*28.4.1684, +1769) in Frankfurt: ISG Ffm, Reichskammergericht, Akten Nr. 522, 19r - 31v.

6   P. Kriedte, 'Vom Großhändler zum Detailisten. Der Handel mit Kolonialwaren im 17. und 18. Jahrhundert', in.: *Jahrbuch für Wirtschaftsgeschichte*, 1 (1994), 11-36.

7   A. Dietz, *Frankfurter Handelsgeschichte*, 162-166; J. Augel, *Italienische Einwanderung*, 42-58; J. Rumpf-Fleck, *Italienische Kultur in Frankfurt am Main im 18. Jahrhundert*, Stuttgart 1936, 16-18.

8   My Ph.D.-thesis on this topic is in progress.

3. Financial standing;
4. Kindred business network;
5. Structure of trade companies and;
6. Acquisition of right of residence.

Place of Origin Situated on a Traditional Trade Route

These citrus fruits and rare commodities merchants came from small rural areas along the west bank of Lake Como and in many cases achieved a considerable economic and social ascent over several generations.

Even though these areas would appear to be remote by today's standards, they were situated on main north-south trade routes since Roman times. The city of Como, which was located not far from this trade route, had, in addition to its key strategic position, a long tradition in trade and manufacturing. Since the Middle-Ages, Como had been connected with northern Europe through its linen production. Natural resources required for production were bought in Germany, manufactured in Como and the finished products sold north of the Alps. In the eighteenth century, Como became famous because of its silk production and manufacturing.[9]

Postal routes in the eighteenth century also contributed to Como's importance. Two postal routes, referred to as the „due corrieri degli Svizzeri", crossed paths on Lake Como. One route led to Milan from France, Geneva, Turin and Savoy. Routes from Spain, Genoa, the region of Veneto, the Holy Roman Empire and the Netherlands all went through Como. One further route led through Zurich, Basle and Lucerne. The postal route from Milan to Lake Constance led directly through the villages from where the merchants originated: Cadenabbia, Tremezzo and Mezzegra. The small towns in the mountains along the west bank of Lake Como above these villages were also not far from this postal route.[10]

---

[9]   G. Mira, 'L'industria della lana a Como nel periodo comunale e durante la dominazione viscontea', in: *Economia Lariana*, vol. 12 (1949); C.A. Vianello, *Il Settecento milanese*, Milano 1934; C.A. Vianello, 'L'industria, il commercio e l'agricoltura dello Stato di Milano nella seconda metà del secolo XVIII, in: *Periodico della Società Storica Comense*, 29 (1932), 113-114, 7-43; B. Fasola, *Tracce della memoria. Una storia del territorio comasco attraverso i documenti*, Lipomo 1996, 15.

[10] B. Caizzi, *Dalla posta dei re alla posta di tutti. Territorio e comunicazioni in Italia dal XVI secolo all'Unità*, Milano 1993, 102-106; A. Carera, 'Gli spazi dello scambio sulle terre del lago', in: *Il difficile equilibrio agricolo-manifatturiero (1750-1814)* (Da un sistema agricolo a un sistema industriale. Il Comasco dal Settecento al Novecento, vol. 1), Como 1987, 269-478.

A Tradition of Trade and Migration

Due to the scope and significance of the emigration to America, and the migration from the countryside to the cities as a result of the industrial revolution in the nineteenth century, the tradition of migration within the regions surrounding the Alps was, for the purposes of historiography, of secondary importance. However, over the past ten years, research has been conducted on earlier centuries pertaining to the migration in the regions surrounding the Alps. Some researchers even base their work on the assumption that migration in the regions around the Alps is part of a traditional way of life, and that the inhabitants of these regions first became settled after World War I.[11]

Research conducted on the citrus fruits and rare commodities merchants from Lake Como confirm these results in many aspects. As early as the twelfth and thirteenth centuries, the researched group of "maestri comacini", or skilled and manual workers, originating from Lake Como can be found as having contributed to important construction projects in many other places in Italy, and partly in Northern Europe.[12]

In the seventeenth century, migration took on a greater dimension. It could vary between one fourth and one third of the entire population of the respective village, and was limited chiefly to males within the population. Whereas those who lived near Como tended to seek seasonal occupation in the city, the migration in more distant regions such as Central and Northern Europe was more typical of those originating from the central and northern banks of Lake Como.[13]

However, in addition to trends in migration, an involvement in commerce was also a long tradition with some families from Lake Como. Most of the inhabitants from Lake Como sought other work outside of their work in the

---

[11] P.P. Viazzo, 'La mobilità del lavoro nelle alpi nell'età moderna e contemporanea: nuove prospettive di ricerca tra storia e antropologia', in: G.L. Fontana, A. Leopardi and L. Trezzi (eds.), *Mobilità imprenditoriale e del lavoro nelle Alpi in età moderna e contemporanea*, (Seminario permanente per la Storia dell'economia e dell' imprenditorialità nelle Alpi, vol. 3), Milano 1998, 21; P.P. Viazzo, *Comunità alpine. Ambiente, popolazione, struttura sociale nelle Alpi dal XVI secolo a oggi*, Bologna 1990; D. Albera, 'Dalla mobilità all'emigrazione. Il Caso del Piemonte sud-occidentale', in: P. Corti and R. Schor (eds.), *L' esodo frontaliero: Gli italiani nella Francia meridionale/ L'emigration frontalière: les Italiens dans la France méridionale* (numero speciale di „Recherches régionales" III trimestre), Paris 1995; P.P. Viazzo, *Ethnic change in a walser community in the Alps*, London 1983.

[12] G.P. Bogneti, 'I capitoli 144-145 di Rotari ed il rapporto tra Como e i „Magistri Commacini"', in: *Scritti di storia dell'arte in onore di Mario Salmi*, Roma 1961, 166-171; G. Merzario, *I Maestri Comacini*, Milano 1893 (reprint Bologna 1967); M. Salmi, 'Maestri comacini o commàcini?', in: *L'artigianato e tecnica nell'altomedioevo*, Spoleto 1971, 409-424.

[13] J. Augel, *Italienische Einwanderung*, 85-95.

fields, since farming was not always sufficient to provide for their daily needs. Therefore, holding several different occupations was quite commonplace. Many did not practice further occupations in their region of origin. Research on the occupations of the male members of the Brentano families, who were quite successful in trade and commerce in the seventeenth and eighteenth centuries in Germany, particularly in Frankfurt and Mainz, revealed that some members of these families were active in trade and commerce as early as the fifteenth century. Though other Brentanos migrated, they did not emigrate as traders, but as bakers or other such skilled-labour occupations.[14]

Still, migration and trade generally did not result in emigration. Instead, many cases, such as those concerning commodities merchants originating from Lake Como, revealed that an extensive return to regions of origin predominated. It was, in fact, this return to regions of origin that was instrumental in laying the foundation for the socio-economic ascent of these Italian merchants in Frankfurt and Mainz. It was in their native country where the business networks of various families interfaced, where migrating family members congregated, where the next generation of merchants was recruited for trade companies, and where previous generations of merchants retired in the bosom of their families, leaving their sons to care for the business abroad.

Moreover, this tradition of migration and commerce on Lake Como is one that reaches as far back as the twelfth century. Thus, migration and commerce was an essential component in life and in many cases did not result in emigration. Rather, it was the return to the native region that was crucial to sustained success and economic ascent abroad. An eighteenth century government official from the province of Como ascertained, for instance, that migration could be observed, "[...] which, however, was not disadvantageous for the region, but, on the contrary, was a benefit, as such industrious people emigrate, who cannot sufficiently be sustained, nor achieve wealth from the natural unfruitfulness of the mountainous terrain, which constitutes the greater portion of this province. They seek and find, as has been the custom of this region as far back as can be remembered, in foreign provinces, and even in the very afar off regions, not merely the most basic sustenance, but even manage to save, as well. After several years of absence, the greater majority returns, whereas previously poor, now more or less wealthy. [...] In this context it is additionally noteworthy that the absentees maintained their houses, and that at least one family member always remained in the hometown. [...]"[15]

---

14 A. Engelmann, *Die Brentano am Comer See* (Genealogia Boica, 2). Munich 1974, 5-6.
15 German Translation see: J. *Augel, Italienische Einwanderung*, 84.

Financial Standing

Migration in the regions surrounding the Alps was in some cases, but not always, due to dire financial circumstances. Particularly with respect to those merchants active in the larger commercial centres and royal seats, such as Frankfurt and Mainz, it can be deduced that migration was often based on a desire to pursue further economic ascent and expansion, rather than emigration merely as a flight from poverty.[16]

On the basis of numerous sources from the regions surrounding Lake Como, it can, in fact, be upheld that insufficient agricultural prerequisites to economic gain existed, such as infertile soil and rocky, mountainous terrain, which made for difficult cultivation and farming. In spite of its mild climate, the region did not provide the adequate acreage necessary to accommodate the alimentary needs of the entire population.[17]

It was precisely this set of circumstances, however, which resulted in many inhabitants from this region not limiting their vocations to farming and the like in order to make a living. Nearly every individual supplemented their income with an additional form of occupation. Research yields therefore incomplete results in concluding that financial status can be determined on the basis of the amount of a migrant's real estate ownership alone. Hence, supplementary incomes also have to be taken into account.[18]

Moreover, it must be proved that those migrant merchants who made their way as far as Central and Northern Europe do not fall under the category of the most impoverished among the inhabitants of their home villages. Research of inheritances, dowries and real estate ownership revealed that merchant families such as the Brentanos were financially quite well off. The Brentanos and other such merchant families were free landowners, who owned both small and large tracts of land, as well as houses. These families were able to generate basic incomes through leasing their property, or by paying seasonal manual labourers to till their land, as well as finding tenants for their houses. The revenues

---

[16] B. Caizzi, *Il Comasco sotto il dominio spagnolo. Saggio di storia economia e sociale* (Centro Lariano per gli Studi Economico, 1), Como 1955; B. Caizzi, *Il Comasco sotto il dominio austriaco fino alla redazione del Catasto Teresiano* (Centro Lariano per gli Studi Economici, 3), Como 1955; F. Braudel, *La Mediterranée et le monde méditerranéen à l'époque de Philippe II*, Paris 1966; 42.

[17] B. Caizzi, *Comasco spagnolo*, 141-169; J. Augel, *Italienische Einwanderung*, 59-71.

[18] Research on these topics is made for my theses based on notary documents from Archivio di Stato in Como.

produced by these activities formed the initial base capital for pursuing trade endeavours.[19]

Following their economic ascent abroad, particularly in the mid eighteenth century, real estate ownership served more as a means of maintaining ties to their places of origin.

Further evidence of an established social and financial standing in the native region is a fact that can be traced back over generations and was still evident in the seventeenth and eighteenth centuries, i.e., as free landowners, these merchants also held positions in municipal administration, positions that were typically held by affluent and influential free landowners.[20] Migration was, therefore, not necessarily crucial for survival, yet vital for the economic ascent and expansion of a network. In order to attain this objective, these merchants were thus dependent upon a certain amount of financial backing which they had secured in their native regions.

The Kindred Business Network

The ascent of the merchants from the Lake Como region was also based for the most part on their capacity to tap into an expansive business network of kindred relationships, a network which was employed and maintained in and outside the native region.

First of all, this allowed the merchants to manage their native estates. The wives, who often did not at first accompany merchants in their initial moves to the foreign regions researched, would commonly remain behind to care for and manage the estate and household, deal with legal matters, manage business affairs or supervise the harvest, often with the help of siblings or cousins. Merchants abroad kept up regular correspondence with their relatives and families at home, relaying in letters the latest news and delegating business-

---

19 As early as in the 15th century, the Brentano were landowners, e.g. ser Martino Brentano (* ca. 1380/1385, + 25.11.1422/1.11.1423) owned property in the region of Tremezzo (Engelmann, Brentano vom Comer See, 223), but ownership of property was still common in the 17th and 18th centuries. Even the heirs of emigrated merchants such as Pietro Antonio Brentano (*19.9.1735, + 9.3.1797), who died in Frankfurt, still kept some land in their home region (ISG Ffm, Kuratelamt, Akten Nr. 671, Peter Anton Brentano 1799-1811, Doc. 5, p. 3, § 6).

20 A. Engelmann, 'Die Brentano vom Comersee. Zu ihrer Soziallage und -entwicklung als Familie', in: K. Feilchenfeldt and L. Zagari (eds.), *Die Brentano. Eine europäische Familie*, Tübingen 1992, 17-28.

related tasks to them. These relatives and family members were then responsible for carrying out transactions in the name of the merchant abroad.[21]

Many merchants did not remain abroad for the entire year, but returned home at least once, if not numerous times. This is evident in the contracts concluded by Dominico Brentano and his sons' trade company, which operated mainly in Frankfurt and by way of subsidiaries in Mainz, Amsterdam and other places. These contracts contain a clause which states that each company employee was only allowed one trip back to the home region, and dictating mandatory attendance at Frankfurt trade fairs.[22]

At home, the practice included meetings with business associates and partners, who were more often relatives owning business subsidiaries in other locations, such as Cologne, Amsterdam or Genoa. One utilized the time at home to discuss business activities in quiet and confidentiality, solve problems, and refresh business contacts that were of great importance both for family as well as business purposes. Blood relatives or in-laws, who came from the same town on Lake Como or a neighbouring town, were present at all main commercial centres. These relatives were instrumental in arranging and conducting numerous business transactions, as common origins and family relationships served as a basis of trust, which was key to harmonious dealings. Such relations were essential to expediting the flow of goods, as familiar business associates could be trusted to manage swift transactions, attest with reliability to the quality of products, as well as responsibly care for both the credibility and the handling of debt recovery.[23] This European-wide network, although not institutionalized, was clearly invaluable. It granted the merchants from the Lake Como region an enormous advantage over the competition in Frankfurt and Mainz in the procurement, transport and sale of their goods.

---

[21] L. Pini, 'Notizie dall'archivio della famiglia Brentano-Semenza di Volesio', in: K. Feilchenfeldt and L. Zagari (eds.), *Die Brentano. Eine europäische Familie*, Tübingen 1992, 29-36. Innumerous „procura" can also be found in the notarial documents at the Archivio di Stato di Como, e.g.: Andrea Brentano, who was living in Frankurt, wrote a „procura" in 1684 through the notary of public Johannes Thomas Abbate on behalf of his father. His father was authorized to sell a property at Lake Como for the payment of debts, which Andrea had with his father and his brother. Archivio di Stato di Como (ASC), notarile cartello 2403, Malagrida, Pietro Francesco, 5 January 1685).

[22] Freies Deutsches Hochstift Frankfurt a.M. (FDH), XP B 1/4, annexes 1-15.

[23] P. Burke, 'Information und Kommunikation im Europa der Frühen Neuzeit', in: *Frühneuzeit-Info 2* (1991), 13-19.

The Structure of the Trade Companies

Supporting this informal business network of kindred relationships, which was not directly based on contractual agreements, a further structure existed that contributed to the ascent of the merchants from Lake Como: the trade companies themselves. These merchants originating from Lake Como did not migrate individually, but were organized into trade companies.[24]

Much information about the structure of the trade companies can be found in still-existing business contracts. Of these, one of the most explanatory sources is a collection of contracts referencing the structure of a trade company which began in 1699 and operated for a long time, mainly in Frankfurt, Mainz and Amsterdam, under the name "Dominico Brentano e figli".[25] Generally, these merchants from Lake Como joined forces, forming smaller trade companies of two to eight partners. These associations typically limited their formation to between three and five years. Upon expiration of the respective contract, all the partners were either released of their obligations under the contract, or permitted to extend the terms. They were free to leave the company, to integrate new partners, or to form an entirely new agreement. The name of a company often remained the same for long periods of time in order to convey continuity, but could be changed at will, and differ in other places. These partners set forth bylaws, to which all of them were obligated to adhere. For example, the bylaws included clauses, wherein the amount of each partner's capital contribution and the interest rates were indicated. The distribution of profits was calculated according to a key that was based on the amount of a fixed "associate's share". This share was not necessarily fixed to the amount of capital contribution, but could be determined according to the amount of influence a partner had within the company, or how keen a businessman he was. Often, there were one or two

---

24 There are few studies on the structure of family trade companies in the early modern era, e.g. R. Hildebrandt, 'Unternehmensstruktur im Wandel. Familien- und Kapitalgesellschaften vom 15.-17. Jahrhundert', in: H.J. Gerhard (ed.), *Struktur und Dimension* (Festschrift Kaufhold, 1), Stuttgart 1997, 93-110; G. Tonelli, *"Vendere, scuodere, comprare, sì per conto del negotio come per qualunque comissione di terza persona". I grandi operatori del commercio estero milanese nella Lombardia spagnola del XVII secolo (1600-1650)*, Ph.D.-thesis, Milano 1999, 126-136; A. Dietz, *Frankfurter Handelsgeschichte*, vol. 4.1, Frankfurt a. M. 1925, 247-254.

25 FDH, XP B 1/4, Beurkundete Darstellung des am Höchstpreislichen Kaiserl. Reichs-Cammergerichts anhängigen Rechtsstreits in Sachen Stephano Brentano, jetzt dessen Söhnen und der Söhne des Dominico Brentano, Appellanten, entgegen Dominico Antonio Brentano, Appellaten, 1798, annexes 1-15; ISG Ffm, Reichskammergericht, file nos. 249-253.

people called "principale", who directed all aspects of the business in a supervisory capacity.

Further conditions were agreed upon, such as who was responsible for a particular branch, who was granted special authority, or what monies could be taken from the company till for what purpose.

This organizational structure yielded a great amount of flexibility. For instance, it guaranteed a relatively large capital pool, out of which much more substantial investments were funded than could have been supplied by any individual partner. The intimate contacts with relatives and neighbours from their home villages, who were brought in as associates, ensured for a responsible handling of company funds and goods. Short contractual periods hindered an associate from exploiting another for great spans of time, since such a partner would be shut out of future business associations upon expiration of a particular contract. Diverse markets could also be occupied relatively quickly, depending on whom one brought into the company as partner.

These trade companies were generally not bound to a particular location, instead, stores were typically rented and bought according to the lucrative nature of the particular business, which gave these primarily mobile trade companies an edge over the local competition who were constrained by necessity to maintaining their local stores.[26]

Even though this system functioned quite well for a relatively long period of time, there were still disputes from time to time, particularly where the distribution of profits was concerned. The more associates were involved, distributions postponed, and the higher the amount of money in question, the more painstaking became the process of running this flexible yet tedious system with its regularly conducted inventories, and increasingly dispersed transactions. For this reason, furious quarrels arose amid the eighteenth century that were sometimes taken before the court.[27]

These very same organizational structures, which had proven to be an asset at the onset of these companies, had become possible snares for dispute. Thus, in many cases, individual merchants broke away from this structure and began running businesses at their own expense, a venture that had become more than

---

[26] For example, the Dominico Brentano e Figli company first had a store in Frankfurt, then in Mainz and Bad Kreuznach, thereafter another in Bingen, and later another in Amsterdam. As the branch in Bingen and Bad Kreuznach generated enough profits, they closed it (FDH, XP B 1/4, Anlagen Nr. 1-15).

[27] The most well documented case is a dispute between Dominico Antonio Brentano (*1724, +1795) and his uncles regarding the inheritance he was to receive out of the company. This dispute lasted more than 50 years (ISG Ffm, Reichskammergericht, Akten Nr. 249-253; FDH, XP B 1/4).

feasible due to the size of the company capital, which had flourished over several generations.[28]

Acquisition of Right of Residence

Here, the focus is on specific local situations which had an impact on the merchants' general success, or the lack thereof. These Italian merchants were not welcomed everywhere they sought to do business in the second half of the seventeenth century. In many places, local businessmen complained about these assertive competitors.

The largest hindrance to commerce for these Italian merchants in most of the German cities was that they did not possess the right of citizenship or residence. However, these permits were necessary for conducting business. As foreigners, they were only allowed to sell their goods on marketplaces and trade fairs. In both cities, Frankfurt and Mainz, the merchants from Lake Como applied for a right of residence with varied success. The problem was that in Frankfurt, as was also the case in Mainz, resident merchants filed complaints against these foreign competitors, stating that they offered goods at less expensive prices and in better quality, and therefore attracted greater numbers of customers.[29]

In Mainz, which was governed by an electoral prince, these resident merchants were ultimately not successful with their complaints. After having fulfilled the formal criteria, such as possessing a certain amount of assets and real estate in the city, having proved marital status and religious affiliation, as well as freedom from serfdom, they often received citizenship without any further difficulty. In Mainz, this process was not only less complicated since resident merchants did not hold positions in city government, but also because Mainz was predominantly Catholic, as were the merchants from Lake Como.[30]

---

28   For example, Pietro Antonio Brentano (*19.9.1735, +9.3.1797) started his own business in 1771 after achieving much success with his father's company (Dietz, *Frankfurter Handelsgeschichte*, vol. 4.1, 249).

29   For Frankfurt, the most well documented of these complaints can be found in ISG Ffm, Handel Ugb Nr. 191, Specerey und Würtzkrähmer Acta contra die Italienische Beysaßen und deren Handel da 1671 a 1736. In Mainz several complaints can be found within: Stadtarchiv Mainz (StA Mz), Abt. 21, 120-164, Krämerzunft und Handelsstand.

30   C. Reves, 'Von Kaufleuten, Stuckateuren und Perückenmachern. Die Präsenz von Italienern in Mainz im 17. und 18. Jahrhundert', in: M. Matheus and W. Rödel (eds.), *Bausteine zur Mainzer Stadtgeschichte; Mainzer Kolloquium 2000*, Stuttgar 2002, 135-159. The government in Mainz also promoted an active immigration policy to improve the economic status of the city, cf. H. Schrohe, *Die Stadt Mainz unter kurfürstlicher Verwaltung (1462-1792)*, PhD-thesis, Frankfurt

The situation in Frankfurt was much more complex, but not only because the region was predominately Protestant.[31] First, it was not possible for the merchants from Lake Como to obtain citizenship. They were only allowed to apply for residence permits, which were restricted in certain ways and could theoretically be repealed. Furthermore, as early as the 1670's, disputes flared up between resident and Italian merchants over what products the Italians should be allowed to deal in.[32] These kinds of disputes occurred in other cities as well, but in Frankfurt they were bitterly intense. Such written complaints had a great impact on the Italian merchants' business activities and on their requests for residence permits. As a result, the merchants from Lake Como were forced in several cases to enter a series of complaints at the court of the Kaiser in Vienna, between 1706 and 1711. In spite of these legal disputes and difficulties in obtaining residence permits, they remained in Frankfurt and continued their lucrative commerce with rare commodities and spices, as Frankfurt was a hub between North and South, East and West in all sectors of trade and commerce.[33] It was therefore crucial to the functionality and the success of Italian commerce

---

a.M. 1932, 126-135; F.G. Dreyfus, *Sociétés et Mentalités à Mayence dans la seconde moitié du XVIIIe siècle*, Paris 1968, 302-303; K. Schwarz, *Der wirtschaftliche Konkurrenzkampf zwischen der Reichsstadt Frankfurt und der kurfürstlichen Stadt Mainz*, Ph.D.-thesis, Frankfurt 1932; H. Scholl, *Kurmainzische Wirtschaftspolitik unter besonderer Berücksichtigung der Handels- und Gewerbepolitik in der kurfürstlichen Residenzstadt Mainz (1648-1802)*, Ph.D.-thesis Frankfurt 1924; R. Schäfer, *Förderung von Handel und Wandel in Kurmainz im 18. Jahrhundert*, Ph.D.-thesis, Mainz 1957, Frankfurt-Höchst 1968.

[31] R. Koch, 'Lebens- und Rechtsgemeinschaften in der traditionellen bürgerlichen Gesellschaft: die freie Reichsstadt Frankfurt am Main um 1800', in: C. Jamme and O. Pöggeler, *„Frankfurt aber ist der Nabel dieser Erde. Das Schicksal der Generation der Goethezeit*, Stuttgart 1983, 21-41; R. Koch, *Grundlagen bürgerlicher Herrschaft. Verfassungs- und sozialgeschichtliche Studien zur bürgerlichen Gesellschaft in Frankfurt am Main 1612-1866*, Habil., Wiesbaden 1983, 106-108.

[32] C. Reves, '"Ich erzählte ihm von den sämtlichen italienischen Familien ..." Die Präsenz von Händlern vom Comer See in Frankfurt im 17. und 18. Jahrhundert', in: *Archiv für Frankfurts Geschichte und Kunst,* (68) 2002, 309-327, C. Peter (Reves), 'Operatori prealpini all'estero: negozianti comaschi a Francoforte nel Settecento', in: *Tra Identità e Integrazione. La Lombardia nella macroregione alpina dello sviluppo economico europeo (secoli XVII-XX). Atti del Convegno di Studio Milano, 10-11 dicembre 1999*, Milano 2002, 195-209.

[33] M. Straube, 'Funktion und Stellung deutscher Messen im Wirtschaftsleben zu Beginn der frühen Neuzeit. Die Beispiele Frankfurt am Main und Leipzig', in: H. Pohl (ed.), *Frankfurt im Messenetz Europas*, Frankfurt 1991, 191-204; R. Koch (ed.), *Brücke zwischen den Völkern – Zur Geschichte der Frankfurter Messe*, vol. 3, Frankfurt a.M. 1991; esp. vol. 2, 122-255; B. Baehring, *Börsen-Zeiten. Frankfurt in vier Jahrhunderten zwischen Antwerpen, Wien, New York und Berlin*, Frankfurt a.M. 1985, 32; F. Lerner, 'Frankfurt im Netz der Handelsstraßen', in: *Brücke zwischen den Völkern – Zur Geschichte der Frankfurter Messe*, vol. 2. Frankfurt a.M. 1991, 103-107.

for some families to establish branches in Frankfurt. With substantial amounts of money, patience and persistence, the merchants managed to resist being driven out.

Hence, the merchants from Lake Como did not primarily apply for residence out of a desire to remain permanently in Frankfurt and Mainz, nor did they necessarily wish to be integrated into urban society. Their main objective was to continue their business without any complications. Particularly in rural villages, these Italian merchants were often integrated rapidly. Nevertheless, in larger commercial centres, they were chiefly interested in expanding their business opportunities. Only after the second half of the eighteenth century did ties with the Italian homeland become looser and the merchants more settled in Germany.

In conclusion, it can be surmised that the success of these merchants from the regions surrounding Lake Como North of the Alps did not only depend upon circumstances in their foreign destinations, such as in commercial centres like Frankfurt and residencies such as Mainz. Their economic and social ascent was more closely related to those elements that comprised their starting position, such as a tradition of trade and migration, their financial standing, the kindred business network, which they were able to tap into, and the flexible structure of their trade companies. On this basis, they were able to manage disputes with competitors abroad, achieve their goals and secure their fortunes. Although this network continued to exist thereafter, it was not until the second half of the eighteenth century that it began to lose importance. Despite this, traces of the network could still be found at the beginning of the nineteenth century, when Italian merchants, who had long since successfully integrated into urban German society, sometimes married descendents of former compatriots. For example, Georg Friedrich Guaita, the descendent of an Italian merchant originating from Lake Como, who was elected Mayor of Frankfurt several times, married Meline Brentano, the daughter of Peter Anton Brentano, born in Tremezzo on Lake Como.[34]

---

[34] J. Rumpf-Fleck, *Italienische Kultur*, 28.

The Organisation and Evolutions of Traders' and Pedlars' Networks in Europe

Laurence Fontaine

In Early Modern Europe networks of Traders and Pedlars were numerous and quite powerful. These networks operated on two levels. The first level was made up of a family network (parents and kinship relations), which traded over a wide geographical area. It was supported by a family banking system and, through opening warehouses and shops in the cities, gained access to a vast geographical web. Credit relations cemented the whole organisation. The second level was a distribution network linked to migratory movements. It had a rigid hierarchical structure and was based upon temporary migration and the labour of men from the home village.

First I would like to give a few examples of those networks, then I shall analyse how they financed and organised themselves and I shall end by following the evolutions of these networks in response to political and economic transformations. The Giraud family, originally from La Grave in Oisans in the Dauphiné, formed, in the seventeenth century, part of a protestant merchant network which operated over Switzerland, Northern Italy and Southern France: between Lyon, Geneva, Mantua and Perpignan. Like his father before him, Jean had a shop in Lyon, his father-in-law a shop in Geneva. The Giraud family was only one segment of a much larger network which linked other inter-related families from the same mountain range, such as the Berard family, the Delor, the Horard and the Vieux families from Mizoen. These men were not small merchants and Thobie Delor was a "bourgeois" (burgher) of Lyon and an influential member of the Consistory. The family had been established for over a century in Geneva, where Antoine, Gabriel, Luc and Etiene Delor, all four small merchants from Mizoen, were admitted as municipal citizens of Geneva in 1572 and where Georges was accepted as a "bourgeois" in 1597. The archives of the notaries in the villages reveal that others established themselves in Grenoble, in Bourgogne, in Italy and on the route to Spain and Germany.[1]

---

1   Departemental archives Isère, 1J 1102, Livre de raizon apartenant à Moy Jean Giraud de Lagrave où est contenu mais affaires emparticulier. Comancé le 17 janvier 1670 à Lion; Departemental archives Rhône, série B, 8 mai 1690; voir O. Martin, *La Conversion protestante à Lyon (1659-1687)*, Genève 1986, 50-65; E. Arnaud, *Histoire des protestants du Dauphiné aux XVIe, XVIIe et XVIIIe siècles*, 3 vols, Paris 1875, vol I, 499-510. L. Fontaine, *History of pedlars in Europe*, Cambridge 1996.

These families were at the origin of a later powerful network of booksellers and book pedlars which operated in southern Europe in the eighteenth century, as François Grasset, formerly chief clerk with the Cramer booksellers in Geneva, made us understand in a letter to Malesherbes in 1754. He stated that: "The bookselling trade in Spain and Portugal, as well as that of many Italian towns, is totally controlled by the French, all of them from a village in a Briançonnais valley in the Dauphiné. Active, hard-working and moderate, they make successive trips to Spain and almost always marry amongst themselves... not only is the bookselling trade in their hands, but also the market for geographical maps, prints, clock-making, cloth, printed calico, stockings, hats and so forth".[2] And he was right: the list of those individuals who had an account with the Cramer bookshop between 1755-60, as published by Giles Barber, reveals at least 38 names of booksellers originally from Monêtier or the surrounding villages who were then established booksellers in France, Italy, Spain and Portugal.[3] The confiscation of goods from the Briançonnais population of Spain during the Terror of 1793 showed that 45 families originally came from Monêtier alone.[4] Similarly, Aristide Albert has published a list of 51 booksellers, originally from the very same villages, who were in business in the same places (as well as extending their activities into the Brazilian market) at the end of the eighteenth and the beginning of the nineteenth century.[5] Naturally, these lists are open to cross-checking. Other names from other sources can be added to this provisional list, revealing nearly 50 Briançonnais family names (referred to 140 times) amongst those who ran bookshops in Europe in the eighteenth century. Roughly speaking, they controlled almost the entire Portuguese market and between 1/3 and 1/4 of the Italian and Spanish markets.

Let me recall the Brentano. They originally came from the valleys surrounding Lake Como. They relied on four family branches – the Brentano-Gnosso, the Brentano-Toccia, the Brentano-Cimaroli and the Brentano-Tremezzo – to form their network. The first Brentanos arrived in the sixteenth

---

2   Bibliothèque National, Ms. fr. 22130, f 37, Novembre 1754.

3   G. Barber, 'The Cramers of Geneva and their trade in Europe between 1755 and 1766', in: *Studies on Voltaire and the 18th Century*, 30 (1964), 377-413; 'Who were the Booksellers of the Enlightenment', in: G. Barber et B. Fabian (eds), *Buch und Buchhandel im 18 Jahrhundert*, Hamburg 1981, 211-224. G. Barber, 'Pendred abroad. A view of the late eighteenth century book trade in Europe', in: *Studies in the Book Trade in Honour of Graham Pollard*, Oxford 1975, 231-277; 'Books from the old world and for the new: the British international trade in books in the eighteenth century', in: *Studies on Voltaire and the Eighteenth Century*, 151/155 (1976), 185-224.

4   *Annales des Alpes*, 12 (1908-1909), 219-225.

5   A. Albert, *Les Briançonnais libraires*, Grenoble 1874, 19-23. et *Biographie, bibliographie des Briançonnais, cantons de la Grave et de Monêtier-de-Briançon*, Grenoble 1877, 97.

century as simple *Höker*, itinerant merchants selling citrus fruit and spices. At the beginning of the eighteenth century, members of the Brentano family established themselves in Amsterdam, Bingen, Brussels, Koblenz, Cologne, Constance, Cracow, Diez, Frankfurt, Fribourg, Heidelberg, Mannheim, Mainz, Nuremberg, Rothenburg, Rotterdam and Vienna. If we also add to the above the towns where their relatives had opened shops, then their establishments could be found all across northern Europe.[6] The history of this family was very similar to that of many other families from the Italian Alpine valleys. And, indeed, from one end of the Alpine curve to the other, one could name similar families from numerous villages in pre-modern times.

In the same way, Scotland scattered her merchants, pedlars, leather craftsmen and weavers across all of northern Europe to Poland, Denmark, Sweden and Norway.[7] The first settlements date back to the second half of the 15th century when Scots were to be found on both sides of the Channel, in western France, Norway and the Baltic. These migrations reached a peak between 1500 and 1650. The Scots who settled in Poland originally came from over 140 locations, mainly in the north and north-east of Scotland. The majority arrived by sea, particularly via Gdansk and the other Baltic ports. Some, however, following the main highways and rivers of Germany and Bohemia, spread out over Poland from the sixteenth century onwards and, in the first half of the seventeenth century, can be identified in more than 420 locations.

Organisation of the Merchant/Pedlars Networks

These merchants were part of a large kinship whose members circulated on the main European routes and markets and who were sedentary and migrant at the same time. This fundamental trait that permitted them to invest efficiently over vast spaces is being reinforced by certain characteristics. These family networks organised themselves into very flexible firms, which could be set up and

---

6   J. Augel's index in: *Italienische Einwanderung und Wirtschaftstätigkeit in rheinischen Städten des 17. und 18. Jahrhunderts*, Bonn 1971, mentions 77 members of the Brentano family who were established in the Rhine area between the end of the seventeenth century and the end of the eighteenth century. See also A. Dietz, *Frankfurter Handelsgeschichte*, Frankfurt 1921, 240-259; J. Rumpf-Fleck, *Italienische Kultur in Frankfurt am Main im 18. Jahrhundert*, Köln 1936, 18 which also looks at the different branches of the Brentano family in Frankfurt (25-28), and lists on 133-135 the members of the four branches of the family in Frankfurt in the seventeenth and eighteenth centuries.

7   T. Riis, 'Scottish-Danish relations in the sixteenth century', in: *Scotland and Europe, 1200-1850*; T.A. Fischer, *The Scots in Sweden*, Edinburgh 1907, 10-17; *The Scots in Germany*, Edinburgh 1902 and *The Scots in Eastern and Western Prussia*, Edinburgh 1903.

disbanded in response to commercial necessity, death, and the relative wealth or poverty of its members. Generally the association lasted between one and four years: each member invested a certain amount of capital and the profits were shared out in proportion to the initial investment. The association looked after its members for a month, provided them with silk stockings, with shoes and with chausses,[8] and allowed them to spend two months a year in the village.[9] So, despite settlement in the towns, it was still a question of temporary migration, progressing imperceptibly from one activity to another more important one, and from one level of wealth to another; the length of absence being in proportion to these variables.

The basic characteristic of these networks relied on the practice of endogamy within the narrow group of merchants who originally came from the same village: this was still the key to the arrangement and the effectiveness of marriages. However, what is important is that marriage brought merchants together irrespective of their business specialization. This system of family alliances proved to be extremely flexible and effective when faced with the weakness of the economic, legal and police machinery of the time, which was unable to control the itinerant merchant population; or when up against illness and death which left families in despair.

Four essential elements are the traditional foundations of the migrant merchant organisations :

1.) A family banking system bound the family network together and enabled it to maximise resources, since each member invested the essential parts of the family fortune into the firm.

Commercial inter-marriage was one of the cogs in a mechanism which aimed to protect the banking system and the loyalty that each member felt towards the merchant network. The exceptions to this rule were the result of compromises that the migrants had to make in order to gain access to the markets of the countries in which they settled.[10]

---

8   Tight-fitting garment covering the feet and legs
9   Departemental archives of the Isère, 1J 1102; Departemental archives of the Hautes Alpes, 4E
      48 39, 6 August 1686.
10 J. Augel, *Italienische Einwanderung*, 202, K. Martin, 'Die Savoyische Einwanderung in das
      alemannische Süddeutschland', in: *Deutsches Archiv für Landes und Volksforschung*, 6 (1942),
      647-658; D. Hemmert , 'Quelques aspectes de l'immigration dans le comté de Bitche, fin du
      XVIIe siècle, début XVIIIe', in: *Actes du 103e Congrès national des Sociétés Savantes, Nancy-
      Metz 1978, Histoire moderne et contemporaine*, Paris 1979, 41-56 (51). P. Guichonnet,
      'L'émigration alpine vers les pays de langue allemande', in: *Revue de Géographie alpine*,
      (1948), 553-576 (565); D. Ozanam, 'La colonie française de Cadix au XVIIIe siècle, d'après un
      document inédit (1777)', in: *Mélanges de la Casa de Vélasquez*, 4 (1968), 259-349 (287). To

2.) A system such as this meant that one could always have someone at the vital points in the network – which can be represented as a tree in which those who were installed on the far end of the branches were likely to be moved if a place fell vacant on a more central branch. An individual did not, therefore, have any geographical stability and, according to the necessities of business and of biological chance, which left family firms without anyone at the top, each individual moved between businesses throughout the Mediterranean basin. The concept of mobility was instilled as early as childhood through apprenticeship. Simon Gravier, who himself always lived in the valley, thus sent his four sons to different countries to learn the merchant profession, both from booksellers and haberdashery merchants.[11]

Moreover, the clerks might move from business to business, depending on the departures of the main shareholders. Whichever family one studies, one comes across such movements within the merchant network. In the Gravier family, for instance, Thomas summoned his nephew Jean-Simon to Rome as a clerk as soon as he himself had been able to establish himself as a bookseller. Ten years later, in 1796, Jean-Simon left for Genoa, where he worked for another bookseller, Yves Gravier, taking the place of Fantin, who had left to set up a bookshop in Paris; another Briançonnais, Billaud, came to take up the post of clerk in Rome left vacant by Jean-Simon. Finally, on 12 July 1801, Jean-Simon joined forces with Fantin in Paris, initially as a clerk, later taking over from him as bookseller at the shop at 55 quai des Augustins; in 1809, Pierre Joseph Rey, a native of Villeneuve-la Salle, a hamlet of Monêtier, and formerly a bookseller in Lisbon, withdrew to Paris to continue his business. There he met up with Jean-Simon Gravier, who had then been in charge of the Fantin bookshop for 12 years, and in 1815 they set up in partnership together and applied for a bookseller's licence.[12] Another example: in 1747, Pierre Gendron and Joseph Reycends were booksellers in Lisbon; ten years later Pierre Gendron set up his business in Paris – again on the quai des Augustins – and Joseph Reycends went back to Turin where he went into partnership with a Guibert; they were replaced in the Lisbon bookshop by two relatives, Bonnardel and Dubeux.[13]

---

trace the development of the legislation, see A. Dominguez Ortiz, *Los extranjeros en la vida española durante el siglo XVII*, Madrid 1960.

11 Gravier family Archives.

12 From the Gravier family archives; M.-H. Piwnik, 'Libraires français et espagnols à Lisbonne au XVIIIe siècle', in: *Livres et Libraires en Espagne et au Portugal (XVIe-XXe siècles)*, Paris 1989, 81-98 (87-88).

13 M.-H. Piwnik, 'Libraires français et espagnols', 81-98.

3.) Mobility assured the continuing activity of the important markets and ensured that families were scattered between the main Mediterranean towns and ports on the one hand, and the Alpine villages on the other. It also meant that if the need arose the mountain routes, neglected by official surveillance, could be used. In this way the networks became effective and flexible, allowing goods and books to be circulated between all markets, without using the traditional channels and away from foreseeable inspection by the authorities. Traditional routes or unofficial channels were used depending on the political circumstances. When Gosse the bookseller had to send his catalogue to Jean Baptiste Reycends in Lisbon, he sent it first to Yves Gravier in Genoa, asking him to make sure it got to Reycends.[14]

4.) The strength of this mutual dependence between members, further bound together by family ties, ensured the greatest degree of security against the extensive web of debt upon which the network was based: in every town there was a relative, haberdasher or bookseller on whom could be bestowed a power of attorney to look after one's interests where the estate of some merchant or pedlar with whom one had done business was concerned. In 1747, Pierre Gendron and Joseph Reycends, then booksellers in Lisbon, bestowed a power of attorney upon Diego Barthélémy so that he could recover as best as he could the money owed to them by Pedro Simond.[15]

In order to develop their business, these merchants relied on village migration. At the top of the hierarchical structure was the *commis* (clerk), who was in fact a salaried pedlar who travelled the town, fairs and surrounding villages selling the goods which the company had imported. Generally the *commis* were relatives of members of the organization who, having completed their apprenticeship, remained in the service of the business until they had the capital necessary to set up their own business or take a share in the company employing them.

Alongside the *commis*, the merchants had numerous apprentices. These young men, sons of members of the organization or of their relatives, came to undertake their apprenticeship as packmen. There were sometimes a fair number of them in the town and this practice was denounced by the native merchants, who complained that not only all these young men were not registered with the town authorities but that they also peddled their wares with impunity.[16]

On a level below that of *commis* and apprentices were many pedlars. It is not always easy to highlight the link between the merchant businesses and peddling

---

14 Geneva State Archives, business, F62, letter of 31 march 1780 to Yves Gravier in Genoa.
15 M.-H. Piwnik, 'Libraires français et espagnols', 87.
16 J. Augel in: *Italienische Einwanderung*, 198.

since the merchants who had succeeded in getting themselves accepted as citizens of the town where they had their shop made every effort to conceal those relations.

Within the peddling group, a hierarchy existed. At the top were a group of travelling merchants who did not have shops, who were always referred to in texts as 'merchants' and who were numbered amongst the richest inhabitants of their home villages. Their periods of absence corresponded to the seasons. From the end of the seventeenth century, notaries' deeds concerning travelling merchants demonstrate the essential role of these men as a pivot between the two halves of the organisation.

In the lowlands, they were part of the network developed by those merchants who had opened shops and from whom they got their supplies. In the mountain villages, the travelling merchants acted as intermediaries by whom one could organize trade in winter. These pedlars, who were very much a part of the economic life of the village, were the pivots of the village migratory system.[17] In their turn, the packmen, who stocked up from the factories and warehouses established in the town by their compatriots, employed servants and apprentices. However, unlike the *commis* in the large firms, the pedlar's employees were not allowed any opportunity to line their own pockets: they were forbidden to act as wholesalers or retailers on their own behalf or to lend money (the other method of building up one's own business); moreover, any social activities likely to divert them from their work - such as dancing, playing billiards, or going to the theatre - were forbidden.

The rulings in Mainz, just as in Cologne and elsewhere, railed against the practice of only employing one's compatriots because it brought about the ruin of the native traders by not allowing them the opportunity to benefit from the merchant network. They also revealed the links which bound the wealthiest to those who could offer only a limited amount of craftsman's knowledge, or who had nothing more than a bear or marmor to exhibit. In their own way, these complaints express the bonds which linked the various migrants from the same village, from the richest down to the most impoverished.[18]

Similar conclusions can be drawn for northern Europe. In Sweden, the relationship between the important merchants, pedlars and craftsmen in the migrant community was a strong one. The pinnacle of social success was establishing a business, but, if things didn't work out, the backpack was

---

17 L. Fontaine, 'Family Cycles, Peddling and Society in Upper Alpine Valleys in the Eighteenth Century', in: S. Woolf (ed.), *Domestic stategies. Work and Family in France and Italy 17-18th century*, Cambridge 1991, 43-68.

18 J. Augel in: *Italienische Einwanderung*, 189, 193-4, 203; A. Dominguez Ortiz, *Los extranjeros en la vida española durante el siglo XVII*, Madrid 1960.

abandoned in exchange for a sword and the army.[19] Everywhere, in North as well as in South Europe, opposition to the migrants was very strong and every country developed a legislation to break the exclusive links between the settled merchants and their employees coming from the same geographical area. In Gothenburg, for instance, the rich Scottish merchants who dealt in the export of wood and iron and the import of fabrics, wine, salt and herrings were said to use 'the many young, foreign merchants' who hovered around the town 'on the pretext of collecting debts relating to their illegal trade' and who stocked up from the vast warehouse owned by the Scots. In Malmö, the inhabitants accused those Scots who had acquired citizenship of being bad citizens since they offered work only to those of their own nationality. The petition, which they sent to the King, refused the Scots the right of citizenship because they did not respect the responsibilities which went with it.[20]

An analysis of the geography and chronology of different rulings against the migrant merchants in northern Europe, Spain and in the Rhine area demonstrates the wide variety of local circumstances and the numerous changes in political direction, and it also reveals the opposite side of the coin – the times and places which were favourable to the migrants, areas where institutions were more relaxed and where the migrant organizations could again gain a foothold.

Enforced Interdependency

Business association, financial guarantees and sponsorship were the main instances of enforced interdependency. From the beginning, the first two had been vital to the success of peddling: at no time would the smaller merchants have had enough capital of their own to be able to open a town warehouse, or obtain the necessary credibility to acquire the *droit de bourgeoisie*, which was indispensable to those doing business in the lowlands. The importance of the business association was such that its various rules were taught in the village school, where children learned to solve the problems that it raised in terms of the capital invested and the duration of the association.[21] Evidence shows that the

---

19 A. Bieganska, 'A note on the Scots in Poland, 1550-1800', in: T.C. Smout (ed.), *Scotland and Europe, 1200-1850,* Edinburgh 1986, 157-165 (156).

20 T. Riis, 'Scottish-Danish relations'; T.C. Smout (ed.), *Scotland and Europe,* 82-96 (87-88); E.-B. Grage, 'Scottish merchants in Gothenburg, 1621-1850', in: T.C. Smout (ed.), *Scotland and Europe, 1200-1850,* Edinburgh 1986, 114.

21 Exercise book belonging to Jean-Baptiste Bompard, Villeneuve la Salle, completed 28 January 1788. Gravier family private archives.

imbalances inherent in interdependency made it more and more difficult to bear in times when economic crises were eroding profits.

The second enforced interdependency developed under pressure from the financial backers: this was the system of financial guarantees. For the smaller pedlars, for whom paying for their own purchases was already difficult even before a slightly poor year came along, interdependency threatened their very existence. The development of financial guarantees, which linked individual fortunes together, meant that the failure of one pedlar weighed upon the others and introduced a further imbalance into the network of relationships. In times of growth, the most fortunate could help those who were less well off, but in times of recession it was the whole economic and social structure of the villages that shook.[22]

The system of sponsorship of newcomers in the commercial network, which was no more than a disguised financial guarantee, could, like this latter option, land the mistaken or over-optimistic sponsor in difficult financial circumstances. By hitching the shakiest fortunes to those of the wealthiest individuals, in times of economic recession guarantees and sponsorship weakened the whole merchant body, or, in other words, the entire fabric of village society. However, this interdependency also had two sides to it: for those who acted as guarantors, it provided a hold over the pedlar's manpower and assets. For the financial backer, the extremely hierarchical structure of village migration, in which the peddling 'elite' classes functioned as anchor, acting both as contractors of manpower and privileged intermediaries between city business and itinerant selling, provided them with as many guarantees as he needed. The financial guarantee, whilst enforcing interdependency, also spawned a climate of denunciation: should a pedlar attempt to escape his creditors, the guarantors, their own existence threatened, would join forces with the merchants to find him and make him pay. Therein lies the first ambiguity of merchant interdependency, which encouraged the elimination of the black sheep and forced the peddling body to shoulder the failure of certain individuals. This moral code imposed on the group was reinforced by the strategies employed by the village elite, who carefully took notes of all changes in an inheritance and were on the alert for any change in fortune.[23]

---

22 L. Fontaine, *Le Voyage et la Mémoire, colporteurs de l'Oisans au XIXe siècle*, Lyon 1984.

23 Departemental archives of the Isère, 1J 829. Registre des copies de lettres du gantier-banquier Nicolet. A detailed analysis is given in L. Fontaine, *Le Voyage et la Mémoire, colporteurs de l'Oisans au XIXe siècle*, Lyon 1984.

Goods, Banking and Smuggling

These small business networks had a certain number of common characteristics. They relied on commercial diversity: merchants and pedlars traded in all types of merchandise, depending on the demand and the opportunities – even though each family had a relative speciality, which had its roots in the broad specialisation of their home region – the southern Tyrol for carpets, Lake Como for citrus fruits, or the Upper Dauphiné for gloves. Three factors forced them to offer a wider selection of goods: the desire to reach a larger clientele by offering the widest possible of products; methods of payment in which exchange and barter played a large part; and the search for new or forbidden goods, which would mean larger profits.

Moreover, the peddling organisations turned all trade circuits to their advantage. The pedlars sold their goods on credit, and demanded repayment in the form of buying or renting fields; or as a share of the harvests, which they stored there in the village in rented cellars and barns. In this way, they multiplied their access to other markets and short-circuited a certain amount of trade between town and countryside. In addition, the itinerant merchants continued to act as moneylenders. Through their financial dealings, the migrant merchants rose above the framework of family and peasants and gradually became merchant-bankers who boasted a clientele where craftsmen rubbed shoulders with lords and members of the lower middle classes.

A last feature was present beneath the surface in all aspects of the merchant organisations: men and merchandise circulated and worked on the fringes of the law. This constant is, of course, the most difficult to establish, even if one can hazard a guess at the profits gained from the skill with which these men manipulated the rules – at all levels. Goods were transported along routes where it was possible to avoid customs and tolls. When a new market opened up or circumstances allowed and, in particular, as soon as war began, smuggling and illicit warehouses multiplied. Armies and war always created places where excellent profits were to be made. The pedlars also circulated in this legal twilight: the richest tried as hard as possible to avoid paying costly registration fees in the city, thus confusing both urban and peddling hierarchies.

Finally, it is more important to take note of the extraordinary capacity of the migrant merchants for exploiting all opportunities for profit, the ease with which they adapted between the diverse locations within their network and the balance between its various axes, than it is to note the diverse receptions which greeted them. This balance between locations was the basis of the migratory structure, at the centre of which were several powerful families from the Alpine villages. Because of this structure, despite the constant friction with the sedentary merchants, and in defiance of the political moves to contain them and change their trading practices, the links established at the end of the Middle Ages between town wholesalers and itinerant pedlars from the same region lingered until the end of the eighteenth century.

Evolution and Collapse of the Migrant's Merchant networks

Between the seventeenth and eighteenth centuries, the vast peddling networks became fragmented and withdrew to regional areas. The chronology of this withdrawal, a result of the encounter between internal changes in the adopted country and those in the home villages, had its own logic and periods of inertia: the break-up was sometimes abrupt and sometimes the result of a gradual change, depending on the region. But by the end of the eighteenth century, this transformation had been accomplished everywhere. In the French and Savoyard Alps, the first crack in the migratory system was a political one. In France, the affirmation and royal sovereignity, centred on religious unity and the war, upset the balance of the mountain economy between 1685 and 1715. The decision to go into exile, taken by the majority of the peddling 'elite' as well as by a significant proportion of the protestant population of the villages, threw the networks into disarray.[24]

The obstacles to free circulation and the increased price of transport now redirected the movement of trade, accustomed to the southern valleys, towards Mont-Cenis. The French Revolution and the Napoleonic Wars completed the process of fragmentation which had begun a century earlier by discontinuing relations between France, Savoy and Germany, thereby forcing the Italians to settle in Germany; but the flow was already greatly reduced through the combined effects of national politics, municipal obstacles and the merchants' growing lack of interest in the highlands.

In addition to the business world's economic swing towards the north-west, a new imbalance was introduced between lowland and mountain: the new coastal and urban centres favoured the development of nearby (and easily accessible) regions and the mountain economies found themselves further marginalized and confined.[25] For those who had emigrated to the city, the profits to be gained from

---

24 A. Albert, 'Le pays briançonnais : les Queyrassins négociants', in: *Bulletin de la Société d'Etude des Hautes-Alpes*, 1ère série, 8 (1889), 313-331 (316-317) ; E. Gothein, *Wirtschaftsgeschichte des Schwarzwaldes und der Angrenzenden Landschaften*, Strasbourg 1892.

25 J.-P. Poussou, *Bordeaux et le Sud-Ouest au XVIIIe siècle. Croissance économique et attraction urbaine*, Paris1983.

mountain manpower were now in competition with what could be gained from investment in the lowlands. In the areas of proto-industrialisation, the strategies of credit and payment-in-kind meant that the pedlars were natural intermediaries in these developments. Moreover, the social make-up of these migratory movements strengthened the traditional practice of the peddling 'elite' investing in – and, in some cases, creating – such forms of industrialisation. The putting down of economic roots in the lowlands and the subsequent impoverishment of the mountain regions spelled the end of their double lives for the important Alpine merchants – the Bettots, Brentanos, Girauds and Delors. Little by little the mountains became obstacles, isolated communities.

Other migratory movements took advantage of the change of direction in the peddling networks to set up their own commercial organisations, as did men from the Auvergne and the Bas Limousin in Spain.[26] Similarly, ethnic minorities – particularly Jews – took a further step towards integration by moving into the place left vacant by the Italians and Savoyards and by extending their activities towards western Europe.[27] The geography of the merchant networks changed and redefined itself as the profession altered. The number of Savoyards to be found in the German-speaking areas of Switzerland fell dramatically after 1750, and even the Valle d'Aosta began to turn its attention towards France (first towards the Dauphiné, then the South and finally Paris); only those communities which had retained the German dialect – both Gressoneys and the Upper Sesia region – remained loyal to Bavaria and Breisgau. This shift took place after a transitionary period in the intermediate zone comprising Franche-Comté, Burgundy and Lorraine. These regions which, from ancient times, had had a certain German-speaking population, now took the ascendancy: in short, now that the great period of migrant settlement which followed the Thirty Years War was over, establishing oneself in even the smaller towns became increasingly difficult. Such changes took place slowly and overlapped each other: the

---

26 J. Perrel, 'Introduction à une étude sur l'émigration corrézienne vers l'Espagne sous l'Ancien Régime', in: *Bulletin de la Société des Lettres, Sciences et Arts de la Corrèze*, 67 (1963), 92-101; 'Les Limousins en Espagne aux XVIe, XVIIe et XVIIIe siècles: les émigrants', in: *Bulletin de la Société des Lettres, Sciences et Arts de la Corrèze*, 68 (1964), 31-40; 'Une région d'émigration vers l'Espagne aux XVIIe-XVIIIe siècle: Le plateau de Roche-de-Vic (Corrèze)', in: *Bulletin de la Société des Lettres, Sciences et Arts de la Corrèze*, 70 (1966), 183-198; 'L'émigration bas-limousine en Espagne aux XVIIe et XVIIIe siècles', in: *Actes du 88e Congrès national des Sociétés Savantes, section d'histoire moderne et contemporaine, Clermont-Ferrand 1963*, Paris 1964, 709-729.

27 B.W. de Vries, *From Pedlars to Textile Barons. The Economic Development of a Jewish Minority Group in the Netherlands*, Amsterdam 1989; T. Endelman, 'L'activité économique des juifs anglais', in: *Dix-huitième siècle*, 13 (1981), 113-126; R. Moulinas, 'Le Conseil du Roi et le commerce des juifs d'Avignon en France', in: *Dix-huitième siècle*, 13 (1981), 169-179.

assimilation of certain migrants did not prevent other families coming to take the place they had vacated, but the influx was greatly reduced. It was not a clean break in the Alps either.

The Demand from Sedentary Business

The break-up of the large networks, the shifting destinations and the return to the regional areas all brought about changes within the profession of travelling merchants. Admittedly, the new methods of peddling did not develop at the same pace everywhere: things began to change in England[28] at the beginning of the seventeenth century following union with Scotland and the border peace treaty, and in the eighteenth century in France and in the Rhine regions. The new peddling model was fully established in France at the beginning of the nineteenth century.

The geography of the places of origin was always the same: border mountain regions or outlying areas.[29] In comparison with the peddling which occurred in previous centuries, this new structure was distinguished by an increase in the number of pedlars; by the use made of pedlars by all urban commerce and no longer just by the village 'elite', who had settled in the towns; by the wider range of goods offered by the pedlars; and by the disappearance of the multiple transactions involving the pedlar (in which payments in foodstuffs and goods bypassed other markets) in favour of credit alone. Eventually large quantities of new products – printed material – became part of the pedlar's range of wares. Initially, this was distributed from centres of production in eastern France and the German regions of the Rhine, from Paris and Lyon; by the mid-eighteenth century, it had reached most of the rural areas. Before specific peddling networks were built up around it, printed matter was an extra commodity much valued by pedlars of haberdashery. Trading in prohibited books became a very attractive business for the pedlars, since there were large profits to be achieved.[30]

Finally, in certain areas the disintegration of the previous migratory movements allowed men from other regions to occupy the positions thus left vacant, and, in their turn, to build up an organisation of shops and pedlars and to

---

28 M. Spufford, *The Great Reclothing of Rural England, Petty Chapmen and their Wares in the Seventeenth Century*, London 1984, 27.

29 A. Poitrineau, *Remues d'hommes. Les migrations montagnardes en France 17e-18e siècles*, Paris 1983.

30 J. Queniart, *L'imprimerie et la librairie à Rouen au XVIIIe siècle*, Paris 1969; R. Darnton, 'Un colporteur sous l'Ancien Régime', in: *Censures, de la Bible aux larmes d'Eros*, Paris 1987, 130-139; J.-J. Darmon, *Le colportage de librairie en France sous le Second Empire*, Paris 1972.

assume a virtual monopoly in a variety of business areas within the chosen region. However, these later networks, like the one found in the Massif Central, only operated within a single country, or indeed, within certain areas.

Slowly marginalized in the business world and discredited in the home villages, peddling began to decline in England as early as the eighteenth cen-tury[31] and in France from the middle of the nineteenth century[32]. On the other hand, in Spain, where there was still a dearth of diversified and easily accessible shops, there was a peddling revival in the nineteenth century.[33] The map drawn up by Rose Duroux showing the places where the Cantal migrants lived in Castile demonstrates that this reduced form of peddling, which was limited to the family unit, none the less had considerable impact, overall, since there were few villages without a settler from Cantal. The slump in Spain in 1898, the war in 1914 and the excellent exchange rate of the peseta in 1920-2 led to the migrants abandoning Spain for good. There was indisputably indigenous peddling which subsequently took over.[34]

Final Changes in the Profession

Following the rejection of organisations based on extended family groups and the withdrawal into a narrow family structure, the end of the profession was distinguished by a double breakdown, which put an end to all future develop-ment: both family tradition and credit structures were demolished. This final stage reveals that behind the continued use of the term 'pedlar', there lay a radi-cally different way of thinking and of operating as a migrant merchant.

An analysis of the censuses of 1896 and 1901 for the peddling villages in the valleys of the Oisans reveals an initial development – the profession, which up to then had been passed down from father to son, now only survived on the margins of families.[35] Certain traditional pedlars, however, managed to continue in their profession for a few decades longer. They survived by specialising in new, luxury goods, or goods which were very much in demand, which

---

31 R. B. Westerfield, *Middlemen in English Business, particularly between 1660 and 1760*, 1915, reprint New York 1968, 313-314.

32 L. Fontaine, *Le Voyage et la mémoire, colporteurs de l'Oisans au XIXe siècle*, Lyon 1984.

33 D. R. Ringrose, *Madrid and the Spanish Economy (1560-1850)*, California 1983.

34 R. Duroux, 'Les boutiquiers cantaliens de Nouvelle-Castille au XIXe siècle', in: *Melanges de la Casa de Velasquez*, 21 (1985), 281-307; *Les Auvergnats de Castille. Renaissance et mort d'une migration au XIXe siècle* (Publications de la Faculté des Lettres et Sciences humaines de l'Université Blaise-Pascal, n.s. 38), Clermont-Ferrand 1992.

35 Departemental archives of the Isère, 1 Mi 155 canton de Bourg d'Oisans.

sometimes reintroduced an element of craftsmanship as in the early days of the profession.

The most profitable forms of specialisation combined luxury goods with the conquest of new markets. A good example are the florist-pedlars from the Oisans. Originally from traditional families of cloth merchants and haberdashers, they gradually discovered new markets, new customers, new ways of selling and of financing their expeditions. The florists sold all sorts of fruit and ornamental trees, decorative plants, rosebushes and various sorts of bulbs and seeds. They packed them in sturdy wooden boxes, added a few baskets, and picked a destination, depending upon the time of year when they were setting out. Those who set out in autumn headed for Latin America, the Mediterranean basin or the Middle East; those who could only leave at the beginning of winter went to countries where spring came later: the Northern States and Russia. Their target customers were dignitaries and the rich middle classes: their sales pitch combined evocations of luxury, the imaginary and the exotic. As well as the plants, they offered dreams to the rich bourgeois classes, and their sales pitch primarily targeted the imagination.[36]

These pedlars thus managed to get round the major problems which beset the pedlars who travelled in France: by choosing countries with loose business networks and a rich clientele, who were able to pay cash, they were able to continue practising the profession profitably without being constrained by the traditional shackles of debt. Village credit was no longer the basis of their wealth. Credit was no longer granted during the campaign and the pedlar's only ties were with the city merchant bankers, who, as long as the market was profitable, were unstinting with their assistance.

At the same time as these individual ventures were taking place, certain villages in the southern Alps had managed to recreate the circumstances of the great peddling era under the Ancien Régime. Admittedly, the trade routes had changed because of the merchant ventures which were being set up in the Americas, but they had merely followed the shifts in the profitable markets. The goods were no longer the same; after silk, citrus fruits, tobacco and printed material, at the end of the nineteenth century, the Alpine merchants turned their attention to luxury goods. Yet the merchant structures remained remarkably faithful to the old way of doing things, which fixed the family and village migratory movements firmly within a network of shops run by their compatriots.

---

36 L. Fontaine, *History of pedlars*, chap. 7.

This return to the great networks of shops and pedlars took place primarily in the southern Alps.[37]

The key to the long lasting success of these networks of migrants is undoubtedly the moral and financial solidarity that bound together migrants coming from the same areas. For centuries it allowed an original and profitable way of trading, in which the family system of alliance and control had proven to be of a powerful flexibility and efficiency when faced with both the weakness of the economic, legal and executive machinery of the time, which was unable to control the itinerant merchant population, and against illness and death which threatened all enterprises of the time.

---

37 P. Gouy, *Pérégrinations des "Barcelonnettes" au Mexique*, Grenoble 1980; Albert, 'Le pays briançonnais'; E. Charpenel, *L'Epopée des Barcelonnettes*, Digne 1978, 15-16.

II.

Between Local and Global Networks:

the actors

The Principal Agent Problem Revisited: Entrepreneurial networks between Finland and "world markets" during the eighteenth and nineteenth centuries

Jari Ojala

A Transaction Cost and Network Approach to the Principal-Agent Problem

Economic actors collaborate with each other either in markets, hierarchical organisations, or within networks, as stated e.g. by O. E. Williamson (1985). According to the classic arguments by Ronald Coase (1937, 1960) the perfect allocation of resources within the markets is impossible due to the transaction costs that are basically induced because of imperfect information. The actors are lacking information, plus the information might be false or in other ways unreliable, or they simply can not use the information in the most appropriate way. Actors seek to find mechanisms to minimise the costs of transacting, and thus, make markets to operate more secure. These mechanisms include hierarchical economic organisations, such as business enterprises, measures made by the state in order to secure efficient economic activities through property rights, and also formal and informal private institutions, such as networks.[1]

Hierarchical organisations are one solution to the problems caused by asymmetric information. Namely, a business enterprise can internalise the whole production chain (from production to sales) through vertical integration, as stated e.g. by A. D. Chandler (1962, 1977), O. E. Williamson (1985) and M.

---

1   R. Coase,`The Nature of the Firm´, in: *Economica*, 4 (1937), 386-405; R. Coase, `The Problem of Social Cost´, in: *The Journal of Law & Economics*, 3 (1960), 1-44; R.A. Pollak,`A Transaction Cost Approach to Families and Households´, in: *Journal of Economic Literature*, 23 (1985), 581- 583; O.E. Williamson, *The economic institutions of capitalism: firms, markets, relational contracting*, New York 1985, xi-xiii, 2-42. One area of focus of the transaction costs approach is the role of the institutions structuring complex, long-term relationships – such as entrepreneurial networks. See especially: O.E. Williamson, *Markets and hierarchies*, New York 1975, 1-8; D.C. North, *Institutions, Institutional Change and Economic Performance*, Cambridge 1990; C. Menard (ed.), *Transaction Cost Economics*, Cheltenham 1997. On the information problematic, see also: G.J. Stigler, `The Economics of Information´, in: *The Journal of Political Economy*, 69 (1961), 213-225.

Casson (1993).[2] However, as stated e.g. by S. R. H. Jones and S. P. Ville (1996), a vertically integrated organisation does not necessarily provide transaction cost advantages, and thus, more efficient business activities.[3]

The networks between individuals and independently acting organisations are stated to be the solution to the information problematic, especially with regards to international trade. Networks between the actors provide a tool for reducing transaction costs caused by imperfect information. It is argued that the entrepreneurial networks operate in certain situations more efficiently than the hierarchical organisations, because networks provide continuity and stability in economic operations. Networks co-ordinate and provide value to information, because they offer several sources for acquiring the information and, thus, an opportunity to analyse the importance of the information.[4]

Within the marketing and entrepreneurship research there is a growing number of studies that concentrate on network issues, mostly based on sociological theories.[5] In these studies of social networks (e.g. K. S. Cook et al. 1983) the actors within the networks are mainly individuals, though inter- and intra-organisational networks are also taken into account. Authors like Mark Granovetter (1973) have stressed the role information plays within the network contacts, whilst e.g. Jeffrey Pfeffer and Gerald R. Salancik (1978) have stressed the resource dependencies between the actors.[6] Sociologically orientated studies

2   A.D. Jr. Chandler, *Strategy and Structure*, Cambridge (Mass.) 1962; A.D. Jr. Chandler, *The Visible Hand*, Cambridge (Mass.) 1962; M. Casson, *The Entrepreneur*, Oxford 1993, 39-40; Williamson, *The economic institutions of capitalism*, 103-130. See also: S. Nicholas, `Agency Contracts, Institutional Modes, and the Transition to Foreign Direct Investment by British Manufacturing Multinationals Before 1939', in: *The Journal of Economic History*, 43 (1983), 676.

3   S.R.H. Jones and S.P. Ville, `Efficient Transactors or Rent-Seeking Monopolists? The Rationale for Early Chartered Trading Companies', in: *The Journal of Economic History*, 56 (1996), 898-915, 912.

4   S. Nicholas,`Agency Contracts, Institutional Modes, and the Transition to Foreign Direct Investment', 675-86; Williamson, *The economic institutions of capitalism*; I. Ruostetsaari, *Energiapolitiikan määräytyminen*, Tampere 1989, 118; M. Casson, `Entrepreneurial Networks; A Theoretical Perspective', in: C. E. Núñez (ed.), *Entrepreneurial networks and business culture*, Sevilla 1998, 13, 17-18.

5   See e.g.: P.R. Beije and J. Groenewegen,`A Network Analysis of Markets', in: *Journal of Economic Issues*, 26 (1992), 87-114; G. Easton, `Industrial Networks: a Review', in: B. Axelsson and G. Easton (eds.), *Industrial networks*, London 1992; J. Brown and M.B. Rose, `Introduction', in: J. Brown and M.B. Rose (eds.), *Entrepreneurship, networks and modern business*, Manchester 1993; A. Äyväri, *Pienyritysten verkostot*, Helsinki 1999.

6   R.M. Emerson, `Power-Dependence Relations', in: *American Sociological Review*, 27 (1962), 31-41; M. Granovetter, `The Strength of Weak Ties', in: *American Journal of Sociology*, 78 (1973), 1360-1380.; J. Pfeffer and G.R. Salancik, *The external control of organizations*, New York 1978; K. Cook, S. Richard, M. Emerson and M.R. Gillmore, `The Distribution of Power

(e.g. J. Scott 1991) concentrate mostly on networks on the national level.[7] There is research on international networks, especially, within the areas of study concerning industrial networks (e.g. B. Axelson and G. Easton 1992) and entrepreneurship.[8] Furthermore, research shows that the practical use of networks in business operations is an ancient practise, as stated e.g. by authors like Avner Greif (1989), Mark Casson (1993), and the articles in this volume.[9]

The reliability of the information is the key question that needs to be answered in order to understand the role played by the entrepreneurial networks. The problem of honest behaviour can be seen through agency theory, which usually concerns long-term contracts in repeated dealings.[10] According to the principal-agent theory the principals cannot be sure whether the agents act in their best interests, and are not opportunistic in their behaviour. Transaction costs occur due to this uncertainty: The more reliable the agent is the lower the costs are. However, perfect monitoring of the agent is impossible because of the imperfect information and costs that are involved. Though it might be in principle feasible to monitor the agent, it is not economically viable due to the transaction costs.[11]

---

in Exchange Networks: Theory and Experimental Results', in: *American Journal of Sociology,* 89 (1983), 275-305.

7   See e.g. Ruostetsaari, *Energiapolitiikan määräytyminen;* J. Scott, `Networks of Corporate Power: A Comparative Assessment', in: *Annual Review of Sociology,* 17 (1991), 181-203.

8   B. Axelsson and G. Easton (eds.), *Industrial Networks,* London 1992; C. Karlsson, B. Johannisson and D. Storey (eds.), *Small business dynamics,* London 1993.

9   See e.g. Casson, *The Entrepreneur;* A. Greif, `Reputation and Coalitions in Medieval Trade: Evidence on the Maghribi Traders', in: *The Journal of Economic History,* 49 (1989), 857-882; J. Ojala, `Approaching Europe: The merchant networks between Finland and Europe during the eighteenth and nineteenth centuries', in: *European Review of Economic History,* 1 (1997), 323-352; Casson, `Entrepreneurial Networks'.

10 Nicholas, `Agency Contracts', 677.

11 S.A. Ross, `The Economic Theory of Agency: The Principal's Problem', in: *The American Economic Review,* 63 (1973), 134, 138; Williamson, *The economic institutions of capitalism,* 29-31, 47-50; A.M. Carlos and S. Nicholas, `"Giants of an Earlier Capitalism": The Chartered Trading Companies as Modern Multinationals', in: *Business History Review* 62 (1988), 406; North, *Institutions, Institutional Change and Economic Performance,* 21, 33, 128; G. Boyce, *Information, mediation and institutional development,* Manchester 1995, 3; D.E. Campbell, D. E. (1995), *Incentives. Motivation and the Economics of Information,* Cambridge (Mass.) 1995, 3-5. The emphasis in agency-literature is usually on the game-theoretical and mathematical modelling (for example: E. Maskin and J. Tirole, `The Principal-Agent Relationship with an Informed Principal: The Case of Private Values', in: *Econometrica,* 58 (1990), 379-409.; S.J. Grossman and O.D. Hart, `An Analysis of the Principal-Agent Problem', in: *Econometrica,* 51 (1983), 7-46). Agency-theories are concentrating on both intra- and inter-organisational hierarchies and relationships (Williamson, *Markets and hierarchies;* Williamson, *economic institutions of capitalism*). Historical studies on the principal agent-problem are especially

Although the literature usually suggests that the main problem is how the agent can secure the interests of the principal, this is not the only problem. Based on previous investigations, we argue that for the foreign agent it was sometimes even harder to monitor the principal.[12] Thus, the principals also had to secure the interests and satisfy the needs of their foreign agents in order to ensure the reliability of the information provided by them. Therefore, in this paper we are not only looking at the situation in a traditional way from the principal's perspective, but also from the agent's point of view. Thus, the common agency problem should be revisited by stressing the interdependencies between the parties in transaction.

This paper aims to analyse the entrepreneurial networks between Finnish entrepreneurs and their business partners within international trade and shipping during the eighteenth and nineteenth century.[13] Specialised shipping services provided a network of contacts to Finnish tradesmen during the initial period of Finnish international trade and shipping. International trade and shipping provides an interesting arena to study the issue due to the global setting and, at least in theory, nearly free market system. Furthermore, for the Finnish merchant houses internationalisation of the activities (like the sales of the products) abroad was impossible. Enterprises owned by Finnish families were too small and the activities they were engaged in were too complex, so that the whole industry could not be integrated into their organisation. Therefore, the use of long term and stable business networks was a matter of necessity.

This paper is based on the archival material of several Finnish trading houses. Mainly correspondence, circular letters and ledgers are used in this

---

interested in international trade (D.C. North, *Structure and Change in Economic History*, New York 1981; D.C. North, *Institutions, Institutional Change and Economic Performance*; A. Greif, 'Reputation and Coalitions in Medieval Trade') and internalising agencies through vertical integration of the business enterprises (G. Boyce, *Information, mediation and institutional development*; Nicholas, 'Agency Contracts, Institutional Modes, and the Transition to Foreign Direct Investment', 676; M. Casson, 'Entrepreneurial Networks'; Carlos and Nicholas, 'Giants of an Earlier Capitalism', 406; Jones and Ville, 'Efficient Transactors or Rent-Seeking Monopolists?'). Agency problems are also discussed in the literature concerning the problem of moral hazard in economic operations (B. Holmstrom, 'Moral Hazard in Teams', in: *Bell Journal of Economics*, 13 (1982), 324-340; Ross, 'The Economic Theory of Agency').

12   For cases see e.g.: J. Ojala, *Tehokasta liiketoimintaa Pohjanmaan pikkukaupungeissa*, Helsinki 1999, 333-337.

13   Finnish ships were used to carry export (mainly tar and timber) and import (mainly salt) cargo, as well as for international freight shipping. See especially Y. Kaukiainen, *Sailing into Twilight*. Helsinki 1991.

study.[14] The paper consists of four parts. Following the introduction basic concepts as well as the research arena are explained and defined. The third chapter aims to analyse certain solutions of monitoring the agent and principal, and following this are the concluding remarks.

Operating Arena and Conceptual Framework

The efficient allocation of resources in the early period of modern shipping and trade was bound by asymmetric information. Specialised trade and shipping services can be characterised as institutional intermediate co-operative modes that economise transaction costs.[15] They were collaborative arenas and social networks for the transfer and accumulation of information. Entrepreneurial networks created by the specialised commercial agencies lowered the costs in foreign market entry. The specialised services were offered at the time as a rationale solution to organise international trade and shipping, though there was also, of course, transaction cost disabilities related to the specialisation and agencies, especially the principal-agent problem.

According to S. A. Ross (1973) an agent can be characterised as someone who is "designated to act for, on behalf of, or as representative for the other, designated the principal, in a particular domain of decision problems".[16] For the purposes of foreign trade the agents knew the language, local customs and laws, and lived in the country where the products were sold. The task of the agencies was to combine foreign trade with up-to-date knowledge of different (two or more) countries. The principal had knowledge of the product, which was imperfectly transferred to the agent. Moreover, the principal owned the capital

---

14 Author has gained an extensive collection of copies from circular letters in various trading house archives from professor Yrjö Kaukiainen (University of Helsinki), originally collected by professor Sven-Erik Åström. The bulk of circulars originates from trading houses and agencies engaged with shipping services in the Mediterranean area (including Portugal), and from Great Britain (especially from Liverpool). For details see: S.E. Åström, *From Tar to Timber*, Helsinki 1988, 138-169. See also e.g. North, *Institutions, Institutional Change and Economic Performance*, 126; Boyce, *Information, mediation and institutional development*, 3.

15 Nicholas, 'Agency Contracts, Institutional Modes, and the Transition to Foreign Direct Investment', 676. The shipping services were specialised, at least to a moderate level, already during the late 18th century. See e.g. Ojala, 'Approaching Europe'; J. Ojala, 'The problem of information in the Late 18th and Early 19th Century Shipping: A Finnish Case', in: *International Journal of Maritime History*, 14 (2002).

16 Ross, 'The Economic Theory of Agency', 134.

and the product in the transaction, and he also had the decisive power in decision-making.[17]

Conflicts tend to develop, as S. Nicholas (1983) states, between the agent and principal over holding stocks in the goods, promotional efforts, pricing, and levels of service.[18] For the principal who was engaged in international trade and shipping in eighteenth or nineteenth century Finland, it was impossible to know how the markets operated in the area where the agent was working. Thus, the principal had to trust the agent. The principals were aware of the gains and returns of the activities, but they were unsure how much of these gains were related to the actual work of the agent, as it was almost impossible to measure the performance and efficiency of the agent.[19]

The capability to transfer and use the information is related to the personal and acquired capabilities (like schooling, apprentice etc.) of the actors. Mark Casson (1982, 1999) argues that an entrepreneur is someone who is actually "specialised in collecting and synthesising information in order to make decisions".[20] There was quite naturally, a major gap between the information that the leaders might have about efficient leadership and their real knowledge and capability to use this information. Though the efficient activity of the merchant was bound to the personal capabilities of the entrepreneur, there were also a lot of practical problems in day-to-day business operations, such as language difficulties or the processing of the large volumes of information arriving from different sources.[21]

The merchants in foreign ports attended the clearance of the vessels and charged a commission for this service called address commission. Later these merchants evolved into specialised brokers, though the work involved was quite similar for a long period of time. Contemporaries protested against the address

---

17 Coase, `Nature of the Firm'; North, *Structure and Change in Economic History*, 201-208; Nicholas, `Agency Contracts, Institutional Modes, and the Transition to Foreign Direct Investment', 677.

18 Nicholas, `Agency Contracts, Institutional Modes, and the Transition to Foreign Direct Investment', 677-678; M. Casson, `Entrepreneurial Networks', 21-22.

19 North, *Structure and Change in Economic History*, 204; Williamson, *Markets and hierarchies*, 26-37; Williamson, *economic institutions of capitalism*, 27-31; C. Jones, *International Business in the Nineteenth Century*, Brighton 1987, 99; Casson, `Entrepreneurial Networks', 17.

20 Casson, *Entrepreneur*, 23-25; M. Casson, `The Economics of the Family Firm', in: *Scandinavian Economic History Review* 47 (1999), 10-23, 12.

21 T. Mauranen, `Porvarista kauppiaaksi', in: Y. Kaukiainen, P. Schybergson, H. Soikkanen and T. Mauranen (eds.), *När samhället förändras - Kun yhteiskunta muuttuu*, Helsinki 1981, 76; Y. Kaukiainen, `Owners and Masters: Management and Managerial Skills in the Finnish Ocean-Going Merchant Fleet, c. 1840-1880', in: *Research in Maritime History*, 6 (1994), 49-66; Jones and Ville, `Efficient Transactors or Rent-Seeking Monopolists?', 906.

commission system, because they regarded address commission as "an unjustified discount off the freight".[22]

The broker was in a difficult position between the owner and the charter. Also the irregularity of the activities was another disadvantage in the brokerage business. Thus, many brokers engaged themselves in a wide variety of services.[23] Frenckell & Comp. from Paris, for example, stated in a circular that agency concentrated on commission trade (both import and export), marine insurance, discount, and credit granting.[24]

The Problems and Solutions of Monitoring the Agent - and Principal

The networks of specialised shipping services produced mechanisms to prevent opportunistic behaviour by the agent – and also possibilities for the agent to monitor the principal. These mechanisms can be divided into "ex-ante" and "ex-post" measures. Ex-ante measures prevent opportunistic behaviour before contracting. They can be characterised as incentives that encouraged agencies to be honest in their behaviour. Ex-post control mechanisms enabled principals to identify and punish bad performers after the activity.[25] In relation to the early modern international trade these measures can be divided into: commission payments, long-term and personal contacts, intermediates, formal contracts, communications, resource dependence, co-operation by the Finnish principals, the competition between the agencies, and the enforcing mechanisms provided by the state. These measures are discussed in more detail below.

---

22 J.F. Myrhe, *About Chartering and Shipbroking Business*, Copenhagen 1917, 6.
23 Myrhe, *About Chartering*, 6-8; P.N. Davies, *Henry Tyrer. A Liverpool Shipping Agent and his Enterprise, 1879-1979*, London 1979, 23-24; Ojala, *Tehokasta liiketoimintaa Pohjanmaan pikkukaupungeissa*, 309. On brokerage business and commission trade see also e.g. I. Chrzanowski, *An Introduction to Shipping Economics*, London 1985, 20–25; F. Braudel, *Civilisationer och kapitalism 1400-1800*, vol. 3, Stockholm 1986, 211–213; Jones, *International Business*, 28, 97; L. Müller, *The Merchant Houses of Stockholm, c. 1640-1800*, Uppsala 1998, 147-151; M.B. Miller, 'Ship Agents in the Twentieth Century', in: *Research in Maritime History*, 22 (2002), 5-22.
24 Oulu Provincial Archives (hereafter OPA): Bergbom, Frenckell & Comp. (Paris), Circular 15 November 1857.
25 Williamson, *Markets and hierarchies*, 26-37; Williamson, *economic institutions of capitalism*, 20-21, 52-56; Nicholas, 'Agency Contracts, Institutional Modes, and the Transition to Foreign Direct Investment', 678.

Commission payments

A prominent assumption of neo-classic economic theory is that behaviour is honest when it is profitable.[26] The most important tool for ensuring honest activity was commission from sales. No fixed salary was paid to the commission agencies and thus their incomes were dependent on the calls for offers by the principals. The problem was, of course, how high the commission ought to be in order to prevent opportunistic behaviour, and at the same time ensure decent earnings both for the agent and for the principal. As S. R. H. Jones and S. P. Ville (1996) argue, the possibilities for cheating were dependent upon the opportunity and costs of such behaviour, which varied over time and between individuals.[27] Commission discouraged opportunism as an ex-ante measure, but at the same time served as an ex-post measure, as S. Nicholas (1983), has stated. According to him, the agencies had to invest in physical and human capital (like warehouses and clerks).[28] All these investments might be unrewarded in cases of bad performance, which could lead to the ultimate punishment: to the termination of the business relationship.

According to the circular letters and price currencies sent by the brokers and agencies, the commission payments to the agencies were usually a percentage of the value of the freight or the shipped cargo. Also, commission payments varied according to the economic situation or according to the freight or cargo in question. Torladés & Co. from Lisbon stated that their commission is usually six per cent, but depending on the time this figure could differ.[29] According to the calculations based on the archives of the merchant house Malm during the period from the 1820s up to the 1870s, different kinds of brokerage and commission payments constituted over ten per cent of the gross value of the freight or cargo earnings.[30]

The commission payments were direct transaction costs for the entrepreneurs engaged in the activities. However, the owners only seldom complained about these costs, as business activity without the specialised agencies was not possible. The savings were usually taken from insurance costs, thereafter from

26 R.H. Nelson, 'The Economics of Honest Trade Practices', in: *Journal of Industrial Economics,* 24 (1976), 281-293.
27 Jones and Ville,'Efficient Transactors or Rent-Seeking Monopolists?', 904. See also Myrhe, *About Chartering,* 6-8.
28 Nicholas, 'Agency Contracts, Institutional Modes, and the Transition to Foreign Direct Investment', 678.
29 OPA, Lang, Torladés & Co. (Lisbon), Circular 1 March 1825; Bergbom, Torladés & Co. (Lisbon), Circular 20 February 1826.
30 Ojala, *Tehokasta liiketoimintaa Pohjanmaan pikkukaupungeissa,* 332-333.

the maintenance and crew costs, and in the last resort the shipmaster also had to be satisfied with lesser earnings. Only in a couple of cases that have been found in various archives, there were direct arguments against the high commission.[31]

Resource dependence

The Finnish principals were dependent on the information, and sometimes even the capital provided by their foreign agencies. At the same time, however, the specialised agencies were also dependent on their principals, because their whole business activity was based on the commission gained from the transactions provided by the principals. The possibility for the agent to monitor his principal – or vice versa – is dependent on the power of exchange. According to the social exchange and inter-organizational theories the power of an actor is dependent on his capabilities and abilities to control the vital resources – like information.[32] Thus, actors are bound to cooperate in order to acquire the vital resources.

Finnish merchants were in a strong position over their foreign agencies with regard to certain trades. The resource dependence was especially significant in the case of the tar trade. Finnish tar was among the "market leaders" in Europe, especially within the British markets throughout this period. In Liverpool during the 1840s, for example, Finnish tar constituted circa one fourth of the imported tar.[33] To some extent Finnish entrepreneurs also had a strong position in relation to the timber trade*s* and freight trade*s*, due to the high volume of these trades, and the fact that especially Finnish ships had competitive advantages in the cost structure (wage level low, price of ships low).

The information itself was a vital resource within the entrepreneurial networks. In order to ensure the dealings the agencies had to offer valuable information. Thus, information was shared quite well, due to the fact that valuable information was the merchandise in these networks. Mark Granovetter (1973) has argued that these kind of impersonal "weak ties" are especially important in transferring information between people and organisations.[34]

---

31 See e.g. Ojala, 'The problem of information'.
32 See e.g. Emerson,'Power-Dependence Relations', 31-41; Pfeffer and Salancik, *external control of organizations*; Cook, Richard, Emerson and Gillmore,'The Distribution of Power in Exchange Networks', 275-305. See also: Williamson, *Markets and hierarchies,* 26-37; Williamson, *economic institutions of capitalism.*
33 K. Hautala, *Suomen tervakauppa 1856-1913*, Helsinki 1956; K. Hautala, *European and American Tar in the English Market During the Eighteenth and Early Nineteenth Centuries,* Helsinki 1963; S.E. Åström, *From Tar to Timber.*
34 M. Granovetter,'The Strength of Weak Ties', 1369—1372.

Reputation: long term and personal contacts

Economic relationships are usually long-term by nature. Though the parties involved in trades and produce more efficient exchange.[35]

Table 1: Letters analysed in trading houses Sovelius, Falander, and J. Lang & Co.

Name (years)	Number of letters	Number of individual contacts	Letters per contact
Matts Johanson Sovelius (1785-1795)	218	56	3
Abraham Falander (1781-1812)	5250	856	6
J. Lang & Co. (1823-1854)	5422	719	8
Together	10890	1629	7

Sources: OPA, Sovelius & Lang, correspondence. VPA, Falander, Correspondence.

Table 2: Letters to the most and least important business partners in trading houses Sovelius, Falander, and J. Lang & Co.

Name (years)	Letters sent to the ten most important contacts	Per cent from total	Number of contacts to whom letters were sent only once	Per cent from letters	Per cent from contacts
Matts Johanson Sovelius (1785-1795)	151	24	32	15	57
Abraham Falander (1781-1812)	1507	30	391	8	46
J. Lang & Co. (1823-1854)	1604	29	391	7	43

Sources: See Table 1.

The aim of the entrepreneurial networks was to create secure and profitable contacts. The most secure contacts were, however, not necessarily the most

---

35 S. Nicholas, `Agency Contracts, Institutional Modes, and the Transition to Foreign Direct Investment by British Manufacturing Multinationals Before 1939´; G. Easton, `Industrial Networks: a Review´, 9–11; J. Ojala,`Approaching Europe: The merchant networks between Finland and Europe during the eighteenth and nineteenth centuries´, 326.

profitable ones. It is evident that with short-term contacts owners could get quick profits, but also the risks involved were higher. Thus, actors would seek for long-term business relationships, even if more profitable ones were available. Seeking for the continuity and trust between the contracting parties in economic operations is the key to understanding the role played by the networks.[36]

According to the correspondence analysed for this study, there was a clear striving for long-term business contacts among the Finnish entrepreneurs. According to Tables 1 and 2, especially in the large trading houses (such as Falander and J. Lang & Co.) the correspondence and thus the network connections concentrated on some central actors. In Falander and J. Lang & Co. cases the ten most important contacts constituted circa one third of all of the letters sent from these houses. Though, at the same time the number of "occasional" contacts to whom only one letter was sent was almost half of the cases. In the case of Matts Johanson Sovelius, who was a minor player in trade, the contacts were more occasionally.

The importance of reputation can be shown through the fact that in several cases Finnish trading houses favoured the same agencies abroad. The reputation of the agencies was well known among Finns, and newcomers in trade trusted the agencies that already had long-term contacts with the older houses. This fact was even used in "marketing", namely, agencies stressed that they are the most important commission agents for the Nordic houses. For example, Fredholm & Ekström from Marseilles stated in the circular in 1856 that 20 out of 50 Nordic ships that arrived in Marseilles used the services provided by them.[37] Of the 22 Finnish ships that docked at the port of Liverpool during the first months of 1831, 14 were addressed to Hornby, five to Leigh & Co., and the rest to other local agencies. Moller & Co. stated that 19 out of 34 Finnish ships that arrived at the port of Lisbon in 1840 were cleared by them.[38]

Intermediates

Intermediates were also used between principals and agents. These "first degree" agencies included shipmasters, Finnish apprentices abroad[39], and "travellers" of

---

36 Brown and Rose, `Introduction', 3; Easton, `Industrial Networks', 9; Beije and Groenewegen, `Network Analysis of Markets', 103; Casson, `Entrepreneurial Networks', 17-18.
37 OPA, Bergbom, Fredholm & Ekström (Marseilles), Circular 30 April 1856.
38 OPA, Lang, Mordwick (Liverpool), Circular 24 March 1831; Hornby & Co. (Liverpool), Circular 1 January 1835; Moller's enka & Son (Lisbon), Circular 1 March 1841.
39 See e.g.: O. Nikula, *Malmska handelshuset i Jacobstad*, Helsingfors 1948, 150, 356-360; V. Hoving, *Henrik Borgström*, Helsingfors 1949, 57-64; Jones, *International Business*, 28, 67.

the foreign agencies that were seeking business opportunities in Finland. The intermediates were personal agents of the principal; thus honest behaviour was measured ex-ante by the personal commitment. The use of personal intermediates in international trade is a traditional way to deal with the problem of honest behaviour, experienced already with the important role of *commenda* in the expansion of Mediterranean trade during the 10th and 11th century.[40]

The role played by the shipmaster was crucial in order to limit agency problems within international trade and shipping. The relationship between the shipmaster and the ship owner was hierarchical. A shipmaster was the personal representative of the ship owner in faraway places. The shipmaster was the intermediate between the owner and the foreign agencies, as well as between the owner and the crew. The shipmaster was not only responsible for the safe journey of the vessel, but also for the economic returns from the journey.[41]

The earnings of the captain were tied not only to a fixed salary, but also to the profits of the vessel through a special merit pay system (*kaplake*). The *kaplake* was usually five per cent of the gross earnings of the ship. Zacharias Franzén (owner of the trading house J. Lang & Co.) even gave an option: in the case of a safe journey without the ship being damaged the shipmaster could gain six per cent *kaplake*.[42] Thus, *kaplake* was based on a similar incentive structure as the commission payments: obtaining the best results will be profitable both to the agent and to the principal.[43]

Occasionally foreign trading houses sent their representatives to visit various Finnish trading houses. Thus, these visitors not only acted as intermediates but also provided personal relationships between the distant partners in trade. For example, the underwriter of Liverpool-agency Robins & Dalmer himself

40 Detailed: A.L. Udovitch, 'At the Origins of the Western Commenda: Islam, Israel, Byzantium?', in: *Speculum*, 37 (1962), 198-207; Greif,'Reputation and Coalitions in Medieval Trade'. See also: R. Brenner, 'The Social Basis of English Commercial Expansion, 1550-1650', in: *The Journal of Economic History* 32 (1972), 361-384; Jones and Ville,'Efficient Transactors or Rent-Seeking Monopolists?', 910-911.

41 Nikula, *Malmska handelshuset i Jacobstad*; P.S. Ville, *English shipowning during the industrial revolution*, Manchester 1987, 68; Kaukiainen, 'Owners and Masters', 54; Y. Kaukiainen, 'International Freight Markets in the 1830s and 1840s: The Experience of a Major Finnish Shipowner', in: *Research in Maritime History*, 14 (1994), 1-27, 7-8.

42 OPA, Lang, Ship Suomi, orders to shipmaster 1849.

43 R. Davis, *The Rise of the English Shipping Industry*, London 1962, 369; Kaukiainen, *Sailing into Twilight*, 114; C. Kindleberger, *Mariners and Markets*, New York/ London 1992, 84.

journeyed to the Baltic area in the early 1820s, whereas the owner of the Liverpool agency P. C. Jager visited Finland in the early 1830s.[44]

State intervention and formal contract

The formal contracts, and related to it, the role played by the state also provided both ex-ante and ex-post enforcing mechanisms between agents and principals. Though, it is evident that the state had only limited legal contract enforceability.[45] The contracts were made under the law and statutes of each country, which sometimes lead to problems. Thus, one important task for the overseas agencies was to also provide information on the legal changes, especially at the practical level such as changes in customs and tariffs.

The domestic state also provided mechanisms to secure the merchant's property rights abroad in order to promote trade and shipping. The commercial services provided by the Nordic states during the seventeenth and the eighteenth century were especially important for merchant activities. The establishment of consular services was, for example, a state's attempt to externalise their own nation's merchants' transaction costs. The consular service on the one hand helped ships in foreign ports, but on the other hand also provided a tool for information gathering. Consular reports sent to the Swedish Board of Trade were circulated to the Association of Wholesale Merchants in Stockholm. This information was then forwarded, at least to some degree, to other merchants in Sweden and Finland as well.[46]

Communications

The networks of specialised shipping services can be characterised as impersonal occupational groups, where the coordination and communication was explicit.[47] This can be detected from the business correspondence. The formulation of the correspondence, circular letters or price currents was fairly similar no matter

---

44 OPA, Bergbom, Robins & Dalmer (Liverpool), Circular 8 March 1824; Lang, P. C. Jager & Co. (Liverpool), Circular 18 August 1831. See also: L.G. Bonsdorff, *En köpman och hans värld*. Ekenäs 1977.

45 See also: Greif, 'Reputation and Coalitions in Medieval Trade'.

46 See especially: L. Müller and J. Ojala, 'Consular Services of the Nordic Countries during the Eighteenth and Nineteenth Centuries: Did They Really Work?', in: *Research in Maritime History*, 22 (2002), 23-41.

47 Casson, 'Entrepreneurial Networks'; J.S. Brown and P. Duguid, *The Social Life of Information*, Boston (Mass.) 1999, 141.

which part of the world the letters came from. The communications also provided a successful tool for monitoring the agencies. Price differences were noted from the different circular letters, and larger problems would lead in some cases to complaints.

The intermediates in international trade basically handled information within the impersonal entrepreneurial networks, as Mark Casson (1998) has argued. They did not, usually, physically handle the products, but rather gave orders or instructions to where the products should be delivered.[48] Agencies did not only provide vital market information, but also all kinds of information concerning practical matters. For example, two agencies in Cadiz stated information about the new customs in Spain in their circulars of 1852.[49] Also, the epidemic of cholera in Marseilles was noted in several circulars sent to Finland in 1835 and 1836.[50] Also profound political changes were widely discussed within the correspondence, as it was the case with the revolutionary year of 1848 in Europe.[51]

Constant flow of information was a way to achieve trust between the parties undertaking transactions. The agencies tried as best as they could to ensure their sincerity – at least at a rhetorical level. "We will take care of our principal's businesses as if they were our own", stated Sancher & Söner from Barcelona in their letter. Pearson & Claude in Liverpool used a similar approach: after a long and detailed description of how trade and shipping was in a crisis, and how all the trading houses in town were near to bankruptcy, they would still act according to the best interest of the principal.[52]

Though the telegraph, introduced during the mid-19th century, provided a fast and secure way to communicate, it did not displace business correspondence but rather supported it. Torladés & Co. of Lisbon stated in their circular of 1860 that they now had more updated knowledge about the market prices thanks to the telegraph. Thus, they recommended to their Finnish "friends" to send ships to "our port", where they could quickly contact other Mediterranean ports in order to get the best prices for the Finnish export cargo.[53]

---

48 Casson, `Entrepreneurial Networks´, 21.
49 OPA, Bergbom, Vivent y. Vives (Cadiz), Circular 1 January 1852; Moumger (Cadiz), Circular 24 February 1852.
50 For example: Finnish National Archives (hereafter FNA), Malm, Wessel & Co (Marseilles), Circular 1 April 1836.
51 For example: OPA, Bergbom, Fölsch & Co. (Marseilles), Circular 26 June 1848.
52 OPA, Bergbom, Sancher & Söner (Barcelona) to G. & C. Bergbom (Oulu) 12 January 1857; Pearson & Claude (Liverpool), Circular 29 November 1819.
53 OPA, Antman, Torladés & Co. (Lisbon), Circular 16th Jun. 1860. See also: J. Ahvenainen, 'The Role of Telegraphs in the 19th Century Revolution of Communications', in: M. North (eds.), *Kommunikationsrevolutionen. Die neuen Medien des 16. und 19. Jahrhunderts*, Köln 1995; Y.

The capability of the agencies and brokerage firms to deliver information with the Nordic languages was a decisive factor in their work.[54] From the 428 circulars in various Finnish trading houses analysed for this study, 398 were written in Swedish or in other Nordic languages (Danish and Norwegian)[55], only 11 were written in English, 16 in German, and three in French. Swedish was at the time the primary language in Finnish bourgeois families both in the home and business – only in domestic trade with Finnish-origin peasantry was Finnish used as the language. Presumably, in some cases circulars were translated in some Finnish or Swedish trading houses, and only after that circulated to other trading houses. Some agencies used several languages in their circulars. Steward, Bald & Co. from Liverpool, for example, usually wrote in Swedish, but also used German and English in some of the circulars.[56]

Domestic merchant networks

J. S. Brown and P. Duguid (1999) divide networks into communities of practice and networks of practice. According to them, the communities of practice are groups where people know each other personally, reciprocity is strong, and communication and co-ordination is implicit.[57] In their hometowns, Finnish tradesmen created typical communities of practice. Though the merchants were rivals to each other, there usually was a lot of co-operation between them too, especially within costly foreign trade and shipping. Ships were often owned together within partnerships, and vital business information was shared, even with rivals. Thus, the activity of the domestic merchants was a mixture of competition and co-operation, as it is also emphasised in the network analysis of markets.[58] The domestic network was utilised to mobilise and transfer knowledge and capital. The transfer of knowledge also included information about the possibilities in foreign trade, e.g. about the foreign agencies.[59]

Kaukiainen, `Shrinking the world: Improvements in the speed of information transmission, c. 1820-1870', in: European Review of Economic History, 5 (2001), 1-28.

54 Mauranen, `Porvarista kauppiaaksi´, 202-203; Kaukiainen, `Owners and Masters´, 57-61.

55 Åström, *From Tar to Timber*, 140; Ojala,`Approaching Europe´.

56 FNA, Malm, Steward & Co. (Liverpool), Circular 20 June 1840. OPA, Lang, Steward, Bald & Co. (Liverpool), Circular 2 August 1835.

57 Brown and Duguid, *Social Life of Information*, 141.

58 Beije and Groenewegen,` Network Analysis of Markets´, 95.

59 M. Kirby, 'Quakerism, entrepreneurship and the family firm in North-East England', in: J. Brown and M. B. Rose (eds.), *Entrepreneurship, networks and modern business*, Manchester 1993, 122; T.A.B. Corley, 'The entrepreneur: the central issue in business history?', in: J.

Circular letters with price currencies especially show the kind of "free information", at least to the people involved within the network. Circulars and price currencies were often printed, but they could also include more personal letters to the Finnish receiver. Circulars often came to some profound Finnish or Swedish merchant houses, which copied and forwarded them to other houses. J.W. Snellman G:son, one of the most important trading houses in northern Finland, for example, summarised and forwarded circulars to other merchant houses.[60] Some Finnish trading houses even specialised in forwarding price currencies and circular letters, thus, forming their own agencies. F. E. Ekebom from Helsinki, for example, compressed information from various foreign agencies, and then forwarded it as a circular to Finnish houses. His network in 1833 included agencies from Nantes, Antwerp, Rochelle, Malaga, Rotterdam, Newcastle, and Bergen.[61]

Obviously the one who had first access to the information had some kind of a competitive advantage, but in reality it was usually almost impossible to take advantage. This was due to the slow speed of the business activities. It took months rather than weeks to equip a ship with Finnish commodities to sail to distant ports, or to get contact with ships already abroad in order to gain freight shipments. Therefore, the sharing of information was better than hiding in domestic competition. On a reciprocal basis the one who had shared the information with their rivals could also get valuable information in return.

Competition

The competition between the foreign agencies was a market mechanism that prevented opportunistic behaviour. The competition can be detected from the correspondence, and especially from the circular letters. Several houses competed for the occasional Finnish ships, and thus, also monitored each other. There is, of course, always the possibility of co-operation between several competing agencies in one port town. It is impossible to say, whether these kinds of informal "cartels" actually existed. The fact that the prices of the commodities were relatively at the same level, and that there were no differences between the

---

Brown and M. B. Rose (eds.), *Entrepreneurship, networks and modern business*, Manchester 1993, 26; Kaukiainen, `Owners and Masters´, 53; Ojala,`Approaching Europe´, 341-343.

60 Turku Provincial Archives (hereafter TPA), Kingelin, J.W. Snellman G:son (Oulu), Circular 27 May 1848. OPA, Sovelius & Lang, J.W. Snellman G:son (Oulu), Circulars 3 June 1850, 28 November 1850; 14 April 1851.

61 OPA, Sovelius, F. E. Ekebohm (Helsinki), Circular 15 July 1833.

commissions indicates on the one hand that the markets operated efficiently (if the prices were dictated at the markets), but can also be signs of co-operation.

The competition between the agencies addresses the strong position of the principal. In fact, the commission agents were changed quite often, though long-term relationships were preferred. Shipbrokers were especially changed quite frequently. However, in relation to money transfers, Finnish merchant houses were trusted for long-term contacts.[62]

The competition between the agents can be seen especially in the cases where Finnish ships arrived uncharted with the owners own export cargoes at foreign ports. In these situations it was the duty of the shipmaster to select the broker that the ship was going to use in a town. J. F: Myrhe (1917) has illustrated, how the representatives of the brokers, namely, "waterclerks", "climbed up the ship's side like monkeys, in order to be the first to get hold of the Captain".[63] There are several examples of competition from the uncharted vessels, even in Finnish trading house archives. The shipmaster of ship Louise, for example, wrote to the ship owner in 1840 of how three local agencies were competing to sell the cargo on the vessel.[64]

Conclusions

The specialisation of the shipping services enabled Finnish ship owners in many ways to undertake efficient business activities, though it also provided agency problems. The fact that the specialised services as a whole remained active throughout the 19th century, and in some parts even to this day, proves that the benefits from this institutional arrangement were higher than the possible losses. Thus, the trading organisation lowered transaction costs more than induced them.[65] Without the entrepreneurial networks and specialised services early modern international trade and shipping would have been impossible to carry out.

Several cases can be found in the archives of the Finnish trading houses where the problems with agencies and their Finnish principals are stated. These problems were caused only seldom by the opportunistic behaviour of the agent, but rather from human errors, failures in correspondence or simply due to the changes in market prices.

---

62 Ojala, `problem of information'.
63 Myrhe, *About Chartering*, 9.
64 FNA, Malm, P.G. Idman (Marseilles) to Peter Malm 3 April 1840.
65 See also Jones and Ville, `Efficient Transactors or Rent-Seeking Monopolists?'.

The interdependencies between the principals and agents lowered the costs of transaction and thus saved equally the interests of both parties. Though Finnish principals had problems with their agencies, they still had quite a strong position within the exchange. First, the agencies were dependent on the resources provided by the Finnish merchants. Secondly, the co-operation between the Finnish merchants, and thirdly the competition between the foreign agencies made the opportunistic behaviour of the Finnish principals possible.

International trade and shipping during the eighteenth and nineteenth centuries was dependent on entrepreneurial networks, but also on hierarchical organisations, and markets. Commodities and freight rates were determined within the markets. In fact, international trade and especially shipping was, during the time period, as near a "perfect" market mechanism as possible. Hierarchical organisations were used in day-to-day business practises; especially important were the structures between the ship owner and shipmaster. The networks were especially important in transferring information and capital between the parties in transaction.

French Merchants and Atlantic Networks:
The organisation of shipping and trade between Bordeaux and the United States, 1793-1815

Silvia Marzagalli

Historians generally assume that the Revolutionary and Napoleonic Wars radically disrupted the trade of French ports and put an end to the prosperity of maritime cities such as Bordeaux, which built their fortune on colonial trade in the eighteenth century. The loss of French Saint-Domingue, which became independent Haiti in 1804, as well as the emergence of new industrial regions in Northern Europe led to the relative decline of the Atlantic cities on the Western coast of France. Focusing on macro-economic developments and on structural changes within the Atlantic and European economies on the eve of the nineteenth century, this assumption widely ignores the action of merchants on a local level and their remarkable capacity to create alternative commercial webs in wartime. In fact, the relative decline of a port in the long run did not imply that its merchants were incapable of finding new ways to carry on lucrative trades.

This essay focuses on the city of Bordeaux. As a case study, it analyses the organisation of a new trade network across the Atlantic, linking this port to the United States from the beginning of the war between France and Great Britain in 1793 to the end of the conflict in 1815. Thanks to their new commercial links with overseas firms, Bordeaux's merchants were able to circumvent both British maritime blockades and French prohibitions, and to sustain transatlantic exchanges in their port throughout the major part of this period. In organising this commercial network, they contributed to the adjustment of the eighteenth-century Atlantic system to new market and political conditions. Their achievements are impressive, if one considers that their trade with the United States before 1793 was scarce.

Such a change in maritime trade and routes deserves our attention, as the establishment of commercial links is a time and energy consuming task. It requires merchants to set up an effective system to circulate payment as well as information that will enable them to make decisions; to organise transport, that is, to dispose of ships carrying goods efficiently across the Oceans; to import and export products according to demand and availability on the new markets; and to find reliable partners in cities to which they had no previous connexion. As Ronald S. Burt puts it, networks are basically "a matter of trust, of confidence in the information passed and the care with which contacts look out for your interests"[1].

Economists, sociologists and historians have been more concerned with the way a network operates than with the question of what happens when economic actors have to create new links. Which factors are determinant, how do merchants choose their commercial partners and decide if they can trust them, how do they organise the circulation of reliable information? The lack of alternatives gave merchants a determinant impulse to establish new links with unknown markets: privateers and war made traditional colonial trade virtually impossible for France after 1793. But organising and supervising new traffic was a worthwhile effort only if it turned out to be profitable and if losses were reasonable. This implied the efficient management of goods, information, market opportunities and legal constraints.

War determined the rise and fall of this Franco-American trade, which was insignificant up to 1793 and changed its nature after 1815. After recalling this context, the paper describes the patterns of this new commercial web and questions the ownership of the ships and cargoes crossing the Ocean, thus discerning whether French or American merchants risked these new trade links. Finally, the paper deals with the strategies merchants adopted, both in Bordeaux and in the different ports on the east coast of the United States, in order to structure their trade. This case study gives insight into the formation of a trade network, the context which determined its rise, and the ways it worked.

Politics, an Explaining Factor for the Rise of New Trade Networks

During the American War of Independence, France actively supported the rebellion against Great Britain, although the conflict was ruinous to French public finances. However, the French government expected some positive results from the independence of North America and hoped that French merchants would replace their British colleagues in the US markets. The reality after 1783 hardly met this expectation. As soon as peace was restored, American merchants turned again to Britain for most of their international trade. A few ships carried

---

1   R.S. Burt, *Structural Holes: The Social Structure of Competition*, Cambridge (Mass) 1992, 13. (Quoted by W.W. Powell and L. Smith-Doerr, 'Networks and Economic Life', in: N.J. Smelser and R. Swedberg (eds.), *The Handbook of Economic Sociology*, Princeton 1994, 368-402, here 371.

tobacco[2] and grains to France, but French products and sale conditions were not competitive on the US markets. During the 1780s, trade between France and the United States was therefore low. French exports to the US were particularly weak, as they dropped from an average of 11.5 millions *livres tournois* (approx. 2.3 million US $) in 1781-1783 to 1.8 million *livres tournois* (0.36 million US $) a year from 1784 to 1789[3]. Americans were much more active in the French West Indies than in France, a situation which French merchants deplored, as they were sensitive to any breach of their colonial monopoly. Their attitude towards American merchants was therefore fundamentally hostile and they did not welcome French governmental concessions to support the trade of some American commodities to France or her colonies. The situation changed abruptly with the beginning of the maritime war in Europe in 1793. Within a few years, hundreds of American ships yearly sailed to France.

The story of Bordeaux's trade to the United States shows that the ambitions of politicians were clearly not sufficient to generate a market. However, political events, such as war, created the context leading to the formation of new trade networks. The conflict which began in 1793 put French merchants in a well known but uncomfortable position. The war of 1793, like the various eighteenth-century conflicts between France and Great Britain, made it too risky for French merchants to send their property across the Ocean. Colonial trade, in particular, became extremely difficult. This situation induced French merchants to rely on neutral ships. Whereas Great Britain did not tolerate any direct trade between two enemy ports, shipping between a non-belligerent country and France was possible, provided both the ship and the goods belonged to a neutral merchant.

In the 1790s, many European countries were neutral. As the conflict increased the demand in their shipping services, the number of vessels sailing under neutral flags rose dramatically. This was the case with Denmark, for instance, or with Ragusa in the Mediterranean. As time passed, however, French expansionism over Europe reduced the number of neutral countries. As a result, the role of the United States in international maritime trade grew. Being the major neutral country up to 1812, the United States profited more than any other nation from war. This was a new element in international maritime trade, as

---

2   J.M. Price, *France and the Chesapeake. A History of the French Tobacco Monopoly 1674-1791 and of its Relationship to the British and American Tobacco Trades*, Ann Arbor (Mich.) 1973, 2 vols.

3   J.F. Stover, 'French-American trade during the Confederation', in: *The North Carolina Historical Review*, 35 (1958), 399-414. Some ships declared a destination in the West Indies, but went thereafter to the United-States; their exports do not appear in the French export statistics to the US: see J. Meyer, 'Les difficultés du commerce franco-américain vues de Nantes, 1776-1790', in: *French Historical Studies*, 11 (1979), 159-183.

North America had previously been involved in all conflicts either as a colony or a rebellious country. This novelty, however, did not affect the traditional strategies of French merchants in wartime, that is, the use of neutral flags and new trade routes: it just added new and extensive opportunities.

Bordeaux was particularly active in establishing diverisfied commercial patterns involving the United States. From the beginning of the war, the city became the most important French destination for American ships. This may be surprising, as from 1783 to 1793 Bordeaux had no prominent position in the ongoing US-French trade. American sources clearly show, for instance, that Bordeaux played an insignificant role in New York maritime trade before 1793 (document 1).

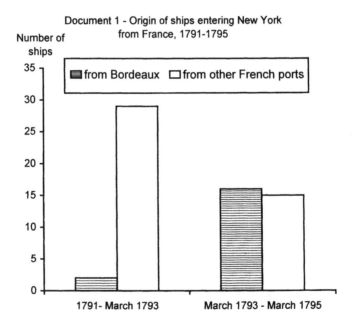

Source: National Archives, Washington, RG 36, 903, New York foreign entries, 1789-1795.

On the Philadelphia market the position of Bordeaux was stronger before 1793 (document 2): the number of ships coming in from Bordeaux equalled those coming from Lorient or Le Havre. The primacy of Bordeaux emerged in both cases only from 1793 onwards, the explanation lying in the nature of Bordeaux's trade.

Document 2: Port of Philadelphia, Origin of ships arriving from France

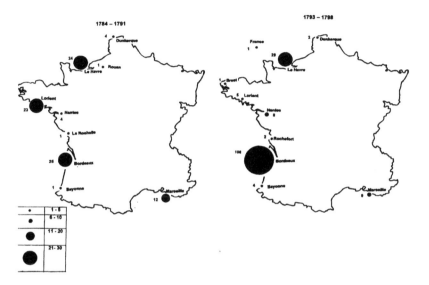

Sources: Pennsylvania State Archives, Harrisburg (PA), RG 41, Registers of Vessels entrances and clearances, 1784-1797; Historical Society of Pennsylvania, Philadelphia, Port of Philadelphia, Captains' Reports, 1797-1801.

Bordeaux was the most important French port in the eighteenth century. By 1789, the value of the trade carried on in the city equalled the value of all foreign trade of the United States. Besides the traditional export of regional products (wine and flour), its primacy was due to the increasing colonial trade. At the eve of the French Revolution, 40% of all French colonial trade was in the hands of Bordeaux's merchants. At the peak of its century-long commercial growth, Bordeaux's shipowners sent around 240 ships to the West Indies and 20 slavers to Africa. Bordeaux re-exported three-quarters of all imported sugar and coffee to Northern Europe – a traffic carried on in foreign bottoms[4]. Bordeaux's

---

4   On Bordeaux's trade in the eighteenth century, see P. Butel, *Les négociants bordelais, l'Europe et les Îles au XVIIIe siècle*, Paris 1974 (reprint 1996); J. Tarrade, *Le commerce colonial de la*

participation as an intermediary in colonial trade was determined by colonial legislation, which gave French ships and merchants a monopoly in the trade with its colonies. War, however, seriously affected this prosperous traffic, because French goods at sea were liable to seizure.

The Revolutionary wars had further disruptive effects. The slave revolts in Saint-Domingue in 1791 and 1793 and the destruction of plantations in the main French West Indian colony reduced the availability of West Indian goods. Moreover, Great Britain occupied Martinique in 1794. As the amount of colonial products arriving in Bordeaux severely diminished, its re-export trade collapsed. Traditional Bordeaux clients, such as the Hamburg merchants, turned to Great Britain and the United States in order to buy these goods[5].

Bordeaux's merchants, however, could rely on a solid and extensive network of correspondents and clients unaffected by the Revolution. War did not modify reduce demand, it just compelled merchants to find new ways to respond to it and to keep maritime trade alive despite all difficulties. Whereas the Royal Navy often blockaded other northern French ports, the southwestern ports such as Bordeaux had a comparative advantage.

Bordeaux's international trade employed all neutral flags, including those of small states like Papenburg and Kniphausen, which in fact covered French goods. Because of its proximity to the West Indies, where it had solid connexions, and because of its long-lasting neutrality, the United States acquired an increasing importance for Bordeaux's merchants. From the very beginning of the war, the volume of the American trade increased enormously. Document 3 clearly shows the path of its growth, as well as the decisive role played by its re-export trade: the United States became an emporium allowing all sorts of transactions considered illicit by the belligerents. American ships carried a great part of the trade between French and Spanish colonies and Europe.

American merchants imported colonial goods from the West Indies, paid the import duties, loaded them on other ships, and re-exported them, thus obtaining a drawback for the duty they had paid. The ships could thereafter sail back to the US with cargo for the West Indian, or any other market[6]. The impressive growth of American re-export trade was determined entirely by international politics. Growth began with the European war in 1793. The peace of Amiens in 1802-03

France à la fin de l'Ancien Régime. L'évolution du régime de l'exclusif de 1763 à 1789, Paris, 1972, 2 vols.; É. Saugera, *Bordeaux, port négrier,* XVIIe-XIXe s., Paris 1995.

5   S. Marzagalli, *"Les boulevards de la fraude". Le négoce maritime et le Blocus continental, 1806-1813: Bordeaux, Hambourg et Livorne,* Villeneuve d'Ascq 1999.

6   The most extensive study on American trade during the French Wars is still: A. Clauder, *American Commerce as Affected by the Wars of the French Revolution and Napoleon,* 1793-1812, Philadelphia 1932 (reprint 1972).

brought a temporary decline, but as soon as Great Britain and France were again at war, American trade exploded. It dropped again to the pre-war level in 1808, under the effect of British Orders in Council of November 1807, Napoleon's Milan decrees and Jefferson's embargo Act. The beginning of war between Great Britain and the United States affected the last part of the period. Given this situation, how did a port of a belligerent country like Bordeaux take advantage of the opportunities provided by American shipping and trade?

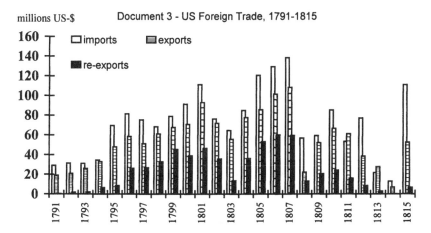

millions US-$ Document 3 - US Foreign Trade, 1791-1815

Sources: D.C. North, 'The United States Balance of Payments, 1790-1860', in: *Trends in American Economy in the Nineteenth Century* (1960). Each year begins on September 30 of the previous year.

American Shipping and Trade at Work: the example of Bordeaux

The study of maritime trade networks is often complicated by incomplete sources and various methodological problems connected with their use. For the study of American shipping and trade activities in Bordeaux, the registers of the American consul in Bordeaux, recording each US ship entering the port with quite an exhaustive set of data concerning the ownership, the voyage, and the cargo (see an example of record, document 4), are an excellent starting point[7].

---

7   The register for 1791 to 1795 is kept at the National Archives of the US (College Park, Maryland) [NA], but it seems to have been misplaced and cannot be consulted at present. As the register from 1795 to May 1797 has only recently be found, I could not include in the

Document 4: Example of Bordeaux consular records

present paper an analysis of all the data the volume provides (NA, RG 84, Bordeaux consulate, C20, vol. 215). I would like to thank Mr. Lawrence Marcus, of Dallas, Texas, who gave me access to the records of the register covering May 1797 to December 1804, which is privately owned. Without his help, this study would have been incomplete, as no other source covers this span of time. The register for December 1804 to November 1806 has disappeared, but lists compiled from this register are to be found in NA, RG 84, Bordeaux consulate, C20, vol. 222. The data in the two sets of documents is the same, but the latter is less complete on the inward cargo, and it makes no mention of the consignee in Bordeaux. The register recording entries from November 1806 to 1816 is kept at the NA, RG 84, Bordeaux consulate, C20, vol. 216.

However, no single source is exhaustive enough to reconstruct the complexity of a trade network. Historians have to cross-check the destination declared by the captain when leaving Bordeaux with other sets of data, such as entries of US-ports or the lists of ships captured by the British. However, there are structural limits to these types of sources, as a ship did not necessarily make a simple return voyage between two given ports. An example shall illustrate this point. The papers of the Brown family in Providence, Rhode Island[8], give insight into the venture of the ship *Charlotte*[9], which left Providence on October 1801, bound for Bilbao, Spain. After discharging freight in Bilbao, the *Charlotte* sailed to Bordeaux, where she entered on February 8, 1802. Tea, iron, nankeens and copper belonging to the shipowner were unloaded and the ship left again on April 25, with wine, brandy and dry goods valued at 45,000 F, declaring New Orleans as her final destination. In fact, the captain sold part of the goods in the West Indies[10], where he bought some rum and coffee, before getting back to Providence, where he entered on September 11 1802. The official records of Providence are not very useful for identifying the voyage of the *Charlotte* to France, as the ship left for Bilbao and entered from the West Indies[11]. On the other hand, the consular record of Bordeaux shows the ship as coming from Bilbao and leaving for New Orleans. No single port source can tell us the complete story of this voyage. In this case, surviving merchant papers made it possible to reconstruct the itinerary, but it is not possible for most shipping activities, for too few merchant papers have survived.

An accurate reconstruction of the trade and the shipping activities of a port is a requisite to analyse the ways a commercial network works. As no single source offers a complete picture, it is necessary to collect as much information as possible from different kinds of sources, the most useful for this case study being: American and French port records, consular reports, merchant papers,

---

8   I would like to express my gratitude to the John Carter Brown Library, Providence (RI), the Institut für Europäische Geschichte, Mainz (Germany), and the Peabody Essex Museum, Salem (Mass.) which have greatly facilitated this research project through their grants, as well as Temiber and the University of Bordeaux 3 which contributed to finance two research missions in the United States.

9   John Carter Brown Library, Providence (Rhode Island) [JCBL], Brown Family Papers, Ship Charlotte, V-C52, Box 52, and ship log; Bordeaux consular records (cp. note 7).

10 "I should have come immediately home from here with the ship & cargo but knowing the duties of the goods must be paid and the goods reshipped which would cause considerable expenses I thought it most advisable for your interest to try the market in Hispaniola", letter dated St. Thomas, July 21, 1802, to Brown & Ives. JCBL, Brown Family Papers, Ship Charlotte, V-C52, Box 52, folder 8.

11 NA, Records of the United States, RG 36, Port of Providence, Entries and Clearances, Custom House, vol. 3, microfilm copy kept at the Rhode Island Historical Society, ser. II, vol. 1.

notarial acts and commercial newspapers[12]. It is a time-consuming but rewarding task, which makes it possible, firstly, to quantify the phenomenon over time, and secondly, to identify trade patterns.

Document 5 shows trends in American shipping to Bordeaux since 1795, when their activities as carriers were impressive. It confirms the evolution shown by document 3, but the negative impact of the "Quasi-War" between France and the United States is much more evident here: diplomatic tensions between the two countries nearly stopped their commercial relations between 1798 and 1800. The first years of the nineteenth century are again a prosperous period; at that time, 150 to 200 American vessels entered the port of Bordeaux, a yearly figure which recalls the number of Bordeaux ships involved in colonial trade before the French Revolution. The American writer Washington Irving remarked during a short visit to Bordeaux in the summer of 1804 that US vessels literally obstructed the port[13].

Document 5 - US ships entering Bordeaux, February 1795 - 1814

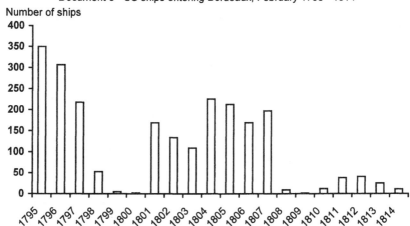

Number of ships

Sources: see note 7.

---

12 I have recorded all the data concerning US-ships entering Bordeaux with FileMaker, a data-base which does not oblige the user to define all the fields in advance. I am indebted to CNRS-director J.-P. Dedieu, of the Maison des Pays Ibériques - Temiber, who introduced me to this programme.

13 J.-P. Young, *Washington Irving à Bordeaux*, Vienne 1946, 160.

The medium-sized ships (177 tons in average for 1805) were perfectly apt for all sorts of trade. Three out of four came directly to Bordeaux from a port of the United States: they carried West Indian goods or North American products, less frequently Asian goods such as tea or nankeens. One US ship out of two entering Bordeaux in those years carried sugar or coffee, and a little more than one out of four arrived with cotton, fish, hides, rice, staves, tobacco, wax or some other American product. The rest arrived mainly from European or French ports, generally on ballast: their captains were looking for a return cargo (or wished to freight the vessel). Between 1807 and 1814, for instance, 333 American ships entered Bordeaux, but only 85 did not arrive directly from a US port. Seventy-nine of them were on ballast: they came from other French ports (44), Spain or Portugal (22) or Northern Europe (16). The 6 remaining ships, which carried cargo but did not arrive from the US, came from Tenerife (2), France (2), Mauritius (1) and Lisbon (1).[14]

American ships transported colonial goods of different origins to Bordeaux. A great deal of them had been produced in the French or former French West Indies. In July 1793, for instance, the house Dutilh & Wachsmuth of Philadelphia sent the brig *Harriot*, James Bently master, to Bordeaux with coffee they had imported on June 20th from Cap-Français (Saint-Domingue); two years later, the house sent on board the ship Harmony sugar and coffee imported from Saint-Pierre in La Martinique two weeks before, a French island which was by then occupied by the British[15]. American merchants acted in this case as intermediaries in customary trade relations between French West Indian planters and Bordeaux's merchants. However, colonial goods arriving in Bordeaux might have could be of different origin. On August 22, 1803, the brig *Humbird*, Kinsmon master, re-exported from Boston to Bordeaux 20 boxes of brown sugar which had been imported two weeks before from Havana by the ship *Veloz*, Nicolin master[16]. According to eighteenth-century colonial legislation, this sugar could have landed in Bordeaux only after having been previously sent to Spain. The war opened colonial markets to neutral trade and the United States replaced European mother-countries in colonial and trans-Atlantic exchanges.

The return cargo charged at Bordeaux generally consisted of wine, brandy and dry goods. The official destination of more than three American ships out of

---

14 See note 7.
15 Historical Society of Pennsylvania [HSP], C.W. Unger Collection, Dutilh & Wachsmuth, volume "*Outward Entries*" (1793-96).
16 Peabody Essex Museum (Salem, Mas.), Newburyport Custom House 282, 496: Abstract of drawbacks of duties payable in the district of Newburyport on goods, wares and merchandise exported from the US, 1802-1804.

four leaving Bordeaux was a port in the United States. Some left for Europe, and a few sailed to the Indian Ocean. The barque *Active* accomplished such a voyage, sailing from Salem on 11 November 1804, to Bordeaux, where she entered on 12 December 1804. Two months later, on 17 February 1805, the ship left Bordeaux for Tranquebar, a Danish and thus neutral port in the Indian Ocean. But the vessel was actually bound for the French colony of La Réunion, where she arrived on 13 October 1805. She was back in Salem on 11 February 1806, after a 15-month voyage[17]. The *Active* was not unique: four other American ships which had arrived in Bordeaux in 1805 left for Tranquebar; but in fact at least three of them sailed to the French Island of Mauritius[18]. Once again, American ships kept the connection between Bordeaux and the French colonies alive.

Even when the cargo was sent to the United States, it was in fact often only the first step to the final market, which was in the West Indies, Europe or Asia. The papers of the ship *Patty*, Egery master, revealed, for instance, that in November 1805 her owner, Isaac Roget, exported from New York to La Guadeloupe dry goods that had been imported from Bordeaux to New York on five different vessels (document 6)[19]. He had acquired these goods either directly in Bordeaux or from New York merchants of French origin, like himself. The very short time these goods stayed in New York confirms that they had been imported only to be immediately re-exported to the West Indies.

American merchants ordered the goods from their correspondents in Bordeaux according to their final market, as shown by the letter Jacob & Thomas Walden of New York who wrote to their Bordeaux consignee, Pierre Couderc junior :

"Our invoice p. the *Thomas* is smaller than we intended, in consequence of having engaged so many goods on freight, but the articles being of good quality we hope will command a good price. The proceeds we wish sent by return of the *Thomas* invested in sixty pipes good high proof Marmande brandy if not exceeding 240 francs, fifty casks good Claret *fit for the French West Indian Market* and such as is usually sent to this port, and the balance in Claret in boxes of 24 bottles each, *the quality suitable for the French West Indian market*, but not to exceed 24, 30 francs the box. [...] but if there should be peace, or very

---

17 Peabody Essex Museum, Logbook of the barque *Active*. See also, for the departure from Salem, ibid. Custom House Records, Salem & Beverly, 139, reel 7, Entrances and Clearances of Vessels. For the call in Bordeaux, see the Consular Records (cp. note 7).

18 NA, RG 84, Bordeaux consulate, C20, vol. 222 ; A. Toussaint, *La route de îles. Contribution à l'histoire maritime des Mascareignes*, Paris 1967. These three ships are the *Eliza*, the *Bordeaux Packet* and the *Ranger*.

19 New York Public Library [NYPL], Prizes Court of Admiralty, New York, ship *Patty*.

strong prospect of it, ship all our funds in brandy in small pipes. We wish the brandy in small pipes & to have it marked "Cognac". Mr. Mc Daniel a broker selected the cargo of the Brig *Patty* last winter for Mr. Jaber, which proved of good quality & *suited this market well.*"[20]

Document 6: Origin of some of the dry goods re-exported by the ship Patty, Egery master, from New York to La Guadeloupe (1805)

Products	quantity	Arrived on board	Imported on (d/m/y)	By	sold to Isaac Roget on
Taffetas	1 bale	ship *Amity*, from Bordeaux	23.10.1805	Jean Figuet, New York	7.11. 1805
Linen	2 bales				
Shoes		ship *Thomas*, from Bordeaux	30.10. 1805	Joseph Icard, New York	7.11. 1805
Flanders linen	1 bale				
Lawns	1 bale	ships *Hiram*, from Bordeaux, and *Mississippi*, from Nantes	26.10. 1805	Bertrand Dupoy, New York	5.11. 1805
Shawls, gloves	1 box				
Silks Stockings	1 bale				
Wine		ship *Nancy*, Olcott master, from Bordeaux	25.10. 1805	Isaac Roget, New York	--
Sugar Boilers	50				
Sugar Pots	910				
Clothes		ship *Maria*, from Bordeaux	5.7. 1805	Isaac Roget, New York	-

In this case, Jacob & Thomas Walden acted on their own account. However, despite official statements and papers stating that both the ship and her cargo belonged to a U.S. citizen, some ships sailing under American colours actually belonged to Frenchmen. More frequently, French merchants owned the cargo, which sailed under the cover of an American citizen. A part of the business

---

20 New York Historical Society [NYHS], BV Walden, 154-55, 31 May 1805.

between Bordeaux and the United States was therefore on account of French merchants, who accepted the risks associated with the trade.

By definition, American ships belonged to citizens of the United States. There were two ways for a Frenchman to put his own ship under American colours. The first one consisted of acquiring American citizenship, a procedure requiring him to settle in the United States. I will analyse this aspect later on, when describing the geographical mobility of Bordeaux's merchants. The second way was for an American citizen to accept formal ownership of the vessel, and receive a commission for this service. In August 1799, the account between Laurens Huron, a citizen of the United States of French origin living in Philadelphia, and Pierre Laguerenne of Bordeaux, showed the former charging to the latter the expenses of fitting out and laying up the brig *Bee*, and crediting to his favour the product of the freight of this vessel. The *Bee*, which carried a wine cargo to Laurens Huron and sailed thereafter to Hamburg, clearly belonged to Laguerenne[21]. The notarial records of Bordeaux provide other examples of French vessels operating under American colours: the *Suzette*, for instance, was a 275-ton ship belonging to the well-known Bordeaux house of Pierre Sauvage & Co., but she sailed as the *Mary Ann*, with John Juhel of New York appearing as the official owner. On the 13 April 1805, she entered Bordeaux from New York, but carried a freight of sugar and coffee charged at La Guadeloupe[22]. When France admitted the use of a flag of truce - the French Marine Department authorised at least 43 Bordeaux ships to sail under the American flag from 1803 onwards[23] - the US-consul in Bordeaux considered this practice as an abuse. Between May 1803 and April 1805, nevertheless, the consul granted American papers to 51 ships fitted out in Bordeaux, although he estimated that at least forty-two were in fact French property[24].

Even when the ships belonged to American merchants they could be used to transport goods on the accounts of Bordeaux merchants, who chose the products and accepted the business risks. The orders given by American shipowners to their captain or supercargo generally instructed them to freight the ship or to load a return cargo according to the freight rate and the prices of goods they would find in Bordeaux. The house Reed & Forde of Philadelphia, for instance,

---

21 HSP, *Laurens Huron papers*, 1 vol., August 1799.

22 Archives départementales de la Gironde, Bordeaux (AdG), 3 E Romegous, 27 and 28 brumaire XIV (17 and 18 November 1805) ; 3 E 24320, 29 brumaire and 1 frimaire XIV (20 and 22 November 1805).

23 Archives Nationales de Paris, Marine FF2 109, "Guerre de 1803 - bâtiments neutralisés - listes générales". ADG, 8M195, "Etat des bâtiments".

24 NA, T 164, reel 2, Dispatches from the United States Consul in Bordeaux, William Lee to the State Secretary Armstrong, 26 April 1805.

wrote to the supercargo of the *Tristram*, leaving for Bordeaux in 1794: "Although it will be very desirable for the Ship to return to Philadelphia early, still if such freight offer as should make the charter a great object, and you can get payment in hand to secure it, we shall not complain if you accept it"[25].

Freight was indeed rewarding. At the end of July 1805, captain Jeremiah Paul freighted his ship *George* for 21,000 Francs (4,200 US-$) to carry passengers to the Swedish Island of Saint Bartholomew[26]. The freight paid in 1805 to export flour and wheat to southern Spain varied from 130 to 150 Francs per ton, plus 15% premium[27]. The house Dutilh & Wachsmuth of Philadelphia gained $3,342 for the freight of the 255-ton *Pilgrim* on a voyage from Philadelphia to Bordeaux in 1806[28]. These examples show that a merchant could repay a ship within a couple of voyages.

It is impossible to ascertain the occurrence of French freights in American ships, as there is no single source recording this aspect exhaustively. Bordeaux's notarial records mention the fact only when a major problem occurred before the ship's departure[29]. I found 10 cases out of a total of 214 American ships sailing from Bordeaux in 1805[30], but references to freight are ubiquitous in merchant correspondence and the actual rate of French property on American ships was certainly much higher.

When they freighted an American ship, Bordeaux merchants traded on their own account. Officially, the goods always belonged to American citizens, as the British seized enemy cargoes even on neutral ships. US-merchants, however, often neutralised goods belonging to their French correspondents, and took a commission. Writing in November 1804 to his correspondent in New York, Dupont de Nemour Victor & Co. – a firm run by the former French consul at Philadelphia, who was the elder son of the famous French economist – the Bordeaux merchant Honorat Lainé asked him to send some Madeira wine and wax, and added: "You will take all possible precautions in order to neutralise this transaction and you will do the insurance at your place, the correspondence will

---

25 HSP, 541, Reed & Forde papers, letterbook, 6 January 1794.
26 AdG, 3E notary Romegous, 5 vendémiaire an XIV (27 September 1805).
27 AdG, 3 E, notaries Maillares and Romegous, different acts.
28 Hagley Museum and Library (Wilmington, Delaware) Dutilh and Wachsmuth papers, 1247.
29 See for instance the declaration of G. Videau, stevedore (*arrimeur juré*) of the port of Bordeaux, declining any responsibility in case of the 600 barrels of flour charged on freight by P. Lucadou on the brig *Nereïde* of Boston for San Lucar. The stevedore has informed Lucadou about the problem. AdG, 3E 31401, Maillares notary, 22 prairial XIII (11 June 1805).
30 AdG, 3 E, Barbarie, Maillares, Romegous and Sejourné. No other mention in the acts of the other Bordeaux notaries.

obviously not show that this goes on account of a Frenchman"[31]. If the correspondence had to mention such invoices, the merchants sent their letters on other ships in order to avoid detection, in case the British visited the vessel carrying the neutralised cargo. On the 13th June 1795, Gouverneur & Kemble of New York wrote to Jona Jones, a Quaker merchant living in Bordeaux since at least 1785: "We shipped you 16 casks of indigo and a few goods on account of Bouquier - apparently on our account to the consignment of c[aptain] Rutgers in the ship *Briseis* who engaged with us upon his arrival to hand over the Invoice and Bill of Loading to you"[32]. Gouverneur & Kemble sent this letter two weeks after the departure of the *Briseis*.

If correspondence was often allusive, account books might reveal the real property of a cargo. On August 16th, 1797, Laurens Huron of Philadelphia declared in the invoice accompanying the sugar, coffee and cotton shipped on the *Benjamin Franklin* to Pierre Laguerenne in Bordeaux that these goods were on his own account. But on the same day, Huron charged these goods to Laguerenne with a 2,5% commission in his account books [33]. Obviously, this shipment belonged to the Bordeaux merchant. Bordeaux's merchants employed the same neutralising practices when exporting from France. When A. Armstrong, a Bordeaux merchant, charged Hugues Wilson, leaving on the *Three Sisters* for Charleston, with selling 232 hogsheads of red wine, 69 cases of 24 bottles each of Médoc wine, and 57 cases of 12 bottles each of white wine, he stated in front of a notary that these goods belonged to Armstrong even if they officially appeared as property of captain Joseph Clark[34].

Although documents concerning neutralised goods were frequent, they cannot provide a comprehensive picture. It is therefore impossible to quantify how often the cargoes sailing in American vessels belonged to French merchants. What is certain, however, is that they were far from being passive in light of the difficulties of the war. At least some of them found ways to carry on trade. Who were they, and how did they act in order to build up their trade network ?

---

31 Bibliothèque Municipale de Bordeaux [BMBx], Mss. 1041, letterbook of Honorat Lainé, 174v, to Dupont de Nemour Victor & Cie, 9 November 1804. Original in French.

32 NYHS, BV Gouverneur & Kemble, letterbook, p. 299, 13 June 1795, to J. Jones (Bordeaux).

33 HSP, *Laurens Huron papers*, 1 vol., 16 August 1797.

34 AdG, 3E 21396, notary Sejournet, 7 messidor XIII (26 June 1803).

Men at Work: building the network

Like most trade networks in modern times, the one linking Bordeaux to the United States was extensively built on human mobility. A striking feature, for instance, is the high number of French surnames amongst the American shipowners sending a vessel to Bordeaux and of English names amongst the consignees in Bordeaux.

The massive departure of the French planters who fled Saint-Domingue in the 1790s contributed to the establishment of links between US-ports and Bordeaux, as many of the West Indian colonists belonged to Bordeaux families[35]. Other merchants came directly from Bordeaux. The result of this migration was a strong presence of Bordeaux merchants in the main ports of the United States, on whom the network between the United States and Bordeaux partly relied.

An analysis of the shipowners of 632 ships fitted out in New York and Philadelphia and arriving in Bordeaux between May 1797 and December 1814 reveals the importance of merchant migration. Nine shipowners in this sample fitted out more than 10 vessels, totalling almost one quarter of all New York and Philadelphia shipments to Bordeaux. In Philadelphia, they were Abraham Piesch (17), Augustin Bousquet (14), John William [later J.B.] Foussat (13) and Louis (Lewis) Crousillat (12); in New York, Stephen Jumel [& Desobry] (40), G. Main & Ebenezer Stevens (individually or in partnership) (20), Elisha Leavenworth (14), Isaac Roget (14) and Gouverneur & Kemble (11).

At least five of these 9 houses – Jumel, Bousquet, Foussat, Roget and Crousillat – were led by Frenchmen who had obtained American citizenship[36]. A sixth one, Abraham Piesch, was a Swiss[37]. Stephen (or rather Étienne) Jumel was born in Bordeaux in 1754; owner of a coffee plantation in Saint-Domingue, he settled in the United States in 1795. Two years later, he acquired American citizenship. At the beginning of the nineteenth century, he took Victor Prosper Benjamin Desobry as his partner, a Frenchman who became an American citizen in 1803[38]. Augustin Bousquet, born in Beaulieu (Hérault), had come to the

---

35 J. De Cauna, *L'eldorado des Aquitains. Gascons, Basques et Béarnais aux îles d'Amérique, XVII-XVIIIe siècles*, Biarritz 1998.

36 A. Ritter, *Philadelphia and her merchants 50 & 70 years ago*. Philadelphia 1860, 71. NA, T 164, reel 2, Dispatches from the United States Consul in Bordeaux: List of Vessels Papers taken from the captain by William Lee and sent to General Armstrong, 1805.

37 Ritter, *Philadelphia*, 20.

38 The partnership between S. Jumel and John Dupan ended on April 30, 1801; after this date, the house name was "S. Jumel": Benjamin Desobry was a partner, but his name did not officially appear. A new change took place on February 11, 1805. NYHS, Jumel papers, Box 4, Business

United States in 1793 and applied for American citizenship in September 1795 [39]. His brother Jean, who lived with him in Philadelphia in 1795, led the house of Bousquet, Anthoine & Co. in Bordeaux for some years afterwards. John William (Jean-Guillaume) Foussat had been in the United States since the beginning of the 1790s and became an American citizen in 1798[40]. His brother Justin was a well-known merchant in Bordeaux[41]. Finally, Isaac Roget belonged to a Jewish family of Bordeaux, where his brother lived. The Roget family had interests in the West Indies[42]. Further research may evaluate the presence of Bordeaux merchants in the United States more precisely, but this sample shows that they were a key element at least amongst the houses of the two major US-ports that were more directly involved in trade with Bordeaux. However, French merchants were undoubtedly less important in smaller ports, for instance in Salem, Mass., which fitted out 65 ships to Bordeaux between May 1797 and December 1814 and where no French surnames appear amongst the shipowners.

Whereas Frenchmen settled in the United States, American merchants came to Bordeaux. Since June 1790, Bordeaux had an American consul, Joseph Fenwick, who moved from his native Maryland to Bordeaux in 1787 and entered into partnership with the Virginian John Mason a year later. After a short stay in Bordeaux, Mason took over the firm in Georgetown, Maryland, whereas Fenwick directed the business in Bordeaux until 1799, when he was suspended from his consular functions because of the quasi-war between France and the United States[43]. William Lee, who took over the consulate in 1801, was also a merchant[44].

mss. See also J. CHASE, 'War on Trade and Trade in War: Stephen Jumel and New York Maritime Commerce (1793-1815)', in: *Bulletin du Centre d'histoire des Espaces Atlantiques*, 4 (1988), 111-161, here 120; and NYPL, Prize Court of Admiralty. New York, ship *Eugenia*.

39 NYPL, *Prize Court of Admiralty*. Philadelphia, vol. 2, ship *Zulema*. Philadelphia Naturalization Records. *An index of records of Aliens' declarations of Intention and/or oaths of allegiances*, 1789-1880 - Philadelphia, ed. by P. W. Filby. Detroit 1982.

40 NYPL, *Prize Court of Admiralty*. Philadelphia, vol. 2, ship *Zulema*.

41 P. Butel, 'Guerre et commerce sous la Révolution et l'Empire: les négociants français et le "refuge" américain', in: *Revue d'histoire économique et sociale*, 55 (1977), 433-451, here 438; Philadelphia Naturalisation Records, in: *An index of records of Aliens' declarations of Intention and/or oaths of allegiances*.

42 NA, T 164, reel 2, Dispatches from the United States Consul in Bordeaux: List of Vessels Papers taken from the captain by William Lee and sent to General Armstrong, 1805.

43 See S. Marzagalli, 'Un Américain à Bordeaux. Joseph Fenwick, premier consul des États-Unis', in: *Revue historique de Bordeaux et du département de la Gironde*, 3rd serie, 1 (2002), 73-90.

44 On W. Lee, see M. Lee Mann, *A Yankee Jeffersonian. Selections from the Diary and Letters of William Lee of Massachusetts, written from 1796 to 1840*, Cambridge (Mass.) 1959.

But consuls were neither the only, nor the first American merchants to establish houses in France. One of the pioneers was Jonathan Jones, born in Philadelphia in 1748, son of John Jones and Sarah Miflin. He arrived in Bordeaux before 1785, when he married Jeanne, daughter of the Bordeaux merchant Pierre Texier[45]. Jones was a Quaker[46], the Texiers were Huguenots. Other American merchants settled in Bordeaux after the beginning of the Revolutionary wars. Robert Andrews of Philadelphia arrived in 1799 and lived in Bordeaux until 1817, when he moved to Le Havre[47]. Although he traded on his own account, he was chiefly a commissioner, the bulk of his business consisting of receiving consignments from the United States[48]. Daniel Strobel, of South Carolina, led one of the biggest merchant firms of Bordeaux at the end of the 1790s, but his house "Strobel & Martini" failed at the end of 1803[49]. By 1805, Gothard Martini entered into partnership with another American merchant, John Archer Morton, who traded extensively with the United States[50]. Daniel Strobel became the next American consul in Bordeaux in 1815. In the 1830s, he was back in New York, his son succeeding him as consul[51].

In order to evaluate the involvement of Bordeaux houses in the trade with the United States, it is necessary to analyse the consignees' names of the cargoes arriving in American vessels. From the end of November 1806 to 1814, two firms were outstanding: John Lewis Brown received 57 of the 330 ships for which the consignee's name was recorded (that is, 18% of the total) and John

---

45 P. Meller, *État civil des familles bordelaises avant la Révolution; mariages. Bordeaux 1909:* protestant marriage of February 8th, 1785.

46 See the process between Jona Jones and the former (Catholic) American consul at Bordeaux, Fenwick, who insisted that Jones should swear in the name of God: BMBx, Factums, J 440/4, 10 'Mémoire pour le Sieur Jona Jones contre les Sieurs Fenwick, Masson et Cie', 1809.

47 J. Campbell, 'Saint-Domingue Refugees in Philadelphia ', in: *Records of the American Catholic Historical Society*, 28 (1917), 97-125; 213-243, here 225.

48 See the oath of R. Andrews, published by Campbell, 'Saint-Domingue refugees in Philadelphia'.

49 The news of this bankruptcy and the amount of the debt (ca. 1 million US $) shocked the merchant world: "Strobel & Martini have failed if I understood geometrical proportion I would understate to tell you the supposed amount", wrote John Crowninshield, then in Bordeaux, to his firm Crowninshield & sons, Salem on 8 January 1804. Essex Institute, Salem (Ma), Crowninshield Family Papers, MSS, MH-15, Box 4, folder 9 - Letterbook of John Crowninshield captain, France 1803-04. The Crowninshield lost 20 000 $ in this bankruptcy.

50 Information provided by Leon Cohen of Bordeaux in a letter to J. Crowninshield of Salem: Peabody Essex Museum, Crowninshield Family Papers, MSS 4, Box 5, folder 1, letter of December 2, 1805. Gothard Martini was born in Mittau, Lettony: AdG, 3L 179, 7 July 1793, passport request to St Thomas (Danish West Indies).

51 Peabody Essex Museum, Crowninshield Family Papers, MSS 4, Box 5, folder 1, letter of Daniel Strobel to J. Crowninshield, New York, 1 June 1833.

Archer Morton 38 (12%). John Lewis Brown was a Scot and his father lived in Denmark. His mother, born a Fenwick, belonged to a Swedish-Danish family related to the Huguenot merchants of Bordeaux, but was apparently no relation of the Catholic American consul of Bordeaux of the 1790s. A letter of 1806 states that Brown's partner was in New York, where he also sent his two sons in 1811, the nineteen-year old Robert David and his eighteen-year-old brother David[52]. John Archer Morton (from 1811 in partnership with Russel) was an American, as were Jonathan Jones (consignee of 15 ships) and Robert Andrews (10 ships). The most important French consignee was Justin Foussat (13 ships), whose brother lived in Philadelphia.

The primacy of American houses amongst the main consignees of US-ships is not at odds with the importance of Frenchmen amongst the American firms involved in this trade network. It is quite possible that American shipowners who sent a ship on their own account preferred to rely on an American house in Bordeaux, whereas Bordeaux merchants freighted American ships, and French merchants settled in the United States kept on corresponding with French houses in Bordeaux.

American shipowners who were not acquainted with the Bordeaux market, charged their captain or supercargo with selling the goods and buying the return cargo. This was, however, a time-consuming task for the captain, and if the prices were low at his arrival, the adventure quickly turned into a loss. Moreover, as the captain tried to acquire a return cargo with as little delay as possible in order to reduce expenses the quality of the products he bought was often low. For these reasons, the establishment of a efficient trade network required merchants to rely on someone at the port of destination who decided to sell the incoming cargo or to store it if prices were low. This commissioner also provided a good return cargo. If he opened a credit account with the American house, there was no need to wait for the sale of the inward cargo in order to buy the outward products, thus reducing the stay of the vessel in Bordeaux and the costs.

There were many ways to find reliable Bordeaux houses. Correspondence, conversation and recommendation were standard practices to find a good commissioner. The Bordeaux merchant Honorat Lainé advised a French merchant who began his trade in New York: "Think carefully before making a decision ; you have to choose good friends and try to find out the solidity of the

---

52 NYPL, Thomas Williams papers, William Williams junior (Bordeaux) to his father William (Stonington), 28 October 1806: "Mr. Brown's partner is in N. Yk, no doubt you will see him"; AdG, passports (see footnote 65); Jean CAVIGNAC, *Les vingt-cinq familles. Les négociants bordelais sous Louis-Philippe*, Bordeaux, (Cahiers de l'I.A.E.S. n° 6) 1985, 107-108.

houses you will be dealing with. The Houses at our place on which you can take bills safely are Jona Jones, J[usti]n Foussat, John Gernon, Bousquet & Antoine, Hourquebie frères. These houses deal with New York and Philadelphia. I might be forgetting some of them, but I advise you to choose amongst those I listed"[53].

A common practice to start trade with a new firm, was to begin with a small invoice, and to see if the commissioner dealt with the business satisfactorily before sending more valuable cargo. Writing to Peter Hurtel, who in May 1805 had sailed to Bordeaux on the *Thomas* and settled there, Isaac Roget of New York encouraged his zeal by promising him future consignments: "I rely on your activity in making me the most expeditions and quick returns, and those very frequently, and well executed, that I might be encouraged to continue my consignments with the greatest confidence which you merit, your first essays will no doubt determine my further Shipments"[54]. With regard to the same 206-ton vessel, her shipowners Jacob and Thomas Walden wrote to Peter Couderc junior in Bordeaux: "Favoured by the introduction of Mr. Delorthe, we have consigned to you the *Thomas*, captain Gardner, together with 25 h[ogshea]ds sugar, ten bales cotton, four thousands staves, & a quantity of logwood (...) p. Invoice and bill of loading, this we wish to sell to the best advantage on our a/c & render us a/c sales of each article separately to enable us to make calculations in future. The vessel is loaded mostly on freight [...]. It is our wish to have the *Thomas* return directly home [...]. We intend the vessel for a regular trader, if on this first experiment our expectations are realised, to do that & render the voyage profitable, every means of dispatch and economy must be used, & as captain Gardner is a stranger in Bordeaux we particularly request you will give him every necessary advice & assistance"[55].

The business turned out not to be very satisfactory. Walden believed that Couderc sold his goods "when the market was the most unfavourable" and complained above all about the price and the duties Couderc charged on the return cargo. In his correspondence, Walden made a comparison with "some wine of equal quality" shipped at the same time, which was considerably cheaper and which was charged lower duties in Bordeaux, therefore showing his correspondent that he was not naïve. "If these are errors you will of course correct them, if on the contrary you have given so very high a price for our wines, we suppose we must submit - yet in this case it appears strange that duties

---

53 BMBx, Ms 1041, Letterbook of H. Lainé, 17, to Dupré at New York , 22.12.03. Original in French.

54 NYPL, *Prize Court of Admiralty*, New York, vol. 1, ship *Enterprize*.

55 NYHS, *BV Walden*, 154-55, 31 May 1805. See note 20 for the following passage of this interesting letter.

on the same kind of wine, at same time & by same vessel should so materially differ. This observation will apply to most of the other charges, which you will observe on comparison of the two invoices. We do not wish to make complaints in a business we are not toughly acquainted with, yet these observations strike us too forcibly to pass without notice"[56].

In November 1805, Walden sent the *Thomas* once more to Bordeaux, but this time he trusted the captain with the sale of the cargo. For the third venture of the *Thomas* to Bordeaux, Walden gave captain Turner "full power to adjust and settle the account with you [Couderc]"[57].

In order to avoid the problems met by Walden, other American merchants preferred to get into personal contact with their correspondents across the Ocean, and acquire some knowledge of the products. The Philadelphia merchant Daniel Coxe, for instance, sailed as supercargo on the *Tristram* to Bordeaux in 1793. It was a joint venture with the house Reed & Forde, and apparently their first venture in Bordeaux. However, Reed & Forde had already sent some shipments to Marseille. Therefore they asked their correspondent in Marseille to introduce Coxe to other French houses, as Coxe "goes under an expectation of making large and advantageous shipments of articles calculated for our Market and the West Indies and probably will visit the principal Manufactures in France"[58]. The young William Williams of Stonington (Connecticut) wrote shortly after his arrival in Bordeaux about his intention of learning to speak French fluently before travelling around in France: "My object is to make myself known"; and therefore asked his father to procure him letters of recommendation from "merchants of good respectability" in New York and Boston to introduce him to their French correspondents. After nine months in France, he claimed in a letter to his brother, a merchant at New York: "at present I have an understanding with the different manufacturing from the interior from whence I shall make all further purchases in case I should be disposed to [...]. I defy almost every Frenchman to dupe me now"[59].

By 1795, Gouverneur & Kemble already had a trustworthy correspondent in Bordeaux in the person of Jonathan Jones. They sent cargoes to him and, among other things, relied on him to assist a young captain: "We have made a considerable shipment in the ship *Briseis*, captain Rutgers, under his direction

---

56 NYHS, *BV Walden*, 255, 27 November 1805.

57 NYHS, *BV Walden*, 358, 3 May 1806.

58 HSP, 541, Reed & Forde papers, letterbook; letter of December 27th, 1793 to Testard & Gerin of Marseille; instruction to Daniel Coxe, 6 January 1794.

59 NYPL, Thomas Williams papers, William Williams junior (Bordeaux) to his father William (Stonington), 28 October 1806, and from Nantes to his brother Thomas (New York), 26 August 1807.

who will probably hand you this letter and we recommend him to you in a particular manner. He is a young man we confide very much in, connected in the House of Mrss. Rutgers, Seaman & Ogden, and who has in great measure been brought up under us. Most probably he will value on you or some other good house to manage his business - as his cargo is valuable".

They relied on Jones also for information: "Great seems the rage of speculations to France and we wish to know from you if some valuable property was sent, can it be sold and the specie had for it - or such bills as would answer to convey to England & by way of Hamburg. It is of such serious moment that a prudent man ought to see his way clear in a thing of magnitude". Probably wishing to increase their trade to France, in 1795 they sent Sam Gouverneur over, the brother of one of the partners of the house, who had just returned from a voyage to the West Indies. His mission was to prospect markets in Le Havre and Paris, before going to Bordeaux to have "a personal interview with you [J. Jones] "[60].

There were in fact a number of American merchants travelling to Bordeaux as well as Bordeaux merchants to the United States. From November 1806 to December 1813, 90 Bordeaux merchants applied for a passport to the United States, their favourite destination at that time[61]. When they left, they probably had power of attorney from other Bordeaux merchants, enabling them to settle business more quickly and at a lower cost. On his return journey to the United States, Joseph Lopès-Dias, a Jewish Bordeaux merchant living in New York, got power of attorney from 29 insurers of the ship *Harmonie* [62]. Another traditional means merchants used to establish new trade relations was to send their children abroad for their commercial training. For instance, the two grandchildren of the most famous eighteenth-century Bordeaux merchant, François Bonnaffé, were both in New York in 1806[63].

In establishing links across the Ocean, religious solidarity might have played a role. Due to the importance of Jews in Bordeaux[64], it is particularly interesting

60 NYHS, *BV Gouverneur & Kemble, letterbook,* 174, 274 and 299, 22 January, 30 May and 13 June 1795, to J. Jones at Bordeaux.

61 S. Marzagalli, 'Les voyages des négociants bordelais à l'étranger à l'époque napoléonienne', in: *Bulletin du Centre d'histoire des Espaces Atlantiques,* 6 (1993), 137-150.

62 AdG, 3E 13289, notary Trimoulet, 4 prairial an XIII (24 May 1805), substitution in favour of J. Lopès-Dias of the power of attorney originally given by the 29 insurers to J.F. Thebaud, a New York merchant then at Bordeaux.

63 ADG, notary Romegous, statement, 18 October 1806.

64 S. Marzagalli, 'Atlantic Trade and Sephardim Merchants in eighteenth-century France: the Case of Bordeaux', in: P. Bernardini and N. Fiering (eds.), *The Jews and the Expansion of Europe to the West, 1493 to 1800,* Providence2001, 268-286.

to follow the strategies of this group. At least 26 Bordeaux Jews sailed to the United States between 1793 and 1815[65], and amongst them Moïse Gradis, one of the two brothers leading the most famous eighteenth-century Jewish house of Bordeaux. Gradis settled in Philadelphia from 1794 to 1801. His correspondence shows him desperately trying to recover his property both in Haiti and in La Martinique, whereas he did not seem to make any serious attempt to organise a consistent flow of trade to Bordeaux[66]. Other Bordeaux Jews, on the contrary, like Jacob Furtado or Benjamin Roget, applied for US citizenship and got involved in trade. By 1808, Benjamin Roget had apparently made some considerable profits in the United States and was back in Bordeaux[67].

Conclusion

The establishment of new commercial links in modern times required high short-term (voyages) as well as long-term mobility (commercial training, acquiring foreign citizenship, founding a firm). Networks largely relied on familial and religious solidarities across the Ocean, and benefited from politically-determined diasporas and migrations (French *émigrés*, the Haitian revolution). This human mobility intensified the network of correspondents, who provided information on markets and prices. Information circulated through travellers, letters and captains. It enabled merchants to make decisions about the opportunities for venturing ships and goods across the Atlantic, thus establishing a regular trade flow. The result of French and American merchant activities at the end of the 18th century was an impressive traffic between Bordeaux and the United States.

---

65 AdG, passports, 3L 179-180; 3L 183-187; 4 M 677 to 692 and Archives Nationales, Paris, F7 3542 (1812-1813). I have considered as Jews only those people listed by Jean Cavignac, *Dictionnaire du Judaïsme bordelais aux XVIIIe et XIXe siècles: biographies, généalogies, professions, institutions*, Bordeaux 1987.

66 The private correspondence of Moïse Gradis is kept at the AdG, fonds Gradis, 1 MI 315(B2), 318(B1), 319(B1) et 332(B1). His letterbook to the West Indies is kept at Roubaix, Archives Nationales du Monde du Travail, 180 AQ 7. I am indebted to Mr. Henry Gradis who kindly authorised me to consult his family archives. On the Gradis family, see J. de Maupassant, *Un grand armateur de Bordeaux, Abraham Gradis, 1699-1780*, Bordeaux 1931; J. Schwob D'Hericourt, *La maison Gradis et ses chefs*, Argenteuil 1975; R. Menkis, *The Gradis Family of eighteenth-century Bordeaux: a social and economic study*, Ph.D.-thesis, Brandeis University, Massachusetts 1988.

67 A letter of Gradis to him states "depuis ton arrivée d'Amérique j'avais appris que tes bénéfices te laissaient le loisir de te livrer à ton goût pour les lettres". Roubaix, Archives Nationales du Monde du Travail, 180 AQ 8, letterbook p. 117, to Benjamin Roget (Castelmoron), 11 October 1808.

For the first time in their history, American merchants were able to participate actively in world-wide maritime enterprises, the international context of war offering them unique opportunities to increase their business. Their trade with the West Indies, which began long before the French Revolution, increased dramatically: this fact can help to better understand the future attitude of the United States in this area.

While there is no doubt among scholars that American merchants and shipowners were dynamic, research shows that merchants of belligerent countries also played an active role. American ships helped to sustain traffic across the Oceans, but often the trade they carried on went on account of French merchants. This study leads to a reassessment of the current image of decline of Bordeaux during the French Wars and of the alleged passive attitude of French entrepreneurs. In fact, many Bordeaux merchants were involved in this traffic. The most active amongst them sent a partner or an agent to the United States. Other French merchants benefited from their international reputation to obtain commissions. For American merchants, Bordeaux and France were just one amongst many possible markets and destinations. But for the Bordeaux merchants, this link was vital. It is therefore understandable that they were eager to contribute to the construction of this new commercial web.

Thanks to this trade network, Bordeaux did not loose its function as an international trade centre during the long-lasting French wars, although the port never recovered the primacy it had in eighteenth-century France. The trade to the United States helped merchants to survive and to continue their business after 1815. Peace weakened their links to the United States, as Bordeaux merchants could establish again direct links to their colonies and to Northern Europe. Some Bordeaux inhabitants still sought their fortune in the United States after 1815[68], but the volume of imports decreased. Later in the nineteenth century, Bordeaux exported consistent quantities of wine to the United States.

Finally, this study shows that merchants were largely able, through their international networks, to circumvent the attempts of the belligerents to stop the enemy's maritime trade. This underlines the potential conflict between merchants' market-oriented logic and official aims, and raises the more general question of the impact of national policies on commercial networks.

---

68 See the references to Bordeaux migrants in É. Saugera, 'D'un Sud à l'autre : exilés, engagés et esclaves en Alabama au début du XIXe siècle', in: *Bulletin de l'Institut Aquitain d'Études Sociales*, 76 (2001), 123-151. This article retraced the activities of the Colonial Society of French Emigrants (1816), whose Vice-President was William Lee, the former US-consul at Bordeaux, and their attempts to settle a plantation colony in Alabama.

The Members of the Mersey Docks & Harbour Board Re-Visited: 1895-1936

Adrian Jarvis

Introduction: the origins of this paper

In 1989 I became interested in a merchant named Harold Littledale, a member of the Mersey Docks & Harbour Board who frequently attacked his colleagues and the Board's Engineer-in-Chief on matters related to the cost and design of new works on the dock estate during the 1870s and '80s.[1] This was, of course, continuously the most important issue facing the Board then and for a considerable time afterwards, because of the implications for future revenue which hung on effective investment.

Almost all of Littledale's charges proved sustainable to some degree, which conflicted with the success stories of dock construction presented by Mountfield and Hyde,[2] but more importantly it raised a different question. G. F. Lyster, the Engineer-in-Chief, appears at first sight to have been personally blamed for major errors, either directly in things which he designed himself or indirectly where he authorised unsuitable designs by his subordinates. However, the buck did not stop there: he was responsible to the Works Committee of the Board, which was in turn responsible to the Board proper.

The question arose, therefore, that if Lyster, for much of his long term in office the highest-paid salaried engineer in the country, could make major errors without incurring the wrath of the Board, what was going on in the meetings which provided him with his brief, approved his plans and oversaw their execution? The Board was, after all, supposedly made up of 28 of the best business brains in Liverpool acting disinterestedly for the furtherance of the trade of the port.[3] Yet I found some decisions of considerable stupidity and,

---

1   A. Jarvis, 'Harold Littledale: The man with a mission', in: H. Hignett (ed.), *A Second Merseyside Maritime History*, Liverpool 1991.

2   S. Mountfield, *Western Gateway*, Liverpool 1965; F. E. Hyde, *Liverpool and the Mersey*, Newton Abbot 1971.

3   The Board was established by the Mersey Docks & Harbour Board Act 1857 to take over the powers and duties, assets and liabilities of the Trustees of the Liverpool Docks, which was effectively under the control of Liverpool Corporation and widely believed to be far from

equally seriously, a *penchant* for wasting time in meetings by discussing issues of mind-numbing triviality.[4]

Some possible explanations occurred to me.[5] One could rule out inherent stupidity or dishonesty: there may have been the occasional stupid or dishonest member, but obviously not enough of them to form a permanent majority on the Board over a period of decades. More likely was that the Board became, in the words of an England rugby captain, a gathering of '57 old farts'[6] through their being too old when first elected, through remaining on the Board too long, or both.

A second hypothesis was that the Members were not the best business brains in the city at all, but sons, nephews or grandsons of earlier generations of best brains, now busily enacting the 'clogs-to-clogs syndrome' by receiving a 'liberal education' at a public school, studying the classics at Oxford or Cambridge, buying a house in the country and making occasional visits to Liverpool for meetings.[7]

A third possibility was that members pursued their own outside interests when making decisions at Board, in other words that they were not disinterested. In theory, acting as the representative of a particular trade was forbidden,[8] but in practice the best way of containing strife between different interest-groups within the Board was to allow specific trade associations to make nominations, and this procedure became increasingly overt. While investigating those hypotheses it became clear that members were, typically, involved in a great many other activities, leading to the testing of a final hypothesis which was simply that members tried to do so many things that the chance of them discharging their considerable responsibilities as Board members was minimal.

---

disinterested. The Board had no statutory objective except making and keeping the port's customers happy and itself solvent.

4 For examples, see A. Jarvis, *Liverpool Central Docks 1799-1905*, Stroud 1991, Chapter 6.

5 The following section is a brief reprise of the arguments advanced in A. Jarvis, 'The Members of the Mersey Docks & Harbour Board and Their Way of Doing Business 1858-1905', in: *International Journal of Maritime History*, 6 (1994), 121-39.

6 W. Carling, speaking of the Rugby Football Union.

7 Even accepting Rubinstein's argument that such cases were rare, they still existed, e.g. Henry Bright, son of the innovative Australia Packet owner Samuel Bright. Bright Jnr. (Rubgy and Trinity Cambridge) is remembered only because his literary work secured him a place in the *Dictionary of National Biography*.

8 M.K. Burton, General Manager and Secretary, specifically denied any question of trade representation in evidence before the Royal Commission to Enquire into the Administration of the Port of London, BPP 1902 (6708), XLIII, 222. He was lying.

The method employed was a simple one which I was surprised to discover had never previously been employed in studying the history of a port. In the Mersey Docks & Harbour Board archive there is a sequence known as *'Antecedent Files'* which contain biographical material relating to Members.[9] I constructed a simple card index from those files that survived for the first hundred men elected to the Board and sorted them according to such criteria as age at election, whether they were first, second or third generation in their particular line of business, and so on. Hypothesis 1 had some, but not much, substance and the weakness of the numerical evidence was compounded by strong contrary qualitative evidence in that some of the ablest individuals were both old and of long standing. Hypothesis 2 was almost without support in either the generational aspect or by place of residence, and Hypothesis 3 also fell: the Members' network ensured that each of them knew where the others were coming from. Only the effective pursuit of *concealed* interests would have substantiated Hypothesis 3, and none was found.

Hence the extempore Hypothesis 4 appeared the most likely, and so it proved. Members were so heavily involved in their principal businesses, in non-executive directorships, in local politics, in charities, clubs, churches, volunteer soldiering, time-consuming hobbies and a host of lesser interests that there was no chance at all of them mastering all the Board paperwork they had to read, understand and remember if they were to be able to engage in policy-making of the quality previously attributed to them.[10] Much less could they monitor the effective performance of their policies. This explained their fascination with trivia: they could attend conscientiously and engage in discussion and decision-making on issues whose determination could proceed in the absence of knowledge and understanding alike. They were neither knaves nor fools: they were simply hopelessly optimistic about how much they could do in a week.

---

9   The Mersey Docks & Harbour Board collection is held at the Maritime Archives and Library, Merseyside Maritime Museum. The *Antecedents Files* are the principal source for this paper, as for the previous one. To avoid repetitious citation it should be assumed that, unless otherwise stated, any statement about a Member is drawn from the *Antecedents File* bearing his name. The files contain, typically, a summary of the Member's 'career' on the Board, press cuttings regarding his retirement, death, funeral and grant of probate, sometimes other details.

10   The quantity may be judged from the fact that 28 Committee Clerks were employed to produce it.

Reform

In 1890, just a year after Harold Littledale died, some of the Members realised that there was much amiss in their organisation, and a Special Committee was appointed to investigate and report on the general conduct of the business of the Board.[11] The report, discussed in January 1891, had many recommendations for the reduction of administrative costs, but it leads one into conjecture as to matters which we may reasonably assume were discussed but which were not minuted.[12] Two things happened quite shortly afterwards. G. F. Lyster 'sought the permission of the Board' to hand some of his responsibilities to his son in return for a reduction of salary from £4,500 to £3,500.[13] The second was the preparation of a Parliamentary Bill to enable the construction of new entrances at Sandon Dock to take the largest classes of vessel using the port, which had already outgrown the almost-new Canada Entrance, Lyster Senior's greatest and costliest blunder. Lyster Junior was later to state that he had in effect been Engineer-in-Chief since 1891.

Now let us imagine that the Board, eyes newly opened, in fact wished to dismiss Lyster Senior. They simply could not do this, just as they had not been able to dismiss their corrupt Secretary Edward Gittins the previous year.[14] The effect of either dismissal on the Board's reputation and hence its credit-worthiness would have been catastrophic, and without being able to borrow there was nothing the Board could do to correct the engineering errors which had been made. Gittins died at a very convenient moment, but Lyster, who had been guilty of some terrible misjudgements, did not. His persistent opposition to any attempt at dredging the Bar had, perhaps unjustly, made both him and the Board extremely unpopular and when he was forced to begin dredging in 1890 he did

---

11 Legal H80: *Discussions at Board* 15, 22, 29 January 1891.

12 There were four levels of confidentiality: meetings of the Board and its committees began with reporters present and the proceedings were public. Next, the reporters withdrew for the confidential business which was often concerned with land acquisition or personnel matters. In just one instance I have found the definite existence of the third and fourth levels: a discussion after the confidential business closed, which was actually minuted, and the minutes end not with 'the discussion closed' but with 'the shorthand writer withdrew'. *Discussions at Board,* 23 April 1908.

13 He was, after all, 69 years of age.

14 Gittins had been supplying sensitive information to his brother who was one of a trio of speculators who made significant money at the Board's expense by trading in land options.

so with a very bad grace. There is at least a strong possibility that Lyster was deliberately (and, overall, justifiably) marginalised.[15]

These events followed on a major re-organisation of the bookkeeping system in the Engineers Department, and on the potentially pivotal death in 1889 of Thomas Hornby, Chairman of the Board. Hornby was the great closer of ranks, when Littledale advocated a more open form of operation by the Board, and had been a Member since 1862, Chairman since 1876. His replacement by Alfred Holt was welcomed by the local press with huge enthusiasm, implying what they could never state, namely that Hornby personified an old order which needed sweeping away.

So the auguries for a great improvement in the performance of the Board were good, and the engineering successes of the '90s, including Sandon Entrance and the modernisation of Canada and Huskisson Docks, seemed to bear them out. The continuing rising trend of Liverpool's tonnage and revenue was coupled with a downward trend in the percentage of earned income spent on interest. But it was too good to last, and the same problem recurred: although some wise decisions undoubtedly were taken indecision and error lingered on.

The decision-making on the Gladstone Dock project was abysmal. In 1904 the Works Committee asked Lyster to design a dock system with an entrance lock at a narrow angle to the River, like the one under construction at Brunswick Dock. Between 27 July 1904 and 16 June 1905 Lyster's team produced six different designs, one of which went to the Parliamentary Committee, who agreed that a Bill should go to Parliament. Drafting the Bill gave time for more doubts, and Lyster had to re-design the scheme to handle a 1000ft ship instead of the 800-850 feet in previous designs. The initial request from the Docks & Quays Committee to the Works Committee, made on 1 January 1902, had been for a dock to handle ships 1,000ft long.

One could continue: suffice it to say that when the Act was obtained, construction did not begin and on 6 November 1906 Lyster was told to scrap the half-tide entrance in the current and previous designs and revert to an entrance lock as in earlier ones. April 4th, 1907 saw another new brief. In February 1908 the Finance Committee re-opened the question of whether it was worth building a dock for giant vessels at all. After six years' discussion, work began on fencing the site on 12 May 1908, and continued until December when it was stopped on

---

15 For more on Lyster's failures see A. Jarvis, 'G. F. Lyster and the Role of the Dock Engineer 1861-97', in: *The Mariner's Mirror*, 78 (1992), 177-99.

financial grounds. When it eventually restarted on 30 June 1911, it was to a completely different scheme from any which had been considered previously.

The Board's fundamental problems, which were great, were greatly aggravated by the Members' inability to make decisions and stick to them. The waste of staff time does not bear thinking about. We are driven back to the same question which arose for the earlier period, of how competent and well-intentioned men could perform badly once they entered the Boardroom.

Reverting to the method of the earlier paper,[16] a quick trawl of Members suggested that they were staying on the board even longer and working to a greater age than before, so the gerontocracy hypothesis merited re-appraisal for this later period. The 'clogs-to-clogs' hypothesis again proved wanting. Just one member, for example, was notable as 'a sportsman' and only one lived out of reasonable commuting range.[17] The 'outside interest' question becomes rather fluid because of shifts in the informal rules governing these matters (as distinct from the formal ones, which did not change but were ignored). This suggested that it was worth re-visiting, especially since the 'Gladstone issue' had involved so much friction between the protagonists of different trades.

Table 1: The Gerontocracy Hypothesis Re-visited

Age at election 2002sample (1992 sample)			Years on Board, 2002 sample (1992 sample)		
Under 30	1	(6)	1-5	8	(7)
30-39	3	(6)	6-10	6	(10)
40-49	11	(24)	11-15	16	(8)
50-59	18	(14)	16-20	8	(8)
Over 60	9	(4)	21-25	2	(9)
			25-30	6	
			Over 30	4	

Source: Maritime Archives and Library, Merseyside Maritime Museum, Antecedents Files

---

16 Jarvis, of the Mersey Docks & Harbour Board.
17 Namely Edward Rayner (1861-1932), a Produce Broker, Member 1911-18, who was noted for the size and success of his bets on horses. Sidney Keymer, the nominee of Manchester Chamber of Commerce, lived in Alderley Edge.

The previously preferred hypothesis, that members simply tried to do too much, still looked strong at the beginning of this later period, but it is clear that in some circles changes were occurring and it became easier to find obituaries of Members who, apart from Board membership, 'took no part in public or social life'. This pointed towards cross-relationship with Hypothesis 1, that those who were more careful about how much they took on tended not to remain on the Board for long periods, so that, for example, Harold Sanderson of the White Star Line stayed only two years as a representative of the passenger liner trade before being replaced by Sir Percy Bates, who also stayed only two years.

The 'sample' is the next fifty members elected following Mr James Barkeley Smith, with whom the previous analysis ended. The information is much fuller for this period, the only significant 'blanks' being that in 8 cases the member's date of birth was not available.

The table shows a clear trend with regard both to age and time served. In the new sample 22 - more than half - served on into their seventies with three into their eighties. Sir Richard Holt, who died at 77, had been on the Board for 45 years. He was one of 25 (exactly half) of the full sample who died in office.

Over the period spanned by the documents, various evolutions occurred in the custom and practice of the Board, and one of these suggests that if the age profile of the Board was a problem, then it was a greater one than at first appears. At first, members were appointed to the various standing committees chiefly on the basis of their known skills, experience or interest, but as time went by a pecking order of committees emerged, at first clandestinely, but later as a matter of public knowledge.[18] At the pinnacle was the Works Committee whose decisions were the most critical to the overall affairs of the port, and sometimes ineptly made. It became exceptional for a new Member to be appointed to the Works Committee: he would start somewhere harmless, like Docks and Quays, and, sometimes after many years, get 'promoted'. 26 of our sample served on the Works Committee at some stage: 19 remained there until they retired or died and only 7 moved on to another committee. Of the 26, date of birth is unknown for 4, and of the remaining 22, 12 remained in office aged over 70, including William Clarke, who died in office aged 87.

It was the same in the Finance Committee: the second most important committee had become by definition the second most likely to have an

---

18 For example, *Syren and Shipping* for 18 March 1908 mentioned the 'annual shuffling up of committees' when Harold Sanderson was promoted from Docks & Quays to Works.

unfavourable age profile.[19] Worse still, the problem was at least self-perpetuating, perhaps self-aggravating. It is noticeable that some of the men elected young did not stay long: the youngest man elected, Sir Percy Bates, lasted two years, Sir Aubrey Brocklebank three. In fairness, however, one must admit the exception of Sir Richard Holt, aged 32 at election, the second youngest of the sample, who stayed 45 years. But how well, on average, would a successful younger businessman react to joining a meeting chaired by the 77-year old Joseph Hodgson?[20]

At last we get to the conference theme. The Dock Board was itself a network, established by Parliament to find out what the customers of the port needed and then give it to them. Membership was a great social honour and in its early years it provided a mechanism for commercial communication - and self-advancement through participation in 'public and social life'. Frequent accusations that Members' firms gained preferential treatment in berthing and porterage show how some non-members saw the Board. Changes soon began, which continued with growing momentum into the twentieth century. Certainly by 1876, Hornby's elevation to the Chair of the Board rested not on ability but on seniority. That was a serious matter, because with no paid 'Chief Executive' the Chairman held - and exercised - considerable executive powers.

Board elections also 'evolved': it became increasingly rare to have a contested election, initially because they were 'organised' by the inner caucus.[21] In the second sample not a single member was voted off: they resigned or they died. When this happened and it was necessary to elect a new member 'In the room of Mr Algernon Henderson, deceased'[22] the process which followed bore little relationship to the intentions expressed in the Mersey Docks & Harbour Board Act, 1857.

---

19 Of our 50 members, 25 served at some time on the Finance Committee and all but one left by death or retirement - and that one was Richard Holt on his being elected Chairman of the Board. Two of the 25 were of unknown age and of the remaining 23, 16 served beyond 70.

20 It was alleged in *Syren and Shipping* 18 March 1908 that Mr Sanderson left the Board because friction arose in the Works Committee '... the one active member was disappointed with the slowness of his colleagues', though Sanderson denied this in a letter of 25 March 1908.

21 Some documents on the subject of elections survive bearing a rubber stamp 'Chairmen's Meeting'. This 'body' had no constitutional basis and although minutes were taken (which we know from fragmentary transcriptions elsewhere) the Minute Books have not survived.

22 It is perhaps telling that this archaism continued in use into the 1930s.

The process by which elections were reduced to farce may be traced back to the practice that one of the Nominee[23] Members of the Board was fairly openly given the brief of watching over the well-being of the Birkenhead interest. The Liverpool Steam Ship Owners' Association was established in 1858 specifically to secure representation of its members' interests on the Board, but 'representation' only really became public knowledge with the election of Hugh Mason in 1872, specifically as the nominee of the Manchester Chamber of Commerce. The practice of allowing, eventually encouraging, outside associations, to make nominations was not illegal, but was in breach of the spirit of the 1857 Act, which expected individual members, as well as the Board corporately, to behave in a disinterested manner. When we reach the period of our sample it was clear what would happen when Alfred Woodall, a fruit broker, resigned: 'The Chairman, after receiving Mr Woodall's letter had seen the President of the Fruit Brokers' Association, Mr Frederick Getty, as to filling the vacancy...' Mr Getty was nominated and elected unopposed. The electoral process had been sub-contracted to the Fruit Brokers' Association.

The only way conflict could arise was where one trade had multiple representation while another, perhaps a young and growing one, had none at all. Great ill-will had occurred among the timber trade when William Smellie was elected in 1915 to represent the oil trade, which had not been represented previously, and when he announced his intention to retire in 1928, a lengthy correspondence ensued between Sir Richard Holt, Chairman, who was away on holiday and Lionel Warner, General Manager & Secretary, of which the outcome was that they persuaded the General Brokers' Association to nominate a timber man. There was no thought of conducting the election other than through the General Brokers, much less of having a contested election. Even the timber men would not suggest that![24]

What this means is that instead of the Board being a primary network of business communication it had in fact moved towards the use of other people's networks. This may be thought to be both cause and effect of the dearth of

---

23 Only 24 of the Board's 28 members were elected by the port users: the other four were nominees of the Conservancy Commissioners.

24 In 1923 the sugar trade was less acquiescent and forced a contested election, which they lost. It was a mark of the cunning of Chairman Thomas Rome and Warner that two years later John Tilman was elected unopposed to represent the sugar trade in place of Mr Willmer, who retired as a mere stripling of 67. The message was 'All you need, young man, is a little patience'.

ambitious men in early middle age seeking to get themselves elected to the Board.[25]

Clearly, many men over the age of 70 are capable of very useful work, and so are a few over 80. In so far as one may generalise, one of the first 'faculties' we lose with increasing age is the ability to come to terms with change, often followed by the loss even of desire to do so. We place more value on experience than on raw talent, which exacerbates our desire to carry on doing things in tried and tested ways - closely followed by a desire to keep the company of our own generation, avoiding young feller-me-lads who think they can mend the world. By the time the men in our sample were getting seriously thinned out by death or retirement, much of what happened in the Board was extraordinarily archaic. Members still 'deplored' the death of an old colleague, using the word in its Victorian (and by 1930 almost entirely forgotten) sense. Minutes were given a familiar ring by the use of expressions like '... That N be appointed, and he hereby is appointed...' dating back to the days of Members' grandfathers.[26] It was not exactly a promising seedbed for the radical and continuous change, which needed to take place in the port, if it was going to maintain its place. We should, in fact, be surprised not at how little change took place in the construction and operation of the docks between, say 1900 and 1930, but how much.

Outside Interests

As before, the largest single principal occupation of members was shipowning in one form or another, totalling of 21 of the 50. However, also as before, if we brigade merchants and brokers as having, for port services purposes, similar needs, we again find that their numbers tie exactly with the shipowners. This is unsurprising, for if it were difficult to replace one kind of merchant by another, replacing either with a shipowner would have been virtually impossible. The result might have been a 'hung' Board, with the balance held by the 'neutrals' - three shipbuilders, two manufacturing chemists, two bankers and one average adjuster - but in fact the interests of the owners of different sizes of ship were so

---

25 In my earlier sample of members, over two thirds were elected before the age of fifty, in the present sample the ratio is reversed.

26 In the cases of John Rankin and William Moss, their fathers and grandfathers had been on the Board.

at variance one with another as to render that a purely theoretical consideration. Where the earlier study concluded that members did, by and large, do as they were meant to and leave their principal business interests outside the Board Room along with their hats and coats, by the time the new sample had got their feet under the table this was no longer always the case.

In the late '90s there was prolonged strife over the facilities for the Irish trade, in which shipowners and merchants with interests in the trade united to oppose the interests of those trades employing larger vessels. Although their primary complaint was the near-monopolisation of the floating stage by large passenger liners, they also fiercely opposed the 1898 'New Works' Bill whose success was crucial to the continued growth of the cargo liner trade. Their actions are understandable, for their trade had been starved of Board investment for decades, but it is also true that they were not acting disinterestedly. In 1898 the entire coastal trade paid the Board tonnage dues of £39,830 and Ismay Imrie alone paid £35,613. Rates on goods handled at berths appropriated to the coastwise trade totalled £26,528 and those paid by Ismay Imrie were £42,822.[27] Of course the Irish Trade was not the only one to try to call the tune without paying the piper, but its abuse of the way the Board was meant to function is conspicuous.

This matters, because although the Act for the Gladstone Dock eventually passed through Parliament unopposed, it was the failure of the factions within the Board to come to an early agreement and then stick to it which caused the prolonged indecision mentioned above. Members simply would not decide what the new dock was for. In short, outside interests, which my earlier study suggested could be largely discounted as a source of poor policy-making, seem to emerge as more important than previously and this again relates to the function of the Board as a network for meeting the needs of port users. By effectively delegating the election process, the Board had also out-sourced its own networking function, with the result that some members clearly no longer felt their loyalty must be first and last to the Board. Now they could - and some believed they *should* - be loyal to the people who put them there.[28]

---

27 MD&HB, *Steamship Owners' Returns*, 1898. Unfortunately these returns aggregate the dues on goods so the comparison is not exactly like with like, but the difference is large enough to be beyond quibbling.

28 This is different from the opposition of the 'Birkenhead Lobby' to the 1873 Bill: those Members could claim that they were working for the best interests of the port as a whole. They

A Busy Life

From the start, nearly all the men elected to the Board were already of substantial achievement in business. This meant they were likely also to be in demand as non-executive directors of companies, members of trade associations and the like, as well as helping manage a host of good causes from orphanages to retirement homes for sailors. Several were prominent fund-raisers or benefactors in two great public projects of the day, the building of the Cathedral and the University. But only seventeen of the 50 were Justices of the Peace as compared with 37 of 52 in the earlier sample, and only six were active in local or national politics.

Far fewer had commitments to charitable institutions and although some gave away very large sums of money, they were less generous than their predecessors, only seventeen having serious commitments, though some had several, making a total of 36 compared with the earlier sample's 67 commitments among 52 men. Involvement in Church activities was markedly less, with only six of the 50 obituaries mentioning any, as against 26 from the 52.[29] By contrast, nine (as against seven) are mentioned as participating in various sports, particularly golf and yachting. Again there is a decline participation in 'public life' as previously understood.

Participation in secondary businesses as non-executive directors fell strikingly, from 92 seats occupied by 40 members to 31 occupied by 50. As before, a handful held several directorships, including Sir Richard Holt and Sir Aubrey Brocklebank with 6 each and John Rankin with 5. The most obvious change, however, is the roughly threefold rise in membership of trade associations from 25 in a sample of 52 to 73 in 50.

Over-commitment is not nearly so convincing an explanation as it was for the earlier period. This unease with my earlier conclusion is compounded by the change in the age profile of the Board. It is one thing to have a body of experienced men, quite another to have one where membership has ossified through lack of turnover. Once the Board had gone a while without voting anyone off, it effectively became impossible to do so at all, because that would

---

were misguided, but that is a different issue. On 'interest' issues in this earlier period, see G. J. Milne, *Trade and traders in mid-Victorian Liverpool*, Liverpool 2000.

29 This refers to working for churches, not merely attending services.

imply that the victim was the most useless Member in living memory. Most Members of the two key committees were voted off by the Grim Reaper. That, in turn, feeds back to the one field in which Members increased their level of activity, namely trade associations, which were now fulfilling part of the networking function of the Board, and it is clear that at times they rendered the Board virtually powerless. The Gladstone Graving Dock, begun in 1911, was designed and built to receive one specific ship, the *Aquitania.* Yet in 1907 White Star had transferred its 'Big Four' express liners from Liverpool to Southampton and in 1911 they were still the second largest payers of dues in the port, behind Leyland & Dominion but ahead of Cunard, which had not yet moved to Southampton.[30] It was not the exceptional ships which made the money for the Board, and members knew this when they took the decision.

Of course nothing above suggests that everything the Board did was wrong-headed or bad,[31] or that all their policies were ill-formed and vacillating. On the contrary, they did some things wisely and well and one aim in both papers has been to explain how a body of such obvious capability in some respects could sometimes get things horribly wrong.

One thing the Board had long been good at was borrowing money, which was absolutely essential because the port's facilities could not be up-dated from revenue. The Members conveyed an image of irreproachable financial probity, and they clearly understood that this was among the most important things they did. In that arena, age and conservatism were strong advantages, as they were when seeking aid from the Unemployment Grants Committee, who paid the interest costs on the programme to modernise the Central Docks. Equipped with their palatial Dock Offices and their steam yacht *Galatea,* they excelled at being dignified. Faced with a problem they had faced before, they could make wise decisions.

That comes with age and experience: the other side of the coin is being panicked by the unfamiliar, and it seems that during the service of our 50 Members we can find both those sides, even, in the case of Gladstone Dock, exhibited in response to the same issue. When the Engineer's men were told they could spend extra money to save time, they successfully met an extremely challenging completion date well within budget and despite severe labour

---

30 *Steamship Owners' Returns 1911.*
31 Bidston Dock, for example, may have been misconceived or badly timed, but at least it was built within budget and schedule.

difficulties. The difference was that, once desperation set in, the Members had no alternative but to trust the engineers: until then they kept on meddling with the scheme.

In short, while the Gerontocracy Hypothesis might not hold up very well for the first 100 members of the Board it seems more convincing in respect of the behaviour of the next 50. It is not a complete explanation, and the Members were clearly not all doddering old fools. In 1908, a vintage year for indecision, the *average* age of the members of the Works Committee was only 60, that of the Finance Committee 59.9. The Busy Life Hypothesis clearly had a part still to play, with most Members attending three meetings a week, some four or five, and this at a time when the amount of paperwork to be mastered was growing fast. The fact is, though, that a typical 60-year old businessman had long since had someone younger handling all the detail for him in his principal business and had probably forgotten how to do it himself. So it was with the Members: there are many instances in the *verbatim* Minutes sequence of discussion getting side-tracked by complete misunderstanding of the situation.

That brings us to the greatest caveat of all: whatever figures one may produce, two individuals who were always on the ball to sort out problems like that, namely Robert Gladstone and Sir Richard Holt, Chairman respectively between 1899-1911 and 1927-29 and 1930-41 and both served into their 70s: so much for gerontocracy. Overwork was, to a conscientious Chairman, a condition of the job: he was an *ex-officio* member of all standing committees and therefore, in theory, required to be present for meetings every day of the week. Both Gladstone and Holt took this seriously. Add the briefing sessions with the General Manager, the informal caballing sessions and such things as representing the Board at funerals[32] and it was definitely a full-time job.

Conclusion

The clash between individual cases and quantitative evidence emerged in the first sample as well. It is here suggested that the sample is large enough to encourage acceptance in general terms of the quantitative evidence. It was, after

---

32 Business funerals were very large-scale: lists of those present were published in the local press. Because the circuit was large, so was the number of occasions on which a Board member would feel obliged to be present. And the older they got ...

all, the membership at large that formed the starting point of this paper and it was their shifting characteristics and capabilities, so far as we can identify them, which set the tone of Board meetings.

But ironically, these characteristics typically included a large measure of acquiescence, which allowed the handful of exceptional characters such as Richard Holt or John Hughes to exert an influence out of all proportion to their numbers.

It is suggested that the increasingly unfavourable age profile of the Members, together with the increasing influence of trade associations did more than provide a sidelight on the efficiency of the Board as a policy-making body. It changed its nature too, from being a disinterested business network to an assembly of delegates whose purpose was perhaps becoming more advisory than determinative. But this did not result in any evident deterioration of the discharge of the Board's functions, indeed if one restricts the field to the largest single issue, continuing modernisation of the infrastructure, performance might be held to have improved. The Clarence Dock modernisation scheme (1929-1933) was (unusually) completed within budget and schedule, in part because, unlike some of its predecessors, it started with a clear notion of what was required and for whom, an insistence on detailed estimates and the presentation of complete working drawings rather than outline plans.[33] When that preparatory stage was completed, the Board left the officers to get on with it.

The earlier paper began by seeking causes of poor decision-making and this paper began as an extrapolation of it. The change in the nature of the Board, which coincidentally begins about the time when the second sample of Members were growing in influence as earlier Members resigned or died, coincides both with the decline of interest in 'public life' identified above and with what appears to be an improvement in performance. The conclusion that an over-developed sense of public duty was a leading cause of the port's earlier troubles may be partially confirmed by its converse.

---

33 It is unlikely that all the Members could read a detailed engineering drawing, but all that was necessary was that one or two could do so well enough to put awkward questions to the Engineer.

International Arms Traders and the British Civil Wars of the Mid Seventeenth Century

Peter Edwards

When the Scottish covenanters rebelled against the imposition of the Anglican prayer book in 1637-8, the event signalled the beginning of a series of insurrections that engulfed the entire British archipelago for a generation. However, because the monarchs had remained largely aloof from the conflicts wracking Europe in the early seventeenth century the native arms industry had atrophied. From the outset, therefore, all sides in the British Civil Wars had to import arms to function effectively. Charles I looked abroad for weapons to meet the threat from the Scottish covenanters and Irish catholics and continued to rely upon foreign supplies in his struggle against Parliament. Parliament, in spite of controlling existing centres of the industry in London and the Home Counties, also had to import arms and armaments. With fewer resources at home, the Scots and, to a greater extent, the Irish, were even more reliant upon foreign supplies. In England the royalists managed to develop their own manufacturing facilities but remained heavily dependent on imports. Parliament, on the other hand, eventually did become functionally self-sufficient in war materials (except for some gunpowder ingredients) but only in the late 1640s.[1]

Fortunately for them, continental arms industries had expanded in the late sixteenth and early seventeenth centuries, stimulated by the demands of war. Buying on the foreign arms market was expensive but it did provide the parties at home access to a larger and more sophisticated industry and allowed them to obtain essential supplies quickly and in bulk. Relying on imports, however, added an element of uncertainty to the proceedings since it placed the warring parties at the mercy of foreign suppliers, whose interests did not necessarily coincide with theirs. Charles I, for instance, expected to receive material support from his fellow-rulers, especially those in Denmark, France and the United Provinces with whom he was related. Their response, conditioned by political considerations, was disappointing. Merchants, on the other hand, were far more amenable. The Dutch even traded with their enemy, Spain.[2] By the time that British troops required arms and armaments for their battles arms dealers had established a complex trading network that enabled them to move raw materials,

---

1 P. Edwards, *Dealing in Death: The Arms Trade and the British Civil Wars, 1638-52*, Sutton 2000, 175.
2 Edwards, *Dealing in Death*, 175-7.

weapons, ordnance and munitions over long distances and crossed frontiers. Only some of the merchants were specialists but others, aware of the financial rewards to be obtained, added arms dealing to a commercial portfolio that might span the whole of Europe and even further afield.

I.

Merchants, dealing in arms, had a mixture of motives. Some of them were partisans, supporting the cause in a material way. For Parliament, they included Londoners like William Pennoyer and Richard Hill. The Royalists used merchants like Nicholas Crispe. For the Scottish covenanters William Dick of Edinburgh was prominent and for the Irish Confederates, Patrick Archer of Kilkenny. Apart from forging direct links with European manufacturers and dealers, they also maintained agents abroad, who could carry out the detailed negotiations with suppliers and arrange for the assembly of the goods at the quayside. Thomas Andrews and Stephen Estwick, for instance, employed their representatives in France and Holland when asked by Parliament to fulfill a large order placed at the beginning of the English Civil War. In autumn 1642 they were asked to obtain 12,000 muskets and rests; 1,500 pairs of pistols; 6,000 pikes; 600 suits of harquebusier armour; and 6,000 corslets. By 4 October their agents had acquired 2,690 muskets and 3,956 rests; 246 carbines; 66 dragoons; 980 pairs of pistols with cases; 401 suits of harquebusier armour; and 2,331 corslets. Pennoyer and Hill, noted above, had an agent at Dunkirk, a local man called Philipe de Pape, who must have carried on a regular business there, if not solely in arms.[3]

Of particular value were the supporters among the expatriate mercantile communities abroad: they were both highly motivated and on the spot and were therefore well placed to give material aid to their side. Thomas Cuningham, the Scottish conservator at Veere, was responsible for supplying the covenanters with shiploads of arms during the Bishops' Wars and later to their forces in England and Ireland. In addition, he arranged financial help from native merchants such as the Lampsins of Flushing and Middleburg. In 1644 the Lampsins agreed to act as guarantors for £168,000 Scots worth of arms that Cunningham had obtained on credit. The covenanters also obtained consignments of arms from Sweden through the good offices of Scottish expatriates, merchants like James Maclean of Stockholm and his nephew, John Maclean of Gothenburg, whom the Swedish government used as intermediaries.

---

3   Edwards, *Dealing in Death*, 60, 177, 198-9, 203, 241; P.R.O., S.P.28/261, III, fo. 284.

In 1638-9 the Macleans sent shiploads of arms and ordnance, as well as iron (and probably copper) to make ordnance. Some consignments were taken direct to Scotland, others were shipped via Amsterdam.[4]

Charles I also had his supporters abroad. Indeed, Parliament was so concerned about the activities of royalist merchants at Amsterdam and Rotterdam so that it outlawed the ringleaders, John Webster, Theophilus Baynham, Edward Manning, Richard Ford and James Yard, on 6 July 1644. In a letter, written the following day, Thomas Strickland, the Parliamentarian envoy to The Hague, added his condemnation. Because of his wealth, standing and range of contacts he was the pivotal figure. He helped provide arms for the king in the Bishops' Wars and continued to send *matériel* in the English Civil War. According to Strickland, he "hath and doth furnish most of the Arms that go to those in Rebellion, whose credit in that Town (Amsterdam), being allied to many in it of Note; but his Credit is likewise much in London". On 11 June 1642, for instance, a Parliamentarian informant had reported seeing him examining and measuring up a mortar piece, adding that he "doth hasten exceedingly with all these things." Apart from supplying arms and armaments to the royalists, he also loaned money to the royalists or use his credit to raise it on their behalf. In addition, he was instrumental in the negotiations leading up to the pawning of the Crown jewels.[5]

Naturally, foreign merchants, without the same commitment, were more likely to promote their own commercial interests. On 1 November 1642 the States-General in the United Provinces declared a policy of strict neutrality in the English Civil War, prohibiting the export of arms to either side. Unfortunately, merchants at Amsterdam and Rotterdam, the ones most affected by the ban, soon found their trade affected. They therefore broke ranks, interpreting the declaration as the right to distribute arms equally to both sides. Elsewhere, merchants were making similar calculations. In September 1642 it was said of French merchants that they were willing to do business with the Irish Confederates because it was "as profitable a voyage ... as unto the East or West Indies". At the same time, Dunkirk merchants, recognising a market opportunity, were buying up great quantities of gunpowder and arms in Holland and Hamburg for resale to Confederate agents in Flanders. The Fleming, Antonio Vanderkipp, who established a privateering business at Wexford, was par-

---

4   E.J. Courthorpe, The Journal of Thomas Cunningham of Campvere, 1640-1654, in: *Scottish Historical Society*, 3rd series, 11 (1926), 54, 65, 95, 204-19.

5   Edwards, *Dealing in Death*, 199; *Calendar of State Papers Domestic (CSPD)*, (1644), 320; *CSPD*, (1644-5), 502; *CSPD*, (1650), 320; *Cal. Clarendon State Papers*, I, 259, 437, 446; *L(ords) J(ournals)*, 6, 260, 619; The Netherlands National Archives, The Hague, Amsterdam Chamber of the Admiralty (A.C.A.), inv. nr. 1385, 4 April 1639.

ticularly unscrupulous. Although a regular supplier of arms and shipping to the
Confederates, he was in essence a freebooter, supplying arms, munitions and
victuals to whoever would pay his price and hiring out vessels at extortionate
rates.[6]

If merchants were more ready to sell arms indiscriminately, there was a price
to pay. Apart from the partisans among them, they would only look at a venture
if it appeared profitable and therefore had to be encouraged to do business. What
they wanted was ready cash (or at least secure bills of exchange), return cargoes
and trading concessions. As William Sandys noted in a letter to John Strachan at
Weymouth in January 1644, "It is the price & good payment and free permission
to export all Commodityes without Restraynt will make that port thriue and the
kinge well supplied with Armes". He also emphasised the importance of
furnishing the merchants with a return cargo. He claimed that if Strachan could
assure his merchant friends of the availability of saleable goods, he had £30,000
worth of arms to ship out but "for fear of the returne ther, hinders It thither".[7]
Merchants liked to be paid promptly too. In February 1644 Lord Digby, at
Oxford, informed Ormond that he was negotiating with merchants to ship arms
and ammunition to Chester, Bristol or Minehead, promising them ready money
if they did so. Unfortunately, some merchants were reluctant to deal with the
Royalists because of their shortage of money and a casualness of approach.[8]

II.

War material, bound for one or other of the combatants, came from many parts
of Europe (and even further afield) but for all parties the Low Countries were the
most important source of foreign supplies. By the mid seventeenth century the
region contained some of the leading arms manufacturing centres in Europe and
all manner of military hardware could be obtained there. The industry, long
established in the southern Netherlands, had spread to the United Provinces by

---

6   P. Geyl, 'Frederick Henry and King Charles I', in: *English Historical Review*, 38 (1923), 17; S.
    Groenveld, *Verlopend Getij*, Dieren 1984, 106. H(istorical) M(anuscripts) C(ommission),
    Report on the Fransiscan manuscripts preserved at the convent, Merchants' Quay, 196, 199,
    202; J. Ohlmeyer, 'The Dunkirk of Ireland: Wexford privateers during the 1640s', *Jnl. Wexford
    Hist. Soc.*, 12 (1988/89), 39; J. Ohlmeyer, *Civil War and Restoration in the three Stuart
    kingdoms: The career of Randal MacDonnell, marquis of Antrim, 1609-1683*, Cambridge 1993,
    194-5, 219; Edwards, *Dealing in Death*, 191.

7   I. Roy, 'The Royalist Ordnance Papers, part 2', in: *Oxfordshire Record Society*, 49 (1971/3),
    381.

8   Bodl. Lib., Carte 9, fo.254; Roy, 'Royalist Ordnance Papers 2', 393; *C.S.P.D.* (1644-5), 469,
    480.

c. 1600 under the stimulus of war with Spain. In the south, Liège was the most important centre, its industry benefiting from plentiful local supplies of raw materials, good communications links and a skilled workforce. The Liègeois made all kinds of war material but they specialised in firearms, edged weapons and armour.[9] Arms production was carried on at other places too; at Mechelen, Maastricht and Namur, for instance.[10] The same pattern was repeated in the United Provinces as arms manufacture developed there in the late sixteenth and early seventeenth centuries. Amsterdam took the lead, producing ordnance, munitions and weapons on a considerable scale. Elsewhere, production was more restricted both in terms of output and in the range of goods made.[11]

Arms were dispatched to Britain from a number of ports in the Low Countries, especially Dunkirk and Ostend in Flanders and Amsterdam, Middleburg, Rotterdam and Veere in the United Provinces. Of these, Amsterdam was by far the most important. In 1643 300 ships were said to have made the journey between Amsterdam and England, (though not necessarily laden with arms), each one completing four trips a year.[12] In the months leading up to the outbreak of hostilities in England thirty-eight of the surviving export licences record the export of arms to England. The set of licences, which runs up to spring 1645, reveals that the warring parties were particularly keen to acquire stocks of munitions. In August 1640 alone the Chardinels, Amsterdam gunpowder makers and merchants, sent 22½ tons of match and, with Celio Marcelis and John Webster, shared in the dispatch of 40 tons of gunpowder.[13] To increase home production raw materials were also imported. All the sulphur had to be brought in, for instance, since it was unobtainable in the British Isles. In 1641 five export licences to Abraham Pietersz, Croock and Company, Jan van der Meulen, Celio Marcelis and Andries Adrieaensz record the shipment of 154 tons of sulphur to England, France and other neutral countries.[14] Foreign saltpetre, moreover, helped to augment home supplies. On 23 November 1644 Lucas Schorer was allowed to export 'a lot of' saltpetre from Amsterdam.[15] In addition, weapons of all kinds were sent. Of particular value were firearms

9   J. Yernaux, *La Métallurgie liégeoise et son expansion au XVIIe siècle*, Liége 1939, 17-20; C. Gaier, *Quatre siècle d'armurerie liégeoise*, Liége 1977, 31, 35-8.

10 Gaier, *Quatre siècle*, 18-21.

11 H. Vogel, De Republiek als wapenexporteur 1600-1650, in: J.P. Puype, M. van der Hoeven (eds.), *Het arsenaal van de wereld: Nederlandse wapenhandel in de Gouden Eeuw*, Amsterdam 1993, 13.

12 Groenveld, *Verlopend Getij*, 238.

13 A.C.A., inv. nr. 2386, 7-8, 26 August 1640.

14 A.C.A., inv. nr. 1387, 3, 8 March, 5 April, 25 May, 9 October 1641.

15 A.C.A., inv. nr. 1400, 23 November 1644.

because foreign gunmaking skills were in advance of those in England. Sword blades were imported in greater numbers than entire swords and these would have been hilted in this country.

Initially, the Dutch arms trade had been import led in order to acquire weapons to fight the Spanish, and Amsterdam came to prominence as a port through which arms and raw materials were shipped into the country. It also had good communications with arms centres such as Liége and Namur in the southern Netherlands and Solingen in Germany. The blockading of Antwerp in the late sixteenth century aided its growth since arms made in Liège were taken up the Meuse to Dutch ports such as Rotterdam and Amsterdam.[16] After the United Provinces developed its own industry, the arms trade throve as part of the general commercial expansion of the country. The Dutch were efficient and effective traders, offering goods and services at competitive rates, and consequently established extensive commercial links with other countries. As part of this business they built up stocks of arms and military equipment and, thus, could quickly put together large consignments and transport them to their destination. Amsterdam benefited from this development and by about 1620 had become a staple market for arms. Further east, the other arms staple markets of Bremen, Hamburg and Lübeck sent some consignments directly to Britain but many of them seem to have been taken to Amsterdam first.[17]

Dutch enterprise was responsible for the development of the Swedish arms industry in the early seventeenth century. Louis de Geer is the key figure; he helped to modernise the industry by bringing in capital and technological expertise, providing essential entrepreneurial skills and opening up European markets to native products. In association with his brothers-in-law, Elias and Jacob Trip, he first became involved through trading in Swedish copper, which the Crown offered as collateral for loans. By 1620 he was leasing ironworks, mines and factories and had begun to cast ordnance, the mainstay of the Swedish arms industry. To ensure that his operations benefited from the most up-to-date techniques he recruited skilled workers and supervisors from home, especially from the Liège area. He expanded his activities in the 1620s, helped by the financial support of his in-laws, the Trips. In return, the Trips obtained cannon, which they sold at Amsterdam.[18] By the end of the decade de Geer was involved

---

16 V. Barbour, *Capitalism in Amsterdam in the seventeenth century*, Baltimore 1950, 35; Gaier, *Quatre siècle*, 57.

17 P.W. Klein, 'The Trip Family in the 17th Century', in: *Acta Historiae Neerlandica*, 1 (1966), 196.

18 J.T. Lindblad, 'Louis de Geer (1587-1652): Dutch Entrepreneur and the Father of Swedish Industry', in: C. Lesger, L. Noordegraaf (eds.), *Entrepreneurs and Entrepreneurship in Early*

in producing armour and firearms, also marketed through Amsterdam. Many of the Swedish arms that were sent to Britain came *via* Amsterdam, at times as a means of disguising their origin.

III.

The continental arms trade was huge and included large-scale dealers like de Geer and the Tripps. For such people the British Civil Wars were a mere sideshow but, nonetheless, they did supply *matériel*, mainly through Amsterdam. In February 1639, for instance, Pieter Trip sent under licence 500 barrels of gunpowder from the port. The Trips continued to supply arms and armaments to the king during the English Civil War, probably using John Webster, a close business associate of theirs, as intermediary. A hint of this connection is revealed in early 1644 when Pieter Trip sold Webster a consignment of muskets, pikes and match. Among other notable arms dealers, operating through Amsterdam, the Marcelis brothers stand out. In April 1639 Celio Marcelis exported to England 25 bronze cannon and a further fifty smaller pieces, nearly nine tons of match, 10¾ tons of musket bullets, 1,500 muskets with rests and bandoliers, 2,500 pairs of pistols, 1000 sabres, 400 hangers and 400 shovels. On 9 June, his brother, Gabriel, received a licence to ship 6,000 lbs. of match, 600 hand grenades, 3,000 pikes and an unknown number of muskets with accoutrements, and swords.[19] Of course, men like these supplied the other parties too. Thus, in January 1644 Laurens de Geer dispatched a consignment of arms to the Scottish covenanters, who that month invaded England. The cargo comprised 300 muskets and accoutrements, 300 swords and belts, 100 pairs of pistols and holsters, 4 pieces of iron ordnance, 600 cannonballs and 400 hand grenades, 120 barrels of gunpowder, and 6½ tons of match. In 1646, moreover, Pieter Trip sent gunpowder to the Parliamentarian forces.[20]

Although Amsterdam dominated the market, dealers, operating at a similar level, could be found elsewhere in Europe. On 1 August 1642 Geoffrey Barron, then in Paris to procure arms for the confederates, wrote that he had spoken with three men, who claimed that they could in a day furnish 10,000 muskets and

---

Modern Times: Merchants and Industrialists within the Orbit of the Dutch Staple Market, The Hague 1955, 78-80; Barbour, *Capitalism in Amsterdam*, 36-7; Klein, 'Trip Family', 197.

19 *C.S.P.D.*, (1638-9), 166; A.C.A. inv. nr. 1385, 23 February 1639, 9 April 1639, 9 June 1639; Barbour, *Capitalism in Amsterdam*, 113; S.P. 84/158/16r-16v; P.W. Klein, *De Trippen in de 17e eeuw. Een studie over het ondernemersgedrag op de Hollandse stapel markt*, Assen 1965, 217-8; Edwards, *Dealing in Death*, 180.

20 A.C.A. inv. nr. 1400, 5 January 1644; Klein, *De Trippen*, 217-8.

bandoliers out of stock in hand.[21] More typically, perhaps, merchants put together consignments over time and from various sources. This is what Daniel Fourment, an Antwerp merchant, did. On 14 February 1643 he obtained a licence to export to Newcastle 3,050 muskets, 2,400 pairs of pistols and 1200 carbines, all with accessories, 3,000 swords, 1,000 grenades, 7½ lasts of match, twelve suits of cavalry armour and 200 saddles with furniture.[22] Details of the weapons and munitions shipped on the frigate, St. Guillaume, reveal that they had come from nine different places in the north as well as the south Netherlands. The goods had mainly been sent from Antwerp, Liège and Rotterdam but 4,823 out of the 12,745 lbs of match had originated at Winocksbergen and Poperinge.[23]

Imported arms were mainly valued because they were readily available. Indeed, because of large-scale troop reductions in the United Provinces in the late 1630s and early 1640s, there was probably surplus capacity in the country.[24] Nonetheless, though the continental market might be larger and more sophisticated, foreign arms were neither necessarily better nor cheaper. In 1639 many of the weapons that the king obtained from John Quarles in the Low Countries and from Sir Thomas Roe at Hamburg were of poor quality. Sir Thomas, ambassador to Denmark, in particular, was duped. Along with other arms, the weapons had been impounded as contraband by the Danish authorities and had been bought by the king. Christian kept the best ones for himself and sold the worst to Roe. In September 1643 Daniel Van Hecke sent a cargo of weapons to Bristol from Dunkirk but on inspection, many of the backs and breasts and all the swords were unserviceable. Van Hecke, however, did agree to pay for the repairs.[25] Because of the extra costs involved, foreign arms should have been more expensive. Strachan reckoned that an allowance of twenty per cent should be made for transport, customs duties and profit, though exemptions did reduce the price. In a consignment of gunpowder and match delivered to King's Lynn and paid for in May 1644 the proportion was one-sixth.[26]

---

21 Franciscan MSS, 167.
22 Belgium National Archives, Brussels, Audiëntie, inv. no. 1062, fo.119.
23 P.R.O., S.P. 84/157, fos.240-5.
24 J. Israel, *The Dutch Republic: Its Rise, Greatness, and Fall 1477-1806*, Oxford 1998, 541, 544.
25 M.C. Fissel, *The Bishops' Wars*, Cambridge 1994, 99; Roy, 'Royalist Ordnance Papers 2', 365.
26 Roy, 'Royalist Ordnance Papers 2', 413; P.R.O., S.P. 28/22, fo.221.

IV.

Although a lucrative business, arms dealing involved risks. Because imports were so vital, all sides in the British Civil Wars sought to cut off supplies to their enemies by detailing ships to patrol the sea lanes and blockade ports. At first, they only searched ships suspected of gun-running in order not to alienate neutral merchants. Eventually, all merchantmen became targets as the scope of the embargo extended to the destruction of a rival's commercial as well as military capability. This shift in policy entailed the capture of foreign ships as well as those sailing from hostile ports.[27] The royal navy began stopping Scottish ships in 1638. After the Irish rebellion broke out in October 1641 there were similar demands in Parliament for a blockade of the Irish coast. Nonetheless, positive action was only taken in January 1642.[28] The defection of the royal navy in July 1642 put its ships at the disposal of Parliament. Its admiral, the earl of Warwick, stationed the bulk of the fleet in the Downs so that it could guard the approaches to London, monitor activity in Low Countries' harbours and intercept traffic sailing through the straits or travelling to north-eastern ports, the main points of entry for royalist arms.[29] Although arms consignments did get through, Warwick's navy did have some success. Thus, a tract of 24 November 1642, entitled *True Newes from our Navie*, reports on the capture in one week of a French ship en route to Sir Ralph Hopton, the royalist commander in Cornwall; the interception of two Turkish privateers taking arms to Ireland; the bringing in of a Dutch ship that had been taking Lord Digby's servant to Wales to deliver a request to the earl of Bristol for money to buy arms; and the seizure on board of two French-built ships of munitions and weapons for the Irish confederates.[30]

Many of the ships sailing under the colours of one side or another were only loosely associated with its navy. Many royalist commanders, for instance, worked under contract or acted as privateers. One such man was Jeronimo Caesar de Caverle, whose commission in November 1643 nominally made him a vice-admiral under the Earl of Marlborough, but which allowed him considerable independence. He was to employ his ships against the rebels and to receive £2,000 a month, payable out of the profits made from the prizes taken.[31] The Irish confederate navy consisted of nothing but privateers. Apart from Irish

---

27 R. Harding, *The Evolution of the Sailing Navy, 1509-1815*, London 1995, 64.

28 Edwards, *Dealing in Death*, 216; *C.S.P.D., 1641-3*; W.H. Coates, A.S. Young and V.F. Snow (eds.), *The Private Journals of the Long Parliament, 3 January to 5 March 1642*, Yale 1982, 50, 55.

29 Edwards, *Dealing in Death*, 216-8.

30 Thomason Tracts, TT 23 E E.128 (4).

31 *C.S.P.D.*, (1641-3), 499.

captains, at least twenty letters of marque were issued to Flemings, mainly the infamous Dunkirkers, in the winter of 1642/3. Hardly responsive to discipline, they were nonetheless very effective. Operating out of ports such as Wexford and Waterford, they wreaked havoc on Parliamentarian shipping. Wexford men reputedly boasted that they would make the town a second Dunkirk.[32]

For international merchants blockades were nothing new. Depending upon the state of Danish-Swedish relations, the Danes used their control of the Sound to allow through or stop traffic coming from the Baltic. The Spanish and the Dutch imposed naval cordons on each during the course of their long-running conflict. Indeed, the Dutch were blockading Flemish ports well before the end of the sixteenth century. When the Irish rebellion broke out in 1641, Charles I and Parliament both hoped to make use of the Dutch embargo to stop arms being transported from the Spanish Netherlands to Ireland. In response, the States-General did agree to deploy its ships against gun-runners to Ireland.[33] For their part, the Spanish authorities turned to this economic weapon after the end of the Twelve Years' Truce in 1621. Privateers, armed with letters of marque, were instructed to prey on Dutch shipping and thereby destroy the basis of Dutch wealth. Dunkirk was the main base and the headquarters of the operation, which, according to the increasing volume of complaints during the 1630s, did seriously damage Dutch commerce. As the bulk of prizes taken were Dutch, their action must have affected the flow of arms to Britain, even if many consignments did get through.[34]

V.

Clearly, international arms dealers played a vital role in provisioning the various parties involved in the British Civil Wars and were courted by all sides. Linked to an extensive network of manufacturers, suppliers and distributors, they could provide *matériel* in bulk to any part of Europe and certainly sent huge quantities of arms and armaments to Britain. Specialist arms dealers and general merchants, engaged in gun-running as a profitable sideline, benefited from the Civil Wars, even if it were only one theatre of war among others. To improve their returns they often wrung trading concessions out of the authorities with whom they dealt and demanded prompt payment. When they did not receive

---

32 Edwards, *Dealing in Death*, 220; J. Ohlmeyer, 'Irish Privateers during the Civil War, 1642-50', in: *Mariner's Mirror*, 76 (1990), 120; Bodl. Lib., Carte 3, fos.473-475v.

33 Edwards, *Dealing in Death*, 216.

34 R.A. Stradling, The Spanish Dunkirkers, 1621-48: a record of plunder and destruction, in: *Tijdschrift voor Geschiedenis*, 93 (1980), 543, 4, 547-57; Edwards, *Dealing in Death*, 201.

satisfactory treatment, as at the hands of certain Royalist officials, they stopped doing business with them. Individuals might support one side or another but most of them, even if they had a preference, did business with anyone who would pay their price. That they could name their own terms is an indication of the dominant position they had attained.

All sides relied upon these merchants to sustain their war effort at a certain level but, undoubtedly, the degree to which they depended upon them did vary and might change over time. The Scottish covenanters, with a comparatively small manufacturing base at home, could not have waged war very effectively without the huge quantities of weapons they acquired from abroad. The Irish were even more dependent upon imports. The king, too, had to import war materials in order to deal with both sets of insurgents. The loss of London to the Parliamentarians during the course of 1642 added to the royalists' difficulties. To supplement the weapons they managed to gather in they had to import arms on a massive scale. They did develop an arms industry and under the circumstances did reasonably well. However, output was much lower than that achieved by Parliament, even when allowance is made for the poor quality of the evidence. Munitions, for instance, always seemed to be in short supply and, as a result, were prominent in overseas cargoes. In general, therefore, the impression one gets is that the arms shipments were vital to the prosecution of the war and that without them the ability of the royalists to carry on the conflict would have been seriously impaired. The loss of their ports in 1644 and 1645, therefore, proved fatal to the king's cause.

Parliament should have been better placed to wage war. In the long term its control of the South-east and its arms industries proved an important asset, but at the opening of hostilities it had problems. It had little gunpowder and none could be produced. Imports from abroad, mostly from the Low Countries, helped bridge the gap. Even greater reliance had to be made on foreign match. Similarly, pressing need meant that most of the weapons had to be imported.

The situation gradually improved and by the end of 1643 home producers had begun to make a real contribution. By early 1645 native manufacturers were responsible for providing well over half of the arms and armaments needed. Imports were still required, of course, especially items such as gunpowder, match and self-igniting firearms for which raw materials or the necessary skills were lacking at home. Although over half of the gunpowder was made in the country, most of the saltpetre and all of the sulphur had to be obtained overseas. In addition, many of the swords had foreign blades.[35]

---

35 Edwards, *Dealing in Death*, 210-1.

From the Baltic to the Atlantic:
British merchants and the development of trade networks in the northern seas during the eighteenth century

Asa Eklund, Chris Evans and Göran Rydén

Recent work on the British economy in the eighteenth century has dwelt upon the importance of Britain's Atlantic Empire. Emphasis has been laid upon the process of economic integration that bound together Britain's North American and Caribbean possessions and the metropolitan economy.[1] The colonies provided new and seemingly insatiable markets for British manufactures. Total exports from Britain to North America and the West Indies grew by an astonishing 2,300 per cent in the course of the eighteenth century. As a result, the distribution of British exports of manufactured goods was increasingly orientated on the Atlantic Empire, rather than continental Europe. Just 13 per cent of such exports had gone to Britain's Atlantic colonies in 1699/1701, but by 1804/06 over 49 per cent went to the USA, Canada and the West Indies. The European share of manufactured exports plunged from nearly 87 per cent to 37 per cent over the same period.[2]

But the Atlantic economy, we are told, did not merely add to the *quantity* of demand, it transformed the *quality* of demand within Britain and its colonies. By bringing tropical and semi-tropical products (sugar, tobacco, dyestuffs, etc) into circulation it stimulated new forms of metropolitan consumerism. It encouraged product innovation. The new commodities from the tropics, produced by enslaved and unseen African plantation workers, required modish presentation in metropolitan salons, hence the proliferation of coffee pots, tea services, sugar tongs and all the other accoutrements of fashionable consumer display. This Atlantic world was, as the phrase has it, a 'world of goods'.[3] It was composed of a great diversity of new fabrics, ceramics, glasswares, semi-precious *objets*, and 'toys' that radiated outwards from specialised manufacturing districts in London and the English provinces to the transatlantic colonies.

---

1   D. Hancock, *Citizens of the world: London merchants and the integration of the British Atlantic community, 1735-1785,* Cambridge 1995; I.K. Steele, *The English Atlantic 1675-1740: an exploration of communication and community,* Oxford 1986; T.H. Breen, 'An empire of goods: the anglicization of colonial America, 1690-1776', in: *Journal of British Studies,* 25 (1986), 467-99.

2   N.F.R. Crafts, *British economic growth during the Industrial Revolution,* Oxford1985, 145.

3   J. Brewer and R. Porter (eds.), *Consumption and the world of goods,* London 1993.

The Atlantic economy sometimes appears as a closed commercial system. The Navigation Acts of the mid-seventeenth century had successfully restricted colonial producers to the use of English shipping and to a dependence upon English merchants, thereby breaking the maritime hegemony of the Dutch. At the same time, the spread of protectionist barriers in Europe in the late seventeenth and early eighteenth centuries must have inhibited the growth of British manufactured exports to Europe. But we should be wary of over-stressing the coherence of the British Atlantic. For all the dynamism of the Atlantic basin, British merchants retained and augmented their links with European markets. European markets were, not least, of critical importance for the re-export of colonial commodities such as tobacco. Moreover, Britain developed ever closer ties with peripheral areas of Europe capable of supplying raw materials that could not be furnished from the Atlantic plantations.

In this paper we propose to examine Britain's relationship with Europe's northern periphery, the Baltic, a major source of bar iron and naval stores such as timber, hemp and pitch. These prosaic commodities would seem to have little bearing on the dazzling new world of eighteenth-century consumerism. But they did. Needless to say, they underpinned maritime expansion. They were also to provide the material basis for much of the busy product innovation that was to characterise the 'world of goods'. Without high-quality Swedish iron there could have been no steel adequate for making of watch springs, scientific instruments, scalpels or steel jewellery. More generally, not only were the luxury and semi-luxury goods of the era to be made from appropriately robust or workable materials, but the new tools and instruments with which they were fabricated – precision lathes, stamps, files, etc – required ferrous components of a high and consistent quality.

Britain's commercial relations with the Baltic were transformed in the late seventeenth and early eighteenth centuries in ways that were intimately connected to broader shifts in the Atlantic economy. As we will demonstrate, the increasing demand for ironwares in the Americas and the emergence of new plantation crops such as Carolinian rice brought the Atlantic and Baltic economies into closer alignment. The Baltic trade and the different Atlantic trades had once been structurally distinct, but by the mid-eighteenth century important strands of mercantile activity in both of these trading zones had become interwoven, with a single set of merchants directing the flow of commodities and goods from one commercial theatre to another. The Baltic and Atlantic have conventionally been studied in historiographical isolation from one another, but, as this case study suggests, a unified history of these two busy areas of mercantile endeavour has much to offer.

I.

Sven-Erik Åström entitled his classic history of Anglo-Baltic trade in the seventeenth century "From cloth to iron".[4] The story he had to tell was thus encapsulated. In the sixteenth century British trade with the Baltic was a matter of textile exports, sold via Danzig in exchange for naval stores. By the mid-seventeenth century, however, English woollen textiles had been ejected from their former markets. From the 1650s onwards a radically new pattern of trade arose, centred upon Stockholm and the buying of bar iron for the burgeoning English market. At first this trade was managed by Dutch and Scottish factors, but by the late 1670s English merchants, overwhelmingly from London, had assumed control.[5] By 1700 the English market took 44 per cent of Stockholm's rapidly expanding iron exports, and the Scottish market a further 5 per cent. Thus, the iron trade between Sweden and Britain became one of the defining features of north European commerce.

The reasons for this striking development are easily found. English metalware manufacture, increasingly concentrated in specialised production zones in the West Midlands and northern England, was advancing fast, but domestic iron producers, hampered by a shortage of wood fuel, could not keep pace with the surge in demand for malleable bar iron. Despite the careful husbanding of coppice woods, English forgemasters could not break through a production ceiling of about 20,000 tons per annum. The shortfall had to be made good by imported iron. English consumers had traditionally looked towards Spain for iron imports. From the 1620s onwards merchants in the ports of the south-west had presided over a triangular trade that involved the despatch of fishing fleets to the Grand Banks, the trading of salted cod to northern Spain, and the importation of Basque iron (together with Castilian wool) into England. Yet by the late seventeenth century the Basque iron industry was in decline. Ironmongers looked to the Baltic instead. So that by 1700 some 15,000 tons of Swedish iron was shipped to British ports. By the 1740s the mean annual import of Swedish iron had reached nearly 23,000 tons, a volume that exceeded the output of the entire British forge sector.[6] In mid-century, when the rise in

---

4   S.-E. Åström, *From cloth to iron: the Anglo-Baltic trade in the late seventeenth century. Part 1: The growth, structure and organization of the trade*, Helsingfors 1963.

5   The Royal African Company purchased the iron it traded on the Guinea Coast in Amsterdam until 1680, but from London merchants after that date. K.G. Davies, *The Royal African Company*, London 1957, 174.

6   K.-G. Hildebrand, *Swedish iron in the seventeenth and eighteenth centuries. Export industry before industrialization*, Stockholm 1992, 26.

Swedish exports levelled off, but demand from British metalware manufacturers continued to rise, British merchants tapped new sources of supply in the Baltic, shipping Russian iron from St Petersburg. Russian exports to Britain had only begun in earnest in the 1730s, but by the end of the 1760s Russian iron had eclipsed the Swedish product. Total imports from the Baltic peaked in 1793 when nearly 60,000 tons of bar iron were landed on British quays.

This Baltic trade was at first a highly specialised field of enterprise. Its seventeenth-century practitioners did not much deal with other aspects of commerce. They remained focused on Europe, and on northern Europe in particular.[7] The Marescoes, for example, an Anglo-Dutch family active in London's Baltic trade in the 1660s and 1670s, imported Swedish iron, copper, pitch and tar on a large scale. Charles Marescoe sent sugar, spices and tropical dyestuffs to Hamburg and Amsterdam in return; but these he bought on the London market; he did not engage directly in the Atlantic trades.[8] Bilateral trade was typical of the late seventeenth century; Baltic merchants did not engage in a multilateral system of exchanges that might unite the Baltic and Atlantic. The activities of Adam Montgomerie, a Scottish factor, who arrived in Stockholm in 1699, were probably typical. Montgomerie shipped iron, brass wire, tar and timber to correspondents in Scotland and the north of Ireland. He balanced his accounts by importing largely Scottish bulk products such as Clyde herring.[9]

After the peace of Utrecht in 1713, separation of the Baltic and Atlantic trades became less pronounced. The process can be demonstrated by the career of a Bristol merchant named Graffin Prankard (fl. 1710-1740).[10] Prankard began as an Atlantic merchant, shipping ironmongery and other 'dry' goods to the North American colonies. But in the 1720s he also started to trade with the Baltic as well, thereby bringing the Atlantic and the Baltic together in a single commercial loop. Prankard pioneered the importation of Swedish iron into western Britain, whilst simultaneously shipping rice and other colonial products to north European markets. In addition he became involved in metalware manufacturing in Bristol's hinterland, using Swedish (and later Russian) iron to produce the steel and nails that he subsequently marketed in North America. In

---

7 And for their part, Atlantic traders were highly specialised. See N. Zahediah, 'Making mercantilism work: London merchants and Atlantic trade in the seventeenth century', in: *Transactions of the Royal Historical Society*, 6th series, 9 (1999), 143-58.

8 H. Roseveare (ed.), *Markets and merchants of the late seventeenth century: the Marescoe-David letters 1668-1680*, Oxford 1987.

9 See Montgomerie's letterbook for 1699-1702: Mitchell Library, Glasgow, SR352.

10 The discussion that follows is based upon Prankard's business papers in Somerset Archives (hereafter SA), ref. DD/DN 423-52. For a biographical sketch see J.H. Bettey, 'Graffin Prankard: an eighteenth-century Bristol merchant', in: *Southern History*, 12 (1990), 34-47.

other words, Prankard constructed a single, articulated production and marketing chain that stretched from *Bergslagen* – the mining district of central Sweden – to the Delaware valley and the low-country of South Carolina.

How is Graffin Prankard's innovative trading pattern to be explained? In part, he was reacting to the opportunities arising through Britain's growing iron deficit. Sven-Erik Åström has assumed that the English iron market in the early eighteenth century could be divided into distinct eastern and western sectors: the east was the domain of Swedish iron, but the west, equipped with more luxuriant woodlands and shielded from import penetration by higher transport costs, remained the preserve of native ironmasters.[11] By the 1720s this was clearly no longer the case. The market for iron in Bristol and the Severn valley could no longer be satisfied by local ironmasters. Hence Prankard's entry into this market was sudden and decisive. In 1721 he imported a mere 4 tons of foreign bar iron into Bristol. Thereafter the figures rose to 198 tons in 1723, then 395 tons in 1726, then to 933 tons in 1728.[12] At first, Prankard's sales seem to have been in the immediate hinterland of Bristol, but from 1725 onwards Swedish iron began to pour into the West Midlands, the heartland of British metalware manufacturing.[13]

Graffin Prankard was also responding to changes in the Atlantic economy that held out the possibility of employing his ships on an annual circuit between the Baltic and the youngest British colonies in North America. The carrying of rice from South Carolina was a key factor here. Rice cultivation took off in the Lower South in the 1690s to become South Carolina's leading export. These exports, which had amounted to less than 0.27 million pounds per annum at the close of the seventeenth century, averaged 3.36 million pounds annually for the period 1713-1717 and continued to climb very rapidly thereafter. This development, which made careful use of slaves taken from West Africa's 'rice coast', was intimately connected to events in the Baltic.[14] The onset of the Great Northern War in 1699 disrupted the movement of cereals from the southern Baltic to western Europe. As supplies of Polish grain slackened, it was

11 S.-E. Åström, 'Swedish iron and the English iron industry about 1700: some neglected aspects', in: *Scandinavian Economic History Review*, 30 (1982), 129-41.
12 Data supplied by Å. Eklund from the Bristol port books in the Public Record Office (PRO), E190 series.
13 D. Hussey, *Coastal and river trade in pre-industrial England: Bristol and its region 1680-1730*, Exeter 2000, 79.
14 J. A. Carney, *Black rice: the African origins of rice cultivation in the Americas*, Cambridge (Mass) 2001.

Carolinian rice that filled the gap, helping to sustain the poor of Holland and Germany.[15]

Swedish iron and Carolinian rice had complementary production cycles, of which Prankard took full advantage. He despatched one of his ships, the *Parham* or the *Baltic Merchant*, to Charleston in the autumn, just as ice was closing the more northerly Baltic ports to shipping. While the *Parham* crossed a rough, winterly Atlantic, the Carolinian rice crop, planted in April-May and harvested in September-October, was being prepared for shipment. Hundreds, perhaps thousands of slaves were engaged in laboriously 'pounding out' the rice in order to separate the husk from the grain, a task that took from November-December. When the *Parham* arrived at the year's end, Prankard's agent in Charleston would dispose of the nails, pots, steel, and gunpowder with which she was loaded. Having taken on hundreds of barrels of rice, a quantity of logwood, and perhaps some indigo, the *Parham* would sail for Europe in February or March.[16]

As Prankard's ship cleared Charleston, bar iron was already on the move from forges in *Bergslagen* to the staple towns from which it would be exported. In the depths of winter, sledges carrying bar iron were being dragged over the frozen lakes and snowy roads of the Swedish midlands. Most deliveries were to be completed by the spring thaw, which re-opened the Baltic ports to international trade. The successful completion of the transatlantic circuit that Prankard had initiated the previous autumn now required careful synchronisation amongst his agents across northern Europe. Rice, as an enumerated commodity under the Navigation Acts, had to be landed at a British port before it could be shipped on to a foreign market. The *Parham* would accordingly make the briefest of stops at Cowes or Poole, where customs officers would be bribed to work through the night. Then on to Hamburg in May, where David Skinner & Co would dispose of the rice for Prankard. The *Parham* would usually pass the Sound in ballast – if Skinner & Co had no onward cargo waiting for her, her master was to sail without delay – tying up at Stockholm in June.

Francis Jennings, Prankard's correspondent in the Swedish capital, assembled a lading of bar iron, timber and tar in readiness, acting on instructions

---

15 R.C. Nash, 'South Carolina and the Atlantic economy in the late seventeenth and eighteenth centuries', in: *Economic History Review*, 45 (1992), 677-702. See also K. Morgan, 'The organization of the colonial American rice trade', in: *William and Mary Quarterly*, 3rd series, 52 (1995), 433-552, and M. Weir, '"Shaftesbury's Darling": British settlement in the Carolinas at the close of the seventeenth century', in: N. Canny (ed.), *The Oxford history of the British Empire. Volume 1. The origins of empire: British overseas enterprise to the close of the seventeenth century*, Oxford 1998, 375-97.

16 In 1731-32 over 54 per cent of sailings from Charleston for Britain and Ireland occurred in the months of February, March and April. Steele, *English Atlantic*, 289.

received from Bristol during the winter. He was under orders to turn the *Parham* around in the fastest possible time, for the ship had to dock at Bristol in time for the city's St James fair at the end of July, when customers from across the southwest and the West Midlands would gather to settle their accounts and place new orders with Prankard.

II.

Graffin Prankard was not just concerned with transporting commodities across the surface of the globe; he was keenly interested in manufacturing and marketing specialised products for consumers around the Atlantic basin. Prankard did not trade in iron as a generic industrial good. He well understood that bar iron came in a variety of different qualities, each of them suiting a different purpose. If the integration of the Atlantic and Baltic worlds was to proceed smoothly, producers in Sweden had to be given detailed knowledge of the requirements of consumers in Britain, the Americas and Africa. For example, one key area of business for Prankard was the supplying of bar iron to Bristol slave merchants, then at the zenith of their power. 'Voyage iron', as it was known, was exchanged for slaves along the Guinea coast. In effect, voyage iron acted as a currency in slave markets. It had, therefore, to be cut to a specific weight and set of dimensions. Not surprisingly, Prankard's letters to Francis Jennings in Stockholm were replete with instructions concerning the shape and quality of voyage iron.[17] Jennings had to ensure that forgemen in remote *Bergslagen's* settlements were *au fait* with the preferences of African traders.[18]

Francis Jennings was able to assert a significant degree of control over production patterns because of the institutional framework within which iron was made in Sweden. The Swedish state had imposed a three-fold social division of labour on the iron industry in the early seventeenth century. Pig iron was smelted on a seasonal basis by peasant miners, whilst the refining of pig into bar iron was the allotted task of professional ironmasters (*brukspatroner*). The export of bar iron was placed in the hands of specialised international merchants. In practice, however, this neat division broke down. The *brukspatroner* tended to become indebted to the powerful merchants of the staple towns, often

---

17 For example, SA, DD/DN 425, Graffin Prankard to Francis Jennings, 28 February 1733.

18 These preferences clearly changed over time. The bars of voyage iron sold by Charles Marescoe in 1668 came at 50 bars to the ton; those exported by the Royal African Company in the mid 1680s were between 75 and 80 bars to the ton (Roseveare, *Markets and merchants*, 35; Davies, *Royal African Company*, 171). Prankard insisted upon 90 to 92 bars to the ton in the 1730s.

chronically. British merchants, by exploiting their links with Stockholm's quayside elite, were therefore able to lay claim to the product of debtor ironworks. Indeed, they were able to stipulate in advance the form of the product. In other words, dealers in Swedish iron were often ordering bespoke goods, tailored for niche markets.

Just as Francis Jennings was responsible for ensuring that forgemen appreciated the requirements of 'Guinea' traders, he had also to acquaint the forgemen who made the elite Öregrund brands of iron with the technical requirements of English steelmakers. Steelmaking was an area of critical significance for Graffin Prankard. Steelmakers in Birmingham or Sheffield insisted upon certain brands of Swedish iron, those from the Vallonbruk ('Walloon ironworks') in the county of Uppland.[19] The bar iron from these works, smelted from the fine, non-phosphoric ores of the famous Dannemora mine and refined by a forging technique that was practised nowhere else in Sweden, was uniquely suited to steelmaking. These Öregrund brands – so called after the local port through which they were shipped to Stockholm – were made in limited quantities and commanded a premium price on international markets. They were therefore the subject of much manoeuvring on the part of iron merchants anxious to corner the market in 'steel irons'. The most prized marks, those of Lövsta, Åkerby and Österby, were usually monopolised by a closed circle of London Baltic houses. It was then something of a coup for Graffin Prankard to edge aside the traditionally dominant London elite and win a monopoly contract for Lövsta and Åkerby bars in 1734. In concert with Samuel Shore of Sheffield, Prankard aggrandised the supply of the best Öregrund brands. By cooperating with the Stockholm-based monopoly consortium comprising Samuel Worster, Samuel Wordworth and Francis Jennings, they hoped to control the flow of Lövsta and Åkerby iron to British consumers.[20]

Prankard and Shore split the British market between them. "Mr Prankard hath the Bristoll London Birmingham and Ireland marketts to himself", crowed Samuel Shore, "I the Hull & New Castle Markettts as we may not prejudice each other...".[21] Amongst Prankard's most important customers was John Kettle, the proprietor of two cementation furnaces on the outskirts of Birmingham. As with voyage iron, quality control was of prime importance for steel makers. Francis Jennings was bombarded with complaints and pleas. Indeed, Jennings was sometimes compelled to travel into Bergslagen to talk to forge managers and

---

19 See K.C. Barraclough, Steelmaking before Bessemer. Volume 1: Blister steel, the birth of an industry, London 1984.

20 Korsäs AB:s arkiv, Leufsta Depån, Leufsta Brukens samteliga Concept Räkningar Från 1730 till 1740, vol. 268.

21 SA, DD/DN 426, Samuel Shore to Francis Bird, 15 August 1735.

workmen, giving encouragement and *douceurs* to ensure that the slag inclusions in the bars were kept to a minimum. By the mid 1730s Prankard was a major actor in the market for Öregrund iron. He estimated that he could annually dispose of between 300 and 340 tons for conversion to steel, roughly equivalent to a third of the British market.[22] Prankard was not merely a supplier of Öregrund iron, however, he was a steelmaker in his own right. At an early stage in his career he had been one of the proprietors of a steel cementation furnace at Tern in Shropshire.[23] Later, he used his steelmaking clients as subcontractors, sending them Öregrund bars to convert into steel on his account, which could then be marketed in North America under his own name.[24]

Graffin Prankard also engaged in the marketing of nails. Some of these were purchased from major Midland nailmasters like the Homfrays of Stourbridge. The Homfrays bought Russian iron, which was ideally suited for this purpose, from Prankard, slit it into nail rods at their mill in Worcestershire, and put the rods out to domestic nailers in the surrounding parishes. The *Heylin*, for example, which sailed from Bristol for Carolina in 1739, carried 24 casks of ironware, containing over 900,000 clasp nails, which Prankard had bought from Mary Homfray.[25] On other occasions the Homfrays acted as subcontractors for Prankard. They took a parcel of his iron, slit it into rods and – acting as Prankard's agents – distributed the material among their outworkers. The Homfrays returned the completed nails to Bristol. Like the cementation furnace proprietors who converted Prankard's iron into steel, they were paid a fee for superintending the manufacturing process.

The making of steel and nails for the American market sees Graffin Prankard as reaching back into the production chain to ensure quality control and the product's conformity with American demand. The same can be said of other Baltic merchants in the first half of the eighteenth century. They did not restrict themselves to importing bar iron; they intervened actively in the manufacturing process. Josias Wordsworth (d. 1749), for example, was one of London's elite Baltic merchants. He was well connected, being a supplier of bar iron to both the Navy Board and the East India Company.[26] He dealt widely in Swedish and

---

22 SA, DD/DN 426, Graffin Prankard to Francis Jennings, 12 April 1735, and DD/DN 427, Graffin Prankard to Samuel Shore, 24 December 1736.

23 B. Coulton, 'Tern Hall and the Hill family: 1700-75', in: *Shropshire History and Archaeology*, 66 (1989), 99-100.

24 See, for example, SA, DD/DN 438 (part 1), 1 March 1732, for Prankard's account with John and William Shallard, the proprietors of the cementation furnace at Keynsham outside Bristol.

25 SA, DD/DN 439, 22 June 1739.

26 See PRO, ADM 106/3592, 3595-98 for his Navy Board contracts, and British Library, Oriental and India Office Collections, L/AG/1/1/17, for his East India Company connections.

Russian iron, supplying numerous ironmongers in the West Midlands and London. Yet he also operated a manufacturing plant of his own. The firm in which he was a partner had its main base at Deptford on Thames, downstream from London, with a rolling mill and an anchor forge, as well as an assortment of warehouses and yards. An additional plant was to be found in the north-east of England: a suite of anchor shops on Tyneside and other workshops at Bebside in Northumberland.[27] Many of the products gathered in at Deptford were clearly earmarked for the New World's markets. Wordsworth and his associates shipped large volumes of nails, chains and agricultural implements to the Carolinas and the Caribbean. They traded directly with their customers, even accepting remittances in sugar from Jamaican planters.[28]

There is clear evidence here, and in the records of other leading iron-trading concerns, of the development of specialised products for the transatlantic markets. The firm founded by Sir Ambrose Crowley (d. 1713) was the largest single customer for Swedish iron in Britain in the first half of the eighteenth century. A massive inventory of the enterprise drawn up in 1728 discloses a formidable productive capacity, including steel furnaces and slitting mills, built up in the north-east of England since the end of the 1690s, and a huge diversity of manufactured articles destined for the plantation economies of the New World.[29] 'Virginia hoes' were made in eight different grades, as were 'Barbados hoes'; padlocks were made in profusion, including those 'Wide – for Negroes Necks'. The debts outstanding at John Crowley's death also reveal the transatlantic reach of the Crowley firm. To take just those overseas customers whose debts were in excess of £ 1,000, six were to be found in Jamaica, four in Antigua, three in Barbados, and one each in St Kitts, Nevis, and Montserrat. Four other major debtors were to be found in the Carolinas.

III.

The century following the restoration of the Stuart monarchy in 1660 saw England, and more especially London, established as the hub of the international iron market in the Northern Hemisphere. English metalware manufacturers drew upon specialised export zones in national economies that were only partially monetised (in the case of Sweden) or reliant on unfree labour (in the case of

---

27 PRO, C 11/822/3; British Library, Oriental and India Office Collection, MSS Eur F 218/115, 'An Inventory of the Stock belonging to Crowley Hallett & Company at Ladyday 1751'.

28 British Library, Oriental and India Office Collection, MSS Eur F 218/114.

29 Suffolk Record Office (Ipswich), HAI/GD/5/1-17.

Russia). In return, the metalware manufacturers churned out a prodigious quantity of tools, fittings, weapons and decorative objects.[30] Many of these were for the domestic market, but many others were for the New World. These ranged from machetes for slaves on Caribbean sugar estates to harpoons and 'Greenland Axes' for the use of whalers sailing out of ports in New England.

British iron merchants, in their efforts to circumvent fuel constraints within the British Isles, constructed an international iron trade that spanned the Northern Hemisphere by the mid eighteenth century. The wood energy deficit that threatened to choke off metal manufacturing in Britain was to be relieved by raiding the energy resources of *Bergslagen*, the Urals, and the North American colonies. Some grades of bar iron had to be drawn from Sweden and from Russia, particularly those brands, such as *Öregrund*, whose qualities could not be reproduced by English ironmakers. At the same time, the domestic forge trade had to continue as an important source of supply for metalware manufacturers. In fact, British bar iron output could be boosted significantly if pig iron was imported from charcoal-rich American colonies instead of being smelted locally. If colonial forests were devoted to smelting pig iron, then British ironmasters could concentrate their resources on the high value-added forge sector. This began on a small scale in the 1730s when Midland forgemasters began to import pig iron from Maryland and Virginia.

The prospects for an integrated, transatlantic iron industry were good in the 1740s and 1750s, when legislation to foster just such a spatial division of labour was passed by the British parliament. Some ironmasters hoped that an imperial iron trade, spanning the Atlantic, might even lessen Britain's dependence upon the Baltic. It was not to be. Most American ironmasters had rapidly growing markets of their own to attend to; they did not see the necessity of shipping pig iron to Britain. Then the American Revolution put paid to any hopes that colonial ironmakers could be subordinated to merchants in Bristol and London.

A critical change in the position of Baltic iron was only to come in the 1790s, when the coal technology revolution swept the British forge sector. Henry Cort's puddling process, patented in 1783-84, provided an effective and expeditious way of using mineral coal to refine iron. It released the British iron industry from the constraints placed upon it by a dependence upon plant fuel. Thus, the prospects for Baltic iron darkened. For the first time in a century and a half, British ironmasters were in a position to take command of their home market. Baltic iron tumbled from a position of dominance, undercut by cheap British-made bar iron and bound by discriminatory tariffs. By the end of the Napoleonic

---

30   M. B. Rowlands, *Masters and men in the West Midland metalware trades before the Industrial Revolution*, Manchester 1975.

wars Russian iron had been entirely expelled from the British market whilst Swedish iron was restricted to niche markets such as that for steel iron. British bar iron output, a mere 32,000 tons in 1788, sprang to 150,000 tons in 1815.[31] The Baltic and the Atlantic trading systems, which had been drawn together in the eighteenth century by British iron merchants at the start of the eighteenth century, were broken off in the early years of the nineteenth century.

IV.

We wish to conclude with some reflections on the function of merchants in the making and manufacturing of iron in the eighteenth-century economy. During the charcoal era merchants played a critical role in the British iron industry – or iron trade, to use the more accurate term that contemporaries employed to designate the web of production from which finished metal goods emerged. As fuel shortages made a geographical concentration of production so difficult, the various processes of ironmaking and metalware manufacturing were spatially dispersed. Raw materials and semi-processed goods were exchanged between producers. In fact, we would argue against the conventional distinction that is made between ironmasters (those involved in the making of commodities) and iron merchants (those involved in the wholesaling of commodities). Mid-eighteenth-century British ironmasters were not industrialists involved in the management of a plant – characteristically, they subcontracted the production process to workmen – they were merchants, concerned with marketing the products that came out of the forges or mills they nominally controlled.[32] Conversely, so-called iron merchants reached back into the sphere of production, having materials made up according to their specifications and then sold under their trademarks.

This ended with the coal technology revolution of the late eighteenth century – with the concentration and integration of processes that it permitted. For the first time the different stages of production could be integrated or internalised within the confines of a single firm, and localised within a coalfield.

---

31 S. Pollard and R.S.W. Davies, 'The iron industry 1750-1850', in: C.H. Feinstein and S. Pollard (eds.), *Studies in capital investment in the United Kingdom 1750-1920*, Oxford 1988, 87.

32 C. Evans and G. Rydén, 'British ironmasters in the eighteenth century', in: H-J. Gerhard, K.H. Kaufhold and E. Westermann (eds.), *Europäische Montanregion Harz*, Bochum 2001, 81-92.

An international division of labour, articulated by merchants, withered away as Swedish and Russian irons were driven out of the British market. In the early nineteenth century, for the first time, a distinction became appropriate between ironmasters as industrialists and iron merchants as actors concerned with the circulation of commodities made by industrialists.

Webs of Information, Bonds of Trust: the networks of early eighteenth-century Chester merchants

Jon Stobart

I.

The history of eighteenth-century trade is often told in terms of imports and exports, shipping and counting-houses, commodities and capital, or else through the biographies of prominent merchants, each with their triumphs and disasters, strengths and foibles. As Hancock argues, both approaches have their strong points, but both fail to recognise the inter-connectedness of individual lives and businesses.[1] We can tell the same history, arguably more effectively, in terms of the webs of information and the bonds of trust that tied merchants together. That is, in terms of their personal and commercial networks.

Networks are increasingly recognised as key elements of both historical and present day economic activity. Whereas earlier analyses portrayed them as exceptional, transient and unstable, so-called 'new institutional' perspectives see networks as an important form of business integration, intermediate between the extremes of markets and firms. Indeed, they are central to Putnam's notion of social capital as a means of improving economic performance.[2] Historians of the eighteenth and nineteenth centuries have noted that, in the absence of formal business institutions and well-developed communication systems, they were a necessary requirement for efficient economic activity. Meanwhile, studies of late twentieth-century economies show that loose informal networks not only persist, but also form an important aspect of regional development and competitive advantage. The reciprocity and trust upon which they are based encourage economically productive co-operation and collaboration.[3] In all these contexts, networks would afford a range of benefits to their members. First and foremost,

1   D. Hancock, *Citizens of the World. London Merchants and the Integration of the British Atlantic Community, 1735-85*, Cambridge 1995, 3-5.

2   M. Casson and M.B. Rose, 'Institutions and the evolution of modern business', in: *Business History*, 39 (1997), 1-8; R. Pearson and D. Richardson, 'Business networking in the industrial revolution', in: *Economic History Review*, 54 (2001), 657-79; R. Putnam, *Making Democracy Work*, Princeton 1993.

3   See, for example, J. Ojala, 'Approaching Europe: the merchant networks between Finland and Europe', in: *European Review of Economic History*, 1 (1997), (Seite?); G. Cookson, 'Family firms and business networks: textile engineering in Yorkshire, 1780-1830', in: *Business History*, 39 (1997), 1-20; M. Porter, *The Competitive Advantage of Nations*, London 1990, 442-5; R. Putnam, *Making Democracy Work*, especially 161.

links within a network form business opportunities. They are contacts with other traders, manufacturers or financiers often in other places, providing connections to supplies and markets, goods and capital. For early-modern merchants, close business links through a network of national and international contacts were essential for the success, indeed for the basic operation, of their trading activities. More than this, they were often a pre-requisite for entry into international commerce, as is clear from the widespread apprenticing of merchants' sons to colleagues in other ports and other countries, and the common use of letters of introduction.[4]

Second, interaction and association, be it social, cultural or political, 'reinforced the web of business connections, and contributed to the development of common value systems'.[5] This can be seen in the solidarity shown by the 'gentlemen merchants' of Leeds, and the anchoring of social and economic networks in chapel attendance in west Yorkshire.[6] The shared attitudes, goals and aspirations thus engendered in a network could help to reduce the risk and thus the cost of commercial transactions. There are two related elements to this: trust and information. As Casson argues, trust is one means of guaranteeing quality and reliability, and thus reducing transaction costs. Consequently, people prefer to deal with people of known repute.[7] This, in turn, places emphasis on the business and moral character of the businessman and the 'regard' in which they are held.[8] Reputation could be established through honest trading, but also through engaging in public life, charitable works and cultural patronage. This important socio-cultural dimension is increasingly recognised in new institutional perspectives which emphasise the role of non-economic institutions in shaping business activity.[9] Thus we see late eighteenth- and early-nineteenth-

---

4   See D. Hancock, *Citizens of the World*, 115-31; R. Westerfield, *Middlemen in English Business, 1660-1760*, New Haven 1915, 394-400; K. Morgan, *Bristol and the Atlantic Trade in the Eighteenth Century*, Cambridge 1993, passim; I. Bull, 'Training as a merchant. Personal networks as an element in the education of young merchants in the eighteenth century', in: unpublished paper given at the *Fifth International Conference on Urban History*, Berlin 2000.

5   R. Pearson and D. Richardson, 'Business networking', 672.

6   R. Wilson, *Gentlemen Merchants. The Merchant Community in Leeds, 1700-1830*, Manchester 1971; S. Caunce, 'Complexity, community structure and competitive advantage with the Yorkshire woollen industry, c.1700-1850', in: *Business History*, 39 (1997), 27-43.

7   M. Casson, *The Economics of Business Culture*, Oxford 1991, 8; Pearson and Richardson, 'Business networking', 657. See also M. Casson and M.B. Rose, 'Evolution of modern business', 4.

8   A. Offer, 'Between the gift and the market: the economy of regard', in: *Economic History Review*, 50 (1997), 450-76

9   See, for example, C. Muldrew, *The Economy of Obligation. The Culture of Credit and Social Relations in Early Modern England*, Basingstoke 1998; Cookson, 'Family firms and business networks', *Business History*; Y. Ben-Porath, 'The F-Connection: families, friends and firms and

century Liverpool merchants investing increasing amounts of time and money in philanthropic enterprises and in trying to create a cultured image for their town and themselves. Similarly, many London merchants took on the trappings of gentile and cultured living, not least through patronage of the arts.[10] Once established, reputation could become a transaction benefit to be communicated and traded upon across the network. This process often reinforced the status of the individual: those with a good reputation could be trusted because it was a valuable asset which they would not want to lose.[11] Third, these notions of reputation and trust link to what Burt terms the 'information benefits' of networks.[12] Knowing where information could be acquired, and the extent to which it could be trusted as accurate and complete, is vital to all businesses. Networks serve to circulate and direct flows of information. In this sense, they can be seen as mechanisms for reducing the transaction costs incurred because of the absence of information, or where its reliability is uncertain.[13] Information from a trusted source – an individual held in regard within the network – would be especially privileged. Much as Shapin has argued – albeit in a very different context – 'truth' was a product of the source of information as much as the information itself.[14] Thus, common values, trust, reputation and information flows were bound up in networks of individuals and together helped to reduce transaction costs. What cemented these networks were close personal relationships, sustained by regular contact and mutual respect, and often built around family and community.[15]

The family is seen as a major foundation for commercial activity in the eighteenth century. Sons followed fathers into trade; wives helped out in shops and inherited their husbands businesses, and inter-marriage between merchant families was commonplace.[16] Wider kinship networks constituted a resource

the organisation of exchange', in: *Population and Development Review*, 6 (1980), 1-30.

10 J. Stobart, 'Culture versus commerce: societies and spaces for elites in eighteenth-century Liverpool', in: *Journal of Historical Geography*, 28 (2002), 471-85; D. Hancock, *Citizens of the World*, 279-381.

11 M. Casson, *Economics of Business Culture*, 16.

12 R. Burt, 'The network entrepreneur', in: R. Swedberg (ed.), *Entrepreneurship. The Social Science View*, Oxford 2000, 286-8.

13 See D. North, 'Transaction costs in history', in: *Journal of European Economic History*, 3 (1985).

14 S. Shapin, *A Social History of Truth*, Chicago 1994. See also R. Burt, 'The network entrepreneur', 288.

15 C. Muldrew, *Economy of Obligation*, 152.

16 L. Davidoff and C. Hall, *Family Fortunes: Men and Women of the English Middle Class, 1780-1850*, London 1987, 52-7; A. Owens, 'Inheritance and life cycle of family firms in early nineteenth-century England', in: *Business History*, 44 (2002), 21-46; R. Wilson, *Gentlemen*

which could be drawn on when occasion demanded. They formed a 'network of trust, the use of which reduced the transaction costs and the dangers and uncertainties of business activity'.[17] Personal and commercial networks were also shaped by community, for example clusters of locally resident friends or as a more formal system structured by church, civic or political affiliations. Pearson and Richardson warn against overly simplistic readings of such communities, arguing that common business interests could bridge political or religious divisions in middle-class society.[18] That said, Anglican-Tory merchants dominated corporate life in early eighteenth-century Liverpool and in Leeds, whilst Quakers formed increasingly important national and international networks of interest.[19]

Moreover, as was argued earlier, involvement in public life, and networking through civic authority, provided useful contacts and enhanced one's reputation. However, this focus on family and community, whilst providing valuable insights, has led to a relative neglect of wider networks which tied individuals, communities and businesses into increasingly national and global economies. And yet the link between local and global, and between social and commercial networks was intimate and mutually formative. Local networks reflected and shaped the social, economic and cultural life of towns, but in ways which have yet to be fully explored. Social and business linkages served to reinforce one another in myriad ways which we are only beginning to appreciate. Accordingly, this paper has two broad aims. The first is to explore the ways in which personal and commercial networks were mutually constructed. To what extent were local business networks structured by family, community and civic life, and how did these link with broader webs tying Chester and Chester merchants to national and global economies? The second is to assess the benefits that accrued to the individual merchant from networking. How useful were networks in enhancing and communicating reputation and trust; and to what extent were transaction costs reduced by this trust and the provision of reliable business information?

Merchants.

17 M. Casson and M.B. Rose, 'Evolution of modern business', 4.

18 R. Pearson and D. Richardson, 'Business networking', 662.

19 M. Power, 'Councillors and commerce in Liverpool, 1650-1750', in: *Urban History* 24 (1997), 301-23; R. Wilson, *Gentlemen Merchants*, 172-7; J. Price, 'The great Quaker business families of eighteenth-century London', in: R. Dunn and M. Dunn (eds), *The World of William Penn*, Philadelphia 1986, 363-99.

II.

In the early eighteenth century, ships set out from Chester to a range of destinations in Europe and North America, but Ireland dominated the overseas trade, accounting for 86 per cent of ships and nearly 80 per cent of goods clearing the port (Table 1). Coastal traffic carried goods to Liverpool, London, Bristol and Plymouth as well as a large number of smaller Welsh ports.[20] By this time, Liverpool had eclipsed Chester as the region's principal port, whilst long-term problems of silting prompted larger ships to use out-ports at Neston and Parkgate. Nonetheless, Chester had a growing volume of overseas and coastal trade, and a buoyant shipbuilding industry employing upwards of 250 men and still constructing 500 ton vessels in the early nineteenth century. There was a prosperous, but small set of merchants engaged in this trade, probably numbering around fifteen to twenty at any one time.[21] Their probate records indicate that the personal networks of these merchants focussed in the first instance onto family.[22] 60 per cent of the executors named were kin: one-quarter being wives or children and one-third drawn from a wider circle of brothers, nephews and cousins. These close family ties are still more evident from the inheritance strategies of these merchants. As frequently happened in north-west England, most bequests were to immediate family members and many testators left their entire estates to their wives and children.[23] In the absence of this nuclear family, the net was spread more widely, but the focus remained on the family. Thus, William Whitfield divided the vast majority of his estate between his sister, nephew and niece, aunt and uncle, and a number of cousins; whilst James Comberbach left land and money to a large number of relations, including seven

---

20 R. Craig, 'Some aspects of the trade and shipping of the river Dee in the eighteenth century', in: *Transactions, Historic Society of Lancashire and Cheshire*, 114 (1963), 99-128; A. Kennett (ed.), *Georgian Chester*, Chester 1987, 18.

21 Twelve merchants are listed as voting in the contested election of 1732 (CCA, CEA/1). A further three, listed as aldermen, are known to have been merchants.

22 Probate records are economic, social and cultural as well as legal documents and so reflect many aspects of an individual's life-world. Mapping the relative social and spatial position of executors and administrators thus gives a good picture of the networks of close social and economic interaction which bound together individuals and places. See A. Owens 'Property, will making and estate disposal in an industrial town, 1800-1857', in: J. Stobart and A. Owens (eds), *Urban Fortunes. Property and Inheritance in the Town, 1700-1900*, Aldershot 2000, 79-107; D. Cressy, 'Kinship and kin interaction in early-modern England', in: *Past and Present*, 113 (1986), 44–53; S. D'Cruze, 'The middling sort in eighteenth-century Colchester', in: J. Barry and C. Brooks (eds), *The Middling Sort of People: Culture, Society and Politics in England, 1550–1800*, London 1994, 190-99.

23 See J. Stobart, 'Social and geographical contexts of property transmission in the eighteenth century', in: Stobart and Owens (eds), *Urban Fortunes*, 117-18, 123-8.

nephews, five nieces, his sister-in-law, a cousin from Ireland and an unspecified number of great-nephews and -nieces.[24] Executorial links and post-mortem gifts also highlight the importance of community in structuring the social worlds of Chester's merchants. They appear to have chosen their closest and most trusted friends from amongst the elite of the city and county. Of the nineteen executors unrelated to the testator, seven were gentry and further four were other merchants. The best connected merchant was probably Charles Mytton, whose estate was administered by his widow, a gentleman of the city and Richard Grosvenor, one-time mayor and then Member of Parliament for Chester. However, several others signalled their close personal ties with the gentry and pseudogentry through post-mortem gifts.[25] Notions of community stretched beyond such friendships to encompass the wider population: a high proportion of merchants giving money to the poor in their wills. Often, as in the case of Henry Bennett and Matthew Anderton, this charitable giving was centred onto Chester, but others left money for the poor of surrounding or more distant villages – reflecting the rural origins of men such as Thomas Williams.[26] As well as being a genuine attempt to improve the lot of the urban or rural poor, these gifts formed part of the social elite's traditional obligation to community and publicly signalled the good character of the merchant. Whatever the precise motive, such gifting signalled the close links that merchants possessed with local community.

Although there is some evidence of inter-generational business links, Chester merchants do not appear to have drawn heavily on either their immediate or their extended family in weaving their commercial webs. William Whitfield left his stock in trade to his nephew, Robert Bulkeley, and Michael Johnson took on his namesake – probably his nephew – as an apprentice, but the wider engagement of kin networks in business is more difficult to discern.[27] Even the extensive correspondence of Daniel Peck includes just six references to family, even though his uncle, cousin and son-in-law were all engaged in trade in London.[28] At no stage does Peck appear to have sent goods to his merchant relatives, although twice he asks London merchants for bills to be paid to his son-in-law John Capper. More important as a forum in which business contacts could be forged and strengthened was the local community. As was typical, Chester merchants drew apprentices predominantly from the city and its environs,

---

24 Cheshire and Chester Archives (CCA), WS 1757 William Whitfield; WS 1738 James Comberbach.

25 CCA, WS 1746 Charles Mytton.

26 CCA, WS 1715 Henry Bennett; WS 1693 Matthew Anderton; WS 1757 William Whitfield.

27 CCA, WS 1757 William Whitfield; MAB/2/19.

28 CCA, CR 352/1.

including north Wales.[29] Amongst the sons of tradesmen, clergy, yeomen and so on, were Robert Pigat and Roger Barmston, sons of Cheshire squires, and Roger Parry whose father was a gentleman from Mostyn – an out-port of Chester on the Welsh coast.[30] Such links served to tie Chester to its hinterland, reinforcing personal with economic contacts. Through the payment of apprenticeship fees, it also drew capital into productive commercial use and from the countryside into town. It was through the civic life of Chester that the networking potential of intra-community linkages was perhaps strongest. Merchants formed an important part of Chester's corporation in the early eighteenth century, comprising at least five aldermen and a similar number of councilmen, and accounting for six of the fourteen mayors elected between 1697 and 1710.[31] The coherence of this grouping is difficult to discern. Their political allegiances seem to have been split: the corporation was in essence Tory, but some aldermen and the majority of merchants were Whig supporters in the contested election of 1732.[32] Civic ties were strengthened, though, by family connections: the merchant-alderman Thomas Partington, for example, was brother-in-law to John Stringer – the mayor of Chester 1713/14 – and his kinsman Edward Partington was a fellow member of the corporation.[33] Whilst they never achieved the domination seen in Liverpool and Leeds, where merchants formed powerful oligarchies,[34] there was a clear nexus of merchant-aldermen forming a strong personal network at the heart of the city's economic, social and political life. They served on committees and acted as auditors; they were involved in planning a number of public works, and many gave gifts to the corporation or to key city charities. For example, following his election as an alderman in 1688/89, William Allen prepared a number of reports, audited several sets of accounts (including those of the first Navigation scheme) and gave gifts of silverware to the corporation.[35]

Public service brought three main benefits to Chester's merchants. First, they could influence the corporation's policies and expenditure. Although they could not match the capital-intensive schemes of Liverpool corporation – which

---

29 See R. Wilson, *Gentlemen Merchants*, 24; R. Westerfield, *Middlemen in English Business*, 402.

30 CCA, MAB/2/34v; MAB/2/43v; MAB/2/53.

31 Chester's Great Charter of 1506 made provision for twenty-four aldermen and 40 councilmen from whom a mayor and two sheriffs would be elected – see R.H. Morris, *Chester in the Plantagenet and Tudor Reigns*, Chester (no date), 525.

32 CCA, CEA/1.

33 CCA, WS 1718 Thomas Partington; A/B/3/93.

34 M. Power, 'Councillors and commerce in Liverpool, 1650-1750', in: *Urban History* 24 (1997), 309-311; R. Wilson, *Gentlemen Merchants*, 9-36.

35 CCA, A/B/3/41v, A/B/3/57; A/B/3/79v; A/B/3/94v; A/B/3/272v.

included the construction of the first commercial wet dock in the country[36] – they were involved in promoting the first navigation of the river Dee. This scheme held clear benefits for the merchant community as bringing goods to Chester was becoming increasingly difficult and costly due to problems of silting. The special committee appointed by the corporation in 1693 to report on the matter included at least four merchants and a further four were co-opted in 1701 to help oversee the work put in motion by the 1699 Act of parliament.[37] The ongoing efforts to keep the channel open to sizeable ships clearly reflected the economic priorities of the merchant community. In addition to these direct political-economic benefits, involvement in civic life increased an individual's social capital: that is, the density and strength of their network of contacts. For Chester merchants, association through the corporation shaped and strengthened mutual trust and reciprocity. These relationships were reflected in the bonds of civic responsibility, kinship, friendship, trust and respect that existed between merchant-aldermen (Figure 1).

Figure 1: Personal links between merchant-aldermen in Chester

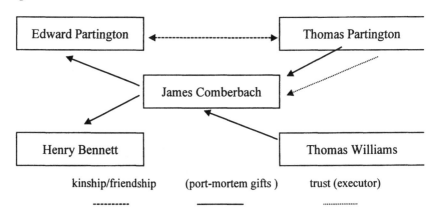

36 M. Power, 'Councillors and commerce', 301.
37 CCA, A/B/3/41v, A/B/3/93. See also A. Kennett, *Georgian Chester*, 18.

They both opened up and cemented reliable, trustworthy contacts with a group of like-minded and well-connected individuals.[38] This links to the last of the principal benefits of serving on the city's corporation: its power to enhance reputation and standing amongst the Chester elite and beyond. Public life in terms of charitable works, cultural patronage and civic duty demonstrated a commitment to the common good and a willingness to contribute to, as well as benefit from, socio-economic networks. "Regard", as Offer argues, "provides a powerful incentive for trust", not just amongst fellow aldermen, but also in wider social, business and mercantile networks.[39]

For all these reasons, being part of the local establishment assisted in the business dealings of merchants in Chester and elsewhere. It is perhaps surprising, then, that such networking does not seem to have generated formal partnerships of the type commonly seen in Bristol and Liverpool, especially amongst merchants engaged in the lucrative, but risky trans-Atlantic trade.[40]

The letter book of Daniel Peck mentions business dealings with just three Cestrians – one of them a fellow alderman – but none appears to have involved partnerships. Indeed, the only reference to such arrangements between merchant-aldermen comes from the will of Thomas Partington where, in leaving him £5, he refers to James Comberbach as "my good friend and partner".[41] There were undoubtedly other partnerships, but it is likely that Chester merchants did not need to draw on local resources and share risks to the same extent as their counterparts in Liverpool, Bristol and London. Any trade was hazardous, especially during times of war, but the bulk of Chester's overseas trade was with Europe (Table 1).

Whilst certain ports or shipping channels might be periodically closed, the routes and markets were more familiar and the shipping times relatively short. The initial investment, and the risks and returns, were probably insufficient to make profit sharing partnerships worthwhile.

It might even be possible to argue that such arrangements would be a wasteful use of time and social capital. As Burt suggests, networks are productively extended only through the addition of useful contact: those with no benefits are not merely unnecessary, they absorb valuable time in their maintenance. In short, 'efficient-effective' networks need to be widened and

---

38 On the importance of building up such networks, see Burt, 'The network entrepreneur', 289-94.
39 R. Pearson and D. Richardson, 'Business networking', 672. See also A. Offer, 'Between the gift and the market: the economy of regard', in: *Economic History Review*, 50 (1997), 450-76.
40 M. Power, 'Politics and progress in Liverpool, 1660-1740', in: *Northern History*, 35 (1999), 119-38; D. Hancock, *Citizens of the World*, 115-42; K. Morgan, *Bristol and the Atlantic Trade in the Eighteenth Century*, Cambridge 1993, 7-33.
41 CCA, WS 1718 Thomas Partington.

diversified to include distant contacts, not 'fattened' with extra links in the local area.[42]

Table 1: Ships cleared in the overseas trade of Chester, 1710-1717

Destination	Number	Per cent	Tons	Per cent
Ireland	1,153	86.0	52,045	79.8
Holland	48	3.6	3,646	5.6
France	47	3.5	3,291	5.0
Portugal/Canaries	33	2.5	1,730	2.7
Isle of Man	15	1.1	308	0.5
Italy	12	0.9	2,180	3.3
Norway/Sweden	9	0.7	735	1.1
Spain	9	0.7	405	0.6
America / West Indies	7	0.5	520	0.8
Newfoundland	4	0.3	200	0.3
Hamburg/Prussia	3	0.2	195	0.3
Total	1,340		65,255	

Source: Craig, 'Trade and shipping of the river Dee', 109. Note: There are no figures available for coastal shipping in the early eighteenth century.

III.

Merchants drew on a variety of institutional, personal and business networks to spin their wider webs. As a garrison, cathedral and county town, Chester had strong links with other parts of the country, especially London. There was a regular movement of soldiers to and from Chester, with large groups being assembled in the city prior to embarkation on military campaigns in Ireland.[43] The clergy of a diocese stretching across three counties were drawn into Chester's sphere, and the bishops, albeit sometimes *in absentia*, tied the city to national ecclesiastical and political life. Such contact was strengthened by the city's Members of Parliament who provided a personal as well as a political link between Chester and Westminster, generally acting in the best interests of the town.[44] More concrete ties with London came in the form of regular coach and mail services. As early as 1673 there were coaches three times each week; a

---

42 R. Burt, 'The network entrepreneur', 289-94.
43 J. Stobart, 'County, town and country: three histories of urban development in eighteenth-century Chester', in: P. Borsay and L. Proudfoot (eds), *Provincial Towns in Early Modern England and Ireland: Change, Convergence and Divergence*, London 2002, 192.
44 A. Kennett, *Georgian Chester*, 21.

century later there was a mail coach every day but Wednesday, a 'flying machine' three times a week and at least six other coaches and nine wagons.[45] These carried goods and people, but also letters and bills of exchange. These were especially important for merchants: the extensive correspondence and financial systems of men like Daniel Peck being dependent upon the speed, security and reliability of these transport services. The wider set of connections engendered by these political functions and articulated by road and coaching networks found their reflection in the individual and collective geographical horizons of Chester residents. They named executors in Holywell, Denbigh and Wrexham; Coventry, Hereford, Oxford and Nottingham; Dumfries, Edinburgh and Islay; London, Dublin and Cork, and dozens of towns and villages in Cheshire, Lancashire and Shropshire. In all, nearly one-quarter of the executorial links with people living outside Chester were to places more than 50 miles (80 kilometres) distant.

Chester's merchants were thus located within an extensive and complex set of social, political and economic networks which helped to structure their own business contacts. Yet merchants operated within commercial webs that spread wider still: to distant, often overseas, trading partners. One common entrée to such national and international networks was through the apprenticing of sons to fellow merchants. Besides the formal training in mercantile activities – indeed, perhaps more important than such instruction – apprenticeship gave exposure and access to masters' local and distant business contacts. Once out of his indentures, a young merchant would commonly start trading as a factor for his former master. This brought experience of overseas markets which could be invaluable in future trading; gave the apprentice recognised status in established networks, and provided a starting point for the construction of his own commercial webs.[46] It marked out the young merchant as someone who was known and trusted. Another means of accessing business networks was via letters of introduction which consciously included the newcomer into a set of trusted contacts. Thus, Daniel Peck wrote to his fellow merchants Messers Day and Cassamajor in Bristol that:

"Yesterday morning set forward for yr City an honest Gentleman of Leverpoole Mr Jno Smallwood, Concerned in the Tobacco Ships arrived in yr Port whom designed to have accompanied to Bristoll. Please to render him what services you can and lett him know I desired you to speak to him and to offer him what

45 P. Broster, *The Chester Guide*, Chester 1782; *Universal British Directory*, vol.II, London 1792.

46 D. Hancock, *Citizens of the World*, 115-24; J. Price, 'Sheffeild v. Starke: institutional experimentation in the London-Maryland trade c.1696-1706', in: R. Davenport-Hines and J. Liebenau (eds), *Business in the Age of Reason*, London 1987, 19-39.

assistances may be requisite to a Merchant Stranger – he desired me to give him a letter of recommendation but was gone before [I] had an opportunity to write."[47]

As with apprenticeship, such personal commendation spread information about the individual to other places.[48] Peck's letter made Smallwood known and therefore someone to be trusted. When Peck himself required assistance in accessing new markets, he turned – as Smallwood had clearly done – to established contacts. Thus, he wrote to his friends in London for help in organising a shipment of deal, tar and iron from Sweden, writing: "please to … think of some friend abroad to recommend this design in my favour".[49]

Once established, these contacts required careful nurturing. Although family members might be called on after years of silence,[50] to keep their relationship alive and meaningful, business contacts had to keep in touch with each other regularly. Over fifteen months, Peck wrote on average two or three letters each week, but this could rise to four or five letters each day. This correspondence was crucial to the success of his trading operations; it also defined and articulated his business world by placing him at the centre of a complex web of commercial and personal linkages. Peck wrote to thirty-five individuals in at least eleven different locations, but over half his letters went to three correspondents: fellow merchants in London, Dublin and Bristol (Table 2). Whilst anxious to cultivate useful new connections, Peck seems to have been careful to use his principal contacts as links into other networks centred on them, rather than simply extend his own network. Such a strategy would have avoided over-stretching his ability to keep in regular contact whilst providing potentially useful contacts across Britain and Europe.[51] Thus, via Rathbone, he tapped into networks spreading from Dublin to the rest of Ireland and back to English ports including Liverpool where Rathbone apparently had business dealings. Similarly, Peck tapped into the networks of Thomas and Michael Carbonell in London, using their contacts in Sweden, Holland and probably Portugal.[52] Such practices allowed merchants to extend their networks in an efficient manner. They were based on the mutual benefits of shared trade, but more fundamentally on trust between merchants; trust built on friendship, integrity and reputation.[53]

---

47 CCA, CR 352/1, 21 October 1704.

48 R. Burt, 'The network entrepreneur', 287.

49 CCA, D/Mc.1, Page from Letter Book of Daniel Peck, 13 November 1703.

50 See D. Cressy, 'Kinship and kin interaction'.

51 R. Burt, 'The network entrepreneur', 289.

52 CCA, CR 352/1 (for example: 2 March 1704, 15 July 1704). CCA, D/Mc.1, 13 November, 1703.

53 See C. Muldrew, *Economy of Obligation*, 186-9.

Table 2: Recipients of letters from Daniel Peck, 1703/04

Location	Number	Percent
London	47	28.8
Thomas and Michael Carbonell	*36*	*22.1*
others	*11*	*6.8*
Dublin	42	25.8
John Rathbone	*39*	*23.9*
others	*3*	*1.8*
Bristol	19	11.7
Day and Cassamajor	*19*	*11.7*
Cheshire and North Wales	13	8.0
Charles Middleton	*5*	*3.1*
others	*12*	*7.5*
Plymouth	5	3.1
Captain John Fisher	*5*	*3.1*
Rotterdam	1	0.6
Unknown	32	19.6
da Silva	*9*	*5.5*
others	*23*	*14.1*
Total	163	

Source: CCA CR 352/1 Daniel Peck's Letter Book. Note: Peck wrote 163 letters between April 1703 and October 1704. Only individuals receiving five or more letters are itemised separately.

Daniel Peck's letters were unusual in their formal tone. We catch few glimpses of the close personal relationships that bound together these merchants. The correspondence of Matthew Anderton – a fellow Chester merchant whose papers survive only in fragments – often mixed business with personal matters. For example, in writing to acknowledge receipt of payment for goods supplied, Nathaniel Atwood of London made Anderton a present of a cock and hen. Similarly, Anderton was asked by Toby Bonnill of London to forward a small box to a mutual acquaintance in Dublin.[54] Whilst Peck rarely included any personal messages or greetings, he frequently referred to his business associates as 'friends'. Notwithstanding the norms and polite language of business and letter writing at this time, this suggests that these were people with whom he had special trusting relationships. Linked to this was Peck's concern for his business

---

54 CCA, CR 656/13, CR 656/7.

and personal reputation.[55] This was carefully built up through involvement in the civic life of Chester – he was Sheriff in 1704/05 – and through his dealings with fellow merchants. It identified him as a man to be trusted, a status which he was quick to defend. For example, responding to a complaint made by Day and Cassamajor that a consignment of lead had been spoiled, he wrote that: "of all the quantity I have sent to Dublin, London and everywhere else no complaint was ever made". The point was not that their grievance was invalid; rather, he was calling on his extensive dealings and the network of merchants that this involved to bear silent witness of his probity as a trader.[56] Perhaps above all, trust was built on familiarity: hence the use of letters of introduction and the regularity of contact, whether in person or by letter. Peck's principal correspondents comprised a set of core, stable relationships. During the nineteen-month-period covered by his letter book, Rathbone and the Carbonells received letters on average about once every ten to fourteen days, and Day and Cassamajor once every three weeks (see Table 2). The relationships thus developed and maintained could operate in a number of different ways, but on just one occasion does he appear to have entered into a formal partnership. On 3 July 1704, he wrote to the Carbonells with news of a ship sailing from Dublin to Lisbon via Kinsale and asked whether they would like to take a half-share. This indicates the geographical scope and organisational complexity of Peck's network: a partnership with London merchants for a voyage from Dublin to Lisbon loaded with north Wales lead being stored at Rathbone's warehouses in Dublin. In its unusualness, this putative arrangement underlines the flexible yet robust nature of Peck's network of merchant friends. Much as Putnam argues in his conceptualisation of social capital, networks of personal bonds forged through mutual trust and obligation could constitute a viable alternative to formal business structures and institutions.[57]

Most Chester merchants dealt in a wide range of commodities. Matthew Anderton imported wines and Brandy via merchants in London, supplied a variety of ironware and guns to a Dublin ironmonger, and appears to have been importing Irish grain.[58] Peck had even broader interests (Table 3). He exported significant quantities of salt, cheese, coal and slate from Cheshire and north Wales, importing wine, manufactured goods, textiles, hides and so on in return.

55 For a more general discussion of the importance of credit and reputation, see C. Muldrew, *Economy of Obligation*, 186-9.

56 CCA, CR 352/1, 12 February 1704.

57 See R. Putnam, *Making Democracy Work*.

58 CCA, CR 656/9, CR 656/14, CR 656/19, CR 656/20, CR 656/10.

His core business, though, was lead: largely from his own mine in north Wales, but also from Chester Corporation's Minerva mine and from Derbyshire.[59]

Table 3: Subject matter of letters from Daniel Peck, 1703-1704

Subject	Number of references	Percentage of letters
Cargoes	144	88.3
lead	69	42.3
salt	17	10.4
coal, timber & slates	17	10.4
textiles	11	6.7
cheese	10	6.1
Dutch goods	7	4.3
other goods	23	14.1
Shipping	42	25.8
arranging ships	20	12.3
insurance	13	8.0
convoys	9	5.5
Business information	44	27.0
news of ships	25	15.3
market/prices	11	6.7
customs	5	3.1
introductions	3	1.8
Bills and Cash	30	18.4

Source: CCA CR 352/1.

Shipments of lead were mentioned in almost half of Peck's correspondence: nearly as often as all other cargoes combined. With many of his irregular correspondents, and with da Silva, and Day and Cassamajor, Peck did little more than send consignments of lead as requested, drawing bills against them as payment.[60] In these cases, most letters were concerned with cargoes dispatched and payments received or outstanding. Rather different were Peck's relationships with John Rathbone and the Carbonells. Both operated, in effect, as factors for the Chester merchant. Rathbone received regular shipments of lead, coal and

---

59 For discussion of the lead trade at this time, see R. Burt, 'The transformation of the non-ferrous metal industries in the seventeenth and eighteenth centuries', in: *Economic History Review*, 48 (1995).

60 See L. Neal, 'The finance of business during the industrial revolution', in: R. Floud and D. McCloskey (eds), *The Economic History of Britain since 1700*, second edition, Cambridge 1994, volume 1, 157-62.

salt, selling these to other merchants in Ireland or organising forward shipment, sometimes in combination with his own goods. For example, in March 1704, a mixed cargo of Welsh lead and Irish beef was sent to Lisbon, wine being imported in return. Similarly, the Carbonells sold Peck's lead on the London market, but also forwarded cargoes elsewhere, including Holland.[61] In addition, they both helped in the organisation of shipping, offering alternative contacts through which information might be had about availability of ships and convoys. It was through the Carbonells that Peck arranged his insurance – an area of some concern as was with France continued.[62] There were, of course, mutual benefits to such arrangements. Peck appears to have operated as a factor for Rathbone and offered a useful link to Cheshire, north Wales and London markets. Yet these relationships were built on trust: Peck relied on the judgement and knowledge of his correspondents. Writing to Rathbone about the demand for salt in Ireland, he confessed that 'I will be govern'd by you who know the matter better than I can guess'.[63] Having reliable contacts in important markets, who knew local trading conditions and could act upon them, was essential to effective commerce, especially at a time when it was impossible for merchants to be as mobile as the goods that they were sending across the seas.

IV.

Important in tying bonds of mutual trust was the provision and receipt of reliable information. Indeed, for Burt, this is the essential purpose of entrepreneurial networks.[64] Information lay at the heart of Daniel Peck's web of contacts. The regular exchange of information about cargoes, shipping, bills, demand and prices helped to reduce risk, and hence transaction costs, and improved the efficiency of trading operations.[65] Four aspects of information appear to be particularly significant in Peck's correspondence. First and foremost was the provision of and quest for intelligence concerning the basic mechanics of trade. Many letters contained information about bills presented or drawn (see Table 3) and prompt payment was clearly expected once a bill reached its date of expiration. Despite this, Peck sometimes had to remind his fellow merchants that

---

61 CCA, CR 352/1, 22 March 1704; 23 March 1704; 3 July 1704.
62 R. Westerfield, *Middlemen in English Business*, 383-6, 391.
63 CCA, CR 352/1, 2 March 1704.
64 R. Burt, 'The network entrepreneur', 286-8. See also M. Casson, *Entrepreneurship and Business Culture. Studies in the Economics of Trust*, Aldershot 1995, 10-12.
65 See R. Pearson and D. Richardson, 'Business networking', 658; J. Ojala, 'Approaching Europe', (page?).

payment was due.[66] In a similar vein, Joseph Stephens wrote to Matthew Anderton asking for payment for wines previously supplied pleading that the delay 'straightens me much for money [as] quick returns is the life of trade'. Conversely, Peck was swift to apologise for delays in paying his bills, suggesting that 'difficultys of business especially with lead in [times of] Warr may be allowed as a reasonable plea'.[67] In addition to this, he was careful to keep his merchant friends informed about the progress of key cargoes and any problems with shipping in general. He thus wrote to Day and Cassamajor assuring them that their consignment of lead would arrive shortly at Bristol, but also to Rathbone that the westerly winds had prevented any sailings from Chester.[68] A perennial problem was finding ships to carry his cargoes as many were converted for military use or were engaged in carrying troops to Ireland. More specifically, he complained of the problems in getting ships to London – because the seamen feared being pressed into the navy when they got there – or to Plymouth – as there was no return cargo to be brought to Chester.[69] In contrast, he was quick to write to the Carbonells that they should expect a large and mixed consignment of goods because 'the benefit of a good convoy makes me more willing to send what the ship will take'.[70]

The rapid communication of such information around the network of personal business contacts could be especially significant in terms of its potential impact both on local markets and on the perceived solvency of the merchant. This links to the second aspect of this networking: the way in which the provision of information could affect reputation. Peck's interest in keeping his good name helps to explain the care he took in providing news about shipments made or delayed. He was at pains to point out that late delivery was due to poor weather or problems in organising ships or convoys; not his inattention to business. On just one occasion did he invoke personal reasons for failing to meet his commitments, writing to Day and Cassamajor that he would have travelled to Bristol to discuss their business in person, 'but for my being elected Sheriff'.[71] Even here, though, the information imparted served to enhance the regard in which he would be held. Messages about integrity could also be shared with

---

66   See, for example, CCA, CR 352/1, 16 November 1703; 24 August 1704. The importance of prompt payment to a merchant's reputation is discussed in C. Muldrew, *Economy of Obligation*, 192.

67   CCA, CR 656/9; CCA, CR 352/1, 14 April 1704.

68   CCA, CR 352/1, 15 July 1704; 22 July 1704; 5 February 1704.

69   K. Morgan, *Bristol and the Atlantic Trade*,(page?); CCA, CR 352/1, 8 March 1704; 22 March 1704; 10 July 1704.

70   CCA, CR 352/1, 22 March 1704.

71   CCA, CR 352/1, 18 October 1704.

third parties, thus spreading and reinforcing one's reputation. Again in a letter to Day and Cassamajor, Peck asked them to forward the payment of his account with one William Pughe, esquire, saying 'I was never so streightned in business since I knew any, but am desirous to comply to the demand of so worthy a friend as you are'.[72]

As was argued earlier, reputation was central to notions of truth and reliability: who could be trusted as holding valid information? At one extreme, official notices supplied authoritative news about losses of ships, and customs documents likewise recorded exports of key goods like salt. Peck assiduously copied both into his letter book. In stark contrast is the advertisement – part of Matthew Anderton's papers – for a London fortune teller who claimed to answer all manner of questions, including: 'Ships at Sea, if safe?' or 'Journies by Land or Voyages at Sea, the success thereof?'.[73] More generally, merchants relied on their correspondents to supply reliable and current information. Within Peck's network, certain individuals appear to have been seen as especially trustworthy sources. Key men here were Thomas and Michael Carbonell, upon whom he relied for much of his insurance and for providing market information on London and Holland. They were critical to Peck's decisions about forwarding shipments of lead to Rotterdam. Moreover, at times of crisis – as when a cargo of goods from Holland was impounded at Plymouth – it was to the Carbonells that he turned for advice and assistance.[74]

Finally, most significant are the ways in which the provision of information could reduce risk and hence transaction costs. In this context, any and all information could be valuable, but information concerning markets, insurance, convoys and cargoes seems to have been especially important. Information about local markets was clearly vital in deciding what goods to ship and when: it reduced the risk of saturating markets or having goods arrive when prices were low. For this, Peck heavily relied on his local contacts to act on his behalf. Yet he also made specific enquiries about market conditions, for example writing to the Carbonells to ask about the price currently obtained in London by two to four year old Cheshire cheese. He also passed on market information of his own, suggesting that the shipment of coal to London 'can never answer' and arguing that they should try salt instead.[75] The risks of trade could be reduced very directly by taking out insurance on cargoes. However, this itself required considerable information: where could insurance be got most cheaply; was the

---

72   CCA, CR 352/1, 5 August 1704.
73   CCA, CR 656/34.
74   CCA, CR 352/1, 5 April 1704; 21 June 1704; 22 July 1704; 7 August 1704.
75   CCA, CR 352/1, 12 July 1704; 19 July 1703.

route recognised and the destination known; how safe was the voyage; what was the quality of the ship and convoy? When organising his cover, Peck sought or offered answers to all these questions. London was the usual source for his insurance, but, on one occasion, he suggested that 'I doe believe you might get it done at Rotterdam cheaper'. On another, he related the problems of getting insurance to Pembroke because the port was not known. Here, and at other times, he chose not to insure the cargo, presumably because he judged that the risks did not merit the costs that would be incurred.[76] When he decided to insure, he was assiduous in providing as much information as possible about the merchant-men and convoys. Escorting vessels were important not just in reducing the cost of insurance – he sometimes opted for Dutch ships because of the quality of their convoys – but also in allowing the movement of ships at all. In writing to George Jackson about the problems in securing ships for his lead, he highlighted the importance of the presence in Chester of a convoy vessel of forty guns which would finally allow return trips to Plymouth, giving 'a small life to our distant port'.[77]

As Peck's correspondence makes clear, information was vital in reducing the transaction costs of eighteenth-century trade. Its importance perhaps becomes most apparent when it was incomplete or imperfect. This is best illustrated by Peck's ill-fated venture into importing goods from Holland. In June 1704, he arranged, in conjunction with John Rathbone in Dublin, for a large consignment of tiles, furniture, wine, hams, gunpowder, mather, stoneware and pepper to be shipped from Rotterdam. This was an important new venture for the two friends and represented 'a great deal of money ... in one bottom'.[78] The shipment arrived safely at Plymouth, but was then impounded because of three bales of pepper ordered by Rathbone. Neither of the merchants were aware of restrictions on the import of pepper and neither had any idea how to extricate the rest of the cargo from the customs officials. These difficulties arose from a lack of information and exposed Peck to considerable risk, both financially and in terms of his reputation. Their resolution through the assistance afforded by the Carbonells relied heavily on his ability to call on reliable sources of information elsewhere in his extensive network.

---

76 CCA, CR 352/1, 16 February 1704; 15 April 1704; 8 May 1704
77 CCA, CR 352/1, 28 June 1704.
78 CCA, CR 352/1, 27 July 1704.

V.

The merchants of eighteenth-century Chester lay at the centre of complex networks of inter-personal linkages which tied them to the local and national economy and society. As their executorial and inheritance practices reveal, family did much to shape the social networks and social reproduction of these men. However, it was communal and civic life within Chester, and a wider mercantile fraternity, that both reflected and structured their business networks. From assured local networks, merchants reached out into geographically wider webs which incorporated fellow merchants across the country and overseas. These networks were both social and economic: based on personal relationships, yet constituting vital business linkages. They frequently involved the same people and were strengthened by the same intercourse. But networks did not happen automatically or accidentally: they were contingent on interaction and communication, either in person or by letter. Merchants were thus bound together by webs of information exchange which at once articulated and gave purpose to their linkages. As Pearson and Richardson argue, such information helped to reduce transaction costs arising from trading in conditions of limited knowledge of markets, prices and supplies. Their friends in other ports were often the only source of local business information, and correspondence with them provided up-to-date and reliable intelligence. At the same time, such interaction was essential in establishing trust between members of the network. These bonds of trust were reinforced by mutual obligation, helping to define reputable and reliable trading partners. They therefore offered some security in an uncertain and unregulated trading environment. Moreover, being part of a network also provided an interpretative structure through which to filter and understand the information received. In other words, networks not only gave access to information, and to national and international trading, but also helped the merchant to shift, order and prioritise knowledge, and to make sense of the increasingly global economy in which they operated.

The Knoop-Family and its International Network

Dittmar Dahlmann

In the last quarter of the eighteenth century Moscow became more and more the centre of the Russian textile industry. At the turn of the century there were roughly 160 enterprises with about 9,000 workers in the former capital.[1] This rise was mainly due to the liberalising policy of Catherine II. After the destruction of great parts of the city in 1812 it took some time before Moscow regained its old position in the hierarchy of the Russian textile industry, but it did so in the course of the second quarter of the nineteenth century.[2] Textile entrepreneurs, who belonged to the Old Believers, a group of religious schismatics, who had left the Orthodox Church in the second half of the seventeenth century, played an influential part.[3]

There were also quite a number of foreigners among the Russian entrepreneurs of the nineteenth century and in particular among the Moscow entrepreneurs.[4] Many of them came from German-speaking countries.[5] The most

---

1   A.V. Koval'chuk, *Manufakturnaja promyshlennost' Moskvy vo vtoroj polovine XVIII veka. Tekstil'noe proizvodstvo*, Moscow 1999, 57, 311.

2   K. Heller, 'Rußlands Wirtschaft in der ersten Hälfte des 19. Jahrhunderts', in: K. Zernack (ed.), *Handbuch der Geschichte Rußlands*, Vol. 2, Stuttgart 2001, 1175.

3   On the Old Believers in the Russian economy, in particular in Moscow cf. A.J. Rieber, *Merchants and Entrepreneurs in Imperial Russia*, Chapel Hill 1982; J.A. Ruckman, *The Moscow Business Elite: A Social and Cultural Portrait of Two Generations, 1840-1905*; DeKalb (Ill.) 1984; T.C. Owen, *Capitalism and Politics in Russia. A Social History of the Moscow Merchants, 1855-1905*, Cambridge 1981; G.N. Ulianova, 'Old Believers and New Entrepreneurs: Religious Belief and Ritual in Merchant Moscow', in: J.L. West and J.A. Petrov (eds.), *Merchant Moscow. Images of Russia's Vanished Bourgeoisie*, Princeton 1998, 61-71; M. Hildermeier, 'Alter Glaube und Neue Welt: Zur Sozialgeschichte des Raskol im 18. und 19. Jahrhundert', in: *Jahrbücher für Geschichte Osteuropas*, n.s., 38 (1990), 504-525; V.V. Kerov, *Konfessional'no-etnicheskie faktory staroobrjadcheskogo predprinimatel'stva*, Moscow 2000, 254-264. In exile after 1917 a young Moscow merchant wrote a collective portrait of the world of Moscow's entrepreneurial community: P.A. Buryshkin, *Moskva kupecheskaja*, New York 1954, reprinted Moscow 1991.

4   V.I. Bovykin, 'Inostrannoe predprinimatel'stvo v Rossii', in: *Istorija predprinimatel'stva v Rossii. Kniga vtoraja: vtoraja polovina XIX - nacalo XX veka*, Moscow 2000, 108-126.

5   D. Dahlmann, 'Lebenswelt und Lebensweise deutscher Unternehmer in Moskau vom Beginn des 19. Jahrhunderts bis zum Ausbruch des Ersten Weltkrieges', in: *Nordost-Archiv*, n.s., 3 (1994), 133-163; J.A. Petrov, 'Deutsche Unternehmer in Moskau um die Jahrhundertwende 1900', in: *Tel Aviver Jahrbuch für Deutsche Geschichte*, 24 (1995), 105-116. An interesting

famous example of a successful German entrepreneur or merchant in Russia in the course of the nineteenth century is Heinrich Schliemann from Ankershagen, who later became the well-known excavator of Troia.[6] But we find other entrepreneurial dynasties in Russia, who came from Germany and stayed much longer than Schliemann and were even more successful.

One of them was Ludwig Baron Knoop, born in Bremen in 1821 as the fourth child of a Lutheran merchant. The family had resided in the city since the end of the sixteenth century; all six generations before Ludwig were merchants. The father was a tobacco merchant who went bankrupt in 1833.[7]

The family belonged to the middle classes. After his father's bankruptcy the effects of social decline were alleviated by the family network, which provided for their empoverished members. Ludwig served his apprenticeship in a company in Bremen for three years. At the age of seventeen he was sent to Manchester where his uncle Andreas Frerichs was partner in the company of the Englishman Carey B. De Jersey. This company dealt with twist yarn that was also exported to Russia.[8]

---

portrait of the German industrialists in Russia before 1914 is given by Georg Spies, *Erinnerungen eines Ausland-Deutschen*, St. Petersburg 2002, originally published 1926.

6   J. Mai, 'Heinrich Schliemann als Unternehmer in Russland', in: D. Dahlmann and C. Scheide (eds.), *"... das einzige Land in Europa, das eine grosse Zukunft vor sich hat." Deutsche Unternehmen und Unternehmer im Russischen Reich im 19. und frühen 20. Jahrhundert*, Essen 1998, 349-360; J. Mai, *"„Ich gelte hier als der schlaueste, durchtriebenste und fähigste Kaufmann"*. Heinrich Schliemann in Russland', in: Dittmar Dahlmann et al. (eds.), *„Eine grosse Zukunft". Deutsche in Russlands Wirtschaft*, Berlin 2000, also in Russian, Berlin 2000; I. Bogdanov, *Dolgaja doroga v Troju. Genrich Shliman v Peterburge*, St. Petersburg 1994.

7   D. Dahlmann, 'Ludwig Knoop: ein Unternehmerleben', in: Dahlmann and Scheide (eds.), *das einzige Land in Europa*, 361-378; D. Dahlmann, 'Ludwig Knoop: Ein Bremer Unternehmer in Rußland', in: Dahlmann et al. (eds.), *Eine grosse Zukunft*, 176-183; cf. J.A. Petrov, 'Nemetskij „chelovecheskogo kapital" v dorevolutsionnoj Rossii (torgovyj dom „L. Knop")', in: *Ekonomicheskaja istorija. Predprinimatel'stvo i predprinimateli*, Moscow 1999, 63-79; S. Martynov, *Manufaktura i fabrikanty*, St. Petersburg 1993, 77-86; M. Gavlin, *Rossijskie Medichi. Portrety predprinimatelej*, Moscow 1996, 231-273; F. Prüser, 'Ludwig Knoop', in: *Niedersächsische Lebensbilder*, vol. 1, Hildesheim / Leipzig 1939, 242-255; F. Prüser, 'Ludwig Knoop. Der Begründer der russischen Webwarenindustrie', in: *Der Schlüssel. Bremer Beiträge zur deutschen Kultur und Wirtschaft*, 4 (1939), 177-184. One of Ludwig Knoop's daughters, Adele Wolde, published a lively portrait of her father at the end of the 1920s: Adele Wolde, *Ludwig Knoop. Erinnerungsbilder aus seinem Leben n.p.n.d.*, reprinted Bremen 1998.

8   Wolde, *Knoop*, 9-10; S. Thompstone, 'Ludwig Knoop. The Arkwright of Russia', in: *Textile History*, 15 (1984), 45-73, here: 47; H. Schwarzwälder, 'Ludwig Knoop (1821-1894). Bremer Bürger und russischer Baron oder „Koopmanns Good is as Ebb und Flood"', in: *Berühmte Bremer*, München 1972, 91-106, here: 93; H. H. Rimpau, 'Johann Hinrich Frerichs', in: *Norddeutsche Familienkunde*, 14 (1965), 111-113.

Ludwig Knoop stayed in Manchester for two years and left for Moscow in 1840, where the representative of his uncle's company needed a clerk.[9] Ludwig worked with the de Jersey house representative company for another four years. He soon became acquainted with many of the German merchants and entrepreneurs in Moscow[10]and established particularly close relations with the family of Johann Christoph Hoyer, a Baltic German by origin.

In 1843 Ludwig Knoop married Luise Hoyer, and the couple lived in the large Moscow home of the Hoyers for eighteen years.[11] Four years after the marriage Ludwig managed to negotiate his first big deal. In 1847 he sold a completely equipped textile factory to Savva Morozov, one of the wealthiest and most influential entrepreneurs in Moscow, a member of the Old Believers. Knoop did not only sell the latest and best English machines, but he also hired British employees and foremen.[12] This kind of business became the basis for Knoop's overwhelming success. Knoop was so convinced of the success of this new factory that he refrained from getting paid directly, but instead opted for a share of 10% in the annual profits of Morozov's factory.[13] Over the next fifteen years Knoop built another 153 factories of which he held a share of 5 to 15% of the annual profits. He equipped another thirty factories with machinery.[14] Knoop not only delivered machinery and technical know-how in the shape of British employees and foremen, but he was also the main importer of cotton that these factories processed.[15]

In 1852 Ludwig Knoop established his own company in Russia, with the main office in Moscow and branches in St. Petersburg and Reval. Another five years later, in 1857, he founded the textile factory "Krähnholm" with Russian and German partners. It was situated directly on the border of the province of

---

9   Wolde, *Knoop*, 9-10; Schwarzwälder, *Ludwig Knoop*, 93.

10 V. Dönninghaus, *Die Deutschen in der Moskauer Gesellschaft. Symbiose und Konflikt (1491-1941)*, München 2002, 58-59; J.A. Petrov, 'Deutsche Unternehmer im ökonomischen Leben Moskaus vom 17. bis zum Beginn des 20. Jahrhunderts', in: Dahlmann et al. (eds.), *Eine große Zukunft*, 106-119; *Nemetskie predprinimateli v Moskve. Sbornik statej*, Moscow 1999.

11 Dahlmann, 'Knoop: ein Unternehmerleben', 368-370.

12 G. von Schulze-Gävernitz, *Volkswirtschaftliche Studien aus Rußland*, Leipzig 1899, 92-95; M. Hildermeier, *Bürgertum und Stadt in Rußland 1760-1870. Rechtliche Lage und soziale Struktur*, Köln / Wien 1986, 528.

13 Svedenija o fabrikach postroennykh v rossi pri posredstve L.G. Knop: Rossijskij Gosudarstvennyj Istorcheskij Archiv (henceforth quoted as RGIA), St. Petersburg, fond 500, opis' 16, delo 509, 12ob-22.

14 RGIA Svedenija, 22ob.; Hildermeier, *Bürgertum*, 530.

15 Schulze-Gävernitz, *Volkswirtschaftliche Studien*, 95-96; Thompstone, 'Ludwig Knoop', 49-50; E. Amburger, 'Der fremde Unternehmer in Rußland bis zur Oktoberrevolution im Jahre 1917', in: K. Zernack (ed.), *Fremde und Einheimische im Wirtschafts- und Kulturleben des neuzeitlichen Russland. Ausgewählte Aufsätze*, Wiesbaden 1982, 97-115, here: 114.

Estonia on the banks of the river Narova, close to the city of Narva.[16] The
company still exists - it is now the biggest company in the whole of Estonia, it
belongs to a Swedish company and is Estonia's biggest exporter: some of the
towels and linen bought in the IKEA-Shops bear the sign of the Krähnholm-
factory.

To go back to Ludwig Knoop in 1857: His five partners in founding of
Krähnholm were three Russians, members of the Moscow Old Believer
community, and two Germans. The Russians were Aleksej and Gerasim Chludov
and Koz'ma Soldatenkov. All of them including Knoop also held shares in the
Emil Zündel Company, another textile company in Moscow, and together with
members of the Old Believer-family Shchukin, they were also shareholders in
the Danilovskaja-factory.[17] Thus Knoop kept up very good relations with his
German compatriots as well as with the Russian Old Believers in Moscow. He
was a well established member in Moscow's business community.

The starting capital of the Krähnholm factory was two million gold roubles,
which was later raised to six million gold roubles.[18] De jure it was a partnership
limited by shares ("Kommanditgesellschaft" - unquoted publicly limited company). All the shares were either in the hands of the founding members and
could not be sold without the others' consent or the shares were in the hands of
members of the Knoop family. Sources on the history of the Knoop family are
poor, because a lot of material was lost during and after the Second World War,
including the family archives and the archives of the Krähnholm factory. So we
have contradicting material concerning the share-holding of the Knoop family:
some sources indicate that Ludwig Knoop's two uncles, who were partners of the
de Jersey company in Manchester, and Ludwig's two brothers Julius and Daniel
held shares of the Krähnholm company.[19]

The rise of the Knoop company continued in the following years. Ludwig
Knoop and his wife together returned to Bremen in 1861 with their three
daughters, whereas the three sons remained in Moscow. The two oldest sons,
Theodor and Andreas, married two sisters of the Zenker family, daughters of a

16 *75 Jahre: 1857-1932. Gesellschaft der Krähnholm Manufaktur für Baumwollfabrikate*, Narva
    1933, 13; *Krengol'mskaja manufaktura. 1857-1907. Istorcheskoe opisanie*, St. Petersburg
    1907, 13-14; Dahlmann, 'Knoop: ein Unternehmerleben', 371-72.

17 Ruckman, *Business Elite*, 54; Rieber, *Merchants*, 210.

18 *75 Jahre: 1857-1932. Gesellschaft der Krähnholm Manufaktur*, 27; *Ustav tovarishchestva
    krengol'mskoj manufaktury bumazhnykh izdelij*, St. Petersburg 1885, § 3; E. Amburger, 'Das
    neuzeitliche Narva als Wirtschaftsfaktor zwischen Rußland und Estland', in: Zernack (ed.),
    Fremde und Einheimische, 41-52, here: 51; B.F. Brandt, *Inostrannye kapitaly. Ikh vlijanie na
    ekonomicheskoe razvitie strany*, 4 vols., St. Petersburg 1899-1901, here: vol. 3, 48.

19 *75 Jahre: 1857-1932: Gesellschaft der Krähnholm Manufaktur*, 27-28.

rich German Moscow banker.[20] Johann, the third son, got married in Bremen. Unfortuntely no information could be gathered about his wife's family. The three daughters married into Bremen's entrepreneurial bourgeoisie: the families of Wolde, Albrecht and Kulenkampff; the Woldes owned a private bank, George Albrecht was the owner of Joh. Lange's Witwe & Söhne, a well-established merchant and shipowner family, and the Kulenkampff-family – which is still well-known in Bremen.[21]

Back in his hometown Bremen, Knoop built a luxurious family residence, called Mühlenthal, on the banks of the river Lesum, which does not exist anymore, but the surrounding Park, in Bremen known as Knoop's Park, still gives an impression of the huge premises of the Knoops.[22] Knoop had his own telegraph as well as his own railway station. He frequently travelled between Bremen, Moscow and Krähnholm by train, as long as he was able to do so. His wife used to say: "Father thinks and dreams only of cotton!"[23]

The network of the Knoop family was more or less exclusively based on family relations. Members of the family took over the British de Jersey & Co. which had branches in Liverpool and Manchester: first the two uncles of Ludwig, his mother's brothers, entered the firm, they were followed by Ludwig's brother Julius, and finally Julius' two sons, Andreas and Ludwig Karl, became partners in the company.[24] Johann Knoop, Ludwig's son, controlled the London trading house Wm. Berkefeld & Co, at least since 1871 together with de Jersey & Co and held shares in the London Banking House H.S. Lefevre & Co.[25] One of Knoop's most important English partners was Platt Bros. in Manchester, where he bought most of the machinery. Ludwig Knoop became a shareholder in the company after E.W. Gromme, his nephew and son of one of his sisters had been nominated to the board of directors.[26] Moreover, he worked with numerous English companies; in many of which he or members of his family had shares. These were in particular: Mather, Platt & Co in Salford, a textile plant, John

---

20 Wolde, *Knoop*, 57.

21 Johann married Gretchen Kern. Wolde, *Knoop*, 57; Dahlmann, 'Knoop: ein Unternehmerleben', 377.

22 Dahlmann, 'Knoop: ein Unternehmerleben', 376; U. Tesch, *Knoops Park. Eine historische Parkanlage in Bremen-Nord*, Bremen 1999.

23 Wolde, *Knoop*, 57.

24 S.R. Thompstone, *The Organisation and Financing of Russian Foreign Trade before 1914*, Ph.D.-thesis, London University 1991, 411-13, 416; Thompstone, 'Ludwig Knoop', 54 and 68, n.35. All partners owning the De Jersey Company were either members of the Knoop or the Gromme families.

25 S. Chapman, *The Rise of Merchant Banking*, London et al. 1984, 144-146; Thompstone, *Organisation*, 417.

26 Thompstone, *Organisation*, 416-17; Thompstone, 'Ludwig Knoop', 54-55.

Musgraves & Sons in Bolton, a steam engine factory, and Hick Hargreaves & Co, another steam engine factory, also in Bolton, and seven other companies.[27] E.W. Gromme was also one of the directors at Musgrave's and was later on joined by Ludwig Knoop's grandson Johann Ludwig Knoop.[28] For the supply of laboratory equipments, valves and pumps Ludwig Knoop relied on two German companies: Keller-Dorian and A. Buttner. There is no evidence that he or members of his family held any shares in these firms.[29]

In America the Knoop family founded the general commission agency Knoop, Hanemann & Co. with branches in New York, Savannah, Charleston, New Orleans and Mobile in 1863.[30] The company was founded by another relative of Ludwig, Gottfried Knoop, and the German Hanemann; several family members became shareholders in it: Ludwig and his brother Julius, Julius' son Andreas and a relative of Ludwig's mother.[31] After Hanemann's retirement in 1879 the company changed its name to Knoop, Frerich & Co. The English De Jersey house was one of the leading partners. The main function of Knoop, Frerich & Co. was to supply the Russian House with raw cotton.[32]

In 1864, during the American Civil War, Ludwig Knoop founded a cotton house in Bombay.[33] De Jersey & Co. and Knoop again were partners in the company of the St. Petersburg German Julius Amburger in Alexandria for the same reason.[34] After Amburger's death in 1881, Ludwig Knoop invested £50,000 in the successor firm Ernest Malleson & Co and remained a silent partner until 1891.[35]

The leading figures of the Knoop family enterprise were the two brothers Ludwig and Julius, the former in Russia and the latter in England. It is also clear that members of the extended family as well as former partners and employees who had capital invested it in L. Knoop and Co. The companies of the two brothers operated on a worldwide scale and supported one another.

In 1877 Ludwig was made a Russian Baron, but the family's outlook was international and cosmopolitan in business affairs as well in their attitudes. Knoop's sons received their commercial training outside Russia, which had

---

27 Thompstone, *Organisation*, 416.
28 Thompstone, *Organisation*, 418.
29 Thompstone, *Organisation*, 416.
30 Dokladnaja zapiska: RGIA, fond 560, opis' 16, delo 509, 30 (backside); Thompstone, *Organisation*, 417-18.
31 Thompstone, 'Ludwig Knoop', 55-6.
32 Thompstone, 'Ludwig Knoop', 55.
33 Thompstone, 'Ludwig Knoop', 55.
34 E. Amburger, *Deutsche in Staat, Wirtschaft und Gesellschaft Russlands. Die Familie Amburger in St. Petersburg 1770-1920*, Wiesbaden 1986, 142-43 and 247.
35 Thompstone, *Organisation*, 417.

become common practice even in genuinely Russian families since the middle of the nineteenth century.

Marriages, as we have seen, were an important means of establishing business relations, though in the first two generations of the Knoop family's Russian branch, religion and national origin were the dominating factors. It was only in the third generation that marriage links with the Russian bourgeoisie were devised: two grandsons of Ludwig Knoop married into two important Moscow entrepreneurial families: the Medved'ev and the Mamontovs.[36]

The family remained the main, but not the only base for Ludwig Knoop's business in Russia. As we have seen, he also had very good connections to Russian, in particular Russian Old Believer entrepreneurs. In general, it can be said that Knoop was well established within Moscow's business circles and had many friends among his Russian colleagues. The German economist Gerhart von Schulze-Gävernitz, who visited Russia and Knoop's factory Krähnholm in the 1890s, wrote that Knoop owed his success to a certain degree to his good stomach,[37] i.e. he frequently visited those places where even in the second half of the nineteenth century many contracts were sealed: the Russian "traktir".[38]

The integration of Ludwig Baron Knoop and his family in the world of the Moscow industrialists is shown by the fact that for many years Knoop was the chairman of the Moscow stock exchange and held various other posts within entrepreneurial organizations. But he and his family also remained part of the German colony in Moscow. They kept to their ancestors' religious belief and were active members of the Lutheran parish of Moscow, as nearly all the other immigrants did.[39] Knoop and his sons donated quite a lot of money to various social and welfare organisations over the years.

Within a time span of 25 years Ludwig Knoop built up an entrepreneurial empire based mainly, but in no way exclusively, on family relations. The network of companies which he owned or in which he held shares was worldwide and intercontinental, connecting Europe with America, Africa and Asia. The production was based in Russia, the supply of the machinery came from England and partly from Germany, raw material, mainly cotton from the USA, Egypt and India, during and after the American Civil War from Russian Central Asia.

---

36 Thompstone, *Organisation*, 419.
37 Schulze-Gävernitz, *Volkswirtschaftliche Studien*, 91.
38 The word is difficult to translate into English. One might called it a pub, but this would be a euphemism.
39 Dahlmann, 'Lebenswelt und Lebensweise', 158-160.

After Ludwig Knoop's death in 1894 the family empire existed until the Russian revolution of 1917. Krähnholm, after 1918/19 in Estonia, belonged to the Knoop family until 1939, but the factory as such still exists today.

In the middle of the 1890s Knoop's position within the Russian cotton industry was very strong. The partners of the Knoop company were on the board of 12 of the leading cotton firms and either controlled them fully or at least partly.[40] Over the next twenty years, until the outbreak of the First World War, the strategy of the Knoop company changed slightly, as Jurij Petrov has shown. Members of the Knoop family or partners of the company entered the boards of 26 Russian companies: 21 were industrial and the remaining five were banks and insurance companies.[41]

But still, the stronghold of the Knoop family's Russian business remained the cotton and textile industry, they retained their overwhelming position by controlling the important Moscow based Emil Cindel-company.[42] The chairman of the company was J. Prowe, Ludwig Knoop's brother-in-law. After his death he was succeeded by one of Knoop's sons, Andreas.

At the turn of the twentieth century and at the time when the second generation of the Knoop family was at the head of business affairs, the world of finance and banking became more and more important. Prowe and the younger Knoops entered the board of some of the most important Moscow banks and thus they could strengthen the financial base of their industrial group.[43]

Before the First World War the Knoops had diversified their business from cotton and textile into banking, and engaged in the newspaper market, financing Golos Moskvy and the Moscow German newspaper "Moskauer Deutsche Zeitung" and turned to new branches, i.e. the automobile and the oil-industry.[44]

But the family enterprise also kept to tradition. De Jersey and Knoop still imported raw cotton for the Russian market, which they bought at the Liverpool cotton stock exchange. Another partner in this business was the Moscow "Kommercheskij Bank", in whose board Theodor Knoop had a seat. The bank provided loans to Moscow textile and cotton companies for the import of raw cotton.[45]

The network still functioned on the eve of the First World War. The Knoops were well established on the Russian market, sought new branches for extending business operations and also kept to the tradition of the founding father of the

---

40 Petrov, 'Nemetskij chelovecheskogo kapital', 72.
41 Petrov, 'Nemetskij chelovecheskogo kapital', 72.
42 Petrov, 'Nemetskij chelovecheskogo kapital', 72-3; Thompstone, 'Ludwig Knoop', 61.
43 Petrov, 'Nemetskij chelovecheskogo kapital', 73.
44 Petrov, 'Nemetskij chelovecheskogo kapital', 74-76; Thompstone, 'Ludwig Knoop', 61.
45 Petrov, 'Nemetskij chelovecheskogo kapital', 75.

"Torgovyj Dom L. Knop", as the company was called in Russian. After the War only Krähnholm remained in the possession of the family. The network had ceased to exist.

Schulze-Gävernitz called Ludwig Baron Knoop "Russia's greatest industrialist" and a mixture of John D. Rockefeller and Sir Richard Arkwright.[46] In any case he was one of the big European industrialists of the second half of the nineteenth century, forgotten in the Soviet Union for obvious reasons. Nowadays Russian historiography deals intensively with him and other great industrialists in Russia in the nineteenth and early twentieth centuries.[47]

---

46 Schulze-Gävernitz, *Volkswirtschaftliche Studien*, 90; cf. Dahlmann, 'Knoop: ein Unternehmerleben', 378 for other judgements on Knoop.

47 Cf. amongst other works: A.N. Bokhanov, *Delovaja elita Rossii 1914g.*, Moscow 1994; M.A. Baryshnikov, *Delovoj mir Rossii. Istoriko-biograficheskij spravochnik*, St. Petersburg 1998; *Istorija predprinimatel'stva v Rossii*, 2 vols., Moscow 2000. Since the mid 1990s the publishing house "Terra" together with the *Ekonomicheskaja Gazeta* publishes a book series "Predprinimateli Rossii" (Russian Entrepreneurs); K. Heller, 'Neue russische Literatur zur Geschichte des privaten Unternehmertums in Rußland', in: *Jahrbücher für Geschichte Osteuropas*, n.s., 48 (2000), 264-272.

III.

Merging Local and Global Functions:
Port cities

The Company and the Port City: Trading centres of the Malay Archipelago and their role in commercial networks during the seventeenth and eighteenth centuries

Jürgen G. Nagel

Introduction

The last decades' research on commerce in Asia during the presence of the European East India Companies is characterised by a dichotomy. No academic schools are represented in this situation but the implicit views of different authors. On the one side scholars basically assume a European dominance in Asian trade since the arrival of the Portuguese or the Western European chartered companies. In that context we find studies on the activities of the companies as well as such on the economy of certain regions. On the other side authors stress the marginal role of the Europeans in Asia during early modern times. This assumption is based on the number of ships or Europeans and their representatives in Asia. Those studies focus on indigenous trade systems leaving out European activities and influences as far as possible. In consequence two more or less wholistic positions describe the development of the indigenous Asian trade between Vasco da Gama and Thomas Stamford Raffels. The idea of a European hegemony in all or most of the important commercial fields in Asia stands against the perspective of an autonomous Asian commerce.

In close relation to the first one a second dichotomy characterises our context as well. Studies from the bird's eye perspective describe global patterns of economic development during the European Expansion and lose sight of the actual situations on the concrete market places in the region – typically done by the older literature with an European and colonial centred view or by studies influenced by world system theories. The opposition is built up by local case studies which often lose contact to the circumstances of and the external influences on the patterns they have in their view. One can observe this situation in a number of recent studies on special trading patterns in South or Southeast Asia.

On the following pages a preliminary attempt will be undertaken to introduce some considerations which might bring together these different positions by a change of perspective.[1] The contribution will use a case study on an important Indonesian port city – Macassar in Southern Sulawesi/Indonesia – but will integrate it in the regional and supra-regional context.[2]

Conceptual Framework

For a differentiated understanding of Southeast Asian trading structures no comprehensive theory is necessary. The use of great theories bears the risk of losing contact to the everyday's experience of the historical subjects and to sort out facts which badly fit to the theoretical assumptions. Nevertheless, clear terms, concepts and models are inevitable in order to describe the complex reality in an appropriate as well as understandable way. Without such a conceptual framework the study would misinterpret the functional contextes and leave its readers with a colorful but more or less useless description.

In the discussion of this chapter as well as in the concept of the whole volume the term 'network' plays a central role. Commercial relations are to be understood as 'networks', commercial activities as 'networking'. Such commercial relations and activities were settled in a certain spatial setting. Thus, 'network' is primarily a greographical term. Certain places of certain economic importance are related to each other by individual or collective commercial acitivities. Accordingly the networks under discussion consist of hooks and eyes. Of course other variations are noted in the geographic network analysis, but it is only the model of 'circuit networks' that offers a useful model for trading relations in maritime Southeast Asia.[3]

All the other networks were based on the structure of the geographical circuit network. Personal relationships in the context of commerce were organised via the threads of the network as well as political relationships. In order to give a

---

1   This chapter is based on the papers 'With, Against and Beside the Company. Port cities in Southeast Asia and their role in commercial networks during the presence of the Dutch East India Company', presented to the conference 'Spinning the Commercial Net' in Düsseldorf (8 March 2002), and 'The Company and the Port City. Official, legal and illegal trade in South Sulawesi (Indonesia) during the 18th century', presented to the European Social Science History Conference in Den Haag (28 February 2002). The author wants to thank all the organisers of the conferences for their kind invitation and all the participants for their engaged discussion.

2   All empirical evidence introduced in the following is based on the author's PhD thesis: J. G. Nagel, *Der Schlüssel zu den Molukken. Makassar und die Handelsstrukturen des Malaiischen Archipels im 17. und 18. Jahrhundert – eine exemplarische Studie*, Hamburg 2003.

3   For the different network models in geography see P. Haggett and R. J. Chomley (eds.), *Network Analysis in Geography*, London 1969, 3-56.

picture of economic reality in early modern maritime Southeast Asia, the importance of sailing routes are to be stressed. The network crossings must be interpreted as port cities. Southeast Asia was one of the regions with the highest grade of urbanisation in the whole world during the early modern period.[4]

Hans-Dieter Evers published a catalogue of criteria to describe trading connections in Southeast Asia systematically as networks. Using these criteria he describes contemporary Asian networks, but due to their durability the catalogue is also valuable for historical analysis. Evers lists the following six preconditions which are necessary for the existence of a trading network: "There is usually an ethnic or religious homogeneity of traders, but diversity of partners, a regular interaction between trading partners along definite trade routes, an evolution of the trading networks over time, a typical inventory of trading goods, the development of distinctive trading practices, customs and types of exchange, including typical ways of travelling and typical means of transport, the utilization of a market place system."[5]

Evers calls his catalogue a "preliminary checklist". Neither he nor the author of this chapter claim this catalogue to be a complete theory. On the contrary, it has to be emphasized that a catalogue of criteria – much simpler than a theory – may be a useful instrument to give historical phenomena a tangible form, even if it might sometimes be dismissed as a "shopping list". Additionally, the verification of a network's existence is only a secondary aim for which the criteria will be used. First of all the reconstruction should provide an analytic framework for phenomena of pre-colonial trade in maritime Southeast Asia.

The market place system of the region was situated in the port cities if we leave out of consideration the small-scale market trade which guaranteed the supply of farmers, fishermen and villages. Again the importance of urban places has to be stressed, particularly of the port cities with central commercial functions. Following Dietmar Rothermund an emporium is "a market place in which a variety of goods is more or less continuously available and in which a plurality of buyers and sellers can meet without undue restraint under predictable conditions of supply and demand."[6] In an early phase a seasonal market place or a fair could fulfil such a function. But due to increasing storekeeping and the

4   A. Reid, *Southeast Asia in the Age of Commerce, 1450-1680. Vol. II: Expansion and Crisis,* New Haven 1993), 62-131. See also A. Reid, 'The Structure of Cities in Southeast Asia. Fifteenth to seventeenth centuries', in: *Journal of Southeast Asian Studies,* XI (1980), 235-250.

5   H.-D. Evers, 'Traditional Trading Networks of Southeast Asia', in: *Archipel,* 35 (1988), 89-100, here 92.

6   D. Rothermund, 'Asian Emporia and European Bridgeheads', in: R. Ptak and D. Rothermund (eds.), *Emporia, Commodities and Entrepreneurs in Asian Maritime Trade, c. 1400-1750,* Stuttgart 1991, 3-8, here 3.

concentration of activities like transport, money exchange and credit, insurance and exchange of 'commercial intelligence' around the actual market place, the usual result of such development was a city.[7]

Some factors arise which can be assumed to be preconditions of the rise of an emporium. Three of them are indispensable: Firstly, the geographic situation of the town, especially concerning the economic and geography of transportation. It was only an appropriate location in the wider region that allowed the integration in expanding or existing networks. Secondly, guarantee of personal and material security for the merchants by the town. Thirdly, the establishment of basic conditions which guaranteed free trade. For these guarantees a local ruler was necessary who was not only willing to follow an appropriate economic policy but was also in the situation to put it into effect.

Two further preconditions are to be added which are not indispensable for the rise of an emporium but strengthen a successful development: Fourthly, the existence of commercial activities by the regional population or the local ruler. Fifthly, the possibility to provide an export commodity of its own on the market. Such a potential became a local advantage at least in the situation of strong competition or economic crisis.

'Emporium' is not the only term we can find in the discussion about urbanisation in Southeast Asia. The Dutch geographer Peter Nas proposed a periodisation for Indonesian urban history: Until c. 1600 he speaks of the 'Early Indonesian Town', followed by the period of the 'Indische Town' between 1600 and 1870. The era of the 'Colonial Town' covers the years from 1870 to 1950, while since 1950 Nas sees the 'Modern Town' as the characteristic urban phenomenon.[8] This periodisation contains two problems. Firstly, the term 'Indische town' is based on the concept of 'Indische culture', which means a culture that emerged through marriage between European men and Indonesian women and is characterised by the dominance of their mestizo-descendents with European values and Indonesian way of life.[9] That concept has been traced back to the urban elite in Batavia in the eighteenth and nineteenth centuries and was afterwards used for urban societies all over Asia. The term 'Indische culture' certainly describes the town during the time of the Verenigde Oostindische Compagnie (VOC) as well as the Dutch colonial rule. But it is insufficient to characterise the port city in the eighteenth century as a whole.

---

7   Rothermund, 'Asian Emporia and European Bridgeheads'.

8   P.J.M. Nas, 'Introduction. A general view on the Indonesian town', in: P.J.M. Nas (ed.), *The Indonesian City. Studies in urban development and planning*, Dordrecht 1986, 1-17, here 5-13.

9   P.D. Milone, 'Indische Culture and its Relationship to Urban Life', in: *Comparative Studies in Society and History*, 9 (1966/67), 407-426.

The second problem is the term 'colonial city'. Generally two definitions are known. One concentrates on the urban society and emphasizes cultural dominance: "mixed cities on the periphery of an empire [...] which carried the core culture to other peoples."[10] The other one centres on the economic function: "The most prominent function of these cities was economic, the colonial city was the 'nerve centre' of colonial exploitation. Concentrated there were the institutions through which capitalism extended its control over the colonial economy."[11] A more open definition is provided by G. A. de Bruijne: "1. a town that was founded or developed under the influence of a Western colonial power; 2. having a central function on the colonial administrative of economic systems; and 3. having a substantial portion of Western elements."[12] In order to include urban concepts of different cultures, an alternative proposal might be allowed: it combines the definition of 'colonialism' as provided by Jürgen Osterhammel with criteria of centrality in the fields of politics, culture and economy.[13] The understanding of a city as a central place allows avoiding difficulties in defining terms like 'city' or 'town' in different cultural contexts.

With respect to the VOC, the whole system – consisting of commercial networks, market places and their urban equivalent in a system of central places – is generally discussed under the condition of monopolies. It is important to differentiate two types. The company's general aim was to achieve a monopoly in the Moluccan spice trade. Criticism of economic theorists is appropriate, if we talk about an absolute or formal monopoly which is characterised by a legal act which contains an exclusion of all competitors of the privileged from a defined market. Although the VOC understood the monopolies which it required in Southeast Asia in that way, the company was never able to actually achieve such a monopoly. We have to differentiate the actual monopoly which is characterised by a hegemony on a special market reached by competition of which kind ever from this version of monopoly. During the two centuries of its history the VOC actually reached some of these actual monopolies in several parts of Asia – partly as the superior competitor on a special market, partly by use of violent

---

10 R. Redfield and M.B. Singer, 'The Cultural Role of Cities', in: *Economic Development and Cultural Change*, 3 (1954), 53-73, quotation 62.

11 T.G. McGee, *The Southeast Asian City. A social geography of primate cities of Southeast Asia*, London 1967, 56.

12 G.A. de Bruijne, 'The Colonial City and the Post-Colonial World', in: R. Ross and G.J. Telkamp (eds.), *Colonial Cities*, Dordrecht 1985, 231-243, quotation 232.

13 J. Osterhammel, *Kolonialismus. Geschichte – Formen – Folgen*, München 1996, 21: „Herrschaftsbeziehung zwischen Kollektiven, bei welcher die fundamentalen Entscheidungen über die Lebensführung der Kolonisierten durch eine kulturell andersartige und kaum anpassungswillige Minderheit von Kolonialherren unter vorrangiger Berücksichtigung externer Interessen getroffen und tatsächlich durchgesetzt werden."

methods. All these actual monopolies had a narrow geographical range in common.

Macassar – Emporium of the Traditional Spice Trade

In 1669 Dutch forces conquered the city of Macassar in South-Sulawesi with their indigenous allies after a longer siege. One of the most important trading places for cloves, nutmeg and mace and at the same time one of the greatest rice-exporting harbours of the region came under Dutch control. The city had offered resistance to the Dutch claim to a spice trade monopoly for more than half a century. To achieve complete control of this trade the VOC saw the possibility of destroying the last great competitor in this field.

In the middle of the sixteenth century the local Sulawesian kingdoms Goa and Tallo were united. This unification allowed the young state to gain independence from the supremacy of Siang in the north and to become a hegemonial power of the wider region with Macassar as capital. In the beginning of the seventeenth century the twin-kingdom adopted Islam. During the following decades Goa-Tallo subjugated the whole peninsula, especially the Bugis-kingdoms of which Boné and Soppeng were the largest. Between 1618 and 1633 several campaigns against the states on Sumbawa incorporated this island to the area of Macassarese supremacy. The islands off the coast of Sulawesi e.g. Selayar or Buton also came under this hegemony. The new religion of Islam was immediately forced on the conquered regions and served as additional legitimation for the new role of Goa-Tallo in Sulawesi and Nusa Tenggara. Next to its rival Ternate Goa-Tallo – often equated with Macassar – was the greatest hegemonial power of the Eastern Malay Archipelago.[14]

---

14 For the rise of Goa-Tallo see: J. Noorduyn, 'De Islamisering van Makasar', in: A. Reid, 'A Great Seventeenth Century Indonesia Family. Matoaya and Pattingalloang of Makassar', in: *Bijdragen tot de Taal-, Land- en Volkenkunde*, 112 (1956), 247-266; L. Tapala, 'L'expansion du royaume de Goa et sa politique maritime aux XVIe et XVIIe siècles', *Archipel*, 10 (1975), 159-171; *Masyarakat Indonesia* 8 (1981), 1-28; A. Reid, 'The Rise of Macassar', in: *Review of Indonesian and Malaysian Affairs*, 17 (1983), 117-160; J. Noorduyn, 'Makasar and the Islamization of Bima', in: *Bijdragen tot de Taal-, Land- en Volkenkunde*, 143 (1987), 312-342; J. Villiers, 'Makassar. The rise and fall of an East Indonesian maritime trading state, 1512-1669', in: J. Kathirithamby-Wells and J. Villiers (eds.), *The Southeast Asian Port and Polity. Rise and demise*, Singapore 1990, 143-159; D. Bulbeck, 'Construction History and Significance of the Makassar Fortifications', in: K. Robinson and M. Paeni (eds.), *Living Through Histories. Culture, history and social life in South Sulawesi*, Canberra 1998, 67-106; J. G. Nagel, 'Vom Stadtstaat zur Kolonialstadt. Grundzüge der Stadtentwicklung Makassars (Süd-Sulawesi) im 17. und frühen 18. Jahrhundert', in: H. Gründer and P. Johanek (eds.),

During that development Macassar became one of the most central port cities of the Archipelago. The place at the Western coast of the Southern Sulawesian peninsula had a long tradition in overseas trading contacts. Archaeological evidence shows early contacts to mainland Southeast Asia and to Southern China; early written sources see the place as a part of the Northern route connecting the Western Archipelago with the Moluccan Islands.[15] The town was emporium for all commodities of significance in Southeast Asia – foodstuff, textiles, metals, potteries, products from the sea and the forests and predominantly spices. Huge quantities of cloves from Ternate, Tidore or Ambon, nutmeg and mace from Banda and pepper from Kalimantan were transshiped in the harbour of Macassar. Together with ports like Melaka, Banten, Palembang or Jambi the capital of Goa-Tallo became the first row of those port cities which controlled the so called luxury trade. Macassar experienced a special, but short boom phase after the fall of Melaka to the Dutch company in 1641 when great parts of the trade abandoned there changed to South Sulawesi. In that situation the emporium Macassar was a serious competitor to the spice trade of the VOC.[16]

Kolonialstädte. Europäische Enklaven oder Schmelztigel der Kulturen, Münster 2001, 109-143.

15 For the traditional trading routes of the Malay Archipelago and their relation to South-Sulawesi and Macassar see: S. Suleiman, 'Maritime Routes in the Classical Period', in: *SPAFA Final Report, Consultative Workshop on Research in Maritime Shipping and Trade Networks in Southeast Asia*, Bangkok 1984, 53-70; J.K. Whitmore, 'The Opening of Southeast Asia. Trading patterns through the centuries', in: K.L. Hutterer (ed.), *Economic Exchange and Social Interaction in Southeast Asia. Perspectives from prehistory, history and ethnography*, Ann Arbor 1977, 139-153; J. Wisseman, 'Markets and Trade in Pre-Majapahit Java', in: Hutterer (ed.), *Economic Exchange*, 197-212; A. B. Lapian, 'The Maritime Network in the Indonesian Archipelago in the Fourteenth Century', in: *SPAFA Final Report*, 71-80; P. R. Abdurachman, 'Observations on the Impact of Trade Goods', in: *SPAFA Final Report*, 273-282; A. Reid, 'Trade Goods and Trade Routes in Southeast Asia, c. 1300-1700', in: *SPAFA Final Report*, 249-272; J. G. Nagel, 'Makassar und der Molukkenhandel. Städte und Handelsnetze im indonesischen Gewürzhandel des 16. und 17. Jahrhunderts', in: M.A. Denzel (ed.), *Gewürze. Produktion, Handel und Konsum in der Frühen Neuzeit*, St. Katharinen 1999, 93-121.

16 For the economic role of independent Macassar see: B. Schrieke, 'The Shifts in Political and Economic Power in the Indonesian Archipelago in the Sixteenth and Seventeenth Century', in: B. Schrieke, *Indonesian Sociological Studies. Selected writings*, vol. I, The Hague 1955, 1-82; C.C. Macknight, 'The Nature of Early Maritime Trade. Some points of analogy from the eastern part of the Indonesian Archipelago', in: *World Archaeology* 5 (1973), 198-208; R. Ptak, 'Der Handel zwischen Macau und Makassar, ca. 1640-1667', in: *Zeitschrift der Deutschen Morgenländischen Gesellschaft*, 139 (1989), 208-226; O. Prakash, 'Restrictive Trade Regimes. VOC and Asian spice trade in the seventeenth century', in: Ptak and Rothermund (eds.): *Emporia, Commodities and Entrepreneurs*, 107-126; Nagel, 'Makassar und der Molukkenhandel'.

The urban character of Macassar was similar to the majority of the Asian port cities. Beside the indigenous population several trading diasporas – in the case of Macassar Bugis, Malay, Indian, Portuguese and an increasing number of Chinese merchants – were not only tolerated but expressly invited by the rulers. Also European factories were allowed to do their business in so far as they accepted the same position as the Asian trading diasporas. The British East India Company (EIC) ran a factory from 1613 to 1666.[17] The VOC started several attempts to establish an own factory, but they failed because of their own arrogant demands towards the rulers of Goa-Tallo.[18]

On the eve of the conquest of Macassar the responsible admiral, Cornelis Speelman, wrote a so called *notitie* which offers the most precise description of Macassar in the seventeenth century.[19] Besides a lot of information about the country, the people and their politics it gives a description of several trading contacts of Macassar during this time. Following a report by Speelman, Buton and other islands off the coast of South Sulawesi delivered mostly slaves and additionally weapons, tortoiseshell and wax. They received predominantly textiles of Indian origin in return. Macassar imported pepper, gold, bezoar-stones, *bilion*-choppers and *parang*-knives from the neighbouring islands Kalimantan or Borneo, while it exported slaves, indigenous and Indian textiles, porcelain and other Chinese products to the port city Banjarmasin and the smaller harbours at the eastern coast. Eastern Nusa Tenggara Macassar had commercial contacts especially to Timor and Flores, where slaves, sandalwood, amber, wild cinnamon and wax were exchanged against indigenous and Indian textiles, Chinese brass and other Chinese products, weapons, jewellery, *bilion* and *parang*. Concerning Java Speelman tells us about the import of Indian and Chinese textiles as well as European and Asian products traded by the VOC, while Macassar exported sandalwood, slaves, wax, tortoiseshell and iron produced in the Bugis country Luwu. Sumatra and the Malay Peninsula were also the origin place of textiles traded by the European companies. The far West of the Malay Archipelago was the destination for sandalwood, wild cinnamon,

---

17 D.K. Bassett, 'English Trade in Celebes, 1613-1667', in: *Journal of the Malayan Branch of the Royal Asiatic Society*, 31 (1958), 1-39; J. Villiers, 'One of the Especiallest Flowers in our Garden. The English factory at Makassar, 1613-1667', in: *Archipel*, 39 (1990), 159-178.

18 J. W. Ijzerman, 'Het ship 'De Eendracht' voor Makassaer in December 1616. Journaal van Jan Steijns', in: *Bijdragen tot de Taal-, Land- en Volkenkunde*, 78 (1922), 343-372; Nagel, 'Vom Stadtstaat zur Kolonialstadt', 117-118.

19 General State Archive, The Hague, Aanwinsten, 1524: 1926 I 10-11, 718-729. See additionally J. Noorduyn, 'De handelsrelaties van het Makassaarse rijk volgens de notitie van Cornelis Speelman uit 1670', in: *Nederlands Historische Bronnen*, 3 (1983), 96-123.

slaves, tortoiseshell, Chinese gold and porcelain as well as pepper which was sold to the companies there.

The report by Speelman also mentions trading contacts of Macassar to regions outside the Malay Archipelago. Thailand was the origin of textiles, indigo, ivory and Japanese copper and received for it sandalwood, besides sulphur and cowries. Macassar imported Chinese products, especially silk and porcelain, Japanese copper-products, benzion, ivory, dyes as well as gum from Cambodia and exported Indian textiles, sandalwood and cotton-yarn. Contacts to the Philippines and the Sulu-Archipelago were – according to Speelman – of great importance for Macassar. From there the Macassarese market received a wide range of commodities like wild cinnamon, wax, slaves, gold, pearles, tobacco, tortoiseshell, cowries, porcelain, copper. On the other hand the Sulawesian metropolis mainly exported Indian and indigenous textiles to the maritime world in the North. Finally, the Sino-Portuguese port city Macau is mentioned by Speelman who reports that only the Portuguese living in Macassar imported porcellain, gold, copper and copper-products, brass, other metals as well as weapons from there and in exchange delivered Indian textiles, sandal- and sappanwood, wax, rattan, ivory and pepper.

A closer look at the European sources of the first half of the seventeenth century – unfortunately indigenous sources with economic evidence are more than scarce – shows that Speelmans notes were not really complete. Especially the spice trade of the Macassarese people is omitted which caused a neglection in the academic literature up to this day. Macassarese merchants were seen by VOC-officials at Ambon as well as in the Northern Moluccas.[20] Moreover, we have some evidence that they sailed to smaller islands in the far East of the

---

20 P.A. Thiele (ed.), *Bouwstoffen voor de geschiedenis der Nederlanders in den Maleischen Archipel, vol. I,* The Hague 1886, 231, no. XVIIk, Steven van der Haghen to the directors, 20 August 1618; ibid., 355, no. XXIIf, Pieter de Carpentier to the directors, 3 January 1624; P.A. Thiele (ed.), *Bouwstoffen voor de geschiedenis der Nederlanders in den Maleischen Archipel, vol. II,* The Hague 1890, 246, no. LVIII, Artus Gysels, governor of Ambon, to the general-governor, 12 June 1633; ibid., 132/133, no. XXX, Philip Lucasz, governor of Ambon, to the general-governor, 10 September 1628; ibid., 40, no. VIII, Jacques le Febvre, governor of the Moluccas (Ternate), to the general-governor, 26 March 1625; ibid., 56/57, no. XI, journal of a VOC-expedition, 14 May - 23 June 1625; ibid., 99, Nr. XX, Jan van Gorcum, governor of Ambon, to the general-governor, 28 April 1626; ibid., 105, no. XXI, journal of Jan van Gorcum, September 1625 - May 1626; ibid., 179, no. XLVII, Antonio van Diemen to the directors, 5 June 1631; ibid., 304, no. LXX, Antonio van Diemen to the directors, 28 December 1636; Ijzerman, 'Het ship 'De Eendracht' voor Makassaer', 370/371; G.J. Knaap (ed.), *Memories van overgave van gouverneurs van Ambon in de zeventiende en achttiende eeuw,* The Hague 1987, 77, no. IX, 'Sommier Verbael' of Philip Lucasz, 23 May 1631; ibid., 153, no. XIV, 'Cort Verhael' of Arend Gardenius, 25 July 1636.

Malay Archipelago in order to trade with spices.[21] Last but not least, we know from the records of the British factory in Macassar that since 1615 there had been a direct connection to China by a regular junk which was abandoned with the fall of Macassar to the Dutch.[22]

The company's general aim was to achieve a monopoly in the spice trade. During the first half of the seventeenth century, the VOC enforced such monopolies in the Moluccas. On Ambon and Banda the Dutch established more or less violently control over the plantation cultures of cloves (Ambon) or nutmeg and mace (Banda).[23] On Ternate they established a customer's monopoly as superior competitor and by contracts with the regional ruler. But the Moluccas were only a part of the Archipelago and the VOC did not achieve an actual monopoly before the middle of the seventeenth century. The strong position of Macassar as an emporium prevented it for a long time.

But the situation in Macassar had become less comfortable. After the Dutch had failed to establish a factory with a legal monopoly in spice trade guaranteed by the ruler of Goa-Tallo they tried to undermine the position of the port city by blockade and bombardments. In 1660 the town was nearly conquered. In the last minute the king yielded, the hegemony in the spice trade of the VOC was recognised by a treaty and the Dutch forces were withdrawn. Nevertheless, trade continued in the harbour of Macassar even under difficult circumstances. The spice market of Macassar reflected the attempts of the company. In 1621 the price of cloves was 150-160 *mas* per *bahar*, in 1651 300-400 *mas* and in 1659 750-850 *mas*.[24]

---

21 W.P. Coolhaas (ed.), *Generale Missiven van Gouverneurs-Generaal en Raden an Heeren XVII der Verenigde Oostindische Compagnie, vol. I*, The Hague 1960, 384, 15 August 1633; ibid., 494, 31 December 1635; ibid., 534, 4 January 1636; W.P. Coolhaas (ed.), *Generale Missiven van Gouverneurs-Generaal en Raden an Heeren XVII der Verenigde Oostindische Compagnie, vol. II*, The Hague 1964, 495, 19 December 1651; ibid., 749, 7 November 1654; W.P. Coolhaas (ed.), *Generale Missiven van Gouverneurs-Generaal en Raden an Heeren XVII der Verenigde Oostindische Compagnie, vol. III*, The Hague 1968, 409/410, 26 December 1662; ibid., 454, 21 December 1663.

22 British Library, London, Oriental and India Office Collections, G/10/1, 2, George Cockrayne (Makassar) to Governor Thomas Smith (Banten), 16 July 1615.

23 J. Keuning, 'Ambonnezen, Portuguezen en Nederlanders. Ambon's geschiedenis tot het einde van de zeventiende eeuw', in: *Indonesië*, 9 (1956), 135-168; G.J. Knaap, *Kruidnagelen en christenen. De verenigde Oostindische Compagnie en de bevolking van Ambon 1656-1696*, Dordrecht 1987; J.A. van der Chijs, *De vestiging van het Nederlandsche gezag over de Bandaeilanden, 1599-1621*, Batavia 1886; T. Beck, 'Monopol und Genozid. Die Muskatnußproduktion der auf den Banda-Inseln im 17. Jahrhundert', in: M.A. Denzel (ed.), *Gewürze*, 71-90.

24 Ijzerman, 'Het wship 'De Eendracht' voor Makassaer', 370/371 (1621); Coolhaas (ed.), *Generale Missiven II*, 489, 19 December 1651 (1651); British Library, London, Oriental and

Finally, the company decided to solve the problem by violence. Therefore an ally who was to attack Macassar simultaneously from land and from sea was necessary. The company found such an ally in Arung Palakka, prince of the Bugis kingdom Boné which was suppressed by the hegemonial power. He was the most charismatic leader of the opposition against Macassar. The military campaign, which started in 1666, was successful in the end. In 1667 the ruler of Goa-Tallo accepted negotiation which resulted in the treaty of Bongaya. Immediately after the contract was signed new fighting started. The VOC and its allies besieged the well fortified city for more than one year before it surrendered. The company's troops destroyed great parts of the town, especially the fortifications. Only one castle, called Ujung Pandang, remained.[25]

The contract of Bongaya manifested the subordination of Goa-Tallo under the VOC's rule, the exclusion of all European merchants from Macassar and several restrictions to the private trade of the Sulawesian people. Officially Asian merchants were not allowed to trade with products in which the VOC had commercial interests. These included all kinds of spice and also textiles. Additionally these merchants were restricted to an area which enclosed little more than Sulawesi, Kalimantan, Java and Sumbawa.[26]

Trade in the Colonial Town

The conquest by the VOC and their allies was not the end of the town of Macassar; but it was re-established by the Dutch as their colonial town. Contrary to the periodisation offered by Peter Nas this colonial town existed since c. 1670.

India Office Collections, G/10/1, 171, 173, Macassar General to Bantam, 12 June 1659; ibid., 183, Agency of Bantam to Macassar, 7 November 1659 (1659). *Mas* was the gold currency of independent Macassar which was equated until 1650 with the Spanish *real* or the Dutch *rijksdalder*; *bahar* was the regional unit of measurement for spices which can be equated with c. 185 kg.

25 For the Macassar War see: F.W. Stapel, *Het Bongaais Verdrag*, Leiden 1922; K.C. Crucq, 'De geschiedenis van het heilig kanon van Makassar', in: *Tijdschrift voor Taal-, Land- en Volkenkunde van de Bataviaasch Genootschap*, 81 (1941) 74-95; L.Y. Andaya, 'A Village Perception of Arung Palakka and the Makassar War of 1666-69', in: A. Reid and D. Marr (eds.), *Perceptions of the Past in Southeast Asia*, Singapore 1979, 360-378; L.Y. Andaya, *The Heritage of Arung Palakka. A history of South Sulawesi in the seventeenth century*, The Hague 1981; F.D. Bulbeck, 'The Landscape of the Makassar War. A review article', in: *Canberra Anthropology*, 13 (1990) 78-99.

26 General State Archive, The Hague, VOC 4785. The treaty has been published several times: J.E. Heeres (ed.), *Corpus Diplomaticum Neerlando-Indico*. Deel II: 1650-1675, The Hague 1909, 370-380; B. Erkelens, 'Geschiedenis van het rijk Gowa', in: *Verhandelingen van het Bataviaasch Genootschap van Kunsten en Wetenschapen*, 50 (1897), 87-90; F.W. Stapel, Het Bongaais Verdrag, Leiden 1922, 237-247; Andaya, *Heritage of Arung Palakka*, 305-307.

It was ruled by officials of the VOC with a governor at the top of the administration. Rebuilt as Fort Rotterdam, the old fortress Ujung Pandang became a manifestation of colonial power. Around 500 soldiers were stationed permanently in the local garrison. Next to the company's fort a new colonial town centre was established under the name Vlaardingen. This relatively small compound was mainly inhabited by Europeans and Chinese and protected by a wooden pallisade. Finally, the Dutch took over control of the harbour by introducing a passport-system. By doing so they achieved their main goal: the actual monopoly in Macassar over the Moluccan spice trade.

Kampung Baru in the South and the Kampung Melayu in the North were more or less secure areas for the colonial administration apart from the neighbouring Vlaardingen and Fort Rotterdam. But Dutch control did not stretch over the whole urban area of Macassar. Especially the numerous *kampung* of the Macassarese und Bugis were situated outside the company's influence and were more or less uncontrollable by the administration. A delegation of the council of law made this experience when it entered the *kampung* of the Bugis in 1727 in order to find some murdered Dutch and to punish their murderers. The members of the delegation found themselves surrounded by angry Bugis people immediately after they had entered the *kampung*. They were very busy to call for help from the Malay quarter and to leave the *kampung* as soon as possible while they completely forgot the reason for their coming.[27] It was the traditional, Indonesian Macassar which still existed in such parts of the city. Parallely, in the centre the 'Indische culture' arose step by step. During the period of the Dutch company all these descriptions were true at the same time: Macassar *was* a colonial city, Macassar *was* an 'Indische town', and Macassar *was* typical Southeast-Asian. And there is no doubt that over all Macassar was a typical case of Indonesian urban history and not an exception of a scheme as that one introduced by Peter Nas. It is not the assignment to a certain typus or period which describes the town in an appropriate way but the ascertainment of its centrality.

Concerning political centrality, Macassar played a central role in the administrative hierarchy of the VOC in the Malay Archipelago. Theoretically the city was the pivotal centre for the whole Eastern Archipelago. Practically the picture was less impressive. The garrison never had more than 500 soldiers who only guaranteed the safety of the fort and did not operate outside the town.[28] The company-fleet of Macassar consisted of two or four chialoups and several

---

27 General State Archives, The Hague, VOC 2050, Macassar, 494-496.
28 General State Archives, The Hague, VOC 2100, Macassar, 1st reg., 49-128, J. F. Gobius' memorie van overgave, 5 March 1727, here 53-56.

indigenous boats. This was enough to carry out some *krijstochten* against smugglers and pirates year by year, but not to control half of Indonesia. Thus, Macassar was of high centrality inside the VOC-administration, but was not able to control the whole region for which it was responsible.

Concerning the economic centrality, a differentiation is necessary. From the VOC's point of view the main positive result of the occupation was the end of the spice trade in the city's harbour. From this viewpoint the most important issue was a kind of "negative centrality". From the private traders' point of view Macassar lost centrality in some trading spheres,[29] but kept, regained or newly established centrality in some others. In a first step the complexity of private trade under the company's rule will be illustrated sketching five aspects which can be observed in the official records of the VOC-factory in Macassar.[30]

The vanishing trade of the Macassarese merchants

In 1717/18 the ships owned by Macassarese merchants held a share of 25.6% of all ship movements in the harbour of Macassar, in 1722/23 even 33.3%. In the 1730s the share was between 22% and 23%. But in 1767/68 only 7.6% of all ship movement were Macassarese vessels. In 1781/82 not one single Macassarese boat approached or left the town port; in 1787/88 the percentage was again about 10%.

After an outstanding role at the beginning of the eighteenth century the local people nearly disappeared from their own harbour. The Macassarese people did not stop their occupation in the commodity trade. A much more probable explanation seems to be that the trading networks of the Macassarese shifted to locations out of the company's control. Contemporary Dutch reports from

---

29 A 'trading sphere' is defined as a context of commercial exchange determined by a single commodity or a group of commodities under recognition of the ethnic, geographic, cultural, organisational and religious connotations brought in by the region and by the participants.

30 The *syahbandhars* (harbour masters) of Macassar conducted a list of all private shipmovements in the port reporting in every single case type, size and amunition, name and nationality of the *nakhoda* (captain) and the owner, destination and the composition of the load. For the PhD thesis of the author ten exemplary years (1717/18: General State Archives, The Hague, VOC 1894 and 1910; 1722/23: VOC 1995; 1727/28: VOC 2072 and 2100; 1730/31: VOC 2192; 1733/34: VOC 2314; 1767/68: VOC 3210 and 3243; 1772/73: VOC 3332; 1777/78: VOC 3493 and 3524; 1781/82: VOC 3623; 1787/88: VOC 3760 and 3809) of the incomplete records in the General State Archives (1717-1719, 1722-1728, 1730/31, 1733/34, 1766-1782, 1783-1785, 1786-1790, 1790/91, 1791/92) were captured in a database and analysed by statistical methods (see Nagel, *Schlüssel zu den Molukken*). For the following paragraphs the evidence is supplemented by the journals of the so called *krijstochten*, the maritime expeditions of the VOC in order to destroy "illegal" plantations and to fight "smuggling" and piracy.

Macassar mention "illegal" harbours in the surrounding area. These could be places under the control of neighbouring rulers as well as places within the urban area of Macassar where the possibilities of the VOC to control economic activities faded to zero.[31] The reports of the Dutch captains who were in command of the *krijstochten* against "smugglers" also mention new places and trading networks outside actual control of the company. For Macassarese merchants the islands between Sulawesi and Sumbawa – like Bonerate – played an important role as well as the Tunkangbesi-Group (Blacksmith-Islands).[32]

The vanishing trade to Kalimantan

In 1717/18 34 private trading ships leaving the harbour of Macassar (12.2% of all) steered for Kalimantan (Passir and Pulo Laut at the eastern coast and the port city Banjarmasin). Ten years later only 10 ships (5.8%) left in the same direction. The 1770s and 1780s generally saw only one ship a year leaving for Kalimantan.

To understand this development a monocausal explanation is not sufficient. Only a number of arguments can explain the fundamental change in such a traditional commercial link. First of all, the VOC held an actual monopoly for pepper, the central export good of Banjarmasin, on the market in Macassar. The drop of the primary good pepper also resulted in a decline of the secondary goods from Kalimantan which were formerly traded together with the pepper. Furthermore, the problems which Banjarmasin had with European pepper-merchants, mostly from the Dutch and English companies, did not only lead to an expulsion of those people but also to worse trading conditions for most of the foreigners.[33] Additionally, the Chinese also gained an increasingly superior role

---

31 General State Archives, The Hague, VOC 2100, Macassar, 1st reg., 49-128, J. F. Gobius' memorie van overgave, 5 March 1727, here 104-106; ibid., VOC 11254, 1-39, C. Sinkelaar's memorie van overgave, 4 June 1767, here 18-20.

32 See for example the journals of Sergeant J. Swanevelt's *krijstochten*: General State Archives, The Hague, VOC 1759, Macassar, 147-169; ibid., VOC 1775, Macassar, 1st reg., 252-283; ibid., VOC 1775, Macassar, 2nd reg., 84-114.

33 For the European contacts to Banjarmasin during the 17th and 18th centuries see: L.C.D. van Dijk, *Neerland's vroegste betrekkingen met Borneo, den Solo-Archipel, Cambodja, Siam en Cochin-China. Met eene levensschets en inleiding van G. W. Vreede*, Amsterdam 1862; J.C. Noorlander, *Bandjarmasin en de Compagnie in de Tweede Helft der 18de Eeuw*, Leiden 1935; R. Suntharalingam, 'The British in Banjarmasin. An abortive attempt at settlement, 1700-1707', in: *Journal of Southeast Asian History*, 4 (1963), 48-72; C. Yoon Fong, 'VOC Relations with Banjarmasin, 1600-1750. A study in Dutch trade and shipping in the 17th and 18th Centuries', in: M.Y. Hashim (ed.), *Kapal dan Harta Karam. Ships and Sunken Treasure*, Kuala Lumpur 1986, 77-87; Nagel, *Schlüssel zu den Molukken*, chapter 7.

in the pepper trade and thus in other economic activities in Banjarmasin. The access to the eastern coast of Kalimantan, where forest products like rattan were traded without being secondary commodities to pepper, became dangerous due to high pirate activity of which the most famous example was Arung Singkang, an exiled Bugis nobleman, and his admiral Tualla.[34] Finally, the connections to the eastern coast that did survive, meant that the trading networks often shifted to places in Sulawesi out of the Dutch company's control.

The persistance and differentiation of the textile trade

In 1717/18 17.6% of the leaving and 24.3% of the arriving vessels transported textile products in their cargo. In 1730/31 the relation was 4.1% to 26.0% and in 1767/68 17.2% to 17.9%. At the end of the period under consideration, 1787/88, the shares were 41.1% of the leaving and 32.9% of the arriving vessels.

Despite the regulations of the Bongaya treaty textiles (from India, China and from the region) still made up the main trading spheres of private merchants in Macassar. They found themselves in competition with VOC which undertook no serious attempts to abolish the private textile trade. In that competition the spheres were differentiated. Some textile products from India were dominated by the company, others mostly by private traders. The company mainly sold Indian textiles on the Macassarese market.[35] A great supply of very different textiles from India existed there. Some of them (like *berthilles*, *haman* or *roemaal*) were only sold by the VOC. The most important sorts of textiles (like *sallamporees*, *chindos*, *guinees*) competed between VOC and private merchants. Generally the sales of textiles by the company shrank in the second half of the eighteenth century. Finally the private traders won. Only the *guinees* remained a domain of the VOC. Furthermore, a trading sphere outside the access of the company should not be underestimated. Regional textiles like *buginees kleeden* from the Bugis countries, from Selayar or from Sumbawa were an export commodity of rising value. This trading sphere in which the products were sold to markets on Java, Kalimantan and the Southern Moluccas was completely run by private

---

34 J. Noorduyn, 'Een Boeginees geschriftje over Arung Singkang', in: *Bijdragen tot de Taal-, Land- en Volkenkunde*, 109 (1953), 144-152; J. Noorduyn, 'Arung Singkang (1700-1765). How the victory of Wadjo' began', in: *Indonesia*, 13 (1972), 61-68.

35 Lists on the commodity trade of the VOC itself (*rendements*) in Makassar can be found in the company's records since 1757. For the case study exemplary years corresponding to the chosen years of the harbourmaster's lists were selected: General State Archives, The Hague, VOC 2933 (1757/58); ibid., VOC 3243 (1767/68); ibid., VOC 3384 (1772/73); ibid., VOC 3524 (1777/78); ibid., VOC 3623 (1781/82); VOC 3760 (1786/87). The rendement for 1787/88 (VOC 3809) is incomplete.

Asian merchants without any share of the company or European privatiers. The same can be said of the import-commodity raw cotton which was planted in South-Sulawesi as well as on Sumbawa. At least in the field of the textile trade, Macassar played the role of an emporium after the VOC's conquest as well as before.

The renaissance of the Chinese junk trade between Amoy and Macassar

Since 1736 one junk from Amoy in China arrived at Macassar annually.[36] Originally such contact was not allowed by the VOC-administration which tried to direct the whole China trade to the harbour of Batavia. Fortunately the incumbent governor of Macassar recognised the mercantile advantages when he allowed the junk of 1736 to enter the port despite such rules. Thus, the governor reinstalled traditional trading contacts which now competed with the Chinese trading routes to Batavia and Banjarmasin.

The annual junk supplied the markets in Macassar with silk and other Chinese textiles, with porcelain and other pottery, with copper products and a lot of cheep articles for everyday use. On the other hand the junk was the greatest consumer of *trepang* (sea-slug or sea-cucumber) which was an essential raw material both for Chinese medicine and cooking. This demand laid the basis for a flourishing *trepang* industry centred in Macassar. Further products the junk annually transported to China were *agar-agar*, tortoiseshell, wax and rattan. The Amoy merchants were not an integral part of the trade with typical Indonesian staple goods like salt, sugar, tobacco or rice. The connection between Macassar and China was linked to its own specialised trading spheres.

The rise of the trepang trade[37]

In 1717/18 Macassar imported 14 tons of *trepang*, in 1733/34 28 tons, in 1767/68 the figure reached 79 tons and in 1787/88 184 tons. The corresponding export-numbers rose from 58 tons (1717/18) via 67.5 tons (1733/34) and 303 tons (1767/68) up to 387 tons (1787/88). About half of the transshipped trepang reached Macassar from harbours which still remained outside the control of the Dutch habourmasters which explains the discrepancies between import and export volume. This trading sphere was interesting for all private merchants who

---

36 General State Archive, The Hague, VOC 2674, Macassar, 30, 108 (for the first arrival 1736). On the Chinese merchants from Amoy and their networks see C.K. Nag, *Trade and Society. The Amoy network on the China coast, 1683-1735*, Singapore 1983.

37 On *trepang* or sea-cucumber (Holothuriidea) see: J.C. Koningsberger, *Tripang en tripang-visschereij in Nederlandsch-Indië*, Batavia 1904.

were active in Macassar. While the company did not take a small part in this trade, and while the Chinese gained more and more control over the *trepang*-export – China and the Chinese diasporas were the only consumers – all trading nations participated in the import and tried to keep some portions of the exports.

The trade with *trepang* developed a supra-regional network connecting the southern parts of the Archipelago (partly including Northern Australia) via Macassar with China.[38] Besides the already mentioned merchants the network included further groups especially in the field of *trepang*-fishing. One of the most famous and at the same time most mysterious people in this context were the Bajau or – as they are often called by Europeans – sea nomads or sea gipsies.[39] Especially under the VOC the port city of Macassar gained a completely new function: that of the central emporium of the *trepang* trade. It was a role which was far away from all trading spheres ever connected to the East India Companies and their trading networks.

These observations can only shed some light on the entire private trade in Macassar, i.e. a complex, colourful and widely differentiated picture. One aspect should have become clearer: the different grades of centrality depend on the trading spheres under observation and their participants. Concerning private trade, neither an elimination or Europeanisation nor an untouched independence be stressed; but rather a shifting of nets and nodes.

Urban and Non-Urban Centres

These officially accepted and recorded aspects of private trade are not able to describe the trading world of early colonial Macassar sufficiently. In a second step four examples from the Malay Archipelago will be introduced in order to show some evidence for comparison and extension of the features discussed above. These examples will be introduced in terms of their different strategies against the VOC, the strategies of the VOC in the specific case, the functions in

---

38 C.C. Macknight, *The Voyage to Marege. Macassan trepangers in northern Australia*, Carlton 1976; H.A. Sutherland, 'Trepang and wangkang. The China trade of eighteenth-century Makassar c. 1720s - 1840s', in: *Bijdragen tot de Taal-, Land- en Volkenkunde*, 156 (2000), 451-472.

39 D.E. Sopher, *The Sea Nomads. A study of the maritime boat people of Southeast Asia*, Singapore 1977; H. A. Nimmo, *The Sea People of Sulu. A study of social change in the Philippines*, San Francisco 1972; C. Sather, *The Bajau Laut. Adaption, history, and fate in a maritime fishing society of south-eastern Sabah*, Kuala Lumpur 1997.

commodity trade and the patterns of centrality. They partly stood in close contact to Macassar, the free as well as the colonial port.

Banjarmasin

The city of Banjarmasin was the centre of a regional empire ruling over the southeast of the island Kalimantan. It was one of the island's most important port cities and at the same time one of the great ports in the Indonesian pepper trade.[40] The kings and their *panambahans* (prime ministers) successfully maintained independence for a long time. At the beginning of the eighteenth century they closed the market for all European companies after the British EIC had made their imperial demands too obvious. Under the impression of the violent outcome of the European-Banjarese relations, the Dutch competitors chose a more cautious manner and attained a careful re-opening to their company during the 1720s. During the second half of the eighteenth century the VOC achieved acceptance without privileges by the Banjarese rulers. The company built up a factory and concentrated itself on the pepper trade in close relationship to the indigenous administration and Chinese middlemen.[41]

The VOC chose a different strategy towards the rulers of Banjarmasin as compared to that of Macassar. The Dutch renunciated violence against the emporium and limited it to actions retaining their access to Banjarmasin, for example against pirates. They restricted themselves to the establishment of regular trading connections. The fact, that Banjarmasin came under Dutch control during the 1780s was not the result of the company's colonial aims but due to inner conflicts of the Banjarese kingdom which allowed the establishment of a king by the company's favour.

Banjarmasin gained its importance from its function as emporium first of all for Kalimantan's pepper exports, in the second place for forest products, textiles and foodstuff. Furthermore, there is some evidence for a role of the city's – or better to say of its hinterland – in the Moluccan spice trade. Sulawesian traders

---

40 For Banjarmasin see the literature in footnote 33 and generally A. van der Ven, 'Aanteekeningen omtrent het rijk Bandjermasin', in: *Tijdschrift voor Taal-, Land- en Volkenkunde*, 9 (1860), 93-133; A.A. Cense, *De Kroniek van Bandjarmasin*, Santpoort 1928; J.J. Ras, *Hikayat Bandjar. A study in Malay historiography*, The Hague 1968; V.T. King, *The Peoples of Borneo*, Oxford 1993; H. Knapen, *Forests of Fortune? The enviromental history of Southeast Borneo, 1600-1800*, Leiden 2001.

41 General State Archive, The Hague, VOC 2072, Macassar, 1st reg., 4-25; ibid., VOC 2072, Macassar, 2nd reg., 19-23; ibid., VOC 2072, Banjermassing; ibid., VOC 2100, Macassar, 1st reg., 2-10, 176-179; ibid., VOC 2100, Macassar, 2nd reg., 123-132, 167-185, 438-447; ibid., VOC 2133, Macassar, 1st reg., 288-341.

especially transshipped cloves, nutmeg and mace on the Banjarmasin river.[42] For contintental Chinese merchants the situation offered a lucrative alternative to the spice markets controlled, restricted or even closed by the Dutch during their seventeenth century's expansion.

Banjarmasin is another example of an Indonesian town with differentiated patterns of centrality. The political and cultural centrality of the city was only of regional scope. It showed a high centrality, despite of this, in several trading spheres especially as emporium of a free pepper trade and as one of several competing central places of the Indonesian-Chinese trading connection besides Batavia and Macassar. An influential Chinese diaspora was one basic feature of that economic centrality. Additionally, we have to mention a certain centrality in the "illegal" networks of the private Moluccan spice trade in competition to the Dutch Moluccan spice monopoly.

Banten

The old merchant metropolis Banten on Java, situated directly at the mouth of the Sunda Street experienced a different fate. Thus the rulers could accept European trading companies as merchant groups with the same rights as their Asian competitors. For a long time they were able to follow a policy of independence and to maintain the position as one of the leading free ports in the Archipelago.[43] After the VOC had removed its headquarter from Banten to Batavia, the city of Macassar became a serious competitor to the VOC for two main reasons: as emporium of the Moluccan spice trade and as host to the competing European nations, especially the EIC. As in Macassar the problem was solved by war and finally by conquest in 1684.

Before 1684, Banten showed a high economic centrality due to its role as emporium of the spice trade; after 1684, Banten's spice trade ended abruptly. The whole private trade was restricted to the connection Banten to Batavia. Between 1774 and 1777 more than three quarters of all ship moves in the harbour of Banten came from or went to Batavia. The other moves were

---

42 General State Archives, The Hague, Collection Radermacher, No. 538, Korte Aanmerkingen van den ondergetekende Raad Extraordinair Reinier de Klerk met Relatie tot het koningrijk Banjer en desselvs aangeleegentheijd voor De E. Comp., 1.

43 On Banten see especially J. Kathirithamby-Wells, 'Banten. A West Indonesian port and polity during the sixteenth and seventeenth centuries', in: Kathirithamby-Wells and Villiers (eds.), *Southeast Asian Port*, 107-125; C. Guillot, 'Libre enterprise contre économie dirigée. Guerres civiles à Banten, 1580-1609', in: *Archipel*, 43 (1992), 57-72; C. Guillot, 'Banten en 1678', in::*Archipel*, 37 (1989), 119-151.

connected to the other Javanese port cities.[44] At the beginning of the seventeenth century the accumulation of a great number of centrality factors like the presence of the Dutch as well as the English companies' headquarters, the link to the intercontinental trade, the function as hegemonial power in Western Java, the role in the spice trade and in a lot of other trading spheres had laid the foundation for Banten's position as leading port city of the Malay Archipelago next to Melaka. During the seventeenth century a step-by-step decline of that centrality became obvious. During the eighteenth century only a regional centrality on Java reminded of the city's former glory. During the period of its independence Banten was a very similar case to Macassar in terms of centrality, commercial function and relation to the Europeans. After the conquest Banten suffered a decline in all these fields, while Macassar changed its face and its role in the region but never completely lost its importance as a central place.

Batavia

Batavia is often regarded as the prototype of all Asian towns under VOC's control, but this is unfortunately only a very superficial view. In no other town was the company as powerful as in Batavia. In no other town were the Europeans and the Chinese as dominant as they were here. Thus, in no other town did the mestizo elites play such an important role. On the other hand, in the majority of the other towns the trading diasporas of the Malay, the Bugis or the Macassarese were much more influential. As a genuine European foundation Batavia was an exceptional case in the Asian urban system. It represented the foundation of its own port city of the Dutch company as administrative and commercial centre at a place with weak indigenous elites.[45] During the predominance of the VOC, Batavia was the only nexus of the Malay Archipelago to intercontinental trading networks, but only one of several competing port cities in supraregional or inner Asian networks.

The conditions of that framework shaped special patterns of centrality. Batavia developed a high political and administrative centrality inside the VOC's structure as well as on Java (by the company's attempt to gain the position of a

---

44 G.J. Knaap, *Shallow Waters, Rising Tide. Shipping and trade in Java around 1750*, Leiden 1996, 198-204.

45 F.W. Stapel, 'Jan Pieterszoon Coen. De stichting van Batavia en de verovering van Banda', in: F.W. Stapel (ed.), *Geschiedenis van Nederlandsch Indie*, vol. 3, Amsterdam 1939, 115-151; H.A. Breuning, *Het voormalige Batavia. Een Hollandse stedestichting in de tropen. Anno 1619*, Utrecht 1981, 9-22; S. Abeyasekere, *Jakarta. A History*, Singapore 1987, 3-19; D. Schott, 'Zur Genese von Kolonialstädten. Batavia und Singapore', in: *Trialog*, 56 (1998), 13-19; H. Lademacher, 'Batavia', in: Gründer and Johanek (eds.), *Kolonialstädte*, 95-108.

hegemonial power on the island). Additionally, the city showed high economic centrality on the world wide as well as on the continental and regional trading levels. The influential Chinese diaspora and the presence of the VOC constituted the foundation of that centrality.[46] Batavia and Macassar were both members of the club of the most central places in the Malay Archipelago – nevertheless, they were cities of very different character.

Bonerate

Originally the island of Bonerate between Sulawesi and Sumbawa was only a place of fishing and small exports of sea commodities.[47] In the first half of the eighteenth century it was nearly unknown to the merchants in Macassar. In the second half the number of vessels, especially Macassarese, steering for Bonerate increased considerably (up to 78 vessels in 1767/68). At the same time the variety of commodities grew and reached its greatest extent during the nineteenth century. All commodities traded in Macassar were also found on the market of Bonerate. Trading contacts connected the tiny island with South Sulawesi, Selayar, Sumbawa, Flores, Bali, Lombok and Singapore.

Bonerate represented the typical features of a non-urban trading place in the context of competition between the company and private merchants. There was no considerable strategical thinking on the part of the island's rulers due to their political weakness. Bonerate was the object of occasional visits by company ships on *krijstochten*, but experienced no real attempt to be forced under Dutch control. Furthermore, there was no considerable political and cultural centrality, but a growing economic centrality during the second half of the eighteenth century as a non-urban centre of most of the Indonesian trading spheres. This development found its peak in the high economic centrality of Bonerate during the nineteenth century.

Hopefully, these short examples could give some impressions of the different possible developments and functions of port cities and the role of non-urban

46 B. Hoetink, 'Chineesche officieren te Batavia onder de Compagnie', in: *Bijdragen tot de Taal-, Land- en Volkenkunde*, 78 (1922), 1-136; L. Blussé, 'Chinese Trade to Batavia during the Days of the VOC', in: *Archipel*, 18 (1979), 195-219; L. Blussé, 'Batavia, 1619-1740. The rise and fall of a Chinese colonial town', in: *Journal of Southeast Asian Studies*, 12 (1981), 159-178; M.S. de Vienne, 'La part des Chinois dans les fermes fiscales de Batavia au XVIIe siècle', in: *Archipel*, 22 (1981), 105-132.

47 For Bonerate and its economic development during the 18th and 19th centuries see J.A. Bakkers, 'De eilanden Bonerate en Kalao', in: *Tijdschrift voor Taal-, Land en Volkenkunde*, 11 (1861), 215-264.

places – a role, which should not be underestimated. It can be asked whether the case of Macassar was typical, in which case, the majority of the Malay port cities must have been very similar. But even the introduced examples speak a different language, and the list of examples could be traced. Possible additions could be the "city of migrants" Kota Ambon, the centre of the most important Moluccan island,[48] it could be the demise of Melaka which formerly maintained the position of a world wide trading centre,[49] or it could be the subordinated centre Alas on Sumbawa which attracted considerable parts of the private spice trade during the eighteenth century.[50] Concerning the non-urban places the role of Seram as origin and trading region of "illegal" cloves could also be mentioned,[51] or the island Balambangan off the northern coast of Kalimantan which the EIC tried to use as a planned emporium.[52]

Conclusion

The regional study shows no coherent trading world shaped by the interests and activities of the VOC. Looking on the indigenous part of this world it reveals very different merchant activities which existed with, against and beside the company. The VOC was a part of that world; not a dominating, but a very influential one. The chosen examples have revealed the following insights:

1) *With the Company*: Within the framework of the country trade which was essential for the VOC, the company took part in several traditional Asian spheres of trade. Private traders were often competitors of the VOC, and often they profited from the company, e.g. from the great supply of Indian textiles in every port city visited by company-ships.

---

48 G.J. Knaap, 'A City of Migrants. Kota Ambon at the end of the seventeenth century', in: *Indonesia*, 51 (1991), 105-128.

49 S. Arasaratnam, 'Some Notes on the Dutch in Malacca and the Indo-Malayan Trade 1641 – 1670', in: *Journal of Southeast Asian History*, 10 (1969), 480-490; M. Dunn, *Kampf um Malakka. Eine wirtschaftsgeschichtliche Studie über den portugiesischen und niederländischen Kolonialismus in Südostasien*, Wiesbaden 1984; B. Harrison, *Holding the Fort. Melaka Under Two Flags, 1795-1845*, Kuala Lumpur 1986; D. Lewis, *Jan Compagnie in the Straits of Malacca, 1641-1795*, Athens 1995; J. Kathirithamby-Wells, 'The Long Eighteenth Century and the New Age of Commerce in the Melaka Straits', in: L. Blussé and F.S. Gaastra (eds.), *On the Eighteenth Century as a Category of Asian History*, Aldershot 1998, 57-82.

50 Nagel, *Schlüssel zu den Molukken*, chapter 8, part III.2.

51 Nagel, *Schlüssel zu den Molukken*, chapter 8, part III.1.

52 A. Dalrymple, *A Plan for Extending the Commerce of this Kingdom, and of the East India Company*, London 1769.

2) *Against the Company*: Those port cities which positioned themselves against the spice-monopoly of the VOC were not at all successful. Free emporia in the Moluccan spice trade hardly existed in the eighteenth century; most of them were forced under the rule of the company as the examples of Melaka, Macassar or Banten have shown. The economic centrality of some of them (like Banten) declined, others maintained it in trading spheres beside the spice trade (like Macassar). The company did not follow the same strategy in every trading sphere in which the VOC participated, as we can see in the cautious attempt to find the way back to Banjarmasin's pepper trade.

3) *Beside the Company*: It was impossible to maintain the indigenous trade with Moluccan spices in immediate confrontation with the VOC. But this did not mean that spice trade became impossible for private Asian merchants. Trade shifted to other sea-routes and less important port cities which had retained their commercial freedom. Perhaps even more crucial: non-urban places like small islands (Bonerate) or flexible harbours unknown to the company also became part of spice trade systems. Those systems were able to attract other trading spheres. Thus, new central places outside the traditional as well as company controlled paths developed. Additionally other trading networks existing independently from the VOC but being of great importance for the Asian economic life are to be taken into consideration. For example: the luxury trade from Indonesia to China centred around other products (e.g. *trepang*) than that from Indonesia to Europe (e.g. Moluccan spices).

Before the European companies reached the Malay trading world two phenomena shaped the merchant frameworks in the port cities. On the one hand, the authorities strived for completely free trade, while administrative control of port and markets was only used to guarantee the free trade. Macassar was one of the most prominent examples of such a policy. On the other hand, the ruling elites participated in special trading spheres, mostly in spice trade and partly with demand for their own monopoly, but without restrictions outside this field. An emporium like Aceh in the north of Sumatra offers a striking example. Restrictions to European chartered companies served to avoid their monopolistic claims or to protect the trade of the ruling elites.

Contrary to the indigenous elites the company wanted to rule the markets in trading spheres by trying to achieve an actual monopoly or by hoping to gain a considerable profit as in the country trade with Indian textiles. In the end the VOC was only willing to use all possibilities to take over control, including military violence in the spice trade. In other spheres the company failed its goal. It did not achieve complete control over spheres like textiles nor the exclusion of unwanted competitors like the Chinese from Amoy. In both cases the company reacted pragmatically. Furthermore, the company was not able to attain real control over indigenous markets outside the ports under colonial administration and had no capacity to avoid the shift of markets, harbours and trading routes.

The indigenous merchants had the least problems with the new situation. The majority were able to come to an arrangement with the conditions under the company's rule. Some unsusceptible communities set up inner ethnic regulations as be seen by the Wajos' captain's purchase in Macassar.[53] Free trade in a port did not mean no restrictions for every individual but the commercial freedom of accepted groups which were able to make their own rules.

This essay demonstrated, that neither the interpretation of the eighteenth century in Southeast Asia as a period of overwhelming Dutch dominance of indigenous economy nor the interpretation of that time as an Asian era with only a marginal presence of Europeans can provide workable access to the complex developments in early modern Asian merchant systems. There was less control over Asian markets by the VOC as insinuated by nowadays school- and handbooks. In order to understand the whole development of the trading world in Asia during the seventeenth and eighteenth centuries, it is essential to take all participants on all levels and especially the function of the nexus points of different levels into consideration.

The given examples were able to shift the discussion of a global trading network to the regional level. Thus, the image of a coherent unit can be ignored for the moment. Unfortunately, a coherent theory coming back to the global level is not yet available. At least, some considerations can be taken.

The model of a network is a two-dimensional concept. In research on trading history, especially during the age of European expansion, the concept leads its user to remain steadily on the same level of merchant activities. From this perspective several developments of trade remain concealed and, thus, the complexity of historical reality cannot be revealed. In order to widen the perspective on the world history of trade, the use of complex, three-dimensional models seems to be necessary. The different levels of trade, their elements and the function of these elements have to be an integral part of the analysis. And research on the nexus-points of those levels seems to be the most crucial work to be done in order to understand global trading systems. The traditional indigenous trading spheres which were unimportant for European companies or merchants should be recognised as functional elements of the whole trading system – even if they seem to be exotic. For the understanding of the nodes of different networks, the concept of centrality which is a standard in European urban history

---

53 J. Noorduyn, 'The Wajorese Merchants' Community in Makassar', in: *Bijdragen tot de Taal-, Land- en Volkenkunde*, 156 (2000), 473-498, here 478. The Wajos were economically the most powerful Bugis community.

should play a greater role in research on overseas port cities. And a last remark: if we want to close the gap characterised at the beginning, the efforts for more bridges between studies on global contexts of trade and specialised studies on specific towns, places, commodities or merchant groups should be strengthened.

Port-City Regions in Context:
The North East of England and Europe's northern seas in the late nineteenth century

Graeme J. Milne

Introduction

This paper is part of a project that aims to locate the port cities of North East England in their regional, national and international urban networks. Unusually in the UK context, the North East had several large ports in close proximity, none of which was able to wholly overshadow its neighbours and establish the multifunctional dominance of a coastal region enjoyed by other provincial ports like Liverpool or Bristol. The North East ports demonstrate a complex pattern of specialisation, interconnection and functional complementarity: coastal and riparian settlements on the North Sea and the rivers Tyne, Wear and Tees often pursued niche activities in coal trading, shipbuilding and fisheries. These in turn gave them very different economic, social and political characteristics from those of their close neighbours.

That profile, locally heterogeneous yet with a broadly common dependence on export industries and maritime services, places the North East urban system at the boundary between a British region and the maritime world of Europe's northern seas. It also, of course, locates it at the boundaries of a number of historiographical schools, including maritime, regional and urban history, which have often not been very communicative with one another. For example, almost every book on the North East, and those on the Tyne in particular, will cite illustrative statistics of coal production from what contemporaries called the Great Northern Coalfield. Virtually none of these books take the next step and analyse where any of that coal went, however, and a similar inwardness applies to many other aspects of the region's historiography.

There are some exceptions, of course. The most recent survey text on the region highlights the wider importance of northern England, and of the North East in particular, and also makes the point that the region's role in 'making the modern world' was accompanied by an increased vulnerability to wider events.[1] Pioneering work by historical geographers in the 1960s located the region's export trade in terms of its marketing and consumption, as well as its more-

---

1   N. McCord and R. Thompson, *The northern counties from AD 1000*, London 1998, 255.

commonly reported production.[2] Nonetheless, such contextualisation remains rare. Large areas of the region's history could be better illuminated through the study of the commercial élites that developed and maintained trading contacts around the North Sea and the Baltic, and, at the other end of the social spectrum, through the multicultural communities of industrial labourers and merchant mariners that grew up in the coastal towns. Ports, obviously, act as the interface between land and sea, but precisely how they do that remains oddly neglected.

The first section of the paper offers a brief overview of the North East of England as a maritime region, in order to explain why it is worth studying in this context, and to demonstrate its broader significance. The second considers the multi-layered interests at work in the management of the North East's maritime trade and connections in the decades before 1914, and in particular, the pressures and tensions that existed in brokering the relationship between hinterland and foreland.

The North East of England as a Maritime Urban Region

The North East is, with good reason, best known for its coal trade and its shipbuilding. These industries, and others related to them, were central to the dramatic development of the region from the mid-nineteenth to the early twentieth centuries, and to its equally dramatic collapse thereafter. Indeed the inter-connectivity of a number of industries, mainly associated with cheap coal and transport, produced a closely-linked complementarity that offered niches to a wide range of specialist manufacturing, trading and service firms.[3] Resulting 'economies of localisation' produced further, cumulative, improvements in labour skills and capital investment capacity which benefited clusters of vertically- and horizontally-connected industries.[4] Contemporaries were well aware of the economic strengths of such an environment, and national opinion-formers pointed to the North East as an industrial type, with an apparently 'multifarious' range of industries which on closer inspection were revealed to be

---

2   N.R. Elliott, 'A geographical analysis of the Tyne coal trade', *Tijdschrift voor economische en sociale geografie*, 59 (1968), 71-93.

3   N. McCord, 'Some aspects of change in the nineteenth century North East', *Northern History*, 31 (1995), 241-66.

4   S. Ville, 'Shipbuilding in the Northeast of England in the nineteenth century', in S. Ville (ed.), *Shipbuilding in the United Kingdom in the nineteenth century: A regional approach*, St. John's, Newfoundland 1993, 35.

'cognate-the logical and practical outcome of each other, a chain of industries whose links are inseparably united to each other'.[5]

This economic profile, combined with the region's geography and topography, also drove a particular pattern of riparian urbanisation, and influenced the distribution of higher urban commercial and administrative functions within the region. Tyneside was, by the later nineteenth century, an almost continuous urbanised or urbanising area running from Newcastle and Gateshead to the sea via Jarrow, South Shields, North Shields, Tynemouth and a number of smaller areas with industrial workforces and urban characteristics. The Tees also had a rapidly developing urban system with the new town of Middlesbrough being created in mid-century downriver from the established Stockton, and with extensive development of the Hartlepool area, just north of the Tees estuary. Sunderland's location at the mouth of the Wear gave it a relatively straightforward position in relation to its upriver towns, none of which were major trading centres by the later nineteenth century: its relative proximity to the Tyne, though, meant that it competed for some hinterland zones with South Shields. The North East also had a number of coastal towns, such as Blyth and Seaham, which were developed as shipping points for local collieries.

If the Tyne was the region's most complex riparian system, Newcastle was by some way its largest town and also the location for most of its higher urban functions. Newcastle's efforts at territorial expansion were often curtailed in this period, however, and the other riparian towns acquired municipal status during the nineteenth century: Tyneside became known nationally as an area of extremely fragmented local government, but continued into the mid-twentieth century to resist rationalisation efforts. Part of the reason for this dedicated localism may lie in economic and demographic specialisation, which influenced the identities of the smaller towns even while limiting their capacity to develop. Jarrow, for example, grew from one shipyard, and its fortunes remained tied to that industry; Gateshead was a dormitory community for some of the lower-paid elements of Newcastle's workforce, but also a major railway town; South Shields was home to a disproportionate concentration of the region's merchant mariners; and North Shields was the base of a significant fishing industry. Much of the riverfront, especially near the mouth of the Tyne, was given over to coal exporting berths and staithes.

The management of the Tyne therefore needs to be considered on a number of levels. As a riparian system, individual towns and industries produced a complex interaction of interests. But the export-orientated character of the

---

5   W.E. Gladstone, quoted in Newcastle and Gateshead Incorporated Chamber of Commerce, *Yearbook and Commercial Review, 1911,* 59.

region's economic development locates such riparian and coastal systems in a broader context. The North East towns had a strategic profile in British politics – they provided much of London's fuel supply, were an important source of material for the Royal Navy, and produced some of the most vocal elements in the shipowning, heavy industrial and overseas-trading lobbies. On another level still, Europe's northern seas were the cradle of carboniferous capitalism, and areas that produced one or more of the staple elements of that economy – coal, iron, timber and ships – had a vital role both in the industrialisation of northern Europe, and in the first era of free trade globalisation in the later nineteenth century.

The question of balancing interests will be discussed in more detail in the second section of this paper. First, can we quantify the wider significance of the North East to the port city networks of northern Europe, and, indeed, the importance of that wider world to the development of the North East? This section offers some outline figures for shipping, the coal trade, and shipbuilding, although a much more detailed profile needs to be built up given the relative absence of previous studies. In addition, most of the material being discussed here relates to the river Tyne, which was relatively well-documented: a broader regional survey needs to be undertaken, however, to offer a more balanced analysis.

In terms of the geographical distribution of Tyne shipping, some of the statistics collected by the port authority (the Tyne Commission) offer a useful broad profile. The Commission characterised its traffic in four zones: regional ports on the North East coast; the rest of Britain and Ireland; continental European ports from the River Elbe to Brest; and everywhere beyond that. Figure 1 shows that the Tyne's major growth patterns in the decades before the Great War were in that last, 'foreign', group, and to a lesser extent in the German Ocean trade between the Elbe and Brest.[6] By the turn of the century, around half of the shipping on the Tyne came from 'foreign' ports, and this was also the category with marked expansion in steamship tonnage, and a terminal decline in the use of sailing ships. The Tyne's second most important zone in this era remained the British coastal trade, although growth rates here were lower, with the major leap to steam shipping having been made some decades previously in the 1850s. The German Ocean ports had closed the gap noticeably in the first decade of the twentieth century. The regional trade accounted for only a small

---

6   'German Ocean' was widely used in British maritime circles in the 19th century, usually to mean the southern part of the North Sea. It was a useful label, reflecting the fact that trades in that sector were often different from those of the northern North Sea and the Baltic. Unfortunately, it went out of use in the era of the 1914-18 war.

proportion of the Tyne's traffic, although it continued to provide a stable living for the operators of small sailing ships.

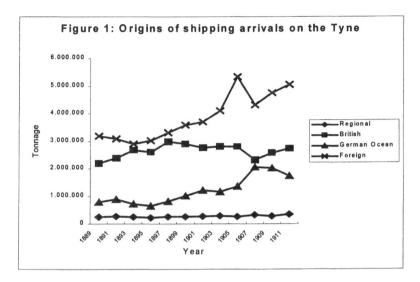

Source: Tyne Commission Annual Accounts, Vessels paying piers dues.

This pattern is also reflected in the Tyne's coal exports, which shifted focus and moved onto a wider stage in the second half of the nineteenth century. The long-established trade to London expanded, but from mid-century the real growth was in northern Europe. This is an important point in the context of British economic historiography, which tends to assume an extra-European and often imperial focus in British trade. Looked at from the perspective of individual port cities and their regions, however, a more subtle pattern emerges. The South Wales coal ports did indeed supply the coaling stations of the long-distance routes, and their fortunes were more dependent on the expansion of global trade and shipping. However, the prosperity of the North East ports in this era was closely tied to industrial growth in Europe, and particularly around Europe's northern seas.

Table 1 shows the profile of the Tyne's seaborne coal shipments. As well as the dramatic absolute rise in quantities, the figure with the greatest implication for the region is the increase in the proportion of foreign traffic. While around 70% of North East coal went elsewhere in Britain in the 1840s, by the early twentieth century the ratio had been reversed, with around 70% going abroad. A further breakdown of that 70% reveals an almost equal division between Germany, Scandinavia, the Low Countries and Russia on the one hand, and

France, Spain and Italy on the other. Over much of the period, only about one ton in eight of North East coal went beyond Europe.[7] More detailed analysis of these patterns is ongoing, because it is important to distinguish between shipments to major port cities, and establish a more appropriate regional framework: obviously, some of the coal registered as going to Holland in the national statistics was in fact bound for German regions further up the Rhine, for example. Even with this level of analysis, however, the interconnection of the North East with its short-sea coal markets is clear.

Table 1: Tyne coal exports

Land/Area	1873		1883		1893		1903		1913	
	Tons	%	Tons	%	Tons	%	Tons	%	Tons	%
France	507,500	14.5	869,400	13.8	762,300	12.1	850,500	8.1	2,559,100	16.3
Germany	483,000	13.8	900,900	14.3	989,100	15.7	2,226,000	21.2	2,700,400	17.2
Italy	336,000	9.6	963,900	15.3	1,266,300	20.1	2,005,500	19.1	2,700,400	17.2
Norway/ Sweden	294,000	8.4	535,500	8.5	396,900	6.3	640,500	6.1	785,000	5.0
Denmark	231,000	6.6	422,100	6.7	233,100	3.7	367,500	3.5	423,900	2.7
Belgium/ Holland	248,500	7.1	220,500	3.5	245,700	3.9	378,000	3.6	1,193,200	7.6
Spain	185,500	5.3	548,100	8.7	648,900	10.3	1,102,500	10.5	973,400	6.2
Russia	252,000	7.2	655,200	10.4	592,200	9.4	630,000	6.0	690,800	4.4
Other Europe	196,000	5.6	441,000	7.0	396,900	6.3	630,000	6.0	1,036,200	6.6
Outside Europe	766,500	21.9	743,400	11.8	768,600	12.2	1,669,500	15.9	2,637,600	16.8
Total	3,500,000	100	6,300,000	100	6,300,000	100	10,500,000	100	15,700,000	100

Source: Derived from N.R. Elliott, 'A geographical analysis of the Tyne coal trade', *Tijdschrift voor econ. en soc. geografie*, 59 (1968), 85.

The North East ports did not collectively have a monopoly on British coal shipments to Europe, of course, nor was the market share of any individual port guaranteed in relation to its neighbours. Within the region, the Tyne felt

---

7   N.R. Elliott, 'A geographical analysis of the Tyne coal trade', *Tijdschrift voor econ. en soc. geografie*, 59 (1968), 71-93, 85.

increasingly threatened by the new specialist facilities built just up the coast at Blyth in the 1880s, while the North East as a whole lost market share in the northern European trade during the last two decades of the nineteenth century. Having been responsible for 63% of British coal exports to the Baltic and North Seas in 1880, the North East ports only provided 42% in 1900, while the coalfields of eastern Scotland increased their share from 17% to 28%, and smaller gains were made by the Humber and South Wales.[8]

Competition for the coal trade manifested itself in other ways, adding to the number of variables that had to be monitored by the trading communities and port authorities of the North East. The railway system had been both a godsend and a curse since the 1850s, in that it brought ever-larger quantities of coal to the Tyne loading staithes, but also threatened to take coal directly by train to London, bypassing the coastal shipping trade altogether. The development, and extremely rapid adoption, of the steam collier ship restored the prospects of the maritime trade in coal to other parts of Britain, as well as bringing new economies of scale to the short sea traffic with the continent. From less than 10,000 tons in 1852, steam colliers were carrying almost one million tons between the Tyne and London only a decade later.[9]

It is clear even from this brief survey of some coal trade issues that the centrality of coal to the North East's exports had a plethora of implications for the region's interconnections with the wider world. Competition at regional and national level meant that coal ports tended to attract a highly heterogeneous traffic in addition to the long-established shuttle service of the coastal trade. The classic pattern is one of ships unloading long-distance goods at ports across northern Europe and seeking a return cargo of what was probably the world's most easily marketable commodity. The North East won a large share of this business. In addition, there was competition and complementarity among the region's ports. Ships carrying, for example, ore from Spain to the iron works on the Tees would often then continue up the coast to the Tyne or the Wear for a coal cargo, despite the availability of coal on the Tees. Prices were monitored constantly, and while coal merchants tried to tie overseas customers and agents to annual contracts, much trade was done *ad hoc* on the basis of information on the day. In addition, 'coal' was not a single commodity, but in fact a wide variety of types, some suitable for domestic use, some for railways, some for industry. Customers specified coal from particular districts, some of which had

---

8   D.A. Thomas, 'The growth and direction of our foreign trade in coal', *Journal of the Royal Statistical Society*, 66 (Sept. 1903), 439-533, 499.

9   J.R.T. Hughes and S. Reiter, 'The first 1,945 British steamships', *Journal of the American Statistical Association*, 53 (1958), 360-81, 379.

only one port of access, while others had railway connections in more than one direction. Ships' captains and agents knew that some types of coal were more marketable in some parts of the world than others.

The cumulative effect of all of these variables was the development of highly complex shipping and commodity markets, which could only be made to work through constant communications and information flows not just in the region itself but across northern Europe and beyond. Newcastle's Commercial Exchange was primarily a coal exchange in this period, and was a major asset to coalowners, merchants and shipowners: 'the pivot...of the North-East Coast ports'.[10] Naturally, though, such face-to-face networking could only handle the relatively local elements of the trading system. The region's coal merchants also had to maintain contacts elsewhere in northern Europe. For example, Pyman Bell & Co., one of the larger North East firms in the late nineteenth century, had offices in Hartlepool and Newcastle, and a number of agencies in Scandinavia. Although archival remains are incomplete, there is evidence that one of the firm's partners visited the Gothenburg office to supervise contracts in 1907, and toured coal merchants in a number of Swedish ports trying to raise the firm's profile and bring in new business.[11] Pyman Bell tendered for large scale contracts advertised by power companies, which provided a predictable income, such as that issued by the Danish Gas Company to supply coal via five Danish ports in 1898.[12] Ultimately, much of the coal trade revolved around the telegraph system by the turn of the century. Coal vessels' logs and ledgers record telegraph messages at every stop, and unpredictable voyage patterns resulted as masters were instructed to proceed to the most appropriate port for the specific quantities and types of coal being requested by their managing agent's customers.[13]

The coal trade needs to be studied not just as a defining element in the economy, society and culture of the North East, therefore, but as a central issue in the relationship between the region and the wider world. This is also true of the other classic heavy industries of the region, which like coal were not just export-orientated, but increasingly so, in the second half of the nineteenth century. Shipbuilding, for example, had relied heavily on local shipowners during the sailing era, but after mid-century ships built on North East rivers were ever-more likely to be bought and operated by shipping firms based elsewhere.[14]

---

10 Newcastle and Gateshead Incorporated Chamber of Commerce, *Yearbook and Commercial Review, 1911*, 14.
11 Pyman, Bell & Co. papers, 145/1/2, Tyne & Wear Archives.
12 Pyman, Bell & Co. papers, 145/1/5.
13 For example, Voyage book of *Mercator* 1898-1903, Witherington & Everett papers, 915/126, Tyne & Wear Archives.
14 Ville, 'Shipbuilding in the Northeast of England', 18-20.

This pattern is symptomatic of the increasing specialisation in port industries and economic profiles which accompanied the development of large steam shipping, but again, these issues are better studied in terms of their impact on port city regions rather than as national aggregates. Those North East shipbuilding firms committed to technological innovation at the largest end of the tonnage scale rapidly outgrew their local clients in the last quarter of the nineteenth century, and indeed all but a few shipping firms operating across northern Europe. Only shipowners working in long-distance trades, and especially those in the passenger liner sector, could operate the very largest ships of this period. Ships on the scale of *Mauretania*, launched on the Tyne in 1906, were only of interest to a handful of firms based in ports like Liverpool, London and Hamburg. A similar, but yet more obvious argument applies to yards specialising in warships: there was (fortunately) no local market for such ships, and builders like W.G. Armstrong had to direct all their marketing and networking efforts towards the Admiralty in London, and towards foreign navies.[15]

Such an increasing focus on extra-regional markets for Tyne shipyards raised complications for the port authority, and for the local economies. The Tyne Commission welcomed the profile given to it by the large yards and their headline-making vessels, and predicted direct and indirect benefits to be had from such activities.[16] It was less impressed when the major builders threatened to take their activities elsewhere during periodic negotiations over river improvement or dry-dock building. Such firms knew that they had more than just local significance, and sometimes behaved accordingly, playing different port authorities off against each other. Historians have suggested that workforces too sensed a detachment on the part of some firms, with owners chasing contracts in distant places rather than paying full attention to their own works.[17]

It is clear, then, that the maritime-orientated economy of the North East needs to be studied more holistically, in terms of distribution and consumption as well as production. In particular, given the functional specialisation of many of the region's towns, changing levels of engagement with the broader European economy point to complex political attitudes towards those institutions that managed port facilities – institutions which were, on some levels, responsible for mediating the relationships between individual communities and the wider world.

---

15 K. Warren, *Armstrong's of Elswick*, Basingstoke 1989.
16 Tyne Improvement Commission, Proceedings, 1907-8, 11. Newcastle Central Library.
17 E. Allen, et al., *The north-east engineers strikes of 1871: The Nine Hours League*, Newcastle 1971, 24.

Interest, Politics and Influence in a Maritime Urban Region

If the profile of the North East's trades became more intertwined with the northern European economy, in some important aspects, the management of the region's ports and trade remained firmly rooted in its hinterland. As such, the region's maritime urban system offers useful evidence for a number of issues facing urban historians. Port towns have been recognised, in Britain and across northern Europe, as occupying a middle way in some of the classification and categorisation attempts of recent historiography. Like the textile and metal industry towns often considered typical of industrial urbanisation, many ports grew dramatically in the eighteenth and nineteenth century, both in population and in economic activity. Unlike most of the manufacturing towns, however, ports often had long-established institutions for government and administration run by existing elites. This was certainly true of Newcastle, although many of the other North East ports, and particularly those riparian towns which developed maritime-orientated heavy industries, lacked these established structures. Within the region, therefore, there are examples of a broad range of maturity in local government.

This is important, because the question of who ran port cities, and how those individuals and groups managed to connect hinterland and foreland, remains unanswered in many cases. With some outstanding exceptions, studies of port cities have focused on economics or demography and paid relatively less attention to politics.[18] Interests of all sorts interacted in port cities, and those managing the cities spent much of their time mediating and brokering these interactions, whether they recognised their role as such or not. The North East offers particularly valuable evidence in this context, because the mercantile and political leadership had to work at riparian and sometimes regional level, as well as in the better-studied municipal context.

The development of the Tyne and of the Tees (rather less so the Wear) involved the interaction of economic, territorial and civic interests, often closely bound together. Newcastle, thanks to its location at the ancient bridging point across the Tyne on the road connecting southern England with the Scottish borders, had held established powers and privileges since the Middle Ages, including the right to manage the Tyne. The identity and prosperity of the towns at the mouth of the Tyne - South Shields and Tynemouth - were inextricably tied

---

18 The classic, but rare, example of a work that deals with all three is R.J. Evans, *Death in Hamburg: Society and politics in the cholera years, 1830-1910,* Penguin edn., London 1990.

to their maritime activities, and to the extent of their influence over the river's trade and shipping: periodically in the early modern era, and with increasing determination in the nineteenth century, these towns sought a share in the administration of the Tyne.

This is important for the current study because the less-developed towns had clear incentives to develop sophisticated institutions for managing riparian resources. It was unlikely that even in an era of rapid population growth, towns like South Shields would come to equal Newcastle in size or prosperity, but they could argue for a voice in new institutions established to manage the river and its facilities. Much of the determination of the smaller towns in the 1840s to improve the river Tyne stemmed from a simple desire for economic betterment, but it is no coincidence that their favoured solution was to establish a Commission with representatives from all the river towns. The creation of institutions for the management of the river, its trade, and the broader prosperity of the region, gave smaller towns a seat at a table previously monopolised by Newcastle.

Any assessment of interests and factions at work in these ports therefore needs to be broadly based, especially because the new institutions often sat alongside the old, rather than replacing them. For example, the Tyne Commission (created in 1850), managed the Tyne and owned some dock and coal-shipping facilities, but much of the river bank remained under the control of the riparian towns, of industrial firms with their shipyards and factories, or of the North Eastern Railway, which had its own coal dock. This meant that the city of Newcastle had to actively promote its own trade, and persuade shipowners and merchants to come all the way up the river to Newcastle Quay, passing several alternative landing places on the way, all of which were being promoted with equal vigour by another town or organisation: such a constitution inevitably built on-going conflict into the management of the port.

In particular, fragmentation of control and authority fed ongoing debates over Tyne Commission expenditure in the later nineteenth century. Arguments about the spending strategies of port authorities are of course almost universal, and the Tyne had all the usual complaints from shipowners and traders that port charges were driving them into poverty. On the Tyne, though, there was another factor, in that the Tyne Commission and Newcastle City Council were in direct competition for some of the port's trade. This was the lucrative and much sought after 'general cargo' trade that many ports wanted. The argument was that only with a broad range of commodities could a port survive temporary crises in particular sectors. Perhaps even more importantly, broader scope was perceived to generate its own trade: once a port had a reputation for having connections with all parts of the world, and a market that could buy and sell almost any commodity, traders would be attracted to it. Newcastle sought a general cargo trade in keeping with its aspirations as a major exchange, commercial and consumer centre, and therefore objected when the Tyne Commission built its own general cargo dock close to the mouth of the Tyne.[19]

If Newcastle resented some of the Commission's dock-building activities, the town of South Shields had a long-running argument with the Commission over the waterfront at the river mouth. South Shields, despite its reputation as a somewhat rough sailor-town, had aspirations as a coastal resort, and was particularly keen to use the Commission's great piers at the mouth of the Tyne as bathing and promenading amenities.[20] This is another aspect of port making and management that is rather neglected by historians, despite the considerable political influence of the Victorian middle classes, who worked in commercial and industrial towns and demanded such leisure facilities nearby. The Commission was challenged over access to the piers, and also over swimming rights in the Tyne, which were obviously a well-established tradition pre-dating the industrialisation of the river.[21] Ownership of, and access to, rivers and beaches was just another in a range of contested aspects of port development.

It needs to be remembered, therefore, that new institutions like the Tyne Commission could not necessarily just exercise their will in the face of opposition from older bodies which had authority rooted in earlier periods and assumptions. Although port authorities seem to be very 'modern' entities, working in a scientific, technological and industrial context, many of their activities in fact required them to engage with much older frameworks. A good deal of the land around the Tyne was owned by the Church of England or various members of the northern aristocracy. The situation on the south bank, in County Durham, was a particular legal maze because of the continued maintenance of some medieval rights and privileges by the Church, and patrician attitudes prevailed. Even in the 1890s, the Tyne Commission despaired of persuading the Ecclesiastical Commissioners to repair their quays at Dunston: 'This thing has been going on for years and years, and we get nothing but politeness'.[22]

The 'old' economy, and its attendant power structures, remained a prominent force in the development and management of the North East ports. Land-owning, which is of course a major issue in British economic and political history, is particularly important in the North East, for three reasons. First, the

---

19 *Newcastle Daily Journal*, 7 Dec. 1887.
20 For example, in Tyne Commission, Proceedings, 1898-99, 577.
21 For example, in Tyne Commission, Proceedings, 1892-93, 268.
22 Tyne Commission, Proceedings, 1891-92, 149.

land itself was productive and the region's agriculture remained an economic force well into the twentieth century despite the common stereotype of the North East as heavy industrial zone. Newcastle had one of England's busiest agricultural markets in the late nineteenth century, but it is worth stressing that it was an international market requiring a close collaboration between farming and maritime transport: for example, half of the cattle sold there came from abroad (mainly Scandinavia), while many of those from the arable belt of central Northumberland had initially been reared in Ireland.[23]

Second, coal mining offered incomes to landowners, either directly through their own mines, indirectly through renting out coal rights, and even less directly through charging wayleaves to allow coal to be transported over their estates to the nearest shipping point. Being coal- *and* land-owners gave the North East élite an unusual political profile in the mid-nineteenth century.[24] The new railway companies of mid-century paid landowners handsomely to buy their support for new lines.[25] Technically, the payment was for the land being used and the disruption to the landowners' estates, but if it made the landowners happy to support the necessary railway bills in Parliament, that was a fortunate coincidence.

Third, and closely related, the great landowners often had estates bounded by rivers, which of course was where industrial and infrastructure development was most likely to be sought in the later nineteenth century. Dock-building schemes in particular tended to bring large landowners into negotiation with the trading interest, often with significant income for the landowners as a result. The Tyne Commission was paying the Duke of Northumberland several thousand pounds a year, and had to negotiate building plans with him in North Shields, in the early twentieth century.[26] At the most extreme, coal owners took the initiative and built their own ports: Cardiff in South Wales is of course the best known example, but the Marquis of Londonderry's harbour at Seaham brought the same phenomenon on a smaller scale to the North East coast.[27] Elsewhere in the region, aristocrats

---

23 W. Richardson, *Visit of the British Association to Newcastle upon Tyne, 1889: Official local guide, industrial section*, Newcastle 1889, 9.

24 T.J. Nossiter, *Influence, opinion and political idioms in Reformed England: Case studies from the North East, 1832-74*, Brighton 1975, 12.

25 D. Spring, 'English landowners and nineteenth century industrialism', in J.T. Ward and R.G. Wilson (eds.), *Land and industry: The landed estate and the Industrial Revolution*, Newton Abbot 1971, 16-62.

26 Tyne Commission Miscellaneous Reports, vol. 4, no. 65, Newcastle Central Library, Local Studies Centre.

27 J. Davies, 'Aristocratic town-makers and the coal metropolis: The marquises of Bute and Cardiff, 1776-1947', in D. Cannadine (ed.), *Patricians, power and politics in nineteenth*

joined in the new administrative structures. Coalowners were the largest single grouping on the River Wear Commission, and repeatedly chose the Earl of Durham as one of their representatives. Not only were his Lambton collieries the Wear's largest coal-shipping client, but the prestige of having the Earl on the Commission was important enough to outweigh his habit of rarely attending meetings.[28]

Landed influence on the institutions managing the North East's maritime trade should not therefore be neglected through a false assumption that agriculture and land-owning were 'legacy' activities in a new industrial world. In a direct political sense, the development of the North East ports was influenced by those owning and managing their hinterland. What of the other potential interests? Both the Tyne and the Wear port authorities had occupational groupings built into their constitutions. By the early twentieth century, after various efforts to increase representation of such groups on the Tyne Commission, five members each were elected by coalowners, shipowners and traders: they therefore made up half the total membership, with the others being elected by the riparian towns. Of course, many of those representing those towns also came from mercantile occupations. On the Wear, the trading classes were much more heavily in control, reflecting the relatively weak role of the town of Sunderland. The 52 River Wear Commissioners included 21 coalowners, three import/export traders and fifteen shipowners. There were also nine riparian landowners, and one representative each from the town of Sunderland, the North Eastern Railway, Customs and Excise, and the Admiralty.

A much more detailed prosoprographical analysis of these individuals, their interests, and the crucial question of 'hat-wearing' needs to be undertaken. Already, though, this continuing involvement of the commercial and industrial elite in the management of ports and rivers raises an important question in the context of British local government. Studies of manufacturing towns have pointed to a retreat from urban government by industrialists in the late nineteenth century, and the corresponding rise of the 'shopocracy'.[29] In the North East, this was certainly true of Gateshead town council.[30] Newcastle, with a still larger retail and small business community, followed a similar pattern, while retaining a Quayside committee to deal with its own wharf and cargo facilities.

---

    century towns, Leicester 1982, 17-68; M. J. Daunton, *Coal metropolis: Cardiff, 1870-1914,* Leicester 1977.

28 River Wear Commissioners, Reports of Meetings, Jan. 1885, Tyne & Wear Archives, 202/3701.

29 J. Garrard, *Leadership and power in Victorian industrial towns, 1830-80,* Manchester 1983, chapter 2.

30 F.W.D. Manders, *A history of Gateshead,* Gateshead 1973.

The mercantile and industrial élite, however, maintained its role in local and regional decision-making through membership of the river commissions, long after its direct involvement in municipal government had waned. Tensions within the ranks of Newcastle Council suggest that the trading classes worked for the development of the town's Quay, and were happy to serve on the Tyne Commission, but that the broader council suspected that they were not always acting in Newcastle's interests. W. H. Stephenson, who held high office in both the Council and the Commission, often had to defend the Commission against criticisms raised during Council meetings, and many clearly feared that Newcastle's representatives on the Commission were no such thing: 'would the six gentlemen recognise our existence after we re-elected them?' wondered one councillor.[31]

The North East may be an extreme case in the persistence of such a complex range of interests, although work on the Humber, Thames and Mersey suggests that similar tensions were in fact widespread. In addition, these cases relate to a single nation-state, and one which was a relatively early developer of unitary legal and administrative systems—comparative examples from more contested maritime regions across continental Europe would be still more illuminating.

Conclusion

The issues raised in this paper will not be surprising to historians of port cities, but they do suggest an alternative agenda for British regional history that may also have resonance elsewhere. With a better understanding of the dynamics of maritime regions, as mediated by the mercantile communities of port towns and cities, should come a more sophisticated picture of the role of regions in European development. The case of the North East of England suggests that port cities played a brokering role on a number of levels apart from the most obvious commercial and mercantile context. As well as standing between hinterland and foreland, they also stood at the administrative and governmental interfaces between municipality, region and nation, and at the shifting and ill-defined boundary between contemporary perceptions of 'home' and 'abroad', of 'internal' and 'external'.

---

31 Newcastle Council, Minutes, 1889-90, 11-17, Newcastle Central Library.

The Growth of Maritime Trade and the Determinants of Port-Hinterland Relations in Nineteenth-Century Germany: the case of Bremen

W. Robert Lee

Introduction

The changing relationship between cities and their hinterlands has seldom attracted the attention of historians, despite the recognition that individual capital cities affected economic demographic development at the national level and that urban systems often facilitated regional specialization.[1] The lack of detailed research on this theme is particularly regrettable in the case of port-cities. Major ports in nineteenth-century Europe often functioned as distinct growth poles, given the rapid expansion of maritime commerce and its overall contribution to urbanization, but their primary function as transit or entrepôt areas has reinforced the view that the links between port-cities and their hinterlands were limited and geographically disconnected.[2]

The relative lack of research on port-hinterland relations is a reflection of a general tendency for urban historians to concentrate on self-contained processes which operate within the boundaries of individual cities and towns.[3] It also reflects the difficulty of distinguishing between the maritime role of a port-city, as defined

1　E.A. Wrigley, 'A simple Model of London's Importance in Changing English Society and Economy', in: *Past and Present* (1967), 44-70; E.A. Wrigley, 'Urban Growth and Agricultural Change: England and the Continent in the Early Modern Period', in: R.I. Rotberg and T.K. Rabb (eds.), *Population and Economy: Population and History from the Traditional to the Modern World*, Cambridge 1986, 123-168; B. Lepetit, *Les villes dans la France moderne (1740-1840)*, Paris 1988; P. Bairoch, *Cities and Economic Development from the Dawn of History to the Present* (Chicago, 1988); D.R. Ringrose, 'Capital Cities, Urbanization, and Modernization in Early Modern Europe', in: *Journal of Urban History*, 24 (1998), 155-183.

2　B. Higgins and D.J. Savoie (eds.), *Regional Economic Development. Essays in Honour of François Perroux*, Boston 1988; R. Lee and R. Lawton, 'Port Development and the Demographic Dynamics of European Urbanization', in: R. Lawton and R. Lee (eds.), *Population and Society in Western European Port-Cities, c.1650-1939*, Liverpool 2002, 1-36; V. Burton, 'Liverpool's Mid-Nineteenth Century Coasting Trade', in: V. Burton (ed.), *Liverpool Shipping, Trade and Industry*, Liverpool 1989, 26-67; A.J. Sargent, *Seaports and Hinterlands*, London 1938; P. Hohenberg and L.H. Lees, *The Making of Urban Europe, 1000-1950*, Cambridge (Mass.) 1985, 161.

3　R.A. Mohl, 'City and Region. The missing dimension in U.S.urban history', in: *Journal of Urban History*, 25 (1998), 3-21; C. Tilly, 'What Good is Urban History?', in: *Journal of Urban History*, 22 (1996), 702-719.

by its import and export trades, and the extent to which this primary function was a result of its location within an internal transport infrastructure which determined the geographical extent of its economic hinterland. The definition of a port-city's hinterland is also problematic. This can be defined as a clearly subordinated territory or region on the basis of political or jurisdictional criteria, whereas a port-city's urban field represented an area where it could influence individual choice depending on the presence or absence of other comparable conurbations.[4] From a purely economic perspective a port-city's hinterland was the area to which it dispersed cargoes and collected export traffic, while its actual supply hinterland was determined by movements in relative prices and transport costs. In a wider context, research on port-hinterland relations has been hampered by conceptual weaknesses, in particular the tendency for historians to analyse a series of individual themes, whether population mobility, transport developments, or the dissemination of urban culture, rather than seeking to develop an interdisciplinary systems approach which embraces the interrelated flows of people, goods, services and information.[5]

The present paper focuses on the port-city of Bremen. Despite substantial industrial development in the late-nineteenth century with the creation of large-scale enterprises in ship-building, machine-engineering and steel production, commerce and trade remained predominant, both politically and in terms of Bremen's employment structure.[6] Indeed, steps were taken to reinforce its maritime function with major improvements to the port's infrastructure and the configuration of the river Weser, as well as the development of more specialized trades.[7] The paper will seek to establish a conceptual framework for analysing the changing relationship between one of Germany's premier ports and its hinterland. It will examine four interrelated determinants of port-hinterland linkages: the political framework of Bremen's long-run development within a federal constitutional system; the structure and pattern of trade between the port-city and its supply hinterland; the extent and significance of population transfers between Bremen and

4   W. Smith, 'Merseyside and the Merseyside District', in: W. Smith (ed.), *A Scientific Study of Merseyside*, Liverpool 1953, 1-19; Ringrose, 'Capital Cities'.

5   M.J. Borges, 'Migration Systems in Southern Portugal: Regional and Transatlantic Circuits of Labour Migration in the Algarve (Eighteenth - Twentieth Centuries), in: *International Review of Social History*, 45 (2000), 171-208.

6   F.J. Pitsch, *Die wirtschaftlichen Beziehungen Bremens zu den Vereinigten Staaten von Amerika bis zur Mitte des 19. Jahrhunderts*, Bremen 1974; K. Löbe, *Seehafen Bremen.: 100 entscheidende Jahre*, Bremen 1977.

7   W.R. Lee, 'Von der Zunftzugehörigkeit zur Deregulierung: Die bremischen Hafenarbeiter von 1860 bis 1939', in: *Bremisches Jahrbuch*, 78 (1999), 148; A. Agatz, 'Hundertjährige Entwicklung der Hafenumschlagsanlagen in Bremen und Bremerhaven', in: Schiffahrtsverlag Hansa (ed.), *100 Jahre Schiffahrt, Schiffbau, Häfen*, Hamburg1964, 121-142.

its surrounding regions; and, finally, the port-city's contribution to cultural innovation as a result of its institutional role and service function, in particular the impact of maritime trade on patterns of consumption in its hinterland.

The Legacy of Federalism for Port-Hinterland Relations

The persistence of a federal structure in Germany throughout the nineteenth century, together with the retention of a substantial degree of autonomy by individual states, even after political unification in 1871, had important implications for regional development. After 1815, many states pursued an independent approach to issues such as tariff and taxation policy, railway development and official support for handicraft production in a manner designed to maximize their own interests.[8] Most economic models of regional development are predicated on the unfettered operation of market forces, the free mobility of both capital and labour, as well as the existence of a responsive transport infrastructure, but few, if any of these preconditions for maximizing the regional impact of urban growth operated in an optimal fashion in nineteenth-century Germany.[9]

Bremen's long-run development and the nature of port-hinterland relations were directly affected by the legacy of a federal state system. In 1815 the city-state of Bremen consisted of the city of Bremen itself, the small township of Vegesack (dominated by maritime activities), together with a limited area of rural settlement. Territory held by the Duchy of Oldenburg and the Kingdom of Hanover constituted Bremen's immediate hinterland and the problematic nature of inter-state relations, specifically in relation to trade and transport policy, affected the port-city's regional role. Separate tolls were retained by the neighbouring states on the Lower and Upper Weser until 1820 and 1857 respectively; there were considerable delays in reaching agreement on the need to improve the depth of the Lower Weser; and Oldenburg sought to limit the growth in Bremen's shipping by the imposition of quarantine regulations and restrictions on the availability of pilots.[10]

---

8   R. Lee, 'Relative backwardness and long-run development: economic, demographic and social changes', in: J. Breuilly (ed.), *Nineteenth-Century Germany. Politics, Culture and Society 1780-1918*, London 2001, 82.

9   B.J.L. Berry, *Urbanisation and Counterurbanisation*, Beverly Hills 1976; Å.E. Andersson, 'Regional Science and Policies in a Swedish Perspective', in: Å.E. Andersson, W. Isard and T. Puu (eds.), *Regional and Industrial Development. Theories, Models and Empirical Evidence*, Amsterdam 1984, 1-14.

10 W. Evers, 'Standorts-Untersuchungen über die industrielle Entwicklung Bremens im letzten Jahrzehnt vor Ausbruch des Krieges', Ph.D.-thesis, Breslau 1917, 39; H. Entholt, 'Bremens Handel, Schiffahrt und Industrie im 19. Jahrhundert (1815-1914)', in: O. Mathies, H. Entholt and L.

Railway development from the 1840s onwards was also characterized by a significant degree of state competition: in particular, the proactive policy adopted by Hanover was designed to promote indigenous trading activity within the region at the direct cost of competitor ports, such as Bremen and Hamburg.[11] Even after political unification in 1871 Bremen's development as a regional centre for trade and manufacturing was affected by the tariff and transport policies of other German states: the Prussian tariff failed to offer the port-city equal treatment in the transhipment of goods; the treaty of 1905 precluded industrial development around Bremerhaven; and there was a further delay in deepening the Lower Weser in 1906 as a result of Oldenburg's opposition and Prussia's preferential treatment of its own port at Emden.[12] To this extent, the persistence of federal autonomy precluded an optimal operation of market forces and affected Bremen's linkages with its hinterland.

The decision not to participate in the Customs Union (*Zollverein*) following its creation in 1834 was of even greater importance in determining the port-city's relations with its hinterland, particularly as an overriding commitment to free trade and the primacy of overseas trading interests meant that Bremen did not seek membership until 1888. The accession of both Hanover and Oldenburg on 1st January 1854 had far-reaching consequences. Many branches of production in Bremen, including the cigar industry, were threatened by a loss of export markets in the port-city's hinterland and exclusion from the *Zollverein* had a negative effect on indigenous industry as a whole. Craft production remained largely stagnant between the mid-1850s and the late-1880s, while the decline in sugar-refining and cotton-printing was directly attributed to Bremen's failure to participate in the Customs Union. Furthermore, specific sectors (including the tobacco and cigar production, silverware manufacturing and jute-spinning) were increasingly relocated in neighbouring territories within the *Zollverein* in order to evade the imposition of restrictive tariffs.

Leichtweiss (eds.), *Die Hansastädte Hamburg / Bremen / Lübeck*, Gotha 1928, 159; K-H. Hofmann, 'Die Weser. Geschichte einer Wasserstrasse', in: H. Roder (ed.), *Bremen: Handelsstadt am Fluß*, Bremen 1995, 302; K. Löbe, *Bremens Holzwirtschaft* (Abhandlungen und Vorträge herausgegeben von der Wittheit zu Bremen 15/4), Bremen 1943.

11 H. Schwarzwälder, *Geschichte der Freien Hansestadt Bremen. Vol.II. Von 1810 bis zum Ersten Weltkrieg (1918)*, Hamburg 1987, 243; J.C. Bongaerts, 'Financing Railways in the German States 1840-1860. A Preliminary View', in: *Journal of European Economic History*, 14 (1985), 331-346; K.-D. Vogt, *Uelzen. Seine Stadt-Land Beziehungen in historisch-geographischer Betrachtung*, Göttingen 1968.

12 K. Löbe, *Bremens Holzwirtschaft*, 64; W. Evers, 'Standorts-Untersuchungen', 113-116; W. Reininghaus and K. Teppe, *Verkehr und Region im 19. und 20. Jahrhundert. Westfälische Beispiele*, Paderborn 1999.

As a result, the potential for exploiting its comparative advantage as a major importer of raw materials and semi-finished goods for manufacturing purposes in order to supply its immediate or more distant hinterland remained largely dormant until the late-nineteenth century, while the relocation of specific branches of production beyond the legal boundaries of the city-state shifted the balance of production between Bremen and its hinterland and affected the long-term development of trading relations within the region.[13]

Maritime Commerce and Regional Trade Patterns

Any attempt to analyse the structure and pattern of trade between Bremen and its hinterland is hampered by substantial data problems, but contemporary estimates and recent research on the foreign trade statistics of Hanover provide the basis for a preliminary examination of this important aspect of the port-city's regional role.[14] Fragmentary data from the first half of the nineteenth century provide an invaluable insight into the pattern of Bremen's trade with its hinterland (*Table 1*).

In 1826 Hanover and Osnabrück accounted for over 20 per cent of Bremen's export trade to other German territories, but their relative share had increased to almost 35 per cent by 1847. There was also a disproportionate increase in the volume of exports to other contiguous regions, such as Oldenburg and Wildeshausen (including Cloppenburg, Löningen and Quakenbrück).

Bremen's trade with its hinterland was dominated by the provision of imported raw materials and colonial goods, including coffee, rice, raw tobacco and unrefined sugar, which accounted for between 40 and 50 per cent of its exports to Hanover / Hildesheim, Osnabrück and Wildeshausen. The only exception was Chemnitz where raw cotton exports represented the bulk of Bremen's trade (*Table 2*).

13 D. Burgdorf, *Blauer Dunst und Rote Fahnen. Ökonomische, soziale, politische und ideologische Entwicklung der Bremer Zigarrenarbeiterschaft im 19. Jahrhundert* Bremen 1984, 70; H. Entholt, 'Bremens Handel, Schiffahrt und Industrie', 170; D. Schmidt, 'Die Großen und die Kleinen. Industrie und Handwerk in Bremen von der Mitte des 19. Jahrhunderts bis zum Ersten Weltkrieg', in: D. Schmidt (ed.), *Gewerbefleiß, Handwerk, Klein-und Mittelbetriebe seit 1850*, Bremen 1997, 16; F. Rauers, *Bremer Handelsgeschichte im 19. Jahrhundert. Bremer Handelsstatistik vor dem Beginn der öffentlichen administrativen Statistik in der ersten Hälfte des 19. Jahrhunderts*, Bremen 1913, 14; F. Jerchow, *1883-1983. Die Geschichte der Bremer Woll-Kämmerei zu Blumental*, Bremen 1983; M. Ellerkamp, *Industriearbeit, Krankheit und Geschlecht. Zu den sozialen Kosten der Industrialisierung: Bremer Textilarbeiterinnen 1870-1914*, Göttingen 1991.

14 F. Rauers, *Bremer Handelsgeschichte*; K.H. Kaufhold and M.A. Denzel (eds.), *Statistisk des Kurfürstentums / Königreichs Hannover* (Quellen und Forschungen zur Historischen Statistik von Deutschland 23), St. Katharinen 1998; K.H. Kaufhold and M.A. Denzel (eds.), *Der Handel im Kurfürstentum / Königreich Hannover (1780-1850). Gegenstand und Methode*, Stuttgart 2000.

Table 1: The distribution of Bremen's German export trade by road and by volume, 1826-1847 (in per cent)

Destination	1826	1837	1847
Osnabrück, Diepholz	13.0	17.2	14.4
Hanover, Hildesheim	8.2	9.1	20.4
Braunschweig, Wolfenbüttel	6.5	4.8	2.6
Göttingen, Münden, Kassel	5.4	6.4	4.1
Minden, Wunstorf	5.2	3.5	5.6
Frankfurt am Main	4.8	3.5	1.6
Hamburg	4.3	4.8	3.8
North Rhine-Westphalia	4.2	2.0	2.1
Wildeshausen, Cloppenburg	3.8	5.0	7.1
Chemnitz, Dresden	3.4	4.1	4.0
Harz	2.6	2.9	2.4
Leipzig	2.2	2.7	3.2
Bamberg, Nürnberg	1.9	5.8	2.7
Oldenburg, Ostfriesland	1.3	2.2	4.0
Prussia	1.2	4.3	4.2

Source: calculated from data contained in F. Rauers, *Bremer Handelsgeschichte im 19. Jahrhundert. Bremer Handelsstatistik vor dem Beginn der öffentlichen administrativen Statistik in der ersten Hälfte des 19. Jahrhunderts*, Bremen 1913, 28-29.

Table 2: Compositional structure of Bremen's German export trade by destination and by volume, 1836-1842 (in per cent)

Product	Hannover	Osnabrück	Wildeshausen	Chemnitz
Coffee	24.4	12.3	15.1	-
Drinks	11.8	6.9	5.4	0.08
Rice	7.1	3.0	3.6	-
Fish oil (Tran)	6.9	9.9	8.0	-
Cigars	1.1	0.1	0.1	1.6
Raw tobacco	6.7	22.8	18.2	0.01
Raw sugar	3.2	4.8	14.1	-
Refined sugar	5.9	4.0	11.8	-
Iron, lead, copper	1.9	5.3	1.5	0.1
Potash	0.6	3.8	11.2	-
Cotton	0.5	0.06	(1.5 dz)	97.8

Source: calculated from data contained in F. Rauers, *Bremer Handelsgeschichte im 19. Jahrhundert. Bremer Handelsstatistik vor dem Beginn der öffentlichen administrativen Statistik in der ersten Hälfte des 19. Jahrhunderts*, Bremen 1913, 64-69.

Bremen, like many other port-cities in the early nineteenth century, failed to develop a strong manufacturing industry and concentrated on processing or refining imported raw materials, particularly colonial products and bulk cargoes.[15] The rapid growth in raw tobacco imports from 1821 onwards provided the basis for development of a significant cigar and tobacco industry, which employed over 10,000 individuals in Bremen by the early 1850s. The port city remained the most important market for tobacco within Germany, but following the creation of the *Zollverein* (1834), production was increasingly relocated to Bremen's neighbouring territories as the exports of raw tobacco to Hanover and Wildeshausen (Oldenburg) confirm (Table 2). By the mid-nineteenth century, Bremen had become a significant importer of rice and the establishment of large-scale rice mills reinforced its comparative advantage in this sector.[16] Coffee imports reached a peak in 1855. Although Hamburg ultimately became Germany's major coffee market, most of Bremen's hinterland drew its supplies largely from the port city. Bremen also failed to establish a dominant position in sugar-refining, whereas its position as a major supplier of alcoholic drinks to the surrounding region, including beer, wine and brandy, was reinforced in the late-nineteenth century by the foundation of new breweries and the adoption of industrial production techniques.[17]

Throughout the first half of the nineteenth century, Bremen's hinterland provided a wide range of products either for export elsewhere (overseas or by ship to other German ports), or for domestic consumption. The most important commodities included linen from Bielefeld, Hesse, Osnabrück, Hanover and Silesia; manufacturing goods from North Rhine-Westphalia; cotton textiles from South Germany (specifically Chemnitz); and local produce from the surrounding rural areas. According to many contemporaries, however, Bremen (unlike Hamburg) was poorly served by its immediate hinterland: it was too small and suffered from an inadequate industrial base. There was an increasing lack of wood supplies from the 1860s onwards and by 1900 Bremen had become Germany's largest importer of overseas wood, which represented a sharp reversal of the earlier pattern of trade. Indeed, throughout most of the nineteenth century emigrants constituted the most

---

15 R. Lee, 'The socio-economic and demographic characteristics of port cities', in: in: R. Lawton and R. Lee (eds.), *Population and Society in Western European Port Cities c.1650-1939*, Liverpool 2002

16 Entholt, 'Bremens Handel, Schiffahrt und Industrie', 187-188.

17 Entholt, 'Bremens Handel, Schiffahrt und Industrie', 193; K. Hoyer, 'Das Bremer Brauereigewerbe', in: *Hansische Geschichtsblätter*, 19 (1913), 193-232; H. Roder, 'Der Wiederaufstieg der Bremer Brauereien im Industriezeitalter (1861-1998)', in: Sparkasse Bremen (ed.), *Bremer Handelsgüter: Bier*, Bremen 1998, 46-55; H. Tappe, *Auf dem Weg zur modernen Alkoholkultur. Alkoholproduktion, Trinkverhalten und Temperenzbewegung in Deutschland vom frühen 19. Jahrhundert bis zum Ersten Weltkrieg*, Stuttgart 1994.

profitable component of Bremen's export trade, rather than manufactured goods or agricultural produce from its hinterland.[18]

By the end of the nineteenth century, the pattern of trade between Bremen and its hinterland had not changed dramatically (Table 3). Bremen provided its hinterland with a wide range of consumption goods, whether from overseas (fruit, wine, rice) or produced domestically, using imported raw materials (beer, chocolate, coffee), together with other raw materials (such as Scandinavian pitch pine) and semi-finished goods.[19] In return, its hinterland enjoyed a positive trade balance in building materials, manufactured goods and industrial products destined for export overseas or for domestic use within Bremen. There were important changes in the component structure of individual trades, including the decline in the cigar industry and the growth of new industries, such as oil-refining and car production, but Bremen's overseas import trade continued to be dominated by staple articles which were either refined in the port-city or supplied directly to manufacturers and consumers in its hinterland.

Table 3: Bremen's imports and exports by land and by river, 1907 (in Reichsmark)

3.1 by commodity type

Commodity type	Imports	Exports	Trade Balance+
consumption items	79,430,000	202,095,814	122,665,583
building materials/fuel	19,474,405	3,144,475	- 16,329,930
raw materials/semi-finished goods	147,880,677	622,366,002	474,485,325
manufactured goods	141,959,257	13,049,470	-128,909,787
other industrial products	197,373,052	30,768,426	-166,604,626

Note: + exports / imports

18 W. Evers, 'Standorts-Untersuchungen', 89-90; H.J. von Witzendorff, 'Beiträge zur bremischen Handelsgeschichte in der zweiten Hälfte des 18.Jahrhunderts', in: *Bremisches Jahrbuch*, 43 (1951), 362; Löbe, *Bremens Holzwirtschaft*; Entholt, 'Bremens Handel, Schiffahrt und Industrie', 199.

19 H. Roder, 'Der Kolonialwarenladen: Ort exotischer Genußverheißung', in: H. Roder (ed.), *Bremen Handelsstadt am Fluß*, Bremen 1995, 290-293; H. Müller, 'Bremer Weinhandel', in: H. Roder (ed.), *Bremen Handelsstadt am Fluß*, Bremen 1995, 232-235.

3.2 Imports by land and river transport in 1907, by volume and value (in per cent)

Commodity type	River		Land	
	Vol.	*Reichsmark*	Vol.	Reichsmark
consumption items	*2.3.00*	*2.3.00*	9.7	18.90
building materials/fuel	*14.20*	*10.30*	46.1	49.60
raw materials/semi-finished goods	*12.10*	*1.60*	22.4	12.90
manufactured goods	*00.05*	*0.001*	80.8	82.40
other industrial products	*6.5.00*	*1.20*	70.7	77.70

Source: calculated from the *Jahrbuch für Bremische Statistik*. Jahrgang 1910, Bremen 1910, 90-91.

In return, Bremen was dependent on its hinterland for a wide range of manufactured goods (including machinery, rubber, tyres, cement and textiles), as well as raw materials such as grain, sugar-beet, leather and building materials.[20] Bremen's economic relations with its hinterland were also affected by improvements to the regional transportation system, as well as by changes in the scale of production and level of specialization. An increasing reliance on land transportation (particularly by rail) had a noticeable impact on intra-regional trade. By the early twentieth century, only a limited quantity of building materials, fuel and low value raw materials was shipped to Bremen from its hinterland using the River Weser and subsidiary rivers, while the role of some traditional market centres had been undermined (as in the case of the wood industry).[21] There was also a noticeable improvement in the comparative advantage of specific industrial sectors in Bremen in relation to other regional producers as a result of increased specialization and the adoption of new technology. Bremen's entry into the *Zollverein* was followed by the development of large-scale production in a number of industries, including jute-spinning, wool-combing, and machine production, while the competitive position of specialist trades in the port-city, such as piano and bronze goods manufacturing, was reinforced by a greater emphasis on mass-production, improved marketing techniques and a greater attention to market

---

20 G. Kadura, 'Das "Kolonialwarengeschäft" im Ostertor', in: H. Roder (ed.), *Bremen Handelsstadt am Fluß*, Bremen 1995, 293-295; W. Weber, *Erdölhandel und Erdölverarbeitung an der Unterweser 1860-1895* (Veröffentlichung aus dem Staatsarchiv der Freien Hansestadt Bremen 35), Bremen 1968; G. Fuhse, *Die freie Hansestadt Bremen in wirtschaftsgeschichtlicher Entwicklung*, Bremen 1927, 230.

21 *Jahrbuch für Bremische Statistik, Jahrgang 1910. Zur Allgemeinen Statistik der Jahre 1905-1909*, Bremen 1910, 91; Löbe, *Bremens Holzwirtschaft*, 62.

demand.[22] As a result, Bremen manufacturers enjoyed a distinct advantage in comparison with other producers in the port-city's hinterland, a trend that was reinforced by the growth of department stores and the declining importance of local markets.[23]

Migration Patterns and Port-City - Hinterland Relations

The nature and range of Bremen's linkages with its hinterland were also affected by contemporary migration patterns. In-migrants already accounted for 56 per cent of the port-city's workforce in 1862, but economic growth and urban expansion in the latter decades of the nineteenth century was accompanied by an increased rate of in-migration with the result that male and female in-migrants constituted 61 and 54 per cent respectively of the local labour force by 1905.[24] Despite some changes in the employment structure of in-migrants, Bremen's relations with its regional hinterland continued to be determined by the persistence of established migration patterns. During the first half of the nineteenth century the majority of in-migrants were either craftsmen or domestic servants who came from the surrounding rural areas or from the towns and cities of central and northern Germany. By the end of this period (1896-1900) the neighbouring territories of Hanover and Oldenburg still accounted for 44 and 55 per cent respectively of the port-city's male and female in-migrants. To this extent, a great deal of in-migration remained essentially local or regional in nature.

It is difficult to assess the complexity of population transfers between Bremen and its hinterland because of the absence of nominative data, but the continued predominance of in-migration from the neighbouring states of Hanover and Oldenburg suggests that a great deal of movement still took place within a familiar

---

22 Jerchow, *1883-1983*; D. Schmidt, 'Die Großen und die Kleinen'; P. Benje, 'Frühe Sägemaschinen, Möbelfabriken und Dampftischlereien. Die Einführung der maschinellen Holzbearbeitung in das Tischlereigewerbe Bremens im 19. Jahrhundert', in: D. Schmidt (ed.), *Gewerbefleiß, Handwerk, Klein- und Mittelbetriebe seit 1850,* Bremen 1997, 90-112.

23 U. Pfister, 'Vom Kiepenkerl zu Karstadt. Einzelhandel und Warenkultur im 19. und frühen 20. Jahrhundert', in: *Vierteljahrschrift für Sozial- und Wirtschaftsgeschichte,* 87 (2000), 38-66; T. Coles, 'Department stores as retail innovation in Germany: a historical-geographical perspective in the period 1870-1914', in: G. Crossick and S. Jaumain (eds.), *Cathedrals of Consumption. The European Department Store 1850-1939,* Singapore 1999, 72-96; H. Homburg, 'Warenhausunternehmen und ihre Gründer in Frankreich und Deutschland oder eine diskrete Elite und mancherlei Mythen', in: *Jahrbuch für Wirtschaftsgeschichte,* (1992), 183-219.

24 R. Lee and P. Marschalck, 'The Port-City Legacy: Urban Demographic Change in the Hansestadt Bremen, 1815-1910', in: R. Lawton and R. Lee (eds.), *Population and Society in Western European Port Cities c.1650-1939,* Liverpool 2002, 252-269.

orbit and that a noticeable distance-decay effect persisted even at the end of the nineteenth century. The persistence of small-scale craft production in Bremen meant that a significant proportion of male in-migrants were craftsmen or unmarried journeymen from the port-city's hinterland, while the recruitment of domestic servants continued to operate on the basis of a well-established pattern whereby small towns and rural districts within Bremen's catchment area provided a regular supply of young women drawn from the families of day-labourers and craftsmen.[25]

Many in-migrants either failed to establish themselves in their new environment or expected to be involved in out-migration after a limited period of residence in Bremen. Single males were highly transient, given the persistence of essentially pre-industrial employment conditions, while many of the constraints which restricted the settlement of in-migrant women continued to operate throughout most of the nineteenth century. By the early-twentieth century there was still a significant degree of labour market segregation. In-migrant women were excluded from most areas of industrial production and from jobs which required training or skill, but they readily found employment in Bremen's numerous bars, inns, guest houses and hotels or in domestic service. Settlement opportunities up until 1871 were restricted by the high cost of acquiring citizenship and the implicit prohibition of marriage to women who had not succeeded in becoming citizens of the city-state.[26] Young in-migrants also remained subject to extensive controls over 'foreigners' and other temporary residents: young women under the age of 21 were required to carry an official work book; all domestic servants remained subject to the *Gesindeordnung* until its abolition in 1918 with its formal justification of patriarchal authority; and 'foreign' domestic servants and short-term residents were far more likely than native-born to be placed in institutional care.[27]

---

25 For the general European context, see L.P. Moch, *Paths to the City. Regional Migration in Nineteenth-Century France,* Beverly Hills 1983; L. Fontaine and J. Schlumbohm, 'Household Strategies for Survival: An Introduction', in: *International Review of Social History,* 45 (2000), 1-19. The recruitment pattern of female domestic servants has been derived from an analysis of the civil death registers, Staatsarchiv Bremen, Sterberegister der Stadt Bremen, 1861-63, 1870-72, 1884-86, 1894-96 and 1904-06.

26 K. Reineke, 'Das bremische Bürgerrecht', in: *Bremisches Jahrbuch,* 32 (1929), 219.

27 J.G. Kohl, *Alte und neue Zeit. Episoden aus der Cultur-Geschichte der freien Reichsstadt Bremen,* Bremen 1871; D. Wierling, '"Ich hab meine Arbeit gemacht - was wollte sie mehr?" Dienstmädchen im städtischen Haushalt der Jahrhundertwende', in: K. Hausen (ed.), *Frauen suchen ihre Geschichte,* Munich 1983, 144-171; *Hundert Jahre Städtische Krankenanstalten Bremen 1851-1951,* Bremen 1951; B. Leidinger, *Krankenhaus und Kranke. Die Allgemeine Krankenanstalt an der St.Jürgen-Straße in Bremen, 1851-1897,* Stuttgart 2000, 96, 161-165; Staatsarchiv Bremen, 7-T.7.d.B.5.a, and 4, 49-3.

In-migration in Bremen, as in other European towns, was accompanied by equally significant outward flows of individuals, and the level of transience by the early twentieth century was substantial.[28] Comparatively little is known of the destinations of out-migrants, but a significant number returned either to their original settlement or to a similar community.[29] For many domestic servants in-migration was a life-cycle phenomenon which would be followed by return migration and probably by marriage. The continued recruitment of domestic servants from the neighbouring territories of Hanover and Oldenburg therefore meant that a high proportion of all moves both into and out of Bremen still occurred within the port-city's hinterland. The impact of age-specific out-migration, as well as return migration, on individual communities in Bremen's hinterland has never been examined, but the nature and extent of migration flows had a visible economic effect. By the early 1860s, almost half of Bremen's merchants had been born elsewhere and in-migrants, as in other port-cities, were an important component of the urban élite.[30] Although a number came from overseas, the majority were from the two states adjacent to Bremen or from its regional hinterland. Many 'foreigners' arrived with some capital, trading experience and an extended network of friends, which was often a prerequisite for commercial activities. The transfer of entrepreneurial talent to Bremen from other areas of northern Germany reinforced its regional predominance, although the economic disadvantages of out-migration for individual source areas may have been offset by the maintenance of personal contacts and family networks.

Maritime Trade, Port-Hinterland Migration and the Diffusion of Urban Culture

The growth of towns and cities in north-west Germany was also a critical factor in the diffusion of urban culture, which has been explained either in terms of an

---

28 I.D. Whyte, *Migration and Society in Britain 1550-1830*, Houndmills 2000, 88; Lee and Marschalck, 'The Port-City Legacy'.

29 S. Hochstadt, *Mobility and Modernity. Migration in Germany, 1820-1989*, Ann Arbor 1999.

30 K. Newman, 'Hamburg in the European Economy, 1660-1750', in: *Journal of European Economic History*, 14 (1985), 57-94; H. Schultz, 'Zur Herausbildung der Arbeiterklasse am Beispiel der mittleren ost-elbischen Handelstadt Rostock (1769-1870)', in: *Jahrbuch für Geschichte*, 13 (1975), 153-201; M. Mahnke, *Rostock zwischen Revolution und Biedermeier - Alltag und Sozialstruktur* (Rostocker Studien zur Regionalgeschichte 1), Rostock 2000; Das Provisorische Bureau für die Staatsstatistik, *Zur Statistik des Bremischen Staats*, Bremen 1862, 14-45; F. Peters, 'Über die Herkunft der bremischen Senatoren von der Verkündung der ersten demokratischen Verfassung bis zur Gegenwart (1849-1955)', in: *Jahrbuch der Bremischen Wissenschaft*, 1 (1955), 312.

acculturation model, with the middle class playing a key role in the dissemination of new cultural values, or as a result of specific innovation cycles, whereby improved living standards in rural areas led directly to an increased acquisition of urban-based prestige objects.[31] Studies of specific communities in Bremen's hinterland provide clear evidence for the increasing diffusion of urban culture. Economic expansion from the late-eighteenth century onwards was accompanied by the adoption and retention of new cultural forms, while there was a noticeable change in rural consumption patterns in the mid-nineteenth century with the assimilation of urban furniture designs and a gradual decline in the use of traditional costume. By the turn of the century the peasantry of north-west Germany had adopted many elements of an urban life style.[32]

Bremen, as a port-city, played an important role in the diffusion of urban culture even if it is difficult at this juncture to assign it a specific weighting. It imported a wide range of colonial goods, which were either processed internally for onward sales or exported directly to its hinterland. As a result, Bremen's trade with its hinterland was increasingly dominated by the marketing of colonial imports (Table 2) and substitute foods and new consumer goods were made available more rapidly and at a lower price than was the case in other more distant territories.[33] For example, Bremen's role as one of Germany's major coffee importers was instrumental in the rapid growth of coffee consumption in its hinterland. Within Germany there was a north-south differential in estimated coffee consumption (with the exception of Baden), while Hanover and Lower Saxony registered a two-fold increase in consumption in the second half of the eighteenth

---

31 M. Maurer, *Die Biographie der Bürgers. Lebensformen und Denkweisen in der formativen Phase des deutschen Bürgertums (1680-1815)*, Göttingen 1996; G. Wiegelmann, 'Novationsphasen der ländlichen Sachkultur Nordwestdeutschlands seit 1500', in: *Zeitschrift für Volkskunde*, 72 (1976), 177-206.

32 D. Sauermann, 'Bäuerliche Brautschätze in Westfalen', in: *Rheinisch-westfälische Zeitschrift für Volkskunde*, 18/19 (1971/72), 103-153; G. Wiegelmann (ed.), *Kulturelle Stadt-Land Beziehungen in der Neuzeit*, Münster 1978; U. Bauche, 'Reaktionen auf städtische Kulturvermittlung, dargelegt an Beispielen aus dem Hamburger Umland', in: G. Wiegelmann (ed.), *Kulturelle Stadt-Land Beziehungen*, 159-174; G. Angermann, *Land-Stadt Beziehungen. Bielefeld und sein Umland 1760-1860*, Münster 1982; R-E. Mohrmann, 'Die Eingliederung städtischen Mobiliars in braunschweigischen Dörfern, nach Inventaren des 18. und 19. Jahrhunderts', in: G. Wiegelmann (ed.), *Kulturelle Stadt-Land Beziehungen*, 297-337; G. Rolfes, *Aus dem Leben einer Bäuerin im Münsterland*, Münster 1986.

33 H.H. Blotevogel, 'Kulturelle Zentralfunktion - theoretische Konzepte und Beispiele aus Westfalen seit dem 18. Jahrhundert', in: G. Wiegelmann (ed.), *Kulturelle Stadt-Land Beziehungen in der Neuzeit*, Münster 1978, 63-114; H-J. Gerhard and A. Engel, 'Preise als Indikatoren von Marktverflechtungen des nordwestdeutschen Raumes 1800 bis 1850', in: K.H. Kaufhold and M.A. Denzel (eds.), *Der Handel im Kurfürstentum / Königreich Hannover (1780-1850). Gegenstand und Methode*, Stuttgart 2000, 101-138.

century.[34] To this extent, spatial proximity to Bremen, together with the availability of river and land transport facilities, were important factors in transforming consumption patterns within the port-city's hinterland.

The transmission of cultural innovations within Bremen's hinterland, however, was not solely dependent on its overseas trading role and imports of colonial goods. Rural settlements were seldom isolated even in the pre-industrial period, and Bremen's public and legal institutions, together with its wider service function, were carriers of urban culture.[35] The development of specialized sectors of production and the lifting in 1861 of residual restrictions on urban-based trade also reinforced Bremen's competitive position within its regional trading network at a time when rapid urban growth augmented the general demand for material goods, while a decline in local fairs and a reduction in rural self-sufficiency strengthened the port-city's market leverage and its ability to influence consumption patterns in its hinterland.[36] At the same time, cultural diffusion was also the result of everyday contacts between Bremen and its neighbouring territories and the impact of return migration in the region, as domestic servants and journeymen sought to emulate the dress code of their former employers and disseminated news of urban fashion. The continued prominence of local migration patterns in the case of Bremen even at the end of the nineteenth century served to maximize the significance of this particular mechanism of cultural diffusion.

---

34 G. Wiegelmann, 'Novationsphasen der ländlichen Sachkultur'; G. Angermann, *Land-Stadt Beziehungen*, 285; P. Albrecht, 'Wie viel Kaffee tranken die Hannoveraner zwischen 1750 und 1850 denn nur wirklich?', in K.H. Kaufhold and M.A. Denzel (eds.), *Der Handel im Kurfürstentum / Königreich Hannover (1780-1850). Gegenstand und Methode*, Stuttgart 2000, 178.

35 H.W. Rohls, 'Großstadt - Wohnungsfrage - Arbeiterkultur. Über Entwicklungstendenzen und Konzeptionen in der Arbeiterbewegung bis 1914', in: *Jahrbuch für Volkskunde und Kulturgeschichte*, 25 (1982), 112. For a similar pattern of urban-rural linkage in Britain, see Whyte, *Migration and Society*.

36 Pfister, 'Vom Kiepenkerl zu Karstadt'; U. Branding, *Die Einführung der Gewerbefreiheit in Bremen und ihre Folgen* (Veröffentlichungen aus dem Staatsarchiv der Freien Hansestadt Bremen 19), Bremen 1951; M.A. Denzel, 'Die Braunschweiger Messen als regionaler und überregionaler Markt im norddeutschen Raum in der zweiten Hälfte des 18. und im beginnenden 19. Jahrhundert', in: *Vierteljahrschrift für Sozial- und Wirtschaftsgeschichte*, 85 (1998), 41-95; J. Kuczynski, *Geschichte des Alltags des Deutschen Volkes*, vol. 3, Berlin 1981, 361. For the operation of these factors elsewhere in Europe, see D.R. Ringrose, 'Capital Cities, Urbanization, and Modernization', 161; G. Rozman, *Urban Networks in Russia, 1750-1800, and premodern periodization*, Princeton 1976.

Conclusion

Urban historians, it has been argued, often accept city limits as well-defined boundaries for analysing 'ostensibly self-contained urban processes' with the result that the mutual interdependence of cities and their hinterlands has been neglected. Theories of regionalism which transcend political boundaries and incorporate the economic linkages between urban communities and their trading areas have also found few exponents.[37] Although it is accepted that capital cities were 'dynamic sources of change', the role of port cities has not been analysed in sufficient detail, despite their importance within international and national trading networks and their mediatising function in importing, marketing and disseminating a wide range of new goods and commodities.[38] A rigorous assessment of port-hinterland relations, however, remains problematic, as the case study of Bremen illustrates. It is difficult to assemble an adequate data base for analysing Bremen's interactive network with its hierarchy of hinterlands: information on its internal export trade before the mid-nineteenth century is sparse and even less is known about the regional impact of urban out-migration in relation to a range of cultural, demographic and economic variables. Moreover, Bremen's relations with its hinterland were directly affected by political factors, in particular by the persistence of a federal constitutional framework in Germany even after political unification in 1871 and by the primacy of overseas trading interests in the port city, which accounted for its exclusion from the Customs Union until 1888.

In the case of Bremen there was a strong degree of mutual interdependence between the port city and its hinterland. Indeed, its trading activities and consumption needs were 'the living principle' for a large part of the neighbouring territories of Hanover and Oldenburg.[39] Although Hamburg enjoyed a more extended natural hinterland, the regional pattern of Bremen's trade was well-established by the early nineteenth century. The hinterland provided Bremen with a range of products, including building materials and manufactured items either for domestic consumption or for export elsewhere, while the port city supplied its hinterland with colonial goods and imported raw materials, some of which had been refined or processed prior to distribution. The underlying pattern of the port-city's trading relations with its hinterland remained essentially unchanged

37 C. Tilly, 'What Good is Urban History', 715; R.A. Mohl, 'City and Region'; A.M. Schlesinger, 'The City in American History' *Mississippi Valley Historical Review*, 27 (1940), 43-66; L. Mumford, *The City in History: Its Origins, Its Transformations, and Its Prospects,* New York 1961.

38 Ringrose, 'Capital Cities, Urbanization, and Modernization', 164.

39 G.W. Marcard, *Zur Beurtheilung des National-Wohlstandes des Handels und der Gewerbe im Königreich Hannover,* Hannover 1836.

throughout the nineteenth century, despite significant improvements in the transport infrastructure, the rise and decline of individual trades, and increasing industrialization in and around Bremen.

The complex web of economic linkages between Bremen and its hinterland was also reinforced by population transfers. In-migration was a key component in Bremen's demographic development, which also extended its range of informal business networks and facilitated the reproduction of its workforce. A very high proportion of Bremen's in-migrants in the eighteenth century came from the neighbouring territories of Hanover and Oldenburg. Despite the expansion of large-scale industrial capacity and rapid urban growth, particularly in the late-nineteenth century, most migrants into Bremen continued to be drawn from its immediate hinterland. By the end of the nineteenth century (1896-1900) Hanover and Olden-burg still accounted for 44 per cent and 55 per cent of male and female in-migrants and the increasing importance of long-distance migration was counterbalanced by the persistence of a clear distance-decay effect. For many domestic servants and journeymen residence in Bremen continued to represent a life-cycle phase and urban transience was reinforced by a range of institutional and legal constraints, which actively discouraged permanent settlement. A strong element of return migration reinforced the interlinkages between the port-city and its hinterland and facilitated the diffusion of urban culture.

The persistence of short-distance migration and the retention of a well-established pattern of trade between Bremen and its hinterland meant that the port-city remained an integral component in a complex system of interactive regional networks. Rapid urban development was accompanied by a further concentration of demand and demonstration effects, which influenced patterns of consumption within its hierarchy of hinterlands. Because of the considerable expansion of overseas trade in the course of the nineteenth century and Bremen's key role as an importer of a wide range of colonial goods, its hinterland wit-nessed a more rapid diffusion of substitute foods and new consumer products than more distant areas of Germany. Regular contacts between Bremen and its hinterland, reinforced by return migration, further accelerated the diffusion process. It is clearly difficult at this stage to assess the precise extent to which the process of cultural change in the port-city's hinterland was determined by the expansion of overseas trade, but this important topic for future research can only be pursued by utilizing an integrated systems approach, which analyses the diffusion of urban culture and changes in consumption patterns in urban hinterlands as a result of interconnected flows of goods and services, human migrations and information dissemination.

Steam and Coal: A forgotten chapter in the history of port cities

Henk van Dijk

Introduction

The image of Bristol as a port city, which the English poet Sir John Betjeman unintentionally evoked in his poem 'Bristol'[1], not only refers to the past but also to the future. Like many port cities during the last decade, Bristol experienced an important transformation.[2] The economic stagnation after World War II as a result of the changes in transport and technology, which led to urban decay, could only partially be halted by efforts taken in urban renovation. This process is generally referred to as 'waterfront development'. During this process, in various port cities throughout the world, specific characteristics of that type of town were used to transform their image. Sites in the neighbourhood of former harbours were appropriated for the construction of houses and prestigious office buildings. Old warehouses were reconstructed into so-called 'lofts', and by offering specific facilities investors tried to attract specific groups of inhabitants, a phenomenon that has often been described in literature as 'gentrification'.

In marketing those urban areas, local municipalities and tourist boards tend to refer back to the period of sailing ships, a time when a relationship between town and harbour still existed. No-one likes to be reminded of the industrial port city, which was mainly related to pollution, overpopulation and recent economic decay - mainly in consequence of the advent of new types of transport technologies.[3] The development of prestigious 'waterfronts' is therefore more than just a

---

1   "Bristol". From "New Bats in Old Belfries" (1945). Reprint in J. Betjeman, *The Best of Betjeman*, London 1978.
2   The tonnage in Bristol ports declined from 9 million tons in 1965 to 3.5 million in 1985. Since then some recovery took place (http://www.shipping.dft.gov.uk/modernports/08.htm).
3   It is clear that the term 'economic decline' could not be used to describe the changes in the ports itself. Most ports, at least the European ones, took advantage from the increase in global trade and transport. The development of the European Market, later Union, stimulated a growing market for goods. Containerisation together with roll-on, roll-off systems made it possible to handle this. However, it not only meant the development of new port areas, outside the traditional port cities, but also a decline in the workforce to be used in handling goods. E.g. the most important British ports showed between 1980 and 1999 an increase in their tonnage of 33%, whereas the workforce in this industry declined from 69,000 in 1985 to 25,500 in 1999 (http://www.bpit.co.uk/pages/employers /news/swdp_txt.pdf). It is important to know, that this

process of revitalising port cities, but at the same time a metaphor of *the port city*.

The results of those changes, however, are not so positive as marketing makes us believe. The lower classes in the port cities hardly ever benefited from the growing market for traditional service-oriented jobs. Port cities suffer as much as typical industrial towns from de-industrialisation. From this point of view therefore, it is not wise to forget the industrial past of the port cities totally.

There is, however, another reason for considering the specific characteristics of the industrial port city on a more theoretical basis. The development of urban planning in port cities is related to a theoretical viewpoint about future developments, which has been based on a (rather simple) understanding of historical developments. The majority of these models can be characterised as stage theories distinguishing three periods in the history of the port cities: a pre-industrial period with a direct link between harbour and town; an intermediate industrial period; and finally a post-industrial one in which living and water are again related. It may be questioned, however, if the development of port cities can be adequately described by a simple stage theory. Especially industrialisation and transport systems led to changes and differences which had not been predominant before. The geographical situation, technological change or the availability of capital (and not to forget political factors) had also repercussions on the image of the town and the spatial development of port cities.

In this article I would like to focus on this 'intermediate stage', the industrial port city. Using comparisons between different European port cities I will sketch a more general historical development.[4] Many ports flourished under the nation states of the nineteenth and early twentieth centuries. National governments could positively influence their own ports, but on the other hand, changing political situations could hamper developments, as the history of Trieste could demonstrate[5] Not only political but also social factors influenced the character of the port cities such as the development of a national system of labour relations.

---

decline was far more dramatic, if one sees that the number of worked hours also declined importantly. The character of employment changed importantly too. Automatisation meant more service oriented jobs.

4   For the use of comparisons of port developments see e.g.: S.A. Andersen, *Dockers' Culture in Three North European Port Cities: Hamburg, Gothenburg and Aarhus, 1880-1960*, Aarhus 1990; V.H. Jensen, *Hiring of Dockworkers and Employment Practices in the Ports of New York, Liverpool, London, Rotterdam and Marseilles*, Cambridge 1964; A. Montarini, 'Barcelona and Glasgow. the similarities and differences in the history of two port cities', in: *Journal of European Economic History*, 18 (1989), 171-89.

5   C. Minca, 'Urban Waterfront Evolution. The Case of Trieste', in: *Geography. Journal of the Geographical Association*, 80 (1997), 225-234.

Most important, however, were changes in technology and changes in the urban networks related to industrialisation in general.

The growth of international trade and transports, already present before industrialisation, speeded up with the coming of industry, thus taking part in the urbanisation process as capital or industrial centres. Port cities became nodes in the network of flow of goods and people. For a long period dependent on geographical factors in almost every respect, particularly the heavy industry could only develop in certain areas of Europe and America, which meant that as well as a part of the basic materials for processing their final products had to pass through ports. These geographical conditions for industrialisation meant that the shift towards the north-western European ports, already visible since the seventeenth century, became still clearer. In particular port cities with good relations to an industrial hinterland – like Liverpool, Antwerp, Rotterdam and Hamburg, but also 'coal ports' like Dundee and others – gained importance, whereas a decline of these industries could later lead to disadvantages. Before industrialisation, it was nearly impossible to have ports very near to sea, only new technology made it possible to construct this type of ports.

Although one can say that in general the north-western port cities gained from the development of industry, some specific situations could help some of the southern ports. Marseilles and Genoa e.g. had profited from the development of railway lines, whereas the development of the industrial area of St. Etienne and Lyon after 1870 proved to be an extra stimulus for Marseilles, but also the making of the Suez canal and the French colonial policy had specific effects. And, within the north-western group important changes took place too. The traditionally important ports like Amsterdam, London, Bremen and Hamburg still kept their colonial trade and their financial strength, but they had to compete more and more with newer ports, which were nearer to the sea and had better connections with the industrial hinterland. The only exception was Antwerp, which could combine the traditional functions with a transport function for the Belgian and northern French industrial zones (in particular the newly developed iron and oar areas of Briey which had to replace the Lorraine fields lost to Germany in 1871).

However, industrialisation not only meant a growth of some port cities and a decline or stagnation of others, but also internal changes for the port cities themselves. It is not true that the industrial port city still had the characteristics of the pre-industrial port city and that only quite recent developments changed the structure of those cities. Industrialisation not only meant that the amount of goods and number of ships in the ports increased, but that new technologies were introduced which resulted in changes in the structure of the city.

The View of the City

Up to the nineteenth century, harbours were an integral part of port cities. The majority of these port cities were not situated directly at the sea, but were located slightly inland on the banks of a river, a lake or an estuary. Arrival in a port city meant that one was received directly in the everyday life of the town. In port cities the presence of sailors was, of course, a normal and daily phenomenon.

With the new technical advances during the nineteenth century (e.g. the construction of larger and faster sailing ships and steamships, and the new docks and specialised warehouses), the appearance of port cities started to change. The cost of transport to and from the working place and the irregularity of the arrival of ships were the main reasons why dockworkers had to live in the vicinity of the ports. Also, for a long time it was impossible to geographically separate economic activities related to the transport of goods from the port activities themselves.

Thus, although the expansion of transport increased the pressure on urban space, the combination of living and working was still the normal pattern in nineteenth-century port cities. Dockers and other labourers lived in the neighbourhood of the ports, which was where the sailors could also be found. The local coffee shops and bars not only had recreational functions, but also served as places for the recruitment of labourers and sailors.[6] However, when organised industrial relations were also introduced into the shipping industry and strikes became an integral part of the negotiating process between employers and employees, these places of recruitment represented a problem for the employers. This applied not only to the dockers, but also to other types of workers such as the labourers in the shipping yards.[7] The employers tried to tackle this situation by controlling the entrance to the port area. Examples of this policy could be

---

6   Andersen, *Dockers' Culture in Three North European Port Cities*; P. Ayers, 'The hidden economy of dockland families: Liverpool in the 1930s', in: P. Hudson and W.R. Lee (eds.), *Women's Work and the Family Economy in Historical Perspective*, Manchester 1990; J. Barzman, 'Port Labour Relations in Le Havre, 1928-1947', in: *International Journal of Maritime History [Canada]*, 9 (1997), 83-106; M. Jackson, *Labour relations on the Docks*, London 1973; Jensen, *Hiring of Dockworkers and Employment Practices*; E.L. Taplin, 'Dock labour at Liverpool: occupational structure and working conditions in the late nineteenth century', *Transactions of the Historical Society of Lancashire and Cheshire*, 127 (1978), 133-54; K. Weinhauer, 'Labour market, work mentality and syndicalism: Dock labour in the United States and Hamburg, 1900-1950s', in: *International Review of Social History*, 42 (1997).

7   M. Cattaruzza, *Arbeiter und Unternehmer auf den Werften des Kaiserreichs*, Stuttgart 1988, 47-51.

found in Rotterdam, where the new ports (built in the 1860s) were closed by means of a gate building which was also including the management's office.

Despite the traditional link between living and working in nineteenth-century ports, the character of the port city changed considerably under the influence of new transport techniques. The former quality of the waterfront was corroded by the construction of docks, large yards, factories for machine building, factories for the treatment of products, and the new methods of storing them. The construction of the new railway yards could only be achieved at the cost of large areas of the waterfront, so that the social character of the waterfront slowly changed. The working class stayed (or even increased in number), whereas wealthier persons moved away to houses in the new suburbs. Their former city villas were converted into offices for shipping lines.

The shipping companies not only acquired new offices, but their business character also changed. Increasingly more ships were becoming part of a large fleet, which meant that the administration could no longer be handled by owner and a few clerks. There was an increasing need for larger offices with a fast-growing staff of bookkeepers, typists and other clerks. Whereas poor travellers (such as emigrants) still used sailing ships, richer persons wanted regular line connections and more comfort. All this demanded efficient organisation and, at the same time, meant that shipping companies had to compete with other firms for presentable office buildings. Ideally, those buildings had to be situated near the ports where the passengers disembarked and the cargo ships arrived, but should not be in the immediate vicinity of industrial buildings. The needs for the transport of goods were different from those for the transport of passengers. At that time the majority of the larger city ports already had a spatial division between a waterfront with prestigious offices and shipping companies, and an area with yards, factories and warehouses.

The Construction of Ports

Urban structure in port cities, however, was mostly influenced by the construction of ports and docks. At the end of the eighteenth century the growth in the maritime circulation of persons and goods was the main incentive for the construction of docks and port structures, which would facilitate the loading and unloading of ships. To a certain extent the ports of the twentieth century were radically new.[8] At least three factors influenced the chronology of the construction, i.e. the amount and type of work to be done: firstly physical geography and

8 A.J. Sargent, *Seaports and Hinterlands*, London 1938, 3.

tidal fluctuations; secondly developments in technology and energy supply; and finally commerce. Initially, dredging of the river mouths was essential, but with the advent of the steamships the capacity for docking increased. In contrast to the smaller works begun at the end of the eighteenth century, much larger and more complicated works were undertaken in the first quarter of the nineteenth century. The growing importance of iron and the steam engine, together with the increase in tonnage, led to the construction of new docks (including locks, dry and tidal docks) accompanied by changes in the loading, unloading, repair and construction of ships. The chronology of the construction of new docks was not identical throughout Europe, neither was the accompanying commercial prosperity of the diverse port cities.

The decline of the Portuguese and Spanish empires had effects on the position of their ports, but it was the development of the railway system in Europe which finally led to a loss of their place in the redistribution of goods originating from South America. A. G. Mendoza considers that the Portuguese ports, and to a certain extent the Spanish ones, benefited from their excellent location for long-distance sea routes until the railway system brought northern and southern Europe closer together, thus distancing them from the international European circuits.[9] Italian ports, such as Genoa, experienced a similar problem after the opening of the transalpine tunnels.

In mid-nineteenth century, the works on Iberian ports were rather small and were a carry-over from plans made in the previous century. In Spain, these works were limited to the small ports of Cantabria, whereas the principal Mediterranean ports (such as Alicante and Barcelona) had only a sea wall to help in the loading and unloading of goods. In Lisbon, before the construction of the Railway Company quay in the early 1870s, only the Navy Arsenal had a proper dock equipped for the unloading of ships. Port cities in peripheral countries with little capital to mobilise (e.g. Lisbon and Venice) often continued to load and unload ships in the harbour or mid-stream by means of barges.[10] Work on the port of Lisbon took place between 1887 and 1890; in the new port in Leixões (5 km from Porto) work began in 1884 and was partially finished in 1892.[11]

The slow growth of shipping in the Mediterranean ports did not stimulate the construction of new docks, which in its turn had effects on loading or unloading. In Marseilles in 1876 the length of its dock was three times that of Genoa. The

---

9   A.G. Mendoza, La modernization des transports dans la Péninsule Ibérique au XIXème siècle, in: *Histoire Économie et Société*, 1 (1992), 145-156, 147.

10 *Regulamento do Porto de Lisboa*, Lisboa 1860, 15.

11 F. Guichard, *Porto la ville dans as région, contribution à l'étude de l'organisation de l'espace dans le Portugal du Nord*, Bordeaux 1982.

average time taken to load a ship in Marseilles was three days whereas in Genoa it was three to four weeks. Although the major works started in Genoa between 1877 and 1888 led to the construction of 6.4 kilometres of docks, this did not suffice to change the situation completely. Similarly the port of Venice had an infrastructure which was inferior to that of Trieste.[12]

The construction of new infrastructures occurred much earlier in English ports. The large tidal fluctuations necessitated the construction of special structures for loading and unloading, such as tidal docks and locks. In 1840, Liverpool had 5 km of tidal docks on the south banks of the river Mersey. The construction of docks started even earlier in London, financed by the city's bankers and businessmen. In the eighteenth century, the Legal Quays ran between London Bridge and the Tower of London. In 1799 the West India Dock Company was created to build docks on Dog Island, between Lime House and Blackwell. Wet docks, basins and locks were built in six years. Ships could now unload their goods into the safety of large warehouses thus avoiding the major losses and thefts. Six docks were built on the south bank of the Thames. By the mid-nineteenth century, London had the best commercial facilities of any port in the world. Work done in the Victorian period extended these facilities down-stream.

In ports like Rotterdam and Hamburg, the construction of canals linking the (inland) port to the sea was a very important development, allowing the presence of ships with a deeper draught and more cargo capacity. The construction of Rotterdam's 'New Waterway' canal to the North Sea dates back to the 1860s. For the ports which were linked to an inland canal or river system, structures to do the transfer of goods to and from the barges were essential. Thus in Hamburg, Bremen and Rotterdam open basins were prevalent in contrast to the closed docks of London. The new ports of that period were rather small to make it possible to load and unload ships immediately to the trains (the new ports on the south bank of the river in Rotterdam as well as the new quays made by Dallmann in Hamburg). During the last decades of the century, however, new types of docks were developed in those cities. Those ports were broad, which meant that ships would only anchor and were loaded and unloaded to river barges 'on stream'. Only when, by contrast, inland transport was done primarily by rail, the tracks came to the quays connecting them to warehouses and train stations, as was the case in Antwerp.

In France similar activities took place during that period, too. Although Marseilles was the most important French port and one of the first nine in Europe,

---

12 A. Schram, L'Italie et l'Europe: une matrice du trafic ferroviaire du Nord de l'Italie, 1867-1884, in: M. Merger, A. Guintini and A. Carreras, *Les réseaux européens transnationaux XIX-XX siècles: Quels enjeux?*, Paris 1985, 363-84, 366.

the project to enlarge the port of Le Havre dated from before the Revolution. Meanwhile, the lengthening of the 'Avant port' and the construction of the docks of Barre (650 meters) and of Commerce (2,800 meters) were only completed in 1834. The work continued, and by 1847 the Florida dock was complete. In 1878 there were eight tidal docks, 13 locks, four wet docks and almost nine kilometres of quays. Marseilles started work on the dock of Joliette in 1844 and it was finished between 1847 and 1853. From the start, the need for a new port was evident. It was started in 1856 by the company "Des Docks et Entrepôts de Marseille" using Parisian capital. The new port had hydraulic cranes, which diminished the work of loading or unloading became the targets for hostility by the dockworkers, which had managed to keep their traditional guild organisation, despite the Allard law.[13] The business community also manifested hostility against the company, a similar phenomenon occurred in Portuguese Leixões when the building of the port there was given to the Peninsular Docks and Railway Company.

In keeping pace with the increased tonnage of ships, new docks had to be larger; this required more substantial investments. The growing complexity of the infrastructure and equipment of ports was linked to the emergence of professionals trained in the planning and direction of their construction. The engineers constituted an elite with diverse social positions in Anglo-Saxon and Latin countries, but with an international circulation between the various cities. Visiting other cities and ports and the writing of reports about technical aspects became routine in the job of engineers. In the second half of the nineteenth century the growth of port expansions took place amid intense competition between public works construction firms, a fact, which also served to advance technological transformations. Powerful cranes now moved the blocks of stone, and more importantly, the foundations were set with increasingly sophisticated drag ships and mechanical digging machines. In the construction of support the labourers could now work under water, thanks to the introduction of long air chambers, which were used for the first time in the expansion of the port of Antwerp in 1878; the technique of working behind a shield was also used here starting from 1880 onwards.

Substantial capital was involved and transferred into the mobilisation of a large unskilled labour force and the presence of skilled labourers who would follow their work from city to city. As work productivity increased, the numbers of employed workers stabilised. Although the distribution of salaries favoured the expansion of the urban economy, the housing situation of these workers was

---

13 W. Sewell, Uneven Development, the autonomy of Politics, and the dockworkers of nineteenth-century Marseille, in: *The American historical Review* 93 (1988), 604-37, 624, 625.

often precarious, mainly situated in degraded neighbourhoods that the growth of public works contributed to. When the construction of the new docks did not involve landfills and the creation of new spaces, the extension of areas to be dedicated to ports contributed to the densification of the central urban neighbourhoods. This applied particularly to cities whose prosperity and large population growth led to significant expansion of the dock areas, such as in Liverpool, which opened three new docks between 1830 and 1844.

Even in the nineteenth century, whenever conditions allowed, new docks were placed on empty land that would allow the city to expand. For those projects which included large landfills, as was the case e.g. in Lisbon, the proposed works aimed at improving urban hygienic conditions by means of a sewerage system, and they foresaw grand avenues, housing for the upper classes and workers, as well as parks and gardens which were never carried out. Discussions about the necessity of constructing new ports or to enlarge existing ones, were rather normal in urban politics of port cities. Sometimes it could led to rather utilitarian reactions, as in Rotterdam, where the opponents to the development of a new park argued that the city needed ports and not trees.

During the nineteenth century, especially for cities with a tradition of autonomy, the construction of the port infrastructure was financed and controlled by the municipality. Cities like Antwerp fought for this control against the growing intervention of the state. In particular the construction of ports in the direction of the Dutch border was seen as a serious weakness of the defence by the central Belgian government. Companies often undertook the management of the ports, which prolonged their construction and which were generally constructed outside the city centre and away from its bourgeoisie. In Rotterdam after a bankruptcy of the most important private dock firm, the local municipality took over this activity with great success.

It is clear that all those construction activities had their impact on the structure of the port cities. Waterfronts, still well to do living vicinities in preindustrial times, were taken over by port and industrial activities and lost their attraction for living. This situation was aggravated by the growing need to link ports by means of railways. The attraction of the Waterfront, as a nice living area diminished, but this development did not lead to a total exodus of the population. Dockers and other port related labourers still had their living areas near to the ships and the yards, and this situation was prolonged until the Second World War.

Hinterlands

The degree to which the hinterland of a port was developed was a determinant factor in the prosperity of the port. Or, as M. B. Amzalak wrote: "the commercial ports were almost always a synthetic expression of the economy of their hinterlands".[14] The quays and docks were part of the new structures with which port cities hoped to respond to the commercial needs of the hinterland, or were an attempt to enlarge it. The growth in port traffic was linked to the characteristics of their hinterland, and technological changes in the system of transportation could restrict or enhance this. The potential 'natural' advantages of rivers, tunnels or railway systems were sometimes offset by tariffs, customs barriers or marketplace advantages.

The existence of a system of canals and rivers served, until the construction of the railway, as the cheapest form of transportation, which favoured the growth of some ports (e.g. in England, the Netherlands, Belgium and Germany). Antwerp and Rotterdam were the new ports which benefited from the enormous long waterway system of the Rhine, together with its secondary streams, that could be served by barge and linked the important industrialised and heavily populated areas with the sea. Although a railway system was also present, it soon became apparent that the barge was the cheapest and easiest way of transporting heavy goods. Although the German government tried to give preferential treatment to their own ports, e.g. Bremen and Hamburg, it was difficult to compete with the Belgian and Dutch ports, as was to be seen in the twentieth century. Only the area around Berlin and the industrial region of Saxony could be served best via the port of Hamburg.

Up to the end of the nineteenth century the transportation of heavy goods via the waterway system was a strong competitor of the railway. In the 1880s the port of Rotterdam predominantly served for the transit of bulk goods, which Germany lacked or exported; Dutch barges became dominant on the Rhine. Both the connection between railway and canals had extended the limits of the hinterland. Between 1884 and 1913, a period in which the navigability of the Rhine was substantially improved, the type of imports and exports at Emmerich at the Dutch-German border changed from mainly agricultural products to iron ore and coal. As a result of these developments, the traditional position of Amsterdam as a port city declined; although the import of colonial goods still continued – with diminishing relative importance, yet.

---

14 M.B. Amzalak, *Portos Comerciais*, Lisbon 1923, 24.

In France, which had a relatively strong internal economy, but a rather weak international trade, the growth of its ports was much slower than in England, the Netherlands, and Germany. The imbalance between incoming and outgoing freight was manifest in ports such as Nantes-Saint-Nazaire and Bordeaux with their un-developed hinterlands. Bordeaux had an agricultural hinterland that exported wine and lumber but which imported mainly food and colonial goods. Ports such as Le Havre, Dunkirk and Rouen, were already more dynamic due to their more industrial settings, and because Paris served as a strong hub from which railway and cheap river transportation radiated. These ports also benefited from the fact that their external trade was mostly with the ports of northern Europe, which were experiencing a rapid expansion in trade. Marseilles, France's largest port in terms of volume had an extensive railway network in the direction of Lyon and expanded steadily thanks to colonial commerce and trade with the Orient (by way of the Suez Canal).

The construction of transalpine tunnels hurt Marseilles, which had until then benefited from oriental trade heading for the French ports on the English channel via the railway links to Lyon. In spite of these changes, the ports of Genoa, Trieste and Venice did not manage to compete with Rotterdam, Antwerp or Hamburg as the commercial hub of trade between Europe and the Orient. The conditions offered by the merchant marine, including port infrastructures and equipment, were the main advantages that allowed the northern ports to become the turning points for big business. Due to the progress in steamship navigation, the transalpine route was not destined to become the sole privileged trade route.

It was above all thanks to the extensive navigable routes of the interior that allowed the ports of north-western Europe to become the principle intermediaries between eastern and central Europe. Twenty years after the construction of the tunnel Sankt Gotthard, Genoa had a traffic volume of 30%, 37%, and 38% compared to that of Rotterdam, Hamburg and Antwerp, respectively. Although a part of the Italian intelligentsia, politicians and economists, believed that their country – thanks to the new railway technology – had the ideal geographical position to become the 'pays de relays' – the expectations greatly exceeded the actual possibilities. This led to the creation of various lobbies of opponents and defenders of the various projects for the different port cities. Only traffic between the Spanish Mediterranean ports and Germany tended to flow through Genoa, to the detriment of Marseilles.[15]

---

15 Schram, 'L'i'talie et l'Europe'. See also M. Merger, 'Mutations téchniques et commerciales: les relations ferroviaires entre l'Italie et l'Europe occidentale de 1867 au début du XX siècle', in: *Revue d'Histoire des chemins de fer*, Hors série, 3 (1992), 211, 227 and 252.

In Spain, largely due to the undeveloped transportation systems, port cities could not aspire to be important points of transit, just as the capital city Madrid (with its population of 167,000 inhabitants in 1800) suffered the consequences in the form of more expensive goods. Barcelona, the main port city of Spain, saw its population of 115,000 inhabitants in 1800 decrease to 83,000 in 1818, only reaching the previous figure again in 1832. By mid-nineteenth century, Barcelona was the only port city in Spain with the function of redistributing colonial products. The city provided itself with food and primary materials through sea trade and its export of industrial products, wines and brandies. The other ports of Spain conducted more specialised trade; e.g. in the ports of Galicia, trade was mainly linked to fishing activity.

The construction of railway lines connecting Lisbon and Madrid, Porto and Salamanca, aimed at being able to attract international traffic via Spain or France on its way to the Americas. The Commercial Association of Porto fought for this construction, convinced that without it the port of Vigo would surpass theirs. The Spanish policy makers also believed that to make Lisbon the port of Madrid (or Porto that of Salamanca) would prejudice their ports at Alicante, Cadiz, Santander or Vigo.[16] So, instead of traversing Portugal, the Spanish railway gave up the advantage of shorter distances in the hope of channelling the internal commerce to their own ports. A tariff war ended up eliminating any advantages that the ports of Porto and Figueira da Foz had over the Spanish ports.[17] However, despite the construction of the railway and the improvement of the ports, Figueira da Foz was not able to transform itself into a port with influence over the region of Salamanca, and even lost its rural hinterland to Lisbon and Porto; the port was thus progressively reduced to fishing and tourist activities.[18]

In general we may say that the structure of the hinterland influenced the position of certain ports. In particular, economic and demographic factors played an important role. The demand for food in the industrialised regions of Europe explained the growth of two other types of port cities: the fishing ports and the ports with an overwhelming agricultural hinterland. In some cases some of the traditional fishing ports on the shores of the Atlantic, the North Sea and the Baltic became a sort of booming towns, although this situation could also turn quite

---

16 Mendoza, 'modernization des transports dans la Péninsule Ibérique', 150.

17 M. Pinheiro, 'L'Histoire d'un divorce: l'intégration des chemins de fer portugais dans le réseau ibérique', in: M. Merger, A. Guintini and A. Carreras, *Les réseaux européens transnationaux XIX-XX siècles: Quels enjeux?*, Paris 1985. See also, M. Pinheiro, Chemins de fer, structure financière de l'Etat et dépendance extérieure au Portugal (1850-1890). PhD-thesis, Paris I 1986, vol. 1, 53.

18 R. Cascão, 'As Vicissitudes do comércio de um Porto secundário: O caso da Figueira da Foz (1850-1920)', in: *Revista Portuguesa de História*, 18 (1980).

quickly depending on the presence of large quantities of fish. Seasonality, however, was an important factor in this booming, as it was in the other type of port cities: those with an overwhelmingly agricultural hinterland. In particular the development of a railway system contributed importantly to this situation. With the development of mining industries in the hinterland the seasonal character of trade diminished, because slowly other products like iron oar, coal and chemicals (fertilisers) etc. passed the port, which would be comparable to some of the Spanish port cities.

Urban Society in Port Cities

The changes in transport not only affected the spatial structures of port cities, but also their social structure; traditionally social life in these cities was connected with shipping and trade. The presence of so many sailors had a specific impact on the urban labour market. Some sailors alternated their work between sailing and working in the docks; they rarely worked constantly on the same ship.

That meant, however, that irregularity of work and income was a typical part of working class life in port cities. This situation was also reflected in family life. The advent of the steamship constituted a major breakthrough in transport. Steamships came into service in the 1840s, and although the old sailing ships adapted and even increased their speed (well-known is the streamlining of the clippers), the coming of the steamship offered regular scheduled travels. Moreover, these ships were able to manoeuvre in ports and small waterways. The steamship not only increased the regularity of transport, but also at the same time represented a new technology with links to other phenomena in port cities. That implied that coal had to be stored close to every shipping route throughout the world. Steam energy gave way to electricity, but both required huge quantities of coal. Until the advent of oil refineries, coal heaps were an ever-present part of the ports' landscape. Most of the coal export from Cardiff, the largest coal port in Europe during the nineteenth century, went to British companies.[19]

But it was not only the steamship that influenced the labour market in port cities. The use of iron, and later steel, led to major changes in the construction of ships and consequently in the way yards were structured. These changes had an impact on the urban character of the port cities and their economic importance, including the labour market. Wooden ships traditionally were built in small yards, using skilled personnel. Thus, experience and skills were important characteristics of shipbuilding. The coming of iron and steel ships created new possi-

---

19 M.J. Daunton, *Coal Metropolis Cardiff, 1870-1914*, Leicester 1977, 8.

bilities for standardisation and industrialisation, which at the same time increased the demand for new technical skills. At the same time a process of centralisation took place; before that time ships were built in various places along rivers or in small harbours at the coast, now the larger vessels could only be constructed in a few places.

A well-known example was the policy of the German empire which not only subsidised the construction of naval vessels, but also shipping companies which were prepared to construct ships locally.[20] However, Germany was not the only country in which state influence in shipbuilding was more a rule than an exception. This policy was also maintained in other countries until long after World War II. The policy of subsidising shipbuilding was generally coupled with a system of tax relief in order to support the national fleet. In the long run this policy was doomed to fail, because the number of ships under a so-called 'cheap flag' increased, which became particularly visible after Word War II. Trade unions could do little against this policy, because the percentage of non-European crewmembers had also increased.

For port cities these were important developments. Yards not only took up an increasing part of urban space which resulted in a tendency to separate the industrial port area from the other parts, but the large-scale character of shipbuilding had an important impact on the local labour relations. Strikes on the shipping yards could easily spread to other port industries, thus in many port cities the yards were seen as a breeding ground for socialism or anarchism. Shipbuilding was, however, not the only industrial activity related to transport in port towns, which affected the social structure and social relations.

Traditionally, processing of imported raw materials played an important role in the economy of port cities. The refining of sugar, tobacco processing, coffee roasting and alcohol distillation were industries, which played a major role in port cities. This was of particular importance when they maintained strong links with their colonial lands. At the same time the demand for specific personnel increased. Wrapping of the goods became increasingly important, and the demand for effective marketing and well-known brands increased as a result of a more anonymous market. Although it was not a highly paid or esteemed work, this gave women of the working class a possibility to escape the traditional work as a household servant. Such a possibility did not exist elsewhere.

---

20 M. Cattaruzza, 'Population dynamics and economic change in Triest and its Hinterland 1850-1914', in: R. Lawton and W.R. Lee (eds.), *Population and Society in Western European Port Cities c. 1650-1939*, Liverpool 2002, 20 and 22 passim.

However, the treatment of trade products was not equally important in all port cities. Ports which were the gateway to an economic peripheral area, or ports which were only used to handle seasonal products, did not develop this kind of industry to the same extent as the ports which were a chain between a (colonial, or semi-colonial) supply area and a home market with a relatively large purchasing power or hinterland. Also, the presence of much first-hand trade as opposed to more intermediate forms of trade played a role.

The Antwerp ports, which served fast industrialising Belgium, had first-hand trade as well as many refinery industries. And the ports of Amsterdam, Bremen and Hamburg, which had fulfilled that role for many centuries, also had large sugar refineries, coffee roasting and other industries related to the treatment of colonial products. That was also the case with Bordeaux and London. However, in the newly emerging ports, like e.g. Rotterdam, where intermediate trade or transshipment was predominant, food-processing industries were not so important.

Comparable differences also existed in the financial services. The presence of capital (and therefore of banking) was more important in the 'old' ports than in the 'new' ones. At that time the number of the upper classes and middle classes was generally small, whereas the lower class was very dominant.

That meant that although port cities were not overall comparable with industrial towns, they did have a predominantly working class population. On top of that, the labour market was characterised by a predominance of temporary and irregular labour and income. Even in ports like London and Lisbon, which were both capital cities, many labourers had to live with the uncertainty of irregular income and jobs.[21]

Conclusion

The transport revolution of the nineteenth century together with the population growth and the industrialisation of larger parts of Europe changed not only the network of port cities, but also their inner structure. Port cities in Europe, how different they might be, underwent remarkable changes over time. With their specific social and economic structure, they represented a unique type of urbani-

---

21 Andersen, *Dockers' Culture in Three North European Port Cities*; Ayers, 'hidden economy of dockland families'; Barzman, 'Port Labour Relations in Le Havre'; Jackson, *Labour relations on the Docks*; Jensen, *Hiring of Dockworkers and Employment Practices*; E.L. Taplin, 'Dock labour at Liverpool', 133-54.

sation; a fast growing population in which the lower class dominated, but without the askew class structure of the industrial centres of the nineteenth and early twentieth centuries. A large proportion of this population still lived and worked for a very long time in the vicinity of the ports. Their living conditions were often deteriorated by the advent of new transport-related industries, such as the yards and the factories for processing goods and food, but they had to stay, because the character of temporary labour gave them little choice.

The urban landscape of the port areas, by origin a mixed area, became more and more specialised and functional. World War II proved to be the watershed in this development: passenger transport – which many European governments and investors hoped would return after the period of the economic crisis of the 1930s – was quickly taken over by air transport, whereas major changes in technology (e.g. containerisation, 'roll-on / roll-off', oil pipelines, etc.) demanded new infrastructures, linked more with national and international transport infrastructures than with the port city itself.

In many cities these developments were linked with a new type of industrialisation; the making of oil refineries and chemical industry.[22] Despite their importance for national income, the contribution of those industries to the labour market was rather small. If those industries needed a workforce, and the number of workers was relatively small compared to more traditional kinds of industry, it was mostly a highly skilled one. This type of industrialisation was not a remedy against the decline of traditional jobs in the ports and the growing segmentation and differentiation of the labour market. Even docking became more and more a very specialised job.

This left port cities with a series of problems, for which the development of a new 'waterfront' was considered an universal remedy.

In the image building of the new port cities they referred to the pre-industrial port city with its nostalgic sailing boats rather than to the 'industrial' part of their history. However, these problems figured largely as a part of the entire process of industrialisation and de-industrialisation of Europe. For example, the decline in shipbuilding was substantially different from the restructuring of the textile industry.

Apart from the differences between port cities in Europe, we may say that it is impossible to assume that only recent technological and economic developments changed the structure and landscape of the port city.

---

22 A well-known example is the industrialisation of the Waterweg area of Rotterdam, but similar developments took place in the ports of other countries.

Although the combination of working and living for a part of the lower class population was a reality for a long time, industrialisation had an important impact on the urban landscape and the population of port cities. Factory towns, mining towns and industrial port cities were all specific urban phenomena belonging to the industrial era.

St. Petersburg, Russia's Gateway to the West: Trade capitalism and its impact on urban change, 1860-1914

Eva-Maria Stolberg

St. Petersburg was founded in 1703 by Peter the Great, the tsar of enlightenment, who envisaged the town as Russia's capital of "spirit and modernity" in contrast to old Moscow, the symbol of backwardness. Since the eighteenth century until nowadays the "Venice of the North" stands in the Russian discourse for Russia's belonging to the West. The rise of St. Petersburg was – like its Italian counterpart – connected with international trade and from the early beginning Russia's capital became a "melting pot". Merchants from Germany, the Netherlands, England, and Italy settled here and contributed to the cosmopolitan flair thanks to St. Petersburg's nearness to the northern sea routes.[1]

It can be assumed that the Great Nordic War with Sweden and the grand tour to Western Europe has influenced Peter the Great's decision for building his capital at the Neva. Maybe the tsar thought of Amsterdam as trade metropolis and, indeed, the architecture of St. Petersburg with its numerous canals reminds of the Dutch town. Despite the non-Russian, Western styled name, the ground plan of the city was modelled after old Russian trade towns like Novgorod. For example, in St. Petersburg the areas of craft and trade were separated.[2] St. Petersburg had traditionally good trade relations with the West, starting with Russia's "open door policy" under Peter the Great and Catherine II. This era was marked with the emergence of the first manufactures for armaments, textiles, and chinaware. Moreover, the tsars envisioned St. Petersburg as an experimentation field for mechanised production and modernisation after the West European model.[3]

St. Petersburg played a significant role in Russia's industrial take-off in the nineteenth century. Nineteenth-century foreign economists convincingly argued that Russia's industrialisation would not be thinkable without the great efforts of

1 B.N. Mironov, 'K voprosu o roli russkogo kupechestva vo vneshnei torgovle Peterburga i Arkhangel'ska vo vtoroi polovine XVIII-nachale XIXv.', in: *Istoriia SSSR*, no. 6, 1973, 129-140.

2 V. Lavrov, *Razvitie planirochnoi struktury istoricheski slovizhivshchikhsia gorodov*, Moskva 1977, 73-75.

3 R. Gosudarstvennyi Istoricheskii Arkhiv (Russian State Historical Archive =RGIA), f. 758, op. 24, l. 141.

investors from abroad who, indeed, represented the nucleus in the formation of a business elite in the Russian empire. Foreigners brought western technology and economic thinking to a country that was connected with backwardness.[4] It is indisputable that the spot in which modernity took place was the city and this also fits to Russia. The history of St. Petersburg delivers in its idiosyncratic as well as generic detail a field that exemplifies Russia's understanding of modernity, progress, and civil society after the western model. Long before Russia's industrial take-off, the English traveller Kohl aptly described the city's outstanding role in Russian history with the metaphor of a "place of rendezvous between East and West".[5] At the eve of the First World War, St. Petersburg numbered 2,000,000 inhabitants, thereby following other European cities like London, Paris, Vienna and Berlin.[6] Tsar Peter the Great and his successors had projected St. Petersburg as a "merchant city" and fascinated by the "luxurious and cosmopolitan" atmosphere of the 1861 trade exhibition in the city, foreign observers felt to be in London or Paris, and noted that "Russian people know the value of refined products like West Europeans."[7] Contemporary reports said that the finest shops on the Nevskij prospekt, St. Petersburg's famous avenue, belonged to Germans and French.[8]

According to official statistics of 1833, among the 442,890 inhabitants of St. Petersburg were 12,059 foreigners and every second of these stemmed from Germany, here especially from the ports of Hamburg and Bremen, and indeed Germans dominated foreign business and trade in the metropolis on the Neva until the First World War.[9] As Rieber has shown in his fundamental study "Merchants and Entrepreneurs in Imperial Russia" in economic entrepots like St. Petersburg and Odessa, the business elite was quite heterogeneous, comprising West Europeans, Russians, but also other nationalities of the Tsarist empire such as Balts, Poles, Caucasians and Tatars which had been attracted to St. Petersburg due to its status as Russia's capital but also due to its nearness to Europe. Foreign entrepreneurs also found a reservoir of a highly qualified working force in the capital.[10] Another factor was that the Tsarist government had always

---

4   G. Shul'tse-Gevernic, *Ocherki obshchestvenogo khozaistva i ěkonomicheskogo poloeniia Rossiia*, St. Petersburg 1901, 43-44.

5   J.G. Kohl, *Russia*, London 1842, 52.

6   J.H. Bater, *St. Petersburg. Industrialisation and Change*, London 1976, 3.

7   M. Ia. Kittary, *Obozrenie vystavki 1861 goda*, St. Petersburg 1862, 7.

8   N.V. Juchneva, *Ětnicheskii sostav i ětnosotsial'naia struktura naseleniia Peterburga*, Leningrad 1984, 67;

9   *Statisticheskie svedeniia o Sankt Peterburge*, St. Petersburg 1836, 125; V.O. Mikhevich, *Peterburg ves' na ladoni*, St. Petersburg 1874, 265-266.

10 A. Rieber, *Merchants and Entrepreneurs in Imperial Russia*, Chapel Hill 1982, 52-73.

hampered the development of an own, Russian native business elite. Moreover, Russian merchants were stigmatised by Russian nobles and bureaucrats as social parvenus.[11]

The Germans replaced the English who had a trade monopoly in the eighteenth century.[12] They had advantages for they, especially the Baltic Germans, were more familiar with the customs in Russia and they showed – in contrast to other foreigners – more patience in dealing with the Russian government. German businessmen were engaged in the production of sugar, paper, and tobacco. Even German beer was produced in Russia's capital by the company "Bavaria".[13] The investment capital of some of these enterprises was quite considerable and amounted e.g. to 500,000 or 700,000 roubles[14] and in the mid-nineteenth century 33.2 per cent of the investments in the city's industry fell to German entrepreneurs.[15] Many of them kept their German citizenship. However, Russian law determined that after a ten-year period foreigners had either to become Russian citizens or to sell their companies with the consequence that foreign entrepreneurs obtained – after a while – Russian citizenship. Like many other foreigners they showed loyalty to Russia and did not feel as "immigrants".[16] Insofar, merchants from abroad who settled in St. Petersburg increasingly assimilated and by this way foreign entrepreneurial spirit entered the capital's society. St. Petersburg became, therefore, a kind of melting pot, thereby playing an outstanding role in spinning the commercial network with the "outer world".

Due to the fact that St. Petersburg was a trade metropolis, banking became an important enterprise in which Germans like the Stieglitz family were engaged. Since the beginning of the nineteenth century the Stieglitz were

---

11 K. Schlögel, *Jenseits des Großen Oktober. Das Laboratorium der Moderne Petersburg 1909-1921*, Berlin 1988, 251.

12 H.H. Kaplan, 'Russian Commerce and British Industry: A Case Study in Resource Scarcity in the Eighteenth Century', in: A.G. Gross (ed.), *Russia and the West in the Eighteenth Century*, Newtonville (Mass.), 325-335.

13 *Ves' Peterburg*, 1913, 33-34.

14 I. Pushkarev, *Opisanie Sankt Peterburga i uezdnych gorodov St. Peterburgskoi gubernii*, *St. Petersburg 1839*, 40-41.

15 N. Overchenko, *Istoriko-geografícheskiij atlas Peterburg-Leningrad, tom 1*, Leningrad 1957 (supplement).

16 N. I. Ivanova, ,Deutsche Handwerker und Unternehmer in St. Petersburg vom Beginn des 19. Jahrhunderts bis zum Jahre 1913', in: D. Dahlmann, C. Scheide (eds.), „... *das einzige Land in Europa, das eine große Zukunft vor sich hat.*" *Deutsche Unternehmen und Unternehmer im Russischen Reich im 19. und frühen 20. Jahrhundert*, Essen 1998, 282; see also W. Blackwell, 'The Russian Entrepreneur', in: *Entrepreneurship in Imperial Russia and the Soviet Union*, Princeton 1993, 24.

Russian citizens, in the 1820s Ludwig Stieglitz obtained the title of a baron. Stieglitz was a prominent figure in the city's business life since he presided over the stock exchange. He possessed the confidence of the Russian ministry of finance and was commissioned to negotiate with foreign governments for loans and investments. Moreover, the bank of "Stieglitz & Co." invested 8,000,000 roubles into the construction of the St. Petersburg-Moscow railway.[17] The Tsarist government patronised the German banker in order to become not too dependent on English and Dutch banks. The press of the capital praised the Stieglitz as the "Second Rothschilds". In 1860 Alexander Stieglitz gained further influence when he was appointed chairman to the newly founded Russian State Bank. In cooperation with M.H. Reutern, the Russian minister of finance, he established a credit system after the West European model in Russia.[18]

By the mid-nineteenth century, 38 per cent of all Russian foreign trade went through St. Petersburg, nearly five times more than in Riga, the other important port on the Baltic Sea.[19] Furthermore, the liberalisation of tariffs stimulated the growth of trade, but also of industries like ship-building, metal-working and textiles.[20] Metal-production with the leading entrepreneur Ludwig Nobel proved to be a booming industrial sector whose production capacity raised from 63 million to 209 million roubles between 1894 and 1913. On the metal-producing sector, mechanical engineering became the dominant part in which nearly every third enterprise of Russia's capital was engaged. At least, St. Petersburg's significance as a gateway to the West was symbolised by the production of steamers that made up 32 per cent at the turn of the century.[21] In 1900 the production of the Putilov company which was the main supplier of steamers for St. Petersburg's port reached 20 million roubles.[22] In the decade before the First World War the greatest customer of the Nobel and Putilov companies was the Russian Ministry of War.[23] Moreover, it is worth mentioning that Russia's industrialisation greatly profited from Western, i.e. German technology. For example, just in 1898 the development of the Diesel motor was undertaken in cooperation with the Technological Institute of St. Petersburg University.

---

17 B.V. Anan'ich, *Bankirskie doma v Rossii, 1860-1914. Ocherki chastnogo predprinimatel'stva*, Leningrad 1991, 14-15.

18 P.P. Migulin, *Russkii gosudarstvennyi kredit, tom 1*, Khar'kiv 1899, 120-122.

19 *Gosudarstvennaia Vneshniaia torgovlia v raznykh eia vidakh za 1852 god*, St. Petersburg 1854, table XII.

20 E. Karnovich, *Sankt Peterburg v Statisticheskom Otnoshenii*, St. Petersburg 1860, 104-112.

21 V.K. Jatsunskii, ,Rol' Peterburga v promyshlennom razvitii dorevoliutsionnoi Rossii', in: *Voprosy istorii*, 9 (1954), 101-102.

22 *Spisok fabrik i zavodov Evropeiskoi Rossii*, St. Peterburg 1903, 314-315.

23 *Mekhanicheskii zavod Ljudvig Nobel' 1862-1912*, St. Peterburg 1912, 11-13.

Moreover, the boom of Russian ship-building industry, especially that of tankers and submarines is not thinkable without the use of German Diesel motors. Insofar, German engineers and entrepreneurs considerably contributed to the equipment of the Russian Navy before the First World War – a fact that has been neglected by recent historiography. In the years 1900-1913 St. Petersburg became the main centre of Russian war industry.[24]

Another important branch of St. Petersburg's industry before the First World War was the production of textiles by foreign enterprises like German Ludwig König and the British Trust of I. and P. Coates Ltd.[25] It is, moreover, impressive that these entrepreneurs produced with no more than 2,000 workers textiles worth of 3 to 4 million roubles a year. Whereas in the 1890s foreign and Russian textile companies imported the raw product cotton from North America, this changed after 1910 in favour of Russian cotton mostly coming from Central Asia. Nearly 50-60 per cent of St. Petersburg's workers had to be found in the metal and textile sector.[26]

Since 1885 Siemens operated in St. Petersburg, thereby bringing electricity to Russia's capital, and it is worth mentioning that Germans stimulated the creation of the first joint-stock companies in the city.[27] Siemens laid the foundation of the electricity industry in the Russian Empire and built the tramway system in St. Petersburg with the help of Russian engineers. Thanks to Siemens, between 1893 and 1913 St. Petersburg became the leading city on the electricity-producing sector. In 1913, nearly 70 per cent of Russia's electric energy had been produced in the capital. On the All-Russian Industrial exhibition in 1896 Siemens presented together with thirty foreign enterprises its technological innovations. With the establishment of the St. Petersburg electric-technological institute two years later the business ties between the German and Russian electric industry were strengthened.[28]

Whereas in 1897 Siemens' investments in St. Petersburg amounted to 4.5 million roubles, in 1913 20 million roubles were invested. Furthermore, the income of St. Petersburg workers employed by Siemens was very high (10 roubles per week) for Russian conditions, it was similar to the wages that Siemens workers earned in Berlin. Due to their high investment capital and

---

24 *Mekhanicheskii zavod Ljudvig Nobel*, 112.

25 RGIA, f. 23, op. 24, d. 90, ll. 106, 215.

26 *Statistika bumagopriadil'nogo i tkatskogo proizvodstva za 1900-1910gg.*, St. Peterburg 1911, 1-2, 8-10.

27 V.S. Diakin, *Siemens v Peterburge. Sbornik tezisov i dokladov i konferentsii „russko-nemetskie kontakty v biografii St. Peterburga*, 2-4 noiabria 1992g., 11-12.

28 50 let Leningradskogo elektrotekhnicheskogo instituta imeni V.I. Ulianova (Lenina), *Leningrad – Moskva 1948*, 20-21.

profits German entrepreneurs like Siemens paid higher wages than their Russian counterparts. Therefore, getting a job in a German company was very lucrative for Russian employees and workers. How deeply Siemens became rooted shows the fact that the daughters of Carl Siemens married Russians. Marriages and family ties were vehicles to cement German-Russian business ties and, moreover, it exemplified how the acculturation of German entrepreneurs to the Russian society went ahead.[29]

Like electricity, chemistry experienced an impressive boom and symbolised Russia's industrial and technological take-off in the last decades of the Tsarist Empire. During the decade between 1894 and 1913 the sum of sales achieved by Russian and foreign companies rose from 5,7 million to 40,8 million roubles. Thanks to cooperation with German firms like IG Farben and BASF the greatest chemical producer, the Tentelevskii factory, refined in Russia's most advanced laboratory the production of chemicals, fertilisers, and lacquers. In the year 1897 alone, 65 per cent of all hydrochloric acid produced in Russia fell on the Tentelevskii factory. Chemicals like sulphuric acid, soda, and chlorine were used as bleach agents in the fabrication of textiles and paper and, at least, the boom of these sectors were not thinkable without the progress of Russian chemistry influenced by Western Europe.[30]

Thanks to railroad construction St. Petersburg became attractive for foreign entrepreneurs. The railroad connected Central Europe and Poland with Russia's capital and the nearby Baltic provinces and made the transportation of goods cheaper and more convenient. Whereas in 1900 180 million pud[31] of commodities were imported to St. Petersburg and its hinterland, in 1913 nearly 368.8 million pud passed the border. Between 1900 and 1913 St. Petersburg's foreign imports from Central and Western Europe via the railroads and the port rose from 236.3 to 422.7 million roubles. In the same period the export rate of agricultural products (bread, butter, fish, meat) to Germany, France, and Great Britain was quite impressive and amounted to 1,520 million roubles.[32]

Despite of this boom beginning in the 1860s (as a result of Russia's inner reforms) and its lasting until World War I, the commerce of St. Petersburg could not compete with West European capitals. As James Bater has shown, 61 per

29 W. Kirchner, *Die deutsche Industrie und die Industrialisierung Russlands 1815-1914*, St. Katharinen 1986, 334.

30 P.M. Lukianov, *Istoriia khimicheskikh promyslov i khimicheskoi promyshlennosti Rossii do kontsa XIX*, tom 3, Moskva 1951, 84-86.

31 1 pud = 16,38 kilograms.

32 *Svedeniia o dvizhenii tovarov po zheleznym dorogom za 1900g.*, St. Petersburg 1902, *Perevozki po zheleznym dorogom v 1913*, Prague 1917. See also V. Pokrovskii, *Znachenie Peterburga vo vneshnei torgovle Rossii*, St. Peterburg 1899, 74-78.

cent of the bourgeois elite of St. Petersburg were engaged in trade and industry in 1869, but in London and in Berlin they amounted to 84 and 79 per cent, respectively.[33] The engagement of German entrepreneurs on various industrial fields resulted in an increasing participation in financial politics. In 1883 Adolf Rotstein had been ordered by the German bank "Diskonto Gesellschaft" to St. Petersburg, as a confident of Otto von Bismarck, he became one of the most prominent figures in the business world of Russia's capital and at last the director of the International Bank of St. Petersburg. Rotstein symbolised more than anyone else the interweaving of politics and economics between Berlin and St. Petersburg.[34] Moreover, Rotstein like Stieglitz advised Finance Minister Sergei Vitte to introduce a currency reform and insofar, the influence of German bankers on Russian economic policy in St. Petersburg, the centre of power, was quite considerable. As sources from the archives in St. Petersburg reveal, Rotstein – and he did not stand alone among German entrepreneurs – regarded himself as a member of the Russian business class. For example, Rotstein refused French participation in the International Bank by arguing that "we remain a Russian enterprise".[35]

Even after World War I, Russian economists like Levin praised the German contribution to Russia's industrialisation, they brought their whole business spirit, individualism and experience into the process of modernisation as Levin concluded in 1918. Moreover, it was striking that the acculturation of German entrepreneurs went further than that of other foreigners.[36] As archival sources reveal, the Russian government and its ministries in St. Petersburg appreciated German entrepreneurs as "trustworthy partners" and here, obviously, bureaucrats of the St. Petersburg administration cultivated the well-known images of the "dutiful and hard-working Germans".[37]

The development of joint-stock companies, of banks and credit cooperations was the prerequisite for a successful industrialisation, which jumped from the Russian capital into the provinces. The dominance of western foreigners in Russian entrepreneurship is reflected by the composition of the First Union of Russian entrepreneurs established in St. Petersburg on 24 October 1906 in which the majority was non-Russian. West Europeans had decisively influenced the

---

33 H. Bater, *St. Petersburg. Industrialization and Change*, 90.
34 E.W. Schmodt, *Männer der Deutschen Bank und der Diskonto-Gesellschaft*, Düsseldorf 1957, 30.
35 RGIA, f. 626. op. 1, d. 1382, ll.207-208.
36 I.I. Levin, *Germanskie kapitaly v Rossii*, Petrograd 1918.
37 See footnote 20.

creation of an industrial élite in Russia's capital.[38] The first intention of the Union of St. Petersburg entrepreneurs was to install a liability insurance in case of industrial accidents.[39] Here, again, German influence was eminent: the chairman, Karl Pohl, championed the idea of a representative body of St. Petersburg entrepreneurs to claim their rights toward the Tsarist government as it was usual at that time in all European countries.[40]

German entrepreneurs like Stieglitz and Siemens were well reputed in the bourgeois society of St. Petersburg as they embodied German industry, moreover they proved to be well-suited to apply the knowledge and experience they had achieved in Germany and Western Europe to Russian conditions. They formed an important and indispensable link between West European and Russian markets. Many of them became millionaires thanks to the flourishing commerce with Russia.[41]

Table 1: Number of foreign entrepreneurs in St. Petersburg, Moscow and Odessa (year 1913)

Country	St. Petersburg	Moscow	Odessa
Germany	99	184	46
Austria	23	45	20
France	39	41	12
Switzerland	12	21	–
Great Britain	19	19	11
Sweden	8	10	–
Others	23	41	169*
Total	223	361	258

Concerning the participation of foreign entrepreneurs, St. Petersburg experienced a sharp competition with its rivals Moscow and Odessa. However, as the centre of the huge ministerial bureaucracy, economic life in St. Petersburg

38 J. von Puttkamer, 'Vorbild Europa? Der Einfluß ausländischer Industrieller auf Entstehung und Politik russischer Unternehmerverbände', in: Dahlmann and Scheide (eds.), *das einzige Land in Europa, das eine große Zukunft vor sich hat*, 101.

39 V.A.P. King, *The Emergence of the St. Petersburg Industrial Community, 1870-1905: The Origins and Early Years of the St. Petersburg Society of Manufacturer*, Ph.D.-tesis., Berkeley 1982, 275 sqq.

40 J. von Puttkamer, 'Vorbild Europa?', 106.

41 Bater, *St. Petersburg. Industrialization and Change*, 222.

*   Due to the nearness of Odessa to the southern border, 74 entrepreneurs came from Greece and 65 from Turkey.

experienced corruption. Petr Kropotkin, for e.g., observed: "As to commercial enterprises, it was openly known that none could be launched unless a specified percentage of the dividends was promised to different functionaries in the several ministries. A friend of mine, who intended to start some enterprise at St. Petersburg, was frankly told at the ministry of the interior that he would have to pay twenty-five per cent of the net profits to a certain person, fifteen per cent to one man at the ministry of finances (...)."[42] Therefore, foreign entrepreneurs had to reckon with the omnipresent bureaucratic apparatus of the Tsarist government which wished to control business life of the capital. German and foreign entrepreneurial spirit has also deeply influenced Russian merchants. Russian merchants like St. Petersburg born Nikolai V. Solov'ev welcomed the idea of spinning a commercial network between Russia's capital and West European countries. Solov'ev, but also other Russian merchants, thought that Russian commerce could learn from the West. However, this thinking stemmed in the case of Solov'ev from his studies at the Sorbonne.[43]

Spinning St. Petersburg into the commercial network with Western Europe made headway in the second half of the nineteenth century. Whereas production of manufactured goods in St. Petersburg valued at nearly 50 million roubles in 1867, it reached 600 million roubles at the eve of World War I (1913).[44] In 1912, over 600 stocks were registered on the exchange with a value amounting to 17 billion roubles. Among the goods exported to Western Europe were grain, canvas, hemp, glass, textiles. The grain exports to West European markets raised from 273.3 million pud in 1900 to 561 million pud in 1913. In 1900, 20 to 25 per cent of Russia's butter exports were embarked in the city's port and nearly one third of all foreign commodities, especially machinery, imported to Russia went via the railways and the port of St. Petersburg.[45] In late Imperial Russia trade capitalism in St. Petersburg met the harsh competition with South Russian ports Odessa and Nikolaev as the following table (table 2) shows:

---

42 J. A. Rogers (ed.), *Peter Kropotkin. Memoirs of a Revolutionist*, New York 1962, 161.
43 'Peterburg kupecheskii', in: *Neva*, No. 1, (1998), 231.
44 Bater , *St. Petersburg. Industrialization and Change*, 222.
45 Bater , *St. Petersburg. Industrialization and Change*, 258.

Table 2: Exports from Russian ports St. Petersburg, Odessa, Nikolaev (1900-1908)[46]

Exports in million pud (without grain)	1900	1901	1902	1903	1904	1905	1906	1907	1908
St. Petersburg	94,6	93,3	73,5	69,3	81,2	108,1	88,7	87,4	88,7
Odessa	53,3	88,2	139,1	155,1	110,9	85,4	107,4	100,0	65,0
Nikolaev	30,0	55,1	85,5	118,5	90,7	99,8	118,7	94,0	76,2

Source: M Fedorov, *Konkurentsiia baltiiskikh i chernomorsko-azovskikh portov*, St. Petersburg 1909, 11-12.

The contemporary Russian historian Fedorov explained St. Petersburg's decline to the fact that the Baltic Sea lost its significance as a trade route to the Mediterranean and Black Sea. In my view, more important was that through railway construction the main grain-producing areas in South Russia were now well connected with the southern ports of Odessa and Nikolaev.[47] Whereas the southern ports played a significant role for exports of agricultural goods, St. Petersburg and other Baltic ports like Riga, Reval became predominately the entrepots for imports of Western European machinery, chemicals, and raw material like coal and coke. 33 per cent of these Western imports were used by the capital's own industry.[48] In Fin-de-siècle Russia, St. Petersburg, at least, owed its prosperity to the consumer industry. In 1913 there existed nearly twenty markets where nearly 800 Russian and foreign cooperatives traded with cloth, furniture, alcohol, tobacco and other goods of daily life[49] and on the main trade centre, the so called "Gostinyi Dvor", were 150 Russian and foreign enterprises present.[50]

46 M. Fedorov, *Konkurentsiia baltiiskikh i chernomorsko-azovskikh portov*, St. Petersburg 1909, 11-12.
47 M. Fedorov, *Konkurentsiia baltiiskikh i chernomorsko-azovskikh portov*, 4-5.
48 Ministerstvo torgovli i promyshlennosti (Ministry of Trade and Industry) (ed.), *Torgovlia i promyshlennost' Evropeiskoi Rossii po raionam, vypusk II. Severno-Zapadnaia zemledel'cheskaia polosa*, St. Petersburg 1913, 8-13.
49 Ministerstvo torgovli i promyshlennosti (ed.), *Torgovlia i promyshlennost' Evropeiskoi Rossii po raionam, 8-13*.
50 *Leningradskii gostinyi dvor, ego proshloe i nastoiashchee*, Leningrad 1925, 4-5.

One of the most important money lender was the Russian State bank and with its residence in St. Petersburg it gave credits to different trade and industry operations in the capital, but also all over the country with any estimated volume from 213.6 million roubles in 1893 to 1,179.4 million roubles in 1913.[51] There were also private banks which number slightly arose from 10 to 12 in the period 1893-1914, but with respectable capital assets from 66.3 (1893) to 506.8 million roubles (1914) due to their manifold contacts with foreign banks and enterprises. In the banking sector of St. Petersburg one can discover a high concentration and it is characteristic that often bureaucrats like A.I. Putilov, director of the chancellery of the Ministry of Finance, headed the banks in the capital – a fact that seems to be plausible (so in the case of Putilov): such men possessed good contacts to the ministries and there existed a dense web between the banks and the state bureaucracy so that it is apt to say that Russia was predominately a country of "state capitalism". Another example is that of the St. Petersburg International Commercial Bank led by A.I. Vishnegradskii, son of the former minister of Finance, I.A. Vyshnegradskii. Such men like Putilov and Vyshnegradskii managed investments into big syndicates in profitable sectors as the booming Russian oil industry.[52] Fin-de-siècle St. Petersburg saw the emergence of trusts in the heavy industry as for example the Russo-Asian Bank (managed by the state) supported the cooperation between French armaments producing enterprises (like Schneider & Cresot) with the Putilov company. Russian banks predominately invested in Russian and foreign syndicates, their interest in small business was marginal.[53]

The emergence of a foreign and Russian business elite also affected the cultural and social life of Fin-de-siècle St. Petersburg and the most prominent representatives of the commercial circles dominated the duma (town council) with the introduction of a municipal census franchise in 1903 which reflected the rising self-consciousness of Russian and foreign entrepreneurs.[54] The significance of entrepreneurial engagement in the town duma is reflected by the fact that the budget of this body climbed from 11,911,000 roubles in 1895 to 57,000,000 roubles in 1915.[55] The last decades of the Tsarist empire show that St. Petersburg played an important role in forming a bourgeois society and a

---

51 RGIA, f. 23, op. 9, d.237, 1.10.
52 I.F. Gindin, *Banki i promyshlennost' v Rossii do 1917g.*, Moskva / Leningrad 1927, 48; see also the standard work of I.I. Levin, *Aktsionernye kommercheskie banki v Rossii*, tom 1, Petrograd 1917.
53 RGIA, f. 23, op. 12, d.1974, 11.22, 39-40.
54 A.D. Bogachev, *Peterburgskaia duma v biografiiakh eia predstavitelei 1904-1910*, St. Peterburg 1904, 2-4.
55 *Izvestiia Petrogradskoi gorodskoi dumy*, no. 5-6, (1917), 100-102.

middle class – an experiment which started much later than in Western Europe and had been interrupted by the October revolution in 1917. Because of a strongly heterogeneous composition of the business elite (predominated by "assimilated" foreigners), the middle class in Russia, including St. Petersburg, differed in its development from Western Europe. As Jürgen Kocka had exemplified for Germany one has to distinguish meticulously the different ways in forming a bourgeois society.[56]

In 1907 the Russian entrepreneur Sergei Petrovich, candidate of the party of Octobrists, had been elected to the Third Municipal Duma. Russian and foreign entrepreneurs of Russia's capital praised him as an outstanding man who supported more than any other "the realization of bourgeois values and peaceful living together of entrepreneurs of different national origin."[57] Sources from the Russian Historical Archive in St. Petersburg reveal that Russian and foreign capitalists closely cooperated in political matters discussed in the municipal duma, and in the revolution of 1905 they sought for a comprise with the striking workers. Russian entrepreneurs learnt from the West to seek the dialogue with the working class.[58]

In the last decades of the Tsarist empire Russian entrepreneurs were not anymore "self-made men" like their predecessors in earlier times, when, for example the son served his apprenticeship with his father, the factory owner. Later in Fin-de-siècle St. Petersburg a prevailing part of the Russian entrepreneurs graduated from business schools or passed their exams in economics at the St. Petersburg University. Besides the university, the famous St. Petersburg business school was another important institution. Most of its students stemmed from the merchant class and were taught in foreign languages and accountancy. The school financed by Russian and foreign entrepreneurs of St. Petersburg trained between 1883 and 1913 nearly 1,600 students with much success as nearly every second graduate found a job in private commerce or founded one's own company. Many of this skilled young people had visited Western Europe during their studies and now as entrepreneurs they additionally showed concern for their workers. They founded schools for children of the working class, thereby fighting against illiteracy. They understood well that a booming industry needed educated workers. Entrepreneurs also led campaigns against alcoholism and better hygienic conditions in the factories. Moreover, learning was regarded as a bourgeois enlightenment that should reach the

---

56 J. Kocka, *Bürgertum im 19. Jahrhundert. Deutschland im europäischen Vergleich*, vol. 1,
     Munich 1998, 11-76.
57 See footnote 42.
58 RGIA, f. 32, op. 2.

workers. Finally, this patronage was - like in many other European commercial cities - a source of social prestige and self-identity of entrepreneurs.[59]

Foreign entrepreneurs like König, Siemens, but also Russians like Nikolai Solov'ev who graduated from the Sorbonne had Western education in mind, when they founded the first factory schools in St. Petersburg. It was their idea to combine school education with productive work, thereby thinking that the industrialization and modernization of backward Russia was not possible without spurring the Russian people on manual work. Therefore, children and juveniles of workers had to learn early at school that manual work was an important element in human maturity. At the eve of World War I there existed in St. Petersburg 53 schools for craft and trade founded by business men and the most gifted pupils received grants. In this context it is worth mentioning that these private schools were not put under the supervision of the Russian Ministry of Education, known for its restrictive policy, but under that of the Ministry of Finance that proved to be innovative in appreciating Russian and foreign entrepreneurs' role in funding schools. However, it often occurred that after the death of a private school founder the financial sources run dry with the consequence that the school had to be closed.[60] In contrast to common factory schools, private business schools were not free of charge, and therefore only the upper and middle classes of St. Petersburg could afford the fees. Whereas between 1910 and 1914 the fee at state-run schools amounted to 70 to 80 roubles per year, parents had to pay for business schools 200 to 250 roubles per year.[61]

Social prestige of foreign and Russian entrepreneurs was, at least, reflected by the aesthetics of St. Petersburg's architecture and fine arts.[62] Business men of Russia's capital sponsored the performances of the Russian Musical Society which regularly invited prominent Russian and foreign musicians like Rachmaninov, Glazunov, Skriabin, Reger, Sibelius, thereby spinning a cultural network between St. Petersburg and Western Europe. Moreover, the "Russian Symphonic Concerts" that took place in the capital since the 1860s, became a "meeting point" between Russian and foreign entrepreneurs knoting not only business ties, but also spending leisure times together. Thanks to St. Petersburg's fine arts, outstanding in the Russian Empire, the capital became an attractive

59   A.G. Timofeev, *Istoriia S-Peterburgskogo komercheskogo uchilishcha*, St. Petersburg 1902, 9-14; Bogachev, *Peterburgskaia duma v biografiiakh eia predstavitelei 1904-1910*, 49-54. See also N. Andreev, 'O vvedenii vseobshchego obucheniia v Peterburge', in: *Uchitel' i shkola*, no. 9, 1914, 1-3.

60   N. Andreev, 'O vvedenii vseobshchego obucheniia v Peterburge', 1-3.

61   Gosudarstvennyi Istoricheskii Arkhiv Goroda Peterburga (Historical State Archiv of the Town St. Petersburg), f. 733, op. 167, d.790.

62   N. Sultanov, *Staryi Peterburg*, St. Petersburg 1902.

"living place" for foreign entrepreneurs that could compete with London, Paris and Berlin.[63]

As my essay has shown, foreign merchants from Western Europe brought their culture to St. Petersburg, but felt – at the latest in the second generation – as Russians, whereas their Russian colleagues learnt of Western bourgeois values and way of living during their studies abroad that finally resulted in sponsoring different social and cultural activities in Russia's capital so that in Fin-de-siècle Russia, St. Petersburg became, indeed, a "Gateway to the West". Insofar, foreign and Russian merchants of St. Petersburg played an important role in "spinning the commercial web" between Russia and Western Europe, they became, at least, "kulturtraeger" of bourgeois values and the idea of a civil society. Moreover, it is worth mentioning that with the October Revolution the old name St. Petersburg was substituted by Leningrad and until the breakdown of the Soviet Union Soviet historiography focused on the city's and their workers' contribution to the revolution, thereby ignoring the bourgeois past, the "Golden Age" of St. Petersburg in the Tsarist era. Not surprisingly, after the dissolution of the Soviet Union the city regained its previous name. St. Petersburg and its citizens again sought access to Western Europe and among Russian cities it became the forerunner in the economic transformation by opening trade with foreign enterprises. Russian and foreign entrepreneurs have opened their companies in the newly restored houses and commercial buildings of the Tsarist "Gruenderzeit".[64]

---

63 See footnote 60.

64 *Sankt-Peterburgskii komitet gosudarstvennoi statistiki: Sankt-Peterburg i Leningradskaia oblast'*, Sankt Peterburg 1996, 75-76.

Colonial Boston and the Commercial Web: One city's dilemma

Sharon Rodgers

The public marketplace, so basic an element of life to most city dwellers, became, for the residents of eighteenth-century Boston, the focus of one of the most bitter, protracted struggles they were to experience. It was a political and economic issue that directly affected their physical survival.

In 1737, the public markets were the object of midnight rioters dressed in clerical robes who proceeded to dismantle them and three years later, the town meeting came within seven votes of refusing the gift of a large brick building – the greatest edifice ever constructed in Boston to that date – because it was to contain a market hall.[1] Although the conflict may have been difficult for outside observers to fathom, the reasons for not wanting public markets were clear to those who sought to avoid or destroy them, and they continued their argument well into the 1760s.

By connecting local markets and businesses to those in distant lands, economic growth throughout the Atlantic trading world created an infinite number of ways in which to make money. The joint commercial ventures, lucrative wartime sales opportunities, new settlements, new markets, and new resources and products not only extended the possibilities for doing business but also for satisfying the innate human quest to improve the quality of life. The siren song of profit was irresistible to the generations that succeeded the Puritan founders. To others, it signaled moral decay and loss of community.[2]

Boston's external trading network during the seventeenth and eighteenth centuries encompassed the entire Atlantic trading world including the American coast from Canada in the north southward into the Caribbean, western Europe, the countries of the Baltic and of the Mediterranean, and the coastal regions of

---

1   *Boston Town Records, 1729-1752*, Boston 1877-1906, 259-60. For a different argument regarding Boston's markets, see Barbara Clark Smith, 'Markets, Streets, and Stores', in: E. Marienstras and B. Karsky (eds.), *Autre Temps Autre Espace: An Other Time An Other Space: Études sur l'Amérique préindustrielle*, Nancy 1986, 181-197 and also B. Clark Smith, 'Food Rioters and the American Revolution', in: *William and Mary Quarterly,* Ser. 3, 51 (1994), 3-38.

2   The English markets that the first Puritan settlers had patronized had been rampant with constraints, abuses, and corrupt public officials - negative memories of these markets were passed from generation to generation in Boston. A. Everitt, 'The Marketing of Agricultural Produce,' in: J. Thirsk (ed.), *The Agricultural History of England and Wales, 1500-1640*, vol. IV, Cambridge 1967, 563-589.

northern and western Africa. Its merchants, among the most adept smugglers in pre-Revolutionary America, pursued illegal as well as legal trade through their close ties with family and friends located throughout this world who provided them with assistance as well as information about distant markets.

The city's internal trading network extended into the farming hinterland around it as well as to the smaller towns of New England. Farmers from the Connecticut Valley and as far away as the Narragansett region of western Massachusetts made seasonal selling trips to the capital.

The first disagreements about Boston's markets occurred during an era that pre-dated the development of formal political parties in colonial Massachusetts. They were discussed at the city's public town meetings by its enfranchised males who met to elect town officers and to establish the regulations by which Boston would be governed. With the growth of the town came new needs and demands for a wider range of public facilities and services. Temporary political groupings evolved naturally from this growth.

The varying affiliations of the city's merchants with different trading networks precluded their forging more than passing ties among themselves to accomplish a particular undertaking. The first group to materialize was, instead, the city's popular party, which sought to protect the interests of the common man and New England's unique form of town meeting government against the interests of the city's powerful residents, most of them merchants, gentlemen, and lawyers. Partisan politics did not emerge fully in Boston until the mid-1760s, when the city's economy was threatened by British economic reforms.

During the seventeenth century, the popular response to the establishment of markets in Boston had augured none of the turmoil that was to beset the town between 1719 and 1763. In a fashion that would come to typify the New England Way, the Bostonians remained true to their moral convictions by neglecting to hold the weekly markets decreed to them by the Court of Assistants in 1634.[3] They preferred to purchase from street hawkers who sold country produce door-to-door[4] and used the designated market area to store munitions. Other towns in the region had also neglected to set up marketplaces, but when the establishment of public markets became an economic necessity for them, the transition was made quietly and effectively.[5]

---

3   J. Noble and J.F. Cronin (eds.), *Records of the Court of Assistants of the Colony of the Massachusetts Bay*, Boston 1901-1928, vol. 2, 40.

4   D.H. Flaherty, *Privacy in Colonial New England*, Charlottesville 1967, 167-168.

5   Weekly or biweekly markets were established at Salem (Ms) in 1634 which was short-lived; at Hartford (Cn) in 1643; at Hampton (Nh) in 1655; in Rhode Island at Newport quite sucesfully by 1672 and at Providence as late as 1774. Lynn and Charlestown were established as market towns during the 1630s but the success of their markets is doubtful. In many of these towns,

New York and Philadelphia, Boston's major commercial competitors during the eighteenth century, also adopted markets more readily than the Puritan city. Their markets were integral elements of the local and regional economies that remained popular as well as profitable despite occasional abuses and conflicts.[6] Unlike Boston, both cities were also incorporated boroughs, which meant that the encouragement of commerce was a primary goal of local government. The creation of large, efficient marketing facilities was fundamental to their commercial growth as it had been in the incorporated English boroughs that they were emulating.[7]

Marketing in New York City dates back to the year 1656, when a Saturday market was established for the sale of country produce. In 1658, the city added a second market housed in its own building that specialized in cattle sales. As a result of popular demand and the growth of commerce, there was a steady proliferation of markets in the city throughout the eighteenth century. Its eleven markets – which included speciality markets for fish and meat – were usually leased to individual proprietors who were responsible for the upkeep of the

fairs were held instead of markets during most of the seventeenth century. W.D. Love, *The Colonial History of Hartford*, Hartford 1974, 296-297; J.H. Trumbull and C.J. Hoadly, *The Public Records of the Colony of Connecticut, 1637-1776*, Hartford 1850-1890, vol. 1, 91; J.B. Hedges, *The Browns of Providence Plantations: The Colonial Years*, Providence 1968, 198-199; C. Bridenbaugh, *Cities in the Wilderness: The First Century of Urban Life in America, 1625-1742*, London 1955, 80-81, 278; N. Bouton (ed.), *New Hampshire Provincial Papers: Documents and Records Relating to the Province of New Hampshire from the Earliest Period of Its Settlement*, Concord 1867-1873, vol. 1, 216; J.B. Felt, *Annals of Salem*, 2nd ed., Salem 1845-1849, vol. 2, 204-206; J.D. Cushing (comp.), *The Laws and Liberties of Massachusetts, 1641-1691*, Facsimile, Wilmington 1976, vol. 1, 27, 100; vol. 2, 275.

6   E.g. City of New York, *Minutes of the Common Council*, New York 1905, vol. 5, 242-244; for Pennsylvania, see *Minutes of the Provincial Council*, Philadelphia 1851-1853, vol. 1, 582; *Minutes of the Common Council of the City of Philadelphia: October 1704-October 1776*, Philadelphia 1847, 155; 188, 210, 279.

7   *Pennsylvania, Minutes of the Provincial Council*, vol. 1, 582; *Philadelphia, Minutes of the Common Council*, 155, 188, 210, 279. J.C. Teaford, *The Municipal Revolution in America: Origins of Modern Urban Government, 1650-1825*, Chicago 1975, 16-44 and passim, discusses early American incorporation and marketing at length, his description of the involvement of the New York and Philadelphia governments in their public markets underscores the impact of the municipal borough - particularly in comparison to the liberal, open town meeting style of government followed in Boston

facilities.[8] The tremendous profits to be made by leasing docks located near the markets kept many dock lessees scrambling for available markets as well.[9]

In New York, the commitment to having good, serviceable markets was much greater than it ever was in Boston. The New Yorkers actually enforced their market rules and, when necessary, took decisive steps to control the prices of produce coming into town. New York's markets were also better equipped to serve overseas trade than those of Boston.[10] They drew on a larger, more fertile hinterland that included not only much of the province itself but also Long Island, part of Connecticut, and East Jersey. They could, therefore, support commercial activity on a broader scale than was possible in Massachusetts. The fiscal environment was also better. New York, learning from the difficulties experienced in Massachusetts when it put its provincial bills of credit into circulation, succeeded in establishing and maintaining a more stable provincial currency than that of its competitor. The greatest shortcoming of New York City's market system was that the number of markets created failed to keep pace with its growing population. Despite the inconveniences that this probably caused some individuals, the food supply remained sufficient for local needs throughout the eighteenth century.

William Penn had included a marketplace in his scheme for the founding of Philadelphia, and it was opened shortly after the first colonists began to arrive there. By 1685, there were two weekly markets in operation; they were merged into one market in 1693. Stalls were also erected and market rules similar to those of contemporary New York were instituted.[11] Philadelphia's first real market house was built in1710 as the basement of the city's courthouse. As contrasted to New York's many decentralized markets, a centralized marketing system remained the preferred system for buying and selling commodities in Philadelphia. Only one or two marketplaces existed at any given time during the eighteenth century, but the Quaker city continually expanded the size of its

---

8 New York had, between 1730 and 1750, a market for every 959 to 1,444 persons: E.B. O'Callaghan, *The Documentary History of the State of New York*, Albany 1850-1851, vol. 1, 471-474.

9 George W. Edwards, *New York as an Eighteenth Century Municipality, 1731-1776*, Columbia University Studies in History, Economics and Public Law, Whole Number 178, LXXVI, 2 (New York: AMS Press, 1968), 77-78; City of New York, *Minutes of the Common Council, passim*, but see particularly rentals to John Ellison in volumes I and II, to Bartholomew Skaats in volumes IV to VI, and to Luke Roome in vol. V.

10 The situation in New York never aroused the animosity that it did in Boston although the competition within the provisioning trade did occasionally provoke loud protests and attempts to prevent food exportation during times of shortage; City of New York, *Minutes of the Common Council*, vol. 5, 242-244.

11 Pennsylvania, *Minutes of the Provincial Council*, vol. 1, 317.

marketing facilities.[12] The Philadelphia market became famous in Europe and throughout America for the quality and abundance of its food and for its affordable prices.[13] Like New York, Philadelphia enjoyed a stable provincial currency on which to base its trading activities and possessed a vast, fertile hinterland that was more than adequate to the needs of local consumers and exporters. The townspeople were so secure in the availability of their food supply that they customarily bought only enough provisions to last from one market day to the next.[14] Although Philadelphia, too, experienced commercial abuses including huckstering, regrating, and engrossing as well as direct conflicts between city and country butchers, these problems never provoked the animosity that they did in Boston.

The critical difference between Boston and its competitors was the absence of a food supply adequate to the needs of its population and its lack of saleable trading staples to support its overseas commerce. These two deficiencies not only provoked the conflict between merchants and consumers that plagued the town throughout most of the eighteenth century but also made it possible for the merchants of other American cities and towns to usurp areas of commerce once dominated by Bostonians.[15]

In 1658, a townhouse was built and equipped to hold a formal market. It was constructed at the bequest of the prominent Boston merchant, Robert Keayne, who left £300 in his will for the purpose.[16] Keayne hoped that a formal market structure that provided such amenities as storage areas for unsold produce and warm, dry marketing stalls would encourage country sellers to use it and attract

---

12 [Philadelphia,] *Minutes of the Common Council*, 69-71, 159, 177-179, 187-189, 363, 638, 644, 647, 683-684.

13 W. Black, *Journal, [1744,]* in *Pennsylvania Magazine of History and Biography*, 1 (1877), 504-506; J. Birket, *Some Cursory Remarks Made by James Birket in His Voyage to North America, 1750-51*, New Haven 1916, 69; G. Middleberger, *Gottlieb Middleberger's Journey to Pennsylvania in the Year 1750*, Philadelphia 1898, 65, 70.

14 P. Kalm, *Peter Kalm's Travels in North America*, New York 1937, 30.

15 The cod fisheries and rum distilleries, which may have provided saleable trading staples for the Bostonians and the means for substantial profits for the city's export trade, had been overtaken by competitors from other areas by 1735. See, for example, *Boston Town Records, 1729-1742*, 120-21. Boston's selectmen petitioned the governor and General Court in 1709, 1710, and 1713 to stop abuses by exporters who shipped off goods needed for consumption within the Boston area, but with very limited success: *Selectmen's Minutes, 1701-1715*, 94, 95, 101-102, 106, 194; see also *Acts and Resolves, 1692-1714*, 724-725.

16 R. Keayne, *Apologia: The Last Will and Testament of Me . . .*, ed. B. Bailyn, New York 1964, 7. Keayne's will was executed on December 28, 1653. See *Boston Town Records, 1634-1660*, 132, 134; Massachusetts Historical Society, *Proceedings of the Massachusetts Historical Society*, 1st ser., 337-344; *Boston Town Records, 1660-1701*, 48.

townsmen to the market. Unfortunately, his hopes were not realized; the market failed to draw popular patronage.[17]

In 1696, when Boston's selectmen once again attempted to establish a public market, they changed their approach by trying to prevent the sales of any commodities outside the official market area during the designated market days, Tuesday, Thursday, and Saturday.[18] Townspeople and merchant wholesalers were to be allowed into the markets when they first opened in the morning; hucksters were barred until noon. This market, like Keayne's, fell into popular disuse within a short time. The market building was later destroyed during the Great Fire of 1711.[19]

During the last decade of the seventeenth century, Massachusetts began regularly importing foodstuffs to feed its population of 50,000. Boston, boasting 6,000 residents, had been forced to follow this course in 1690, when it experienced its first food shortage in many years.[20] The participation of the city and province in King William's War had not only depleted the manpower necessary to produce goods but had also siphoned away large quantities of provisions to feed the American forces who participated in the war. By 1714 a town granary had to be created in Boston to ensure that this basic foodstuff would be available to all inhabitants. The granary sold wheat, rye, and Indian corn at a set price per bushel on certain days of the week. Eventually, in 1737, the selectmen were given the right to force grain sales to the town from any vessels sitting in Boston Harbor that might be laden with grain.[21]

17 D. Neal, *The History of New England*, vol. 2, London 1720, 587; J. Josselyn, 'An Account of Two Voyages to New England,' in: *Massachusetts Historical Society, Collections*, 3rd ser., 319.

18 Petition of Boston selectmen to the General Court, May 27, 1696, Massachusetts Archives CXIX, 106, Trade 1645-1754; *Boston Town Records, 1660-1701*, 224; Acts and Resolves, 1692-1714, 237-239.

19 See Captain Uring's comments as quoted in S.G. Drake, *The History and Antiquities of the City of Boston: The Capital and Metropolis of New England. From Its Settlement in 1630 to the Year 1760*, vol. 2, Boston 1854, 555. *Acts and Resolves, 1692-1714*, 253; *Boston Town Records, 1690-1701*, 160; *Selectmen's Minutes, 1742-1753*, 12. Selectmen's petition requesting that markets be set up in Boston, May 27, 1696, Massachusetts Archives, CXIX, 106.

20 See, for example, *Boston Town Records, 1660-1701*, 84, 99; *Selectmen's Minutes, 1701-1715*, 101-102, 106, 143, and 196; B. Walker, Diary, Massachusetts Historical Society, particularly the entries for March 1733, June 1735, March 1737, April 1741, July 1744, and April 1747. Nash, *The Urban Crucible*, 57-60, 315.

21 See *Boston Town Records, 1700-1728*, 99, 206, and 210 for proposals regarding the granary; see also *ibid.*, 84, 101, 110-111, 113, 121, 127, 131, 163, 171, 185, and 197 for examples of efforts to secure grain. There had been privately-run granaries in Boston before the public ones were established. See *Selectmen's Minutes, 1701-1715*, 19, 174; *Selectmen's Minutes, 1736-1742*, 79.

The year 1719 produced a full-length disquisition on the subject of public markets for Boston. The Reverend Benjamin Colman, pastor of the wealthy Brattle Street Church, attempted to launch a discussion promoting re-establishment of markets in the city by publishing his pamphlet, *Some Reasons and Arguments Offered to the Good People of Boston and Adjacent Places for the Setting Up Markets in Boston*. The pamphlet reflected the ideas then being debated among the merchants in his congregation and Colman's belief in the superiority and primacy of merchant interests in Boston. He envisioned a market where possible transactions between farmers and chapmen could be initiated based on small samples of produce brought into the market.[22] Colman believed that the promise of large sales to merchant exporters would motivate farmers to produce more provisions without prompting them to raise their prices. In his sophisticated, affluent markets, luxury items would also be available for purchase by the town's wealthy residents. He chastised Boston's poor and middling residents against aspiring to compete for these goods with those more privileged. Like the previous attempts to popularize marketing in Boston, Colman's effort failed to attract adequate support, and the issue was dropped for another thirteen years.

Competition for provisions between exporters and consumers varied according to the nature of the commodity in question. During this era, the average colonial diet consisted primarily of starches supplemented by 20% dairy products, 20% meat, and 10% fish, fruits and vegetables. Poorer families consumed a proportion of breadstuffs higher than the 50% average.[23] Since farming in eastern Massachusetts was small-scale and unsophisticated, fruits and vegetables were available in Boston in limited quantities.[24] The highly perishable

---

22 This is the only place in the market literature where explicit mention is made of such arrangements, but it is implied elsewhere. Colman did not consider contracting of goods to be a source of conflict. B. Colman, *Some Reasons and Arguments Offered to the Good People of Boston and Adjacent Places for the Setting Up Markets in Boston*, [Boston 1719] or *Boston Gazette*, 19 and 26 February 1733.

23 L. Harper, *Consumption Study, Introduction* [unpubl. research project report, Dept. of History, Univ. of California, Berkeley 1961], 11-13; K.J. Friedmann, 'Victualling Colonial Boston,' in: *Agricultural History*, 47 (1973), 189-205 passim; C. Bridenbaugh, 'The High Cost of Living in Boston, 1728,' in: *The New England Quarterly*, 5 (1932), 800-811 passim. The most frequently consumed food items in colonial Boston included bread, milk, butter, cheese; Indian corn, peas, onions, roots including turnips and on occasion, carrots; flour, sugar, molasses, rice; fish; small amounts of poultry, meat including fresh and barreled beef and pork, mutton; lamb and veal, which were considered luxury items; apples, dried fruits such as raisins, currants, and cranberries; and lemons, which were a luxury item.

24 The soil in New England had been virtually exhausted by the turn of the eighteenth century. Active attempts to renourish it were not common, farm labor scarce, and farming practices were still relatively primitive. The owner of an average 100-acre farm could cultivate only 6.4 to

quality of these foods, the need to consume them within weeks after ripening, and their availability throughout the Atlantic seaboard made them poor export commodities. Onions and peas, on the other hand, had good longevity and became important basic staples for export since they could be used to feed the vast markets of consumers that included military personnel and slaves.

Merchants made their greatest profits through their sales of salted meats – a particularly important victualling item for the military. Salted pork or beef could be stored in barrels for several months so could be shipped to Europe and the West Indies where they would bring handsome prices. Boston's merchants preferred to purchase salted meat in the markets from country butchers, who charged prices lower than those demanded by the city's butchers.[25]

Crowd action often occurred during particularly difficult times in pre-Revolutionary Boston and was used occasionally to prevent legal exportations of foodstuffs that townsmen considered immoral. For example, in 1706, 1710, and 1713, Andrew Belcher and his son Jonathan, the future governor of the province, were accused of not only exporting food during a period of shortage but also of shipping it to enemy ports. Angry townsmen retaliated by commandeering their ship on one occasion and by ransacking their warehouse on another.[26]

The demand for meat in Boston was so great that the city's butchers enjoyed a thriving trade despite the competition from country sellers. This was not due to their reasonable prices, high quality, or exemplary service, but buyers had few alternatives. Efforts to enhance the fishing trade so that it could support retail sales failed. The Massachusetts fishing industry – particularly the commerce in

---

12.8 acres of it - depending on the soil - and would have to either leave the remaining 87.2 acres dormant or use it for pasturage. Of the 6.4 to 12.8 acres planted, some of the tilled portion was used to raise food for the farm household itself, which averaged seven people. M.G. Schumacher, *The Northern Farmer and His markets during the Late Colonial Period,* New York 1975, 24.

25 It is probable that Boston's butchers and victuallers were among the regular complainants against the prices and activities of the country butchers in the public markets. They opposed the markets in Boston because they facilitated townsmen's access to country butchers. When the markets were open, the town butchers - who were not allowed into the market yard because it was feared that their presence would discourage their country counterparts from occupying stalls - always crowded the immediate environs of the market squares making themselves and their meat dressing habits a source of annoyance to fellow townsmen. They became such a nuisance that in 1734, only three weeks after the markets had been re-opened, a petition against the town's butchers containing twenty-four signatures was submitted. Petition to the Freeholders and other Inhabitants of the Town of Boston, 25 June 1734, Original Papers, 61, 61A-61B, CAPBL.

26 See Massachusetts Archives, LXII, 534 and LXIII, 151. For discussions of these conflicts G.B. Nash, *The Urban Crucible: Social Change, Political Consciousness, and the Origins of the American Revolution,* Cambridge 1979, 77-80.

salted fish – grew steadily but continued to cater primarily to the province's export trade.[27]

Whether or not Boston's markets were in operation, its swindlers thrived. The townsmen remained powerless to control these cheats largely because many of them were the employees of the city's powerful merchants. The laws passed and fines set by numerous town meetings to battle forestallers, regrators, engrossers, and hucksters had no substantial effect. Even fines designed to discourage the sale of adulterated meat failed.[28] The first law against marketing abuses was passed in May 1711 to counter the dearth of supplies produced by the expedition to Port Royal during the previous year. It had been in force for only a few weeks when an emergency call was made in June to provide men and provisions for another expedition.[29] The lust for wartime trading profits again overwhelmed the needs of townsmen for a proper supply of food.

The Boston Neck, a small peninsula 120 feet wide between the Charles River and Boston Bay that linked Boston to the mainland, was particularly notorious as the site of many abuses against the Boston markets. It held the affection of forestallers, regrators, engrossers, and others interested in illegal transactions for provisions who frequented it throughout the century. It was also favoured by sabbath-breaking shoppers who would stop to buy from the farmers who waited there and then continue on to the farms of nearby Roxbury in search of food and

---

27 L. Harper, *Import-export index to the Massachusetts segment of Colonial Office 5 for the period, May 1686 to January 1760* [inconsecutive; unpubl. research project, Dept. of History, Univ. of California, Berkeley, n.d.); R.C. Berner, *"the Means of Paying for Colonial New England's Imports"*, (M.A.-thesis, Univ. of California, Berkeley 1960), 9-1. After lumber, wood products, and European goods, fish was Boston's most profitable export or re-export commodity. The production levels of the city's cod fisheries were surpassed by competitors during the mid-1730s, but the port remained New England's premier exporter of fish for another generation. *Boston Town Records, 1742-1757*, 221.

28 The town order passed ca. 1713, which levied a 20 shilling fine against anyone selling bad milk or meat within the city bounds, was typical: "Ordered, that every such person or persons that at any time or times hereafter within the Neck or town of Boston shall presume to sell and offer to sale any sort of meat of what nature or kind soever that is perishing or that is not fit for sale shall forfeit and pay the sum of 20 shillings for every transgression of this order to the help of the poor of this town." Town Papers, 1713-1733, 29, City Archives, Boston Public Library (CABPL hereafter).

29 Victuallers' petition, 1 July 1735, Original Papers, 1715-1734, 62, CAPBL; Town Meeting Minutes, 25 June 1734, Original Papers, 1715-1734, CAPBL; *Selectmen's Minutes, 1701-1715*, 94-95, 101-102, 106, 143; T. Hutchinson, *The History of the Colony and Province of Massachusetts-Bay*, ed. L. Shaw Mayo, vol. 2, Cambridge (Ma) 1936, 142; Nash, *The Urban Crucible*, 59.

goods for their households.[30] In 1743 and again in 1745, watches were set up to prevent townspeople from trading outside Boston, but they failed to have any lasting effect.[31] Whether or not the markets were open, determined, enterprising Bostonians always found their way out to the Neck and beyond in search of bargains.

Although the Bostonians attempted to promote the use of officially set weights and measures – particularly for transactions involving wood, coal, and foodstuffs – they failed to discourage the employment of steelyards and other fallacious weights and measures. The temptation towards dishonesty – like the temptation to sell adulterated meat – was too much to resist for many of those trying to make a sale among rich Bostonians. *Caveat emptor* persisted in the City upon a Hill.

The effort by the *Boston Gazette* to begin publishing the daily prices of selected provisions in 1719 was aborted immediately, probably in response to pressures from powerful merchants trying to protect their position as buyers.[32] The fact that the listing included important export trade items such as barreled meat, butter, cheese, hay, wheat, and Indian corn explains the speed of the merchants' actions. They argued that any prices published would necessarily be inaccurate since prices were constantly changing and varied widely throughout Boston on any given day. It is also obvious that the opportunity for comparison and uniformity in pricing that would have been promoted by publishing price lists would have impaired the merchants' ability to manipulate food prices. By making it possible for readers to estimate the just prices of individual items before going to the markets to shop for them, these listings would have made it more difficult for merchants to outbid townsmen when buying large quantities for export (and to maintain profit margins at resale). The country produce sellers who connived with the merchants in wholesaling transactions would have lost handsome profits as well.[33]

---

30 A. Haven Thwing, *The Crooked and Narrow Streets of the Town of Boston, 1620-1822*, Boston 1920, map facing page 228; 228-231.

31 By 1738, the problem had become so serious that Chief Justice Benjamin Lynde asked the Grand Jury to investigate. It is noteworthy that the jury sidestepped the judge's request. Nash, *The Urban Crucible*, 454, note 14; *Selectmen's Minutes, 1729-1742*, 31, 117.

32 See, for example, the *New York Mercury* for the years 1753 to 1761 for market price lists. Attempts to control prices in Boston date back nearly to the founding of the port when, in November 1635, William Hutchinson, William Colborne, and William Breton were appointed to set the prices for all cattle, commodities, and victuals as well as the wages paid to laborers and certain tradesmen. The effort was short-lived. *Boston Town Records, 1634-1660*, 5.

33 Without knowledge of current prices, it was impossible for anyone to determine what, precisely, constituted the just price for any given commodity. Farmers wanting to sell dear or merchants buying cheap or dear - depending on their needs - could negotiate among themselves

In February 1733, Boston's merchants used Benjamin Colman's pamphlet from 1719, *Reasons and Argument* ... to revive the issue of markets for the city.[34] Having caught at a disadvantage the powerful Elisha Cooke faction, which had led the previous onslaught against markets, they were able to push through the town meeting a vote in favour of re-opening the markets. A record number of voters attended, and the vote was a close one, 364 to 339.[35] The rules passed were strict and provided a solid basis for regulating Boston's markets. There were three designated market locations: at Dock Square, at the North End, and at the South End. The new markets were to be open six days a week from sunrise to sunset. Meat, grain, fish, apples, onions, turnips, milk, and cider – major items in the Bostonians' diet – could be sold outside the markets as previously. Unwholesome, stale, blown, or leprous meat was not to be exposed for sale; fines for violations of the market rules were set at 20 shillings per offense.

Although the pro-market men had rallied their forces successfully after the setback of June 26, 1733, their victory was short-lived. The new market rules failed to receive confirmation by the Massachusetts Court of General Sessions of the Peace in April 1734. The final, revised version of the rules submitted that month was considerably weaker than the initial draft and the guidelines to promote and strengthen the three new markets in Boston were no longer adequate. Only in their restraint of hucksters and retailers were the new rules as rigorous as the old ones. This was probably due to the petition submitted to the town meeting in June that sought to keep the butchers out of the markets – and thus from huckstering for their retailing interests.[36] Forestalling and engrossing, the practices most useful to merchants seeking to preempt large quantities of foodstuffs continued unrestricted.

---

freely and to the satisfaction of both parties under these circumstances. The stigma of usury could be sidestepped. The diary of Benjamin Walker, a Boston shopkeeper who took a great interest in the cost of provisions between 1728 and 1749, is the most comprehensive list of provisions prices for provincial Boston currently available, moreover with comments on possible determintants. Walker's diary provides evidence that neither the value of money in Massachusetts nor the opening or closing of the public markets necessarily affected provisions prices. The diary of Reverend William Smith of Weymouth includes yearly prices for beef, pork, wheat, Indian corn, and rye for the period, 1737 to 1763, and also includes a small amount of commentary. His price quotations are in agreement with those recorded by Benjamin Walker. Diary of Benjamin Walker, June 1768 to July 1759, Massachusetts Historical Society; Diary of Reverend William Smith, 1728 to 1763, Massachusetts Historical Society.

34 *Boston Gazette*, 19 February and 26 February 1733.
35 *Boston Town Records, 1739-1742*, 46-48.
36 Petition against Boston's butchers, 25 June 1734, Original Papers, 1715-1734, Boston Public Library, 46-48 for the first market rules proposed, 80-82 for the final revised rules. The wealthy district of Rumney Marsh, which had desired a total separation from Boston, was specifically exempted from participating in the marketing plan.

Boston's three markets remained open for only twenty-three months after their inauguration. In March 1735, the first petition against them was submitted to the town meeting but failed by a wide margin.[37] By the meeting of 11 March 1736, the gap between the opposing sides had closed. Under the leadership of Elisha Cooke, Jr., once again the moderator, the employment of market clerks and the ringing of the market bells were discontinued, thereby effectively shutting down the markets. Although John Checkley's motion to reconsider this decision carried by three votes later during the same day, it lost at the vote, 278 to 398, and Boston's public markets were closed.[38]

The climax of the argument over markets in Boston occurred at midnight on March 24, 1737 when approximately one hundred townsmen dressed in clerical gowns dismantled the Middle Market at Dock Square, sawed apart the floor in the North Market House, and destroyed several butcher shops located near both markets (the South Market House was left intact).[39] This event was followed by a successful petition that the market buildings be put to another use.[40] Governor Belcher's efforts to locate the culprits behind the destruction met with a threat of full-scale rioting and murder by "above Five Hundred Men in solemn League and Covenant." The sheriff and his deputy were also threatened. Even when closed, the markets posed a menace to the opposition. Talk at the time of reopening just one market drew additional threats.[41]

The significance of the clerical gowns donned by the rioters has been a matter of speculation among historians. It is most probable that the gowns were meant to insult Reverend Benjamin Colman, author of the pamphlet that had championed the creation of public markets in Boston. Since the markets had been closed during the eleven months previous to the riot, it is probable that the pro-market faction had grown in strength and was on the verge of pressing to reopen them before the end of the annual town meeting. The hard winter of 1736-1737 and the food and fuel shortage, which had already been the occasion

---

37 *Boston Town Records, 1739-1742*, 98.
38 *Boston Town Records, 1739-1742*, 133-136; *Selectmen's Minutes, 1716-1736*, 288, 318-319. The clerks were paid for their services and then dismissed. Assertions by modern authors that the use of paper money was also banned from the markets at this time have not been substantiated. G.B. Warden, *Boston 1689-1776*, Boston 1970, 120-121.
39 *Boston Evening Post*, 20 June 1737; *Boston Newsletter*, 24 March - 5 April and 15-21 April 1737. Benjamin Walker reported the riot in his diary and estimated the number of rioters to be 200; Walker, *Diary*, entry for 24 March 1737. For comments regarding the high meat prices, see the *Boston Evening Post*, 21 March 1737.
40 Petition to the Selectmen of Boston to Appropriate the Markets to Some Other Use, 30 March 1737, Loose Papers, 1709/10-1747, Box 4, 20, CAPBL; *Boston Town Records, 1729-1742*, 164, 170-172.
41 *Boston Newsletter*, April 14-21, 1737.

for grain rationing and closer regulation of hay and wood transactions, may have provided the needed impetus for the anti-market vigilantes to take action.[42] They probably expected the reopening of the markets to exacerbate the food shortage. Their efforts to keep the markets closed, like those of the merchants to keep the markets open, succeeded for only a few years.

Since both sides of the market controversy were evenly matched in strength, neither was able to remain predominant in Boston for very long – consequently the erratic opening and closing of the public markets. The votes in the town meetings and the petitioning that occurred between 1733 and 1763 reflect this instability.[43]

The pro-market faction attracted very little popular support but succeeded in rallying an unusually large segment of the city's merchants as well as many prominent lawyers and gentlemen. Most of these men were exporters, importers, and shipowners who could benefit from the presence of public markets.

Those against the markets enjoyed wide popular support and, consequently, were in a better position to manipulate voting in the town meetings. This group drew much of its primary impetus from the political machine of the wealthy Dr. Elisha Cooke, Jr., from 1733 until 1737, when Cooke died.[44] The Cooke organization undoubtedly had a hand in undermining the original market rules of 1733, in promoting the riot of March 1737, and in organizing the closure of the markets in April 1737. Although such highly organized protests against the markets did not take place after 1737, their antagonists continued to successfully rally support from many of Boston's unenfranchised males.

Attempts to establish public markets in Boston after the successful effort of March 1733 would come in July 1740, March 1748, August 1752, July 1759, February 1762, and May 1763. Besides February 1735 and March 1737, major arguments for the closure of Boston's markets would surface in September 1740, February 1742, March 1747, February 1752, and April 1752. The petitions introduced in each of these instances were produced in response to the city's current marketing problems and the blame placed conveniently on the presence or absence of formal markets. The petitions were not circulated in response to

---

42 See, for example, *Boston Town Records, 1729-1742*, 153; 155-156. Additionally, there had been a lingering threat of smallpox aboard ships arriving from Philadelphia and London that extended from the fall of 1736 through the spring of 1737. See *Selectmen's Minutes, 1736-1742*, 15, 16, 18, 33, 34. The city was also having financial problems and had to borrow money from Edward Hutchinson; *Selectmen's Minutes, 1736-1742*, 6-7.

43 A larger number of petitions were actually generated in favour of the markets than against them. The higher level of political activity among market supporters accounts for this.

44 The fact that the vote establishing markets was carried during a town meeting at which Cooke was moderator attests to the comparable strength of the two sides.

each other or solely to open or close the markets. Throughout the thirty years of conflict, both sides used duplicate arguments about the connection of the markets to abuses in buying and selling and about the impact of markets on the city's economy. The accuracy of these assertions varied with the changes in marketing conditions from year to year.

Those who favoured the establishment of marketplaces in Boston frequently cited the fact that the city was the only major port in America – probably in the British world – without proper markets. This group perceived the creation of markets to be economic progress and a means of enhancing Boston's reputation as the centre of British civilization in America. They argued that buyers would no longer have to wait indefinitely at home for a hawker to pass by or waste time searching for the necessary commodity; instead, householders could go to the market and purchase what they wanted. Servants being sent to make purchases there could not easily loiter in their errand if expected back within an easily estimated amount of time. In a formal marketplace, shoppers could make comparisons and find bargains, thus saving money and forcing food producers to maintain the quality of their goods. Farmers could be saved the indignity of running about town, loudly hawking their goods and, with the time that would be saved, they could return home to other labours.

The detractors of the markets complained strongly against the market tolls and taxes. They believed that markets, as areas of congregation, would provoke arguments and disorder, encourage loitering and lying among vendors and servants, and would foster materialism among the populace. Their primary concern – based on the belief that the demand for foodstuffs in Boston was greater than the supply – was that the presence of markets would make townsmen vulnerable to the exorbitant prices charged by farmers.[45] They also feared that the opening of marketplaces in specific locations throughout the city would draw business away from other areas.[46] This group did not accept the argument that Boston would be considered a backward frontier outpost if it had no markets.

---

45 W. Chauncey Ford (ed.), 'Communication of Two Documents Protesting against the Incorporation of Boston,' in: *Publications of the Colonial Society of Massachusetts, Transactions* 1904-1906, 10 (1907), 346-347. See especially "A Dialog between a Boston Man and a Country Man," [1714], 346. I question the assertion by Warden that merchants wanted to establish public markets to use them as a means of outselling the farmers. Boston's merchants were not allowed to sell in the markets and retailers were not allowed to make purchases in the markets until after the ringing of the second bell, which signaled that private buyers and wholesalers had completed their purchases. Warden, *Boston 1689-1776*, 54.

46 The fact that most shopkeepers had a regular clientele and relied primarily on bookkeeping credits and debits in their business transactions challenges this argument. The goods available and terms of credit were more important factors in attracting business.

The farmers who sold produce in Boston initially opposed the public markets because they feared that they would be unable to sell their goods at a reasonable profit. They also resented the idea of carrying out transactions under the observation of market clerks whose presence they interpreted as a judgment of their untrustworthiness.[47] They quickly realized, though, that the demand for produce in Boston was, in fact, greater than the supply, that it would continue to be so, and that they could make handsome profits within the system.

The early 1740s appeared to be a particularly propitious time for Boston's merchants. Despite their differing individual trading interests, they remained unified in the wake of a monetary crisis that ruptured the entire region and were still enjoying the active political support of Governor Jonathan Belcher as well as that of the elitist advocate of merchant interests, Thomas Hutchinson, Jr., who was returned to the Assembly. Their efforts to improve public works in Boston – including creation of a workhouse to put the dependent poor to work, construction of a bridge, and passage of new laws to combat deception in fuel sales – had succeeded.[48] In mid-1740, a group of them solicited a gift from the prominent merchant, Peter Faneuil, to finance a new market house for Boston.

The matter required a vote in the town meeting. It drew a record turnout of participants and onlookers. Although the gift would cost the town nothing and a concession had been made to allow street hawkers to continue selling produce outside the market, the vote was uncomfortably close, 367 to 360.[49] The merchants, prepared for a struggle and intent on ensuring success, had asked the municipal assessors to attend the meeting with their valuation lists in hand to

---

47 The people of Watertown voted to boycott the Boston markets in 1734 and levied a 20 shilling fine on any townsman who failed to comply. See [Watertown Historical Society, comp. and ed.,] *Watertown Records, Comprising the Fourth Book of Town Proceedings and the Second Book of Births, Marriages, and Deaths, from 1738 to 1833*, Boston 1904, 106-108.

48 *Boston Town Records, 1729-1742*, 223-34, 259-260; 312-313; Petition to the Selectmen to Make a Further Representation of the Distressing Circumstances of the Town and Their Inability to pay the Tax Now Laid on Them to the House of Representatives, *ca.* December 27, 1742, Town papers, 1741-1748, 51, CAPBL. The population of Boston was approximately 17,000 in 1740; there were 3,043 polls in the city that year which suggests a voting population of basically the same size. Bostonians with estates valued at £ or more who were age twenty-four or older were allowed to vote. By 1742, Boston's population had declined to 16,382; of that, there were 1,375 slaves. The city had 1,719 houses. New York and Philadelphia, by comparison, each had slightly more than 9,000 residents in 1740. *Boston Record Commissioners, Report 22: Statistics of the United States' Direct Tax of 1798*, Boston 1890, iv; *Selectmen's Minutes, 1736-1742*, 369-370; Nash, *The Urban Crucible*, 102; *Acts and Resolves, 1692-1714*, 65; Cushing (comp.), *The Laws and Liberties of Massachusetts, 1641-1691*, vol. 2, 56.

49 *Boston Town Records, 1729-1742*, 259-260.

prevent unenfranchised persons from casting ballots.[50] This tactic was challenged later by one hundred and seventy-five members of the market opposition who presented a petition questioning the validity of the vote two months later.[51] They asserted that the screening of voters by tax assessors was neither fair nor legal and that the vote was, therefore, invalid. At no other time was a market vote challenged in this way. The petition was forwarded to Jonathan Read, one of Boston's most prominent lawyers. Read's legal opinion was that the vote had been legal and was binding upon the town. He suggested that no further action be taken on the petition. Boston's selectmen followed his advice.[52]

A formal petition to shut Faneuil Hall Market was presented in May 1746, but it was not until April 1747 that a four-month closure was actually effected. The markets did not reopen in September of that year but instead remained shut until September 1748. During these months, provisions prices rose steadily and forestalling and engrossing practices remained rampant. Boston's merchants appropriated goods for illegal export to France and Spain as well as for the legal trade to Louisbourg while the city's trade and economy deteriorated in the face of growing expenditures for warfare and poor relief.

In March 1747/48, an attempt was made to reopen Faneuil Hall Market, but the opening was delayed again. Faneuil Hall Market was finally reopened in April 1748 under new rules. The town's economic fortunes, meanwhile, continued to deteriorate. March 1752 produced a petition to close the markets and to appoint a special committee to "Consider what Method is best for the Inhabitants to take in order to Reduce the present Excessive price of Provisions, and to prevent the persons, [sic] that bring provisions for Sale to Town, Incumbering the Lands and Highways about and near to Faneuil Hall market and the Nusances [sic] on Dock Square. ..."[53]

In July 1759, the pro-market faction carried a vote, 158 to 132, to reopen Faneuil Hall Market. With the reopening, they presented a new by-law and introduced shortened hours – their strategy being to give farmers less time in which to make sales thereby forcing them to sell sooner at lower prices. This

---

50 *Boston Town Records*, 260.

51 Subscription to the Gentlemen the Selectmen of the Town of Boston to Consider Whether to Adhere to the Vote Accepting Peter Faneuil's Gift of a Market, 10 September 1740, Loose Papers, 1709/10-1747, Box 5, 1, CAPBL. The petition was signed by 175 people.

52 Jonathan Read, Legal Opinion Concerning Boston Markets, 17 September 1740, Loose Papers, 1709/10-1747, Box 5, 2-3,CAPBL.

53 *Boston Town Records, 1742-1757*, 208-209, 213-215.

new rule was reinforced by a prohibition against sales of provisions in the area of Dock Square after the market had closed for the day.[54] Throughout the next eighteen months, an undercurrent of tension over markets continued in Boston. The Great Boston Fire of March 1760 diverted the attention of most townsmen away from them. Faneuil Hall suffered no damage in this fire. On January 13, 1761, though, Faneuil Hall, including the market area, was gutted by fire. This fire may have been an inspired solution to a problem that the market opposition believed had gone out of control. The destruction of the town hall section of the building was probably an unfortunate by-product of the fire. Not to be caught unawares, the anti-market faction immediately blocked the repair of Faneuil Hall Market on March 23rd when the vote to renovate the rest of the building was passed.

More than two years lapsed before a vote to repair the market section of Faneuil Hall succeeded. It came in May 1763, two months after the town had resumed holding its annual meeting in the building. Financing for the repairs had to be raised by lottery rather than by subscription, which suggests that the opposition to the markets remained strong. The absence of a wealthy patron to voluntarily pay the costs for repair of Faneuil's building may have been due to the merchants' preoccupation with the arguments over the writs of assistance, the controversy over Benjamin Barons, and the series of ship seizures that had been carried out by local customs officials against several prominent merchants – all critical issues that threatened their livelihoods directly. Their interests in the markets had begun to wane for other reasons as well. Boston's export trade had continued to deteriorate throughout the 1750s. Meanwhile, its import trade was thriving. During the 1760s, this trend consolidated further. The markets had lost their importance as a source of export commodities.[55]

The increase in the import business being enjoyed by Boston's merchants is evident in the shipping records. During the years 1714 and 1717, 2,100 bushels of grain were imported to help feed the province's 80,000 residents. By the 1760s, the population of Massachusetts had tripled to 240,000. Had its need for

---

54 Petition to Reopen Faneuil Hall Market, July 1759, Loose Papers, 1747-1761, Box 11, 9; Report of the Committee to Consider Further Regulations Touching Faneuil Hall Market, [ca. 27 July 1769,] Loose Papers, 1747-1761, Box 11, 22, CAPBL; *Boston Town Records, 1758-1769*, 27, 28, 29, 30-31. The market supporters' promotion of shortened market hours was significant as an acknowledgement of the opposition's correct assessment that some of the problems in the marketplace were due to selling periods that were too long.

55 The selectmen had actually resumed their meetings in Faneuil Hall in October 1762, which suggests that the section of the building that housed the town offices had been repaired completely by that date. *Selectmen's Minutes, 1754-1763*, 143; 226; *Boston Town Records, 1758-1769*, 54, 90.

grain remained uniform to the earlier pattern, only 6,300 bushels would have been necessary. The change, though, was drastic. During the years 1761 to 1765, 250,000 bushels of grain had to be brought in to the province to feed its populace.[56]

Although the import trade was booming to the benefit of the province's merchants, particularly those in Boston, this increase in grain importation signaled the severity of economic difficulties that many other residents were experiencing. The number of impoverished individuals in need of public assistance had grown throughout Massachusetts; it was worst in Boston.[57] The high level of grain sales probably reflects greater per capita consumption of starches and a heavier reliance on breads and grain-based meals as a source of nutrition.[58]

Boston, always in the forefront of the bad as well as the good that visited eighteenth-century Massachusetts, faced an onslaught in the 1760s. In addition to province-wide problems, the Bostonians had to recover from the Great Fire of 1760, faced a smallpox epidemic, and saw their city become heavily involved in the French and Indian War. In June 1759, the selectmen had been forced to borrow money at interest from private creditors to cover basic town expenses and the burgeoning costs of the almshouse and welfare relief. They had to ask

---

56   See C.O. 5/918-921, Entry Books, 1714-1774, 916-1143; Boston specifically, is covered on pages 916-938, 1047-1087, 1115-1118. See also C.O. 5/848-851, Abstracts of English Shipping Records Relating to Massachusetts Ports, from Original Records in the Public Record Office, London, Compiled for the Essex Institute, Salem, Massachusetts, 1686-1719, 1752-1756, 1752 [sic]-1765, and 1756-1762. See e.g. pages 192-212, 213-219; 238-239, 240-245; 269-272, 273-283 which present cargoes and ports.

57   This is obvious from a reading of the annual accounts of the Massachusetts treasury, specifically, the dischargeth sections for each year. The province reimbursed its towns and private residents for the maintenance of poor and distracted individuals. There are also entries showing reimbursements for sending impoverished families as well as individuals back to their places of origin - in Britain as well as in other English colonies. By the time one reaches the accounts of the 1770s, payments for public welfare constitute the majority of entries. See microfilm copies of the Massachusetts treasury accounts for the years 1761-1773 available from Massachusetts Archives and from the Public Record Office. Massachusetts Archives Collection, vol. 125, Treasury, 1759-1770, dischargeth sections located on pages 310-324, 333-335, 349-360, 374-394; Public Record Office, Colonial Office 5: C.O. 5/853, 197A-226B; C.O. 5/854 9B-35A, 44B-70A, 79B-98A, 106B-121B, 131B-144A, 154A-164B, 174A-183B, 190B-199B, 207B-214A; C.O. 5/894, 90B-100B, 112B-119B; C.O. 5/895, 18B-25A, 99A-107A. The Great Fire of 1760 had produced such a large number of sufferers that the province provided it with funds to assist in the recovery. This was supplemented by donations pouring in from outside the province to aid the victims. Some of the individual losses were recorded and can be read on microfilm available from Boston Public Library. Ms. Am. 1809 (1-211), Town Papers 1760, and Town Papers 1759-1764, nos. 60-133, CAPBL.

58   Nash, *The Urban Crucible,* 315; Harper, *Consumption Study,* 11-13.

for help from private creditors again in March 1763 and began seeking ways to reduce the city's annual expenses.[59]

While the markets were closed, Dock Square had continued to function as a marketing area, market clerks were still elected to office, and the complaints about markets continued. The next re-opening of Faneuil Hall Market was significant for the quiet that surrounded it.[60] There were no new market rules and the conflict between consumers and exporters had finally dissipated. Boston's populace, now united in its hostility towards the country sellers, finally gave the selectmen and market clerks adequate powers to enforce the market rules. Price controls were imposed, stall rentals were resurrected, and the behaviour of the country sellers was monitored closely. By April 1765, Faneuil Hall Market was providing Boston with substantial profits and the complaints about the markets had been reduced considerably.[61]

Despite the strict regulations, the country sellers continued to frequent the markets. The advantage of selling in well-known, centralized locations in the city outweighed the freedom of walking about town trying to make sales. Boston's public markets had become popular areas for transacting business in their own right. Traffic congestion in and around Faneuil Hall Market finally led to the enlargement of adjacent streets and the opening of additional market areas.[62]

---

59 *Acts and Resolves*, 1757-1768, 515-516; *Boston Town Records, 1758-1769*, 53, 102-103, 110 (smallpox); 119-122 (trading acts); 29, 85 (loans). In 1759, the town solicited as much money as it could get on loan and in 1763, it sought £900 for the almshouse.

60 The exact date of the reopening is not evident from the records. It probably occurred in mid-1764. See *Boston Town Records 1758-1769*, 90 and *Selectmen's Minutes 1764-1768*, 101. The latter citation suggests that the markets had reopened by August 1764.

61 Stalls rented for 6.3 shillings to 10 shillings Legal Money per month - slightly higher than the fees of 1742; *Selectmen's Minutes, 1764-1768*, 101, 104, 108. Between May and October 1765, the market earned £549.19.02 Old Tenor and from October to December that same year, an additional £695.14.00 was earned. This money was collected from salespeople for their use of the market facilities and included fees for setting up stands, wharfage, taxes levied on beef and hides brought to market, and so forth. The profits were used to pay for the repairs to Faneuil Hall following the 1761 fire. *Selectmen's Minutes 1764-1768*, 145; Miscellaneous Accounts and Receipts of Cash Revenue from Faneuil Hall Market, 1765, Town Papers, 1765-1776, 2B-3C, 311.

62 *Boston Town Records, 1758-1769*, 48, 58; *Selectmen's Minutes, 1754-1763*, 142; Petition to the Selectmen for Repairing Faneuil Hall Market and Purchasing the Adjacent Lands in Order to Enlarge the Square Around the market and Fill in the Dock, March 2, 1761, Loose Papers, 1761-1767, Box 12, 44, CAPBL; Petition to the Selectmen to See That the Dock is Filled As May be Judged Proper and Necessary, Allowing the Abutters Adequate Compensation for Any Inconvenience It May Be to Them, August 1761, Loose Papers, 1761-1767, Box 13, 52, CAPBL. *Boston Town Records, 1758-1769*, 19, 23, 27, 48, 64-65, 86, 88, 90, 305-308.

Although a petition requesting that Boston's markets be closed or properly regulated surfaced in 1778, the markets were, by that time, an accepted fact of life in the city. In 1783, a town ordinance restricting provisions transactions to prescribed marketing areas in Boston was passed.[63]

Improvements in communication and transportation occurring in the eighteenth century not only made it possible for more people to participate in buying and selling but also tightened the bonds between men living throughout the Atlantic trading world. There was growth in consumer demand and also in the ability to satisfy that demand despite the increased distances between producers and consumers. Agriculture became commercialized and labour forces more mobile and independent in response to the evolution in business.

The intensification of trade and the accompanying commercialization of agriculture produced fundamental changes in the social as well as economic structures of the societies that were part of that world. The improvements in communications and the technological advances eroded the old mercantilist restraints and gave the broader marketplace a new, more self-perpetuating character. Incentives to engage in highly profitable petty machinations led many to turn their backs on traditional standards of morality; people found that great wealth was no longer the inherited prerogative of a few but was within the reach of anyone with intelligence, stamina, and opportunity. The fabulously wealthy John Erving, who had come to Boston in 1706 as a poor sixteen-year old sailor was living proof of this possibility.

Not only did individual interest gain respectability because it fostered creativity and progress but it also finally took precedence over the collective interest – with the *de facto* blessings of the larger society. Eighteenth-century merchants began to believe that what was best for them was best for their community and, to a large extent, this became true. Accumulation of money and luxuries was easier but the danger of financial ruin was also greater. The increased interdependence between debtors and creditors that was nurtured by the expansion and diversification of business meant that a monetary disaster in one part of the world would affect persons living thousands of miles away within a matter of months. In the context of purely local business, financial vulnerability was heightened through the expanding economic interconnections.

The Bostonians were full participants in the transition. The desire for material acquisition and the Puritan work ethic complemented the drive towards financial success. In the course of pursuing their ambitions, the city's merchants promoted the creation of public markets that they could use to facilitate their procurement of goods for sale outside the city and otherwise encroached on the

---

63 *Boston Town Records, 1778-1783*, 301-304.

needs of their fellow townsmen. Even those who sought to preserve traditional institutions and values found that to survive, if not to improve their prospects, they had to adjust to the changes.

Letwin has said that " ... every economic act, being the act of a human being, is necessarily a moral act," and the events in Boston confirm his words.[64] The abuses by the city's forestallers, regrators, and engrossers and the insistence of its merchants on exporting foodstuffs during times of shortage are glaring examples of actions that were economically acceptable but morally questionable. Although endemic to public marketplaces throughout Britain and America, forestalling, huckstering, and similar problems seem to have been more rampant in Boston than elsewhere because local arguments over the markets and their general unpopularity had made it impossible to enforce even minimal market regulations to control the violations.

The shrinkage of Boston's agricultural hinterland, the labour shortage produced by constant warfare, several natural and manmade disasters, and internal political conflict intensified the difficulties of securing adequate provisions and compromised the abilities of the city and the province to compete with other commercial regions. These negative conditions were exacerbated by the transition of many markets where sales had once been made into competitors backed by large, fertile hinterlands.

The persistence of illegal food sales at the Boston Neck as well as forestalling and huckstering at the country farms in the environs of the city actually relieved some of the pressures on its inadequate marketing system. Despite their illegality, they provided alternative means by which inhabitants and wholesalers could obtain provisions.

The continual infighting of the Bostonians led them to sacrifice their ability to act in unison to solve the problems of chronically high food prices in their town. The city was left vulnerable to merchants, farmers, and anyone else who wanted to take advantage of the unregulated buying and selling practices that occurred there. Where Boston's provisioning difficulties would have been solved by the creation of an efficient, well-run marketing system, the city instead found itself immersed in a dilemma in which the usefulness of the markets could not be realized. The perpetual shortage of provisions that had been caused by the merchants' propensity to export goods needed in the market and the farmers' willingness to sell their goods to the highest bidders lay at the heart of Boston's provisioning problems. Since those in power condoned the marketing abuses, it was impossible to eradicate them.

---

64 W. Letwin, *Origins of Scientific Economics: English Thought 1660-1776*, London 1963, 148.

The riots, petitions, newspaper commentaries, and pamphlet literature produced by more than seventy years of bitter quarrels over markets in Boston provide a striking contrast to the popularity of marketing institutions elsewhere in the Atlantic trading world.[65] In other environments, they were a source of pride and enjoyment; among these Puritans, markets were a medium for fostering immoral behaviour and for violating individual privacy. The conflict over markets in Boston reflects the clash between the values of a more simple world still rooted in the mores of mediaeval society and the rapid, inexorable evolution towards the industrial world about to emerge on both sides of the Atlantic.

---

65 Two pamphlets were written in favor of the markets and one against: B. Colman, *Some Reasons and Arguments Offered to the Good People of Boston and Adjacent Places for the Setting Up Markets in Boston*, [Boston 1719], repr. in: *Boston Gazette*, 19-26 February 1733; *Some Considerations Against the Setting Up of A Market in This Town: With a Brief Answer to the Reasons That Are Offer'd In Behalf of It*, [Boston 1733]; 'Observations on a Paper Called "Considerations Against Setting Up a Markett in This Town",' *Boston Gazette*, 29 May 1733.

Americans, Germans, or Simply Capitalists?
Independent Merchants and the Atlantic Port Cities: 1770-1830

Sam A. Mustafa

In 1783 the Senate of Hamburg sent a letter of congratulation to the newly independent United States. After initial pleasantries, the senators got down to business. The letter's real purpose was to explore trade relations with America's harbours:

"In order to show that such mutual commerce with the merchant houses of this place may undoubtedly be of common benefit, your high mightinesses will be pleased to give us leave to mark out some advantages of this trading city. Here reigns a free, unrestrained republican commerce, charged with but few duties."[1]

Like the German Hanseatic ports, the American port cities were centred upon the commercial action at the waterfront. Boston's main trading-place in Faneuil Hall stands only one block downhill from the old State House. In Philadelphia the merchants and their ships plied their trade three blocks east of the building that housed the Continental Congress. Similarly, prior to the construction of the modern industrial-age dockyard downstream, Bremen's *Rathskeller,* centrally located on the little island of the Altstadt, was no more than four blocks in any direction from the merchant ships at anchor in the Weser. In every sense, these were societies where business and politics – capitalism and republicanism – were inextricably bound together.

The Hamburg senators who were writing to the new American government understood this arrangement perfectly. It was the same system that had existed in the free Hanse cities for generations. They were writing to men who might have been separated by an ocean, but whose "world" was much the same as their own.

By 1900, when a young Thomas Mann was writing *Buddenbrooks,* his portrait of the German Hanseatic elite, independent merchants (like the fictional firm of Johann Buddenbrook & Sons) were all but gone, replaced by broadly-based international trading lines like the North German Lloyd and the Hamburg-Amerika. But at the time of the American Revolution, they had been at the zenith of their powers. Between the liberation of the Americas and the onset of European industrialisation, the independent merchants dominated the trade of the

---

1   Hamburgische Landesbank, Girozentrale, The First Exchange of Diplomatic Notes, 5-6.

western world. The men who ran these families and firms belonged to an energetic new class that was establishing commercial linkages across the globe.

These worldly entrepreneurs held positions of power in the port cities of the Atlantic World. In the Hanseatic cities of Bremen and Hamburg, as well as the American harbours like Boston, New York, Philadelphia, and Baltimore, independent merchants stood in the front ranks of a new, international class of politically-active Bourgeoisie. They not only dominated the cities where they based their affairs; they had indeed *created* a "merchant society" which was frequently very different from the German or American heartlands. In fact, this paper will argue that a businessman in Hamburg often had more in common with an American merchant in Boston, than he did with a German from Bavaria or Baden. Among the Atlantic merchants in the late 18th and early 19th centuries, there was a capitalist *lingua franca* that transcended language and created a new international society of bourgeois capitalists.

Merchant Cities and "Merchant Princes"

In the early United States and the German Hanseatic cities of Bremen, Hamburg, and Lübeck, prominent merchants were invariably well connected socially and politically. Businessmen were often active in politics. Examples abound: William Molineux of Boston, Peter Grotjan of Philadelphia, Isaac Sears and John Lamb of New York. Thomas Fitzsimmons was a merchant, a banker, and sat on the board of directors of the Insurance Company of North America. He was also a congressman from Philadelphia who drafted the excise tax bill. Thirteen of the 56 signers of the Declaration of Independence were merchants, second in number only to lawyer/jurists.[2]

The economic, social, and political linkage of the merchant class was a relatively recent development in America, but a long-standing tradition in the Hanse.[3] For centuries, the most successful merchant houses had provided the largest part of the social and political leadership of Bremen and Hamburg. Johannes Lange, who founded the first tobacco-importing firm in Bremen in 1642, was an alderman, later a Senator, and his family produced a number of

---

2   A. Rochester, *American Capitalism 1607-1800*, New York 1949, 77.
3   Opinions differ among historians as to when the merchant classes became a political force in the American seaports. Gary Nash's comprehensive analysis of the northern harbors, G. Nash, *The Urban Crucible: The Northern Seaports and the Origins of the American Revolution*, Cambridge 1986, 167, argues that the period roughly 1730-60 witnessed the ascent of the "mercantile elite" to dominate the politics of Boston, New York, and Philadelphia.

other civil servants over the next two centuries.[4] The Oelrichs family, originally from East Prussia, entered the independent shipping business shortly after American independence, specialising in *Kolonialwaren*. They rose to become one of Bremen's most prominent and influential families, who in the course of three generations produced a Senator, a General-Consul, and an alderman. The merchant dynasty founded by the Kulenkampff brothers in 1806, which operated the biggest tobacco import house in Bremen, contributed two Senators, several consuls, and a number of prominent attorneys and judges.[5]

The Wichelshausens of Bremen were a perfect example of the kind of family which dominated the Hanseatic cities for centuries.[6] In the two generations prior to the French Revolution, they had produced a Bürgermeister, two Senators, and two noted magistrates. In addition, the family boasted some of Bremen's best-known private persons, including three physicians, a writer, and several prominent merchants.[7] Friedrich Jacob Wichelshausen served as the US consul to Bremen for 33 years. His brother Hieronymus Daniel moved to Baltimore, where he became a successful merchant, a prominent leader in the German-American community (serving on the boards of most of the German-American associations), and ultimately Bremen's consul in that city.[8]

Although wealthy merchants in most proto-capitalist societies were often prominent citizens, the US and especially the Hanse provided them with unparalleled opportunities to dominate their society and state. Bremen and Hamburg were governed by Senates, which comprised representatives from the most wealthy and powerful merchant families. After 1712, in fact, a minimum of one of Hamburg's four mayor's positions and half of the twenty-four Senators' seats were reserved exclusively for merchants.[9] The franchise was limited to a moneyed elite, which ensured that the Senate was re-elected, generation after

---

4   R. Bargman (ed.), *Bremen: die Tabakstadt Deutschlands,* Bremen 1939, 41.

5   The brothers were Peter Andreas and Caspar Gottlieb. See: H. Kellenbenz, "Der Bremer Kaufmann: Versuch einer sozialgeschichtlichen Deutung", in: *Bremisches Jahrbuch,*51 (1969), 39-40. See also: Bargman, *Bremen,* 44. Finally, Staatsarchiv Bremen (SAB), Die graue Mappen: Kulenkampff.

6   F.J.. Pitsch, *Die wirtschaftlichen Beziehungen Bremens zu den Vereinigten Staaten von Amerika bis zur Mitte des 19. Jahrhunderts,* Bremen 1974, 20. The Kulenkampffs also were relatively recent arrivals, having lived in Bremen only since the late 1600s.

7   The death-notices of the Wichelshausen family read like a Who's Who of Bremen in: *Neuer Nekrolog der Deutschen,* Altona 1856, 124-128.

8   In addition to his consular file in the SAB, see the Maryland Historical Society (MDHS): Ms1846, in which H.D. Wichelshausen is one of a dozen Baltimore notables who raises money to outfit the "Baltimore Horse Artillery."

9   S.D. Uhalde, *Citizen and World Citizen: Civic Patriotism and Cosmopolitanism in 18th Century Hamburg,* Ph.D.-thesis, Berkeley 1984, 50.

generation, as the representatives of the merchant class. It was customary for men to ascend into the positions held by their fathers, moving up from the position of consul to Senator, for example, assuming that the family and its business had not suffered any untoward developments such as scandals or financial reverses. Over time, Hamburg's system became more democratic than Bremen's, involving a lower chamber elected by all male citizens, and legislation limiting the number of members of one family who could hold prominent offices.

The political/economic arrangement of the Hanse was thus the reverse of that in most German states, where the merchant class was decidedly subordinate (and frequently subservient) to the nobility, church, and even the scholarly and professional elites. Indeed, it more closely resembled the situation developing in young America, where budding capitalism had created a patrician class of well-educated merchants who were interested in worldwide trade and local politics. Business and politics meshed in many families in both the Hanse and the American seaboard.

Prominent politicians and businesspeople moved in the same circles, whether at home or abroad. In the 1790s, John Adams instructed his son John Quincy to seek out the most prominent American businessmen when travelling to London and Hamburg. T.H. Perkins, a wealthy Boston merchant, stayed as the guest of James Monroe in Paris in 1793, along with the merchant and newspaper magnate John Russell, whose wife Lydia, in turn, also came from a prominent merchant family with political connections in Virginia (hence the link to the Monroes).[10] Peter Grotjan, a Hamburg merchant transplanted to Philadelphia, provides a fascinating example. Grotjan was an ambitious 21-year-old entrepreneur when "a prominent German" introduced him to George Washington at an outdoor concert.[11] Grotjan became both a wealthy businessman and an active player in Democratic politics, funding a number of political clubs and campaigns, including those of Jefferson and Jackson. He was also "intimately acquainted" (in his words) with Aaron Burr. The two men shared a lover for several years, yet remained close friends.[12]

---

10 C. Seaburg and S. Patterson, *Merchant Prince of Boston: Colonel T.H. Perkins, 1764-1854* Cambridge 1971, 109-110. See also the papers of Lydia Smith Russell in the Mass. Historical Society (MAHS); her husband John owned the *Boston Gazette*.

11 In his (handwritten) memoirs, Grotjan never specifies who made the introduction; Peter Grotjan Memoirs, Pennsylvania Historical Society (PHS).

12 Peter Grotjan Memoirs (unpublished, no page numbers), Pennsylvania Historical Society (PHS). The woman was one Maria Clements. The three seemed to have had a strange triangular friendship, even after the sexual aspect of the relationship passed. In later years, when Clements came upon hard times, both Grotjan and Burr gave financial assistance to her, and Grotjan

By any definition these people constituted a recognisable class: intermarried, socially distinct, financially and politically connected. The three sons of the wealthy Salem merchant Richard Derby, for example, all married young women whose fathers were either merchants or sea captains. Two of Derby's three daughters likewise married ship owners. Only his daughter Martha wed outside the immediate sphere of commerce, marrying a local physician.[13] The elder Derby, after passing the reins of his business to his oldest son, became involved in politics, first for the king's government, and then after 1775, against it. Peter Grotjan's family in Hamburg provides another example. At fifteen Peter was apprenticed to his uncle's merchant house. In addition to becoming a merchant himself, Grotjan's brother and sister both married into merchant families.[14]

In both America and the Hanse, marriage and family alliances often marked the influence of a particular merchant house. These alliances gradually spread out all over the world, including the United States, in a sense being the eighteenth-century equivalent of multinational corporations, with branches of the family firm in all the major ports where the merchant houses transacted business.[15] The trend towards this internationalisation had been underway since the early 1600s, when the English, Dutch, and to a lesser extent the French, all established chartered companies to manage trade in outposts and colonies, such as the East India Company, whose "outposts of progress" brought increasing profits home to London. Independent merchant firms began employing these tactics somewhat later, in the eighteenth century, when families settled younger sons or brothers in distant lands to manage their firm's affairs and protect their interests in the new markets.

An International Merchant Culture?

Between the liberation of the Americas and the onset of European industrialisation, independent merchants dominated the trade of the western world. The men who ran these families and firms, both in Germany and the United States, belonged to an energetic new class that was establishing commercial linkages across the globe. Crucially for the future of German-

---

helped find a job for her younger son (who was not, apparently, either Burr's or Grotjan's child.)

13 J.D. Phillips, 'The Life and Times of Richard Derby,' in: *Essex Institute Historical Collections*, 65 (1929), 276-277.

14 PHS, Peter Grotjan Memoirs.

15 Uhalde, *Citizen and World Citizen*, 19-20 and 42-45.

American relations, these worldly entrepreneurs held positions of power in both the Hanse and the American port cities.

As the Enlightenment gave way to the West's "bourgeois century," the role of the independent merchant took on new significance.[16] This era witnessed the last phase of bureaucratic absolutism, which was replaced by a rapidly spreading capitalist revolution, a liberation of what would become the investing class.[17] Independent merchants, usually operating in the major seaports, stood in the front ranks of these liberated capitalists in both Germany and North America.

The merchants themselves usually represented only small percentages of the total populations of the harbour cities. Bremen in 1796 had only 156 registered independent merchants and 60 major commercial houses. These men and their families accounted for slightly fewer than 2,000 people, or under 5% of the city's roughly 40,000 inhabitants. They owned the most expensive homes, virtually all in the Altstadt, the oldest, most central district of Bremen, closest to the major religious and government structures. In Lübeck, with a total population of approximately 25,000, roughly the same percentage were members of this economic elite. Hamburg, which had over 100,000 inhabitants in 1800, had a slightly larger merchant class of over 8,000 people who lived primarily in the St. Nicolai and St. Katherine neighbourhoods. In no case did this group exceed 10% of the total population of any Hanseatic city.[18]

Although the merchant class itself was not large, the number of citizens either directly employed by the merchants or connected to their enterprises was very high. In 1790, nearly half of Bremen's population was employed in work related in some way to either shipbuilding or international trade.[19] Since industry in these cities was small and limited to a few fields, it is logical to conclude that a majority of working men were normally involved in one or another facet of commercial activity, and that a good number of the working women were employed by these wealthy families as domestic help.

The Hanse usually represented German commerce in the wider world, since Germans imported and exported largely through Hanseatic harbours. In the

---

16 The expression is Percy Ernst Schramm's, from: P.E. Schramm, *Hamburg, Deutschland und die Welt: Leistung und Grenzen hanseatischen Burgertums in der Zeit zwischen Napoleon I und Bismack, ein Kapitel deutscher Geschichte,* Hamburg 1952, 10.

17 E. Fehrenbach, 'Der Einfluß des napoleonischen Frankreich auf das Rechts- und Verwaltungssystem Deutschlands', in: A. von Reden-Dohna (ed.), *Deutschland und Italien im Zeitalter Napoleons,* Wiesbaden 1979, 23-40.

18 H.-E. Bödecker, 'Marchands et Habitat: Le Nord-Ouest de l'Allemagne vers 1800', in: *Revue d'Histoire Moderne et Contemporaine,* 41 (1994), 577-579.

19 A. Schulz, 'Das Bremer Bürgertum in der Umbruchzeit', in: *Historische Zeitschrift,* Beiheft, 14 (1991), 23.

1790s, Bremen and Hamburg alone accounted for more than half of all imports to German-speaking lands from non-German states.[20] Apart from the Hanse, the rest of Germany's merchants were inward looking. Saxony, for example, had a healthy trade in the 1780s and 1790s, and the Leipzig Fair attracted merchants from across northern and eastern Europe. Such German markets, however, dealt primarily with other German-speaking states, and most of what Saxony did receive from the trans-oceanic world came via Hamburg.[21] The Hanse was thus uniquely suited among all the German states to serve as interlocutors between Germany and the United States. In many ways the Hanseatic business class had more in common with its counterpart on the American seaboard than with most regions of Germany.

Whether or not we accept the portrait drawn by Thomas Mann in *Buddenbrooks*, it is clear that we can speak of some sort of "merchant culture" extent in the seaports of both Germany and the US. Merchant culture was by no means unique to the Hanse and the young United States; many historians have written on the emergence of merchants in the seaports of the western world and its trade outposts in this period. It was rare, however, to find a society like the Hanse, where the merchants so utterly controlled the activities of the state, or even one like the young US, where the merchants had such a substantial amount of direct political power. Holland, for instance, was a "merchant society," although the Dutch political system (and indeed, Dutch sovereignty) did not demonstrate nearly as much stability and continuity as that of the US and the Hanse in the years 1785-1835. Dutch merchants rarely called the political shots during this period. Even in (relatively) democratic Great Britain, where the merchant class was as healthy and active as in these places, direct access to power remained largely beyond their grasp until the ascent of liberalism in the middle of the nineteenth century.

The common ground shared by German and American merchants served as a catalyst for German-American relations as a whole. Although they would have been attracted to the new and expanding markets of North America in any event, the Hanseatic merchants were additionally drawn to the very *idea* of the American "commercial republic" (as a French representative to Congress had described the US in 1779). A trans-national collegiality existed among these men

---

20 P.E. Schramm, 'Die deutschen Überseekaufleute im Rahmen der Sozialgeschichte', in: *Bremisches Jahrbuch*, 49 (1964), 35. It is admittedly somewhat futile to speak of "German commerce" in this era; there was no such thing, rather a number of competing states.

21 W. E. Lingelbach, 'Saxon-American Relations, 1778-1828', in: *American Historical Review*, 17 (1912), 517.

of business. German and American merchants spoke a mutual second language: liberal capitalism.

In both the Hanse and the American port cities, the merchant elites who dominated public affairs were the *hautes citoyens* in republics, which officially disdained nobility. In late-18th century Germany, in areas of great mercantile activity, the nobility was either weak or altogether non-existent. Instead, the high bourgeoisie often filled the role of nobility.[22] Hanseatic society was dominated first by merchants (a great many of whom had studied law as young men) plus a few early industrialists and a few Protestant clergy.[23]

As in the United States, Hanseatic society was led by businessmen and lawyers who claimed to love and defend democracy and republicanism. In reality, of course, both societies' franchises and electoral systems were carefully restricted to allow only members of the existing elite to ascend to power. The structure of the American electoral college, and the fact that only Representatives were to be popularly elected, remind us that early American democracy was every bit as exclusive as the elections to the Senates of the Hanse. The American merchant elite supported the city incorporation movement of the 1780s and 1790s because it helped to place political power more firmly in their own hands. By 1800, Boston was the only major American city *not* incorporated, primarily because its relatively small size and slow growth allowed for the survival of the more democratic town meetings. The Federalists, particularly Hamilton, openly distrusted democracy as one short step from the abyss of mob-rule, and thus sought to narrow the definition of "liberty" in order to preserve the sanity and self-discipline of the republican system. Interestingly, German-Americans (many of whom were first- or second-generation transplants from authoritarian states) were in the vanguard of those who resented and rebelled against the exclusive and "monarchist" impulses of the Federalists in the 1790s.[24]

Thus the Hanseatic and American republics were *de jure* republics, but *de facto* oligarchies administered by a jurisprudent merchant "nobility." While working class Germans (and many Americans) were initially enthusiastic and supportive of the democratic ideals of the French Revolution, the wealthy

---

22 J. Diefendorf, *Businessmen & Politics in the Rhineland*, Princeton 1980, 43. Rheinisch elites seem to have been more divided along scholarly, juridical/political, and mercantile lines than in the Hanse, where all three blurred together.

23 M. Lindemann, *Patriots and Paupers: Hamburg 1712-1830*, New York / Oxford 1990, 10.

24 For a comprehensive analysis of the role of German-Americans in anti-Federalism, see: P.D. Newman, *The Fries Rebellion of 1799: Pennsylvania Germans, the Federalist Party, and American Political Culture*, Ph.D.-thesis, University of Kentucky, 1996, 4-20.

bourgeois leaders of the Hanse (and the Federalists in America) were immediately sceptical. Revolution, after all, is usually bad for business.[25]

Despite the many similarities, American democracy, even in its earliest and most restrictive forms, did not institutionalise the kind of class limitations that characterised the Hanseatic republics. There were no places in the US Senate reserved for "Notables," who could only be elected by a certain class of people, determined by ownership of significant amounts of property. Nonetheless, it is clear that both societies had constructed republics in which the moneymaking and money-managing elites controlled virtually all policy initiatives, unless their hands were forced by the occasional popular rebellion.

However tentative and qualified their commitments to democracy, both societies were nonetheless wholly devoted to capitalism. Commerce, of course, is not the same thing as capitalism, although these merchants frequently embraced the emergent ideas of capitalism because they reinforced and gave rational sanction to a mercantile lifestyle. Thus in the Hanse and in the American seaports, a commercially dominant class reinforced the capitalist ethos. A mid-eighteenth-century German visitor to Hamburg commented that:

"The importance of business in Hamburg and the variety of things connected with it are so great that one could profitably spend an entire year here and learn something new each day. There are few European seaports which Hamburg's ships do not enter, and there is no seafaring people in this part of the world which does not traffic with Hamburg. Its superb location has made the city the emporium of all Germany.... The Elbe and the canals...are almost blanketed over with ships. The assembly on the Stock Exchange is one of the largest [in Europe] and the place teems with negotiants. In a word, one finds here a perpetual motion of all nations and peoples caught up in the business of moneymaking."[26]

A similar scene awaited visitors to the major American seaports. Congressman Samuel Mitchell noted that his New York constituents were "bred to commerce. They are devoted to navigation; barter and sale are their delight. The spirit of business warms them."[27] America may have been broadly rural and

---

25 Walther Vogel has written: "The men at the highest ranks of the small Hanseatic republics were far too sober politicians to allow themselves to become carried away [by]... careless writings." See: W. Vogel, 'Die Hansestädte und die Kontinentalsperre', in: *Pfingstblätter des Hansischen Geschichtsvereins, Blatt 9,* (1913) an annual published in Leipzig by the Verlag von Duncker & Humblot.

26 Lindemann, *Patriots and Paupers*, 3.

27 S. Watts, *The Republic Reborn: War and the Making of Liberal America, 1790-1820,* Baltimore 1987, 69: "In other words, the development of America after the Revolution involved the consolidation of a market economy *and* a market society.... By 1820 a distinctly bourgeois culture had crystallized in the young republic."

agrarian, but a sizeable proportion of Americans were either capitalists or capitalists in the making. The period 1790-1820 witnessed an explosion in the size of the merchant class, the development of the first factories, and a change from household economies to inter-regional and international markets spreading from the rapidly growing urban centres. The development of North America after the Revolution involved the growth of both a market economy *and* a market society. By 1820, the United States – particularly the coastal regions – had a distinctly bourgeois culture.

Both the Hanse and the American ports were the urbanised, ocean-going fringes of nations whose interiors were deep, relatively provincial and out-of-the-way, and generally far less interested in commercial activity than their seafaring cousins. Nonetheless, the port cities depended upon the interior country, where most of the buyers of their imports lived. Relations between the two zones were sometimes fractious, owing to a cultural gulf, which caused mistrust and resentment. In 1784, George Washington (who was a coastal planter, and thus not a member of either camp) advised his merchant-legislator colleagues to make attempts to cultivate better relations between the ports and the hinterland. "The western settlers," he said, "stand as it were upon a pivot.... smooth the road, and make easy the way for them, and see what an influx of articles will be poured upon us; how amazingly our exports will be increased by them, and how amply we will be compensated for any trouble and expense we may encounter to effect it."[28] A decade later, an Irish visitor in Baltimore wrote that, "The size of all towns in America... has hitherto been proportionate to their trade, and particularly to that carried on with the back settlements."[29]

Germany's interior differed as profoundly from her ports as did America's. The area surrounding the Hanseatic cities, however – as far south as Kassel – had a number of things in common with the port cities, including an enlarged bourgeoisie much more numerous and developed than in other parts of Germany, even by 1800. (reference, see my remarks)This had been the case for over two centuries, almost entirely because of the mercantile economy of the Hanseatic ports, which attracted businessmen from other parts of Germany. Farming existed in the German lowlands around the Hanse, and small industry was present, as in all areas of Germany, but the North was notable for its dominant merchant class and the resulting concentration around the few major seaports. The area was fairly urbanised by contemporary German standards; some 25% of the population lived in towns or cities in 1800 – a much higher

---

28 J. W. Livingood, *The Philadelphia-Baltimore Trade Rivalry 1780-1860*, Harrisburg 1947, 8.
29 Isaac Weld, 1797, quoted in: S.W. Bruchey, *Robert Oliver, Merchant of Baltimore 1783-1819*, New York 1979, 30.

percentage than in the rest of Germany.(reference) Just as in the early United States, the most prominent men of affairs could be found in the port cities. Indeed, one could argue that this arrangement has not changed greatly in either country over the past two centuries. The culture and politics of Boston, New York, or Philadelphia remain deeply suspect in the more conservative American heartland, just as conservative Bavaria often snorts contemptuously at the left-wing press based in Hamburg.

A list of German merchants published in 1798 attests to the dominance of the Bourgeoisie in what one historian has called the "Greater Hanse" area: "it constitutes, if you will, the Who's Who of the German bourgeoisie."[30] The multifaceted and multi-national nature of their businesses meant that the merchant firms were linked to virtually all the other bourgeois occupations, if not involved in them in some way directly. Many firms performed all the services of market scouting, contact, transportation, storage, wholesaling, and retailing. Inevitably for merchants who enjoyed success in one kind of commerce, temptations arose to branch out into new markets and new commodities.[31]

Merchants and a Widening World

Proximity to the sea, the highway of world commerce, created a worldly and cosmopolitan bourgeoisie in the Hanse and the American ports. Incoming ships meant constant contact with other nations and their citizens and wares. Ferdinand Beneke, moving from Bremen to Hamburg in 1796, remarked on the latter's "Venetian splendour," and its massive and chaotic multinational waterfront.[32] John Quincy Adams, who as scion of a prominent Boston family was certainly no stranger to wealth or busy harbours, wrote of the impressive size and sophistication of Hamburg when he visited for the first time in 1797. John Parish (the Scottish merchant turned Hamburg entrepreneur turned American consul turned British double agent) entertained Adams for a week at the luxurious homes and salons of his many business friends from Britain and a half-dozen European countries.[33]

---

30 Bödecker, 'Marchands et Habitat', 573-575.
31 J.G. Hutchins, *The American Maritime Industries and Public Policy, 1789-1914: An Economic History*, Cambridge 1941, 241.
32 Uhalde, *Citizen and World Citizen*, 22-23.
33 C.F. Adams (ed.), *Memoirs of John Quincy Adams*, Vol. I, Philadelphia 1874, 201. Parish's astonishing career is thoroughly investigated in: R. Ehrenberg, *Das Haus Parish in Hamburg*, Jena 1905. Parish's secret role as a British agent, however, was not discovered until the 1950s,

S. A. Mustafa

In these salons, which were essentially coffee-houses, Adams would have found other men of his class and educational level from a variety of nations, reading newspapers and magazines from all over Europe. As the eighteenth century ended, a new generation of "cultural patricians" was emerging in Hamburg: more worldly, extravagant, educated, and enlightened than their fathers.[34] In clubs like "Harmonie," which by 1800 had over 500 members, these gentlemen drank coffee and tea, played cards, exchanged foreign books and journals, and entertained visiting foreign persons of note like the young John Quincy Adams. The Harmonie soon spread to other German cities, first in the Hanse, then elsewhere.[35] The fictitious Senator Thomas Buddenbrook in Mann's novel was a member of the Lübeck chapter of the Harmonie, which Mann described as "a gentleman's reading club" in which all the prominent merchants gathered to smoke their pipes, exchanging journals, gossip, and *bons mots*.

The young United States had its share of coffeehouses too, also frequented by the business-political classes. Charles Buck, a transplanted Hamburg merchant who would later serve as Hamburg's consul to the US, remarked happily that Philadelphia's coffeehouses made him feel at home. Later, on a visit to New York, Buck "found the city much engaged in business," but still made the rounds of the various coffee-houses, stopping in to give his regards to fellow merchants, and to gather useful information or gossip. There were so many Hanseatic merchants in New York by 1800 that Buck found gentlemen's clubs in which English was rarely heard; one tavern he frequented was called "The City of Hamburg." When Buck returned to Hamburg after years in America, he went straight to a coffeehouse to catch up on the news.[36]

Other clubs for gentlemen were dedicated to more scholarly or philosophical interests, and had names like "The Museum Club" or "Ressource." [sic][37] In Bremen, the well-known historian (later Bürgermeister) Dr. Liborius Diderich von Post was a scholar from a mercantile family, which had interest and family members in the United States. He was a founding member of a society for the study of new ideas in science and the humanities. He and the other men of this group corresponded frequently with Benjamin Franklin regarding the latter's

---

by cross-indexing references from Karl Sieveking's diary reference, encoded British consular reports, and mysterious omissions in the British *Bullion Report* of 1810.

34 The phrase is from Uhalde, *Citizen and World Citizen*, 60-64.

35 By the 1900s, most chapters of "Harmonie" in German cities were little more than music-appreciation societies. See: M. Kirschstein, *Die Harmonie*, Hamburg 1913.

36 Charles N. Buck, Diary (no page numbers), PHS.

37 An interesting analysis of the social dynamics of these gentlemen's clubs can be found in: T. Maentel, 'Zwischen weltbürgerlicher Aufklärung und stadtbürgerlicher Emanzipation', in: D. Hein and A. Schulz (eds.), *Bürgerkultur im 19. Jahrhundert*, Munich 1996, 140-154.

experiments with electricity and lightning. In the well-read circles of the coffeehouses, people often perused journals like "Bruchstücke von Gedanken und Geschichte", which for its motto tackled the ambitious questions: "Woher bin ich? Wer bin ich? Warum und wozu bin ich? und wohin soll ich?" Its enlightened assault on "old thinking" attempted to offer a perspective, "for every man, for every business, and for the whole world."[38]

As John Quincy Adams discovered, Hamburg was a hub for travelling men of affairs, where nationality was less important than class. Thomas Aston Coffin, an exiled American Tory, arrived there in the summer of 1784, on his way from London to Brunswick. He spoke no German, and had apparently arrived at the height of the business cycle when all the major inns and hotels were full. Coffin proceeded to a gentleman's club, where he met a German merchant who was fluent in English and happy to assist him in finding both lodging for the night and travel arrangements on to Brunswick. The next morning Coffin met a second merchant "who was so kind to take me with him on his journey."[39]

Cosmopolitanism and fascination with foreign ideas, particularly new and controversial ones, were hallmarks of most of America's founders and many of their mercantile colleagues. (Consider the way Franklin cultivated scholarly European friends and devoured the latest European scientific journals, or the excitement and care with which Jefferson planned his sightseeing tour of the Rhineland.)[40] Stephen Girard was fascinated by European systems of education, and collected pamphlets in German and French on the subject.[41] He also prided himself on his expertise in European styles of horticulture, planting with his own hand several impressive vineyards and orchards, and writing articles on tree surgery. He did his best to import European plants and husbandry techniques to the New World; one of his biographers credits Girard with introducing the artichoke to America. Like John Quincy Adams, Girard learned German on a business/pleasure trip. While Adams spent his off-duty time away from Berlin touring Silesia and Saxony, Girard preferred the mercantile aura of Hamburg, where he made several business contacts and collected some German literature. Clearly, this Philadelphia businessman felt quite at home in the largest Hanseatic

38 Staats- u. Univ.-Bibliothek Bremen, Zeitschriften und Journale: file 510.
39 Thomas Aston Coffin to Francis Coffin, 7 June, 1784. MAHS: Coffin. Hamburgh, Germany - 6 letters, 1784.
40 For a fascinating perspective on Jefferson as the archetypical American ingenue in Europe, see: G.G. Shackelford, *Thomas Jefferson's Travels in Europe, 1784-1789*, Baltimore 1995.
41 APS: Stephen Girard papers. Microfilm. Reels 435-436 and 474 contain several of these pamphlets as well as Girard's notes on European education models he was considering for what would become Girard College.

port. He returned in 1798 and visited his friend Johann Berenberg Gosseler, a sugar merchant.[42]

Convergence

Although most of the early American politicians could be counted upon to wax poetic on ideological points (and some, like Patrick Henry and Thomas Paine, could approach hysteria), America's merchants had supported the Revolution largely for more fundamental and practical reasons of economics. The Salem shipping magnate Richard Derby provides a typical example. Frustrated at his inability to expand his rum and molasses exports, feeling cheated by unscrupulous British agents in the Bahamas and the West Indies, Derby was by 1776 an open supporter of rebellion. He turned his fortune to the aid of the revolutionary cause, smuggling guns, powder, and other supplies for the rebels, and hoarding them in his warehouses. Derby was a "patriot" because the British restricted his business ambitions.[43]

Had ideology been the foremost concern of the American merchants, more of them would probably have heeded the urgings of Jefferson and Madison to abandon their dealings with Britain and to shift American commerce in the direction of France, Holland, Spain, and other friends in Europe. That no such shift occurred after 1783 indicates the relative lack of enthusiasm among American businessmen for any kind of ideology that would impinge upon their pocketbooks. The American bourgeoisie was, above all, *practical.*

The primacy of profit was the hallmark of the merchant culture, which the Americans shared with their counterparts in the Hanse. Some historians have made a case for the Hanseatic cities being culturally and ideologically detached from the rest of Germany, which varied wildly from ultra-conservative feudalism to woolly-headed philosophical flights of fancy. The Hanse focused entirely upon the ideology of moneymaking. Once French society began to disintegrate into chaos in the 1790s, the perceived dangers of ideological loyalties became even more pronounced, and the Hanse clung more staunchly than ever to the sensible capitalist examples of Britain and the United States. The

---

42 It is unclear to what degree Girard actually had any "friends." He was, according to all witnesses, a profoundly lonely and solitary man, unusual among the members of his class in that he loathed and avoided society. The notes on the trip to see Gosseler, however, indicate that the visit was social as well as professional. American Philosophical Society: Stephen Girard papers. Microfilm, Reel 63.

43 Phillips, 'The Life and Times of Richard Derby,' 280-289.

Hanse, "are not idealists, but rather materialists. They are realistic and industrious... none of these German dreamers."[44]

Bremen was somewhat less attached to the Anglo-American model than was Hamburg, where more than one pamphleteer had described the city as merely "one of the suburbs [*Vorstädte*] of London."[45] Napoleon would later weigh in with his own damning agreement on the matter: *"Hambourg? Ne me parlez pas de cette ville anglaise!"*[46] Nonetheless, the Bremer merchants shared with their American counterparts a general scepticism for any ideology that had no practical economic applications. One German historian concluded:

"Herein lies the key to Bremen's politics. Only within the context of trade can one understand it. The striving for neutrality, the search for backing from the great powers which was to have guaranteed its position... shows Bremen's guiding principle. Neither nationalism, nor cosmopolitanism, nor even religion, but rather a purely practical point of view motivated the thinking of Bremen's civic leaders."[47]

In his last years, the eloquent and prolific Adam Duckwitz, one of Bremen's most famous statesmen and a vehement defender of free trade, looked back at his sprawling business and political career and concluded that while he had lived among Americans and Englishmen, "I was in my own element."[48]

Thus we find that, by time of American independence, the Hanseatic merchant families were ideally poised to serve as the intermediaries between the German and American people and economies. They shared a host of social, political, and cultural traits, and above all a mutual thirst for free trade. Via their common merchant culture, German and American businessmen began to establish the first ties between their nations. They were often well aware of this cultural heritage that gave them a commercial *lingua franca*. A 1783 letter from a group of Hamburg Senators to Benjamin Franklin emphasises the many things which Hanseatic and American society have in common, concluding with a "hope and wish that a solid foundation can be laid for the strong basis of friendship and community between the citizens of our republics."[49]

---

44 "Sie sind keine Idealisten, sondern Materialisten. Sie sind realistisch und tatkräftig... keine deutsche Phantasten", in: R. Engelsing, 'England und die USA in der bremischen Sicht des 19. Jahrhunderts', in: Jahrbuch der Wittheit Bremen 1 (1957), 33-65, 35.

45 Engelsing, 'England und die USA', 36.

46 Cited in E.J. Clapp, *The Port of Hamburg*, Yale 1911, 20.

47 H. Wiedemann, *Die Aussenpolitik Bremens im Zeitalter der Französichen Revolution 1794-1803*, Bremen 1960, 27-28.

48 Engelsing, 'England und die USA', 38.

49 E. Baasch, *Beiträge zur Geschichte der Handelsbeziehungen zwischen Hamburg und Amerika*, Hamburg 1892, 56-57: "Mit tiefgefühlter Freude mache ich diese Mittheilung und hoffe und

To this day, remnants of the mercantile heritage linger on both sides of the Atlantic. We find it in the statue of Sam Adams gesturing out over the entranceway to the preserved 18th-century Quincy Market in Boston. It is inescapable in the upper-middle class suburbs of northern Bremen, where virtually every major street carries the name of a bygone merchant firm: Kulenkampffallee, H.H. Meier Allee, Crüsemannallee, Gröningstraße.[50] In a dozen other places in America and the Hanse, the old merchant culture remains at the intersection of the very different roads on which German and American history has travelled.

---

wünsche, dass ein solider Grund möge gelegt werden für die feste Gründung der Freundschaft und Gemeinschaft zwischen den Bürgern unserer Republiken."

50 Most of these are in quite affluent areas. For example, Kulenkampffallee (named for the most prominent tobacco-importers of the nineteenth century) and Crüsemannallee (named for the first director of the Lloyd) are spacious tree-lined boulevards in Bremen's upper-class neighborhood of Neu Schwachausen.

IV.

Appendix

Index to persons, firms and places

About the Authors

Marcel Boldorf, Dr.phil., Priv.-Doz.; Lecturer in Economic and Social History (University of Mannheim). His publications include 'Sozialfürsorge in der SBZ/DDR 1945-1953. Ursachen, Ausmaß und Bewältigung der Nachkriegsarmut' (VSWG-Beihefte 138), Stuttgart 1998. In 2003, he completed his Habilitationsschrift on the transition of proto-industrial textile regions into the Industrial Age (a comparison of Northern Ireland and Lower Silesia).

Dittmar Dahlmann, Dr.phil., Professor of Eastern European History at the Rheinische Friedrich-Wilhelms-Universität Bonn. His research is on the history of Russia and the Soviet Union from the 18th to the 20th centuries. Areas of interest are the history of science in the 18th century and entrepreneurs in the Russian Realm in the 19th and early 20th century. His publications include: ',,... das einzige Land in Europa, das eine große Zukunft vor sich hat." Deutsche Unternehmen und Unternehmer im Russischen Reich im 19. und frühen 20. Jahrhundert', Essen 1998 (with Carmen Scheide); `Migration nach Ost- und Südosteuropa vom 18. bis zum Beginn des 19. Jahrhunderts. Ursachen - Formen - Verlauf - Ergebnis´, Stuttgart 1999 (with Mathias Beer), `Eine große Zukunft. Deutsche in Rußlands Wirtschaft´, Begleitband zur Ausstellung, German and Russian version, Berlin 2000, (with Klaus Heller, Tamara Igumnowa, Jurij A. Petrow and Kai Reschke).

Henk van Dijk, Dr.phil., Historian, Professor of Geschiedenis van industriele samenleving at Erasmus University Rotterdam, published widely on urban history in the age of industrialisation, demography and social history. His publications include: 'De modernisering van Europa: twee eeuwen maatschappijgeschiedenis', Utrecht 1994.

Peter Edwards, Ph.D., Professor of History at the University of Surrey Roehampton. Research interests: logistics of the British Civil Wars; early modern British agriculture and rural society; the role of horses in early modern British society. Recent publications: 'The Arms Trade and the British Civil Wars 1639-52', Sutton 2000; 'Arming and equipping the Covenanting armies 1638-1651', in: S. Murdoch / A. Mackillop, eds., Fighting for Identity: Scottish Military Experience c. 1550-1900, Leiden 2002; 'Turning ploughshares into swords: the arms and equipment industries in Staffordshire in the First Civil War, 1642-1646', Midland History 27, 2002.

Chris Evans, Ph.D., Principal Lecturer in History at the University of Glamorgan in South Wales. His current research is on the place of Baltic iron in Britain's Atlantic empire in the eighteenth century. He is the author (with Göran Rydén and Owen Jackson) of 'Baltic iron and the British iron industry in the eighteenth century', Economic History Review 55, 2002, 642-65.

Laurence Fontaine, Dr. phil., Historian, director of research in the CNRS and attached to l'Ecole des Hautes Etudes en Sciences Sociales (Paris) was Professor in the department of history and civilisation at the European University Institute (Florence) till 2003. Areas of research are the cultures of economics in early modern Europe, survival strategies in past and present Europe, migrations and mountain societies are a third area of research. Her publications include: 'History of pedlars in Europe', Cambridge 1996; 'Antonio and Shylock: Credit and Trust in France, c. 1680 - c. 1780', The Economic History Review 1, 2001, 39-57; Household Strategies for Survival, 1600-2000: Fission, Faction and Cooperation (with Jürgen Schlumbohm, eds.), Cambridge 2000; Pouvoir, identités et migrations dans les hautes vallées des Alpes occidentales (XVIIe-XVIIIe siècles), Grenoble 2003.

Sakis Gekas, Teaching Fellow at the London School of Economics. His interests of research include social and economic history of the Mediterranean.

Adrian Jarvis is Curator of Port History, Merseyside Maritime Museum and Co-director of the Centre for Port & Maritime History at Liverpool. Most of his previous research has been in the relationship between policy-making, management and engineering in the Port of Liverpool, but he is currently Co-directing a large project with Robert Lee which seeks to reconstruct the late nineteenth century merchant community of Liverpool. His most recent book is 'In Troubled Times: The Port of Liverpool 1905-38' and he is just completing the co-editing of 'British Ships in China Seas', being the papers given at an international conference held in Liverpool under the same title.

W. Robert Lee, Ph.D., Historian, Chaddock Professor of Economic and Social History at the University of Liverpool. He has published widely on the demographic, economic and social history of Germany. His recent publications include: 'Population and Society in Western European Port Cities, c. 1650-1939' (with R. Lawton, eds.), Liverpool 2002; 'Infant mortality in Bremen in the 19th century' (with Peter Marschalck), The History of the Family 7, 2002, 557-585; 'Official Statistics, Demography and Population Policy in Germany, 1872-1933', in: R. Mackensen (ed.), Bevölkerungslehre und Bevölkerungspolitik vor 1933,

Opladen 2002, 253-272; 'Neue Sichtweisen auf ein altes Thema: Die Industrielle Revolution in Großbritannien' (Kölner Vorträge und Abhandlungen zur Sozial- und Wirtschaftsgeschichte, NF 2), Cologne 2003; 'Official Statistics and Demography in the Third Reich', in: R. Mackensen (ed.), Bevölkerungslehre und Bevölkerungspolitik im Dritten Reich, Opladen 2003, 101-124. He is currently working on three projects: mercantile business culture in Liverpool in the nineteenth and early twentieth century; the politics of demographic statistics in Germany, 1810-1989; and a social history of urban parks.

Graeme J. Milne, Ph.D., research fellow in the School of History at the University of Liverpool. He is the author of 'Trade and traders in mid-Victorian Liverpool: Mercantile business and the making of a world port', Liverpool 2000, and is writing a monograph on the North East of England as a maritime region for publication in 2005. Since January 2004, he has been working for the Mercantile Liverpool Project (funded by the Leverhulme Trust), reconstructing the port's trading and business communities in the 1850-1914 era.

Sam A. Mustafa, Ph.D., Assistant Professor of History at Ramapo College of New Jersey. His research interests are in U.S.-German relations and Germany during the Napoleonic period. He is the author of 'Merchants and Migrations: Germans and Americans in Connection, 1776-1835', London 2001. His most recent article, 'The Long Ride of Major von Schill' is forthcoming in the Proceedings of the Consortium on Revolutionary Europe. He is currently working on a book about the commemoration of German heroes of the Napoleonic Wars.

Jürgen G. Nagel, Dr.phil., formerly Research Fellow at the University of Trier and member of a project on early regional industrialisation. His main fields of research are: European expansion, trading structures of the early modern world, urban history, maritime history, early industrialisation. Presently he is working on Southeast Asian slavery systems in the colonial context. His publications include: 'Der Schlüssel zu den Molukken. Makassar und die Handelsstrukturen des Malaiischen Archipels im 17. und 18. Jh.', 2 vols., Hamburg 2003; 'Zwischen Kommerz und Autarkie. Sklavereisysteme des maritimen Südostasiens im Zeitalter der Ostindienkompanien', Comparativ 13:4, 2003, 42-60.

Alexander Nützenadel, Dr.phil., director of a research group on the history of globalization at the University of Cologne. He is the author of 'Landwirtschaft, Staat und Autarkie. Agrarpolitik im faschistischen Italien', Tübingen 1997, and 'Nationalökonomie, Expertenkultur und Politik im Wirtschaftswunder 1950-1970', Göttingen (forthcoming). He also co-edited 'Zeitgeschichte als Problem. Nationale Traditionen und Perspektiven der Forschung in Europa', Göttingen 2004 (with W. Schieder).

Jari Ojala, Ph.D., Docent in Economic History, University of Jyväskylä. Current research projects are concentrating on the role played by information and social capital in the long term. Latest publications include: 'International Networks of Shipping information in the Late 18th and Early 19th Century: A Finnish Case', International Journal of Maritime History 14:3, 2002 and 'Consular Services of the Nordic Countries during the Eighteenth and Nineteenth Centuries: Did They Really Work?' (with L. Müller), in: G. Boyce / R. Gorski (eds.), Resources and Infrastructures in the Maritime Economy, 1500-2000, Research in Maritime History 22, 2002.

Cátia Alexandra Pereira Antunes, Researcher and lecturer at the Department of History, University of Leiden. Ph.D. thesis on Globalisation of the Early Modern economy: the economic relationship between Amsterdam and Lisbon, 1640-1705. Her current interests of research are Early Modern Urban and Network History, as well as Early Modern Economics in general and perspectives on globalisation as a historical process.

Christiane Reves, public relations officer in the Bundestag. Doctoral dissertation on the social and economic ascent of merchants from Lake Como in the 17th and 18th century in progress. Recent publications: 'Von Kaufleuten, Stuckateuren und Perückenmachern. Die Präsenz von Italienern in Mainz im 17. und 18. Jahrhundert', in: M. Matheus / W. G. Rödel (eds.), Bausteine zur Mainzer Stadtgeschichte, Stuttgart 2002, 135-159; 'Operatori prealpini all'estero: negozianti Comaschi a Francoforte nel settecento', in: Tra identità e integrazione nella macroregione alpina dello sviluppo economico europeo (secoli XVII-XX). Atti del convegno di studio, Milano 10-11 dicembre 1999, L. Mocarelli (ed.), Milan 2002, 105-208.

Sharon Rodgers, Princeton University, Ph.D.-thesis on the economic and social history of Boston, Massachusetts.

Margrit Schulte Beerbühl, Dr.phil., lecturer in social and economic history at the University of Düsseldorf. She is the author of 'Vom Gesellenverein zur Gewerkschaft. Entwicklung, Struktur und Politik der Londoner Gesellenorganisationen 1550-1825', Göttingen 1991, and has since published several articles on the development of a consumer society in Britain, on British nationality and immigration between 1660 and 1820, on German merchants and their commercial networks in Britain in the seventeenth and eighteenth centuries. Currently she is working on a research project on Nationality and Commerce in Eighteenth-century Britain.

Jon Stobart, Ph.D., Historical Geographer, senior lecturer at the School of Science and the Environment, Coventry University. His research interests are in urban and industrial development in the eighteenth and nineteenth centuries: the role of urban systems in structuring the space economy, particularly through specialisation, spatial integration and urban-rural linkages, shopping, leisure and consumption in the eighteenth century. His publications include: 'The First Industrial Region, north-west England, 1700-1760', Manchester 2004, and 'Leisure and shopping in the small towns of Georgian England', Journal of Urban History, 2004.

Eva-Maria Stolberg, Dr.phil., lecturer at the Institute of Eastern European and Russian History at the University of Bonn. Her research is on Russia under Mongolian rule, Russian / Soviet foreign policy, the history of Siberia from the 17th to the 20th centuries (with respect to the East Asian - Pacific area). Her recent publications include `Stalin and the Chinese Communists, 1945-1953´, Stuttgart 1997

Jörg Vögele, Dr.phil., Priv.-Doz., Historian, Director of the Institute for the History of Medicine at the University of Düsseldorf. He is the author of `Urban Mortality Change in England and Germany, 1870-1910´, Liverpool 1998, `Sozialgeschichte städtischer Gesundheitsverhältnisse während der Urbanisierung, Berlin 2001´. Currently he is working on research projects on European Port Cities in the Nineteenth and Twentieth Centuries and on `Der Wert des Menschen in den Bevölkerungswissenschaften´ (The "Value of A Human Being" in Demographic Sciences in Germany, 19th-20th Centuries, supported by the DFG).

Peter Lang · Europäischer Verlag der Wissenschaften

Matthias Hardt / Christian Lübke / Dittmar Schorkowitz (Hrsg.)

Inventing the Pasts in North Central Europe

The National Perception of Early Medieval History and Archaeology

Frankfurt am Main, Berlin, Bern, Bruxelles, New York, Oxford, Wien, 2003.
345 pp., num. fig.
Gesellschaften und Staaten im Epochenwandel. Vol. 9
ISBN 3-631-50538-8 / US-ISBN 0-8204-6091-5 · pb. € 56.50*

This volume relates to a comparative research of historical developments and structures in North Central Europe, which is directed to the exploration of an early medieval design of this historical region beyond the Roman Empire's culture frontier. One point of the editorial concern thus was building bridges to overcome long existing dividing lines built up by divergent perspectives of previous scientific traditions. In addition, the recent come back of national histories and historiographies call for a scrutiny on the suitability of postulated ethnicities for the postsocialist nation building process. As a result, the collected papers – presented partly in English, partly in German – have a critical look into various influences, responsible for the realization of images of the past as of scientific strategies.

Contents: Archaeology and Ethnicity · Symbols of Ethnicity and their Perception · Images of the Other · National Perception of History in the 20th Century

Frankfurt am Main · Berlin · Bern · Bruxelles · New York · Oxford · Wien
Distribution: Verlag Peter Lang AG
Moosstr. 1, CH-2542 Pieterlen
Telefax 00 41 (0) 32 / 376 17 27

*The €-price includes German tax rate
Prices are subject to change without notice
Homepage http://www.peterlang.de